Broken Links, Enduring Ties

Broken Links, Enduring Ties

American Adoption across Race, Class, and Nation

Linda J. Seligmann

Stanford University Press
Stanford, California

Stanford University Press
Stanford, California

Printed in the United States of America on acid-free, archival-quality paper

Library of Congress Cataloging-in-Publication Data

Seligmann, Linda J., 1954- author.
  Broken links, enduring ties : American adoption across race, class, and nation / Linda J. Seligmann.
    pages cm
  Includes bibliographical references and index.
  ISBN 978-0-8047-8605-8 (cloth : alk. paper) -- ISBN 978-0-8047-8606-5 (pbk. : alk. paper)
  1. Adoption--Social aspects--United States. 2. Intercountry adoption--United States.
  3. Interracial adoption--United States. 4. Families--United States. I. Title.
  HV875.55.S44 2013
  362.7340973--dc23
                              2013009277

ISBN 978-0-8047 8725-3 (electronic)

Typeset by Bruce Lundquist in 10/14 Minion

Contents

Photographs appear following page 136

Acknowledgments

I owe my deepest gratitude to the adoptive parents, children, and teens who took the risk and time to share with me their experiences, and their struggles and dreams. Many people took an avid interest in this project, providing encouragement and quiet counsel. I thank, especially, my friends and colleagues Amy Best, Andrew Bickford, John Dale, Makalé Faber, Kathleen Fine-Dare, Christine Harris, Sally Herman, Cortney Hughes Rinker, Marlene Samuels, Joseph Scimecca, and Jane Zhang. Samira Alikadiyeva, an undergraduate student at George Mason's New Century College, and Brian Estes and Emilia Guevara, my anthropology graduate research assistants, proved indefatigable. They collaborated with me in conducting interviews, and helped me to process and code them. Their enthusiasm was contagious. Sociology graduate students Whitney Nicole Jorns and Marisa Allison also assisted me in organizing my data.

George Mason University's Department of Sociology and Anthropology, College of Humanities and Social Sciences, and the Provost's Office generously supported my research. Susan Trencher has that rare peripheral vision that allows her to see what others have overlooked, ignored, or never seen before. I thank her for sharing that vision with me, as well as for her storytelling and hilarious jokes. Rutledge Dennis has been in the forefront of research on biculturalism. Our philosophical discussions pushed me to reconsider my perspective or stick to my guns. Either way, they were always enriching. I benefited greatly from the work and conversations of others who had already spent far more time than I thinking about and doing research on family-making across the globe, among them Alma Gottlieb, Jessaca Leinaweaver, Christine Ward Gailey, Ellen Herman, Elena Kim, Barbara Yngvesson, and the two anonymous reviewers of the book manuscript. Any missteps in the pages that follow are mine, the result of being foolhardy enough to embark on an entirely new field of research.

Family-making through adoption has involved my own family directly. Through thick and thin, through the cycles of life and death, they have sustained me. My thanks to Sue Seligmann Moreno, Ann Lyons, Wendy Seligmann, and my parents, Albert and Bobbie Seligmann; to John Cooper, who never ceased to encourage me time and again; and to Mina Mei Li Cooper, who will read this and, I am sure, tell me what she thinks! Last, but not least, I am grateful to the staff at Stanford University Press—to Joa Suorez, who saw the potential of this project; Kate Wahl, who picked up graciously where Joa left off; Michelle Lipinski and Frances Malcolm, who shepherded the book to the production stage; Judith Hibbard, who oversaw the production itself; and Janet Mowery, who sharpened its prose.

Introduction

Adoption is an ancient practice that has received renewed attention as the ability to create ties between parents and children has become more detached from biological descent. In the United States, surrogate, gay, and single parenthood, facilitated by new reproductive technologies, is no longer rare. Family-making has burst out of a rickety frame that assumed the need for blood ties and heterosexuality. In the case of adoption, these reproductive practices have provoked searching questions and experiments that are most visibly striking when the adoptions are transracial, transnational, or both.

In the following pages, I inquire into the kinds of families and communities that are emerging as a result of these adoptions. My interest in writing about transracial and transnational adoption in the United States was sparked by my own experiences with adoption. In 2000, I became the Euroamerican mother of a daughter, whom my husband and I adopted from China. As was true of so many other transracial and transnational adoptive families, we became the focus of a range of sentiments—affection, celebration, naked curiosity, ignorance, and a dose now and then of discrimination. My training and perspective as an anthropologist fueled my desire to better understand my experiences. I began to pursue more deeply and systematically questions about family-making through transnational and transracial adoption in the United States. It rapidly became clear to me that all adoptions were not alike; that issues of class, race, place, and gender led adopting and adoptive parents along different paths of family-making; and that the practices and narratives that emerged among them were inflected by how power circulated in society.

Anthropologists are well aware that people build their lives using cultural models. These models are conceptual, but they take material form as they are put into practice. They carry meanings that people take for granted. Yet what people take for granted is far from straightforward, common-sensical, or natural. How people make a family, who they deem are its "members," and what is expected of them are good examples of this. The broad purpose of this book, thus, is to explore the tensions surrounding the making of American families—how they are constituted, the forms they take—and the activities of those who are considered "members" of families, through the lens of transnational and transracial adoption over, roughly, the twenty years between 1990 and 2010. In it, I focus on the experiences of Euroamerican parents who have adopted children from China, parents who have adopted children from Russia, and white parents who have adopted African American children in the United States, within a comparative perspective.[1]

My own subject positioning as an anthropologist and a mother who has participated in and experienced much of what I write about informs the narrative I develop. Each step of the way, over the long making of this book, I have reflected on how what I have learned could be personally incorporated into or brought to bear on my own family-building practices. A second defining thread of the narrative is the power of what I call broken links—what is missing or unknown—in the lives of birth parents, adoptive parents, and their children. These broken links attest to power at work that permits severing some people from one another and uniting others; they speak to assumptions people hold about "blood ties," and they are indicators of how secrets, intimate or very public, are heavy burdens indeed. I argue that adoptive parents and their children are affected by these broken links and that they have catalyzed a burgeoning movement among many adoptees to call into question what *is* taken for granted in American family-building, to give it a name, and to act on it.

"Blood Ties"

To better understand the cultural context of transnational and transracial adoption, it is important to situate it within larger debates about family-making in the United States. The ways Americans make their families provide insight into basic building blocks of American culture, offering glimpses of what the ingredients of biology and culture or nature and nurture have to do with how Americans think about family and the recipes they rely on to make them. Prominent anthropologists, most notably David Schneider (1980), argued that biology was the template on which American kinship relationships and the family were built, underlying American social norms about who was related to whom. Yet transnational and transracial adoption practices in America have raised questions about whether "biologism" is the sole ground in which kinship ties are rooted. Schneider's assertion catalyzed scholars to take a fresh look at taken-for-granted constructs such as household, family, child, sibling, and parent, realizing that they might, indeed, constitute American folk models. They began to pay greater attention to the meanings of biogenetics and culture across societies. The growing interest in what, then, exactly constituted "kinship ties"—where did kinship relationships end and other kinds of social ties begin?—were questions Schneider did not address (Yanagisako and Delaney 1995), but they led scholars to wonder why and how assumptions about family-making became naturalized (Carsten 2000: 13–14).

Judith Modell, in her work on American adoption, argued that if Schneider was right about the predominant model of "family" and of "kinship" in America, then "adoption makes absolutely no sense without the biological relationship." Further, she claimed, "adoption makes sense of the biological relationship. The 'made' relationship delineates the terms of the natural relationship: a child born of two parents, the product of their sexual relationship. Fictive kinship tells participants that real kinship means 'blood ties.' These determine the structure of a family and also the emotions of its members: the feelings of being a parent and a child" (Modell 1994: 225–26). At the same time, Modell found her informants were struggling with the assumed relationship between biological family-making and "as if" family-making through adoption. She noted that "natives" themselves were articulating and revising theories of kinship and that they "constructed a critique that very much resembles those made by anthropologists, confronting (as these do) the 'biologism' that dominates the construction of American kinship" (see, e.g., Schneider 1984). Modell found that her informants were "fish out of water—people well aware of, and interested in probing, the contradictions in their lives" (Modell 1994: 13–14).

The discourse that adoptive and birth parents, children, and social workers used about families created intense paradoxes for participants in Modell's study. They desired to replicate the sentiments, characteristics, and functions associated with biologically constituted families, yet also wanted society to recognize their distinctiveness as adoptive families. As Modell put it, all participants were initially engaged in creating "as if" families, grounded in security and love. However, the ideal "as if" family remained just that, as families themselves struggled with the construction of roots through routes and pathways, rather than essences, especially across borders erected by race, class, and nation.

Cross-Cultural Studies of Family-Making through Adoption

Anthropologists realized that one way to investigate the roles that nature and nurture—biology and culture—played in family-making was to explore the premises underlying family-making and the valorization of adoption and fostering in other cultures. They found many examples that stood in sharp contradistinction from those structuring American family-making. In some societies, adoption and social parenthood were as highly valued as biologically constituted families, sometimes more so. In others, adoption was a requisite practice for strengthening lineage ties, ensuring an heir, and creating pathways to valued resources.

In northern Benin, the norm is social parenthood. Almost all children live with non-biological parents and the identity of their biological parents is kept secret, similar to sealed adoption records in the United States. Nevertheless, biological parents take an avid interest in their child. The degree and kinds of social parenthood in Benin often correlate with labor needs and status, creating patterned kinds of inequalities (Alber 2004: 33–47). In yet other cultures, children move among households of adoptive and biological parents throughout the course of their lives. In Micronesia, adoption is common as a practice integral to the sexual division of labor, as well as a system of land exchange and joint use; adopted children are highly regarded, and if obligations to them are not fulfilled, the adoption can be reversed (Treide 2004: 127–42). In Ifaluk, also located in Micronesia, parents seek to adopt because of loneliness or sorrow, and if a childless couple asks to adopt a child from his or her birth parents, their wish is usually granted. If the birth parents have other children and refuse the request to give up one of them, they are considered stingy and become a target of the wrath of the gods (Le 2000: 208).

Among the Wogeo of Papua New Guinea, according to Astrid Anderson (2004: 111–26), adoptions do not imitate other social relationships but rather are essential to the constitution of the social landscape. Children who are adopted continue to belong to their natal matrilineage but also to the locus, the place, where they are raised by their adoptive parents. Not unlike some adoption practices in the United States, childless parents in Wogeo pressure others to give up their children for adoption. And among the Beng of the Ivory Coast, Alma Gottlieb (2009: 115–38) found that mothers quickly turn over their babies to multiple caretakers, including older children and strangers. Because the Beng believe that all babies return to this world as reincarnated ancestors from the afterlife, they are already familiar with existing social ties and relationships. Beng mothers encourage infants to be open and accepting of strangers, forging "satisfying emotional attachments to many people," and they discourage infants from forming "singular emotional attachments" to their mother (Gottlieb 2009: 131).

At the other end of the spectrum, anthropologists have also found cultures that stress "blood ties" and biological descent even more than Americans do (Sorosky et al. 1978: 26). In Morocco, Bargach (2002) writes that adoption is a marginalized activity experienced by marginalized people who experience great anguish. The Moroccan state has made it a crime for adopted children to assume their new family's name. There, being adopted is conflated with being illegitimate; mothers who give up their children for adoption are shamed; and adopted children experience a permanent sense of liminality.

Many examples of family-making principles and practices could be cited in which surrogate and alloparenting are the norm, not the exception; the concept of "family" as a unit with clearly defined boundaries responsible for nurturing may not exist; "love" and "good deeds" are not necessarily taken into account as important reasons for adopting a child; neither is adoption stigmatized or excessively focused on, even though it is an important strategy among families in adjusting to the economic and political implications of differing family composition and events (Borneman 2001: 43). At the same time, as Astrid Anderson (2004: 119) has observed, adoption, and what Americans likely would label "fostering," is not uncomplicated, even if all children are loved the same. As we can see from just the few examples above, forces from afar have considerable impact on adoption and fosterage practices, and all societies filter the pragmatics of adoption through their moral values, customary laws or legal tenets, and economic and political practices.[2]

Being Related

Given the evidence for such a wide range of family-making practices, not surprisingly, anthropologists began to question Schneider's assumptions about American family-making, especially as different kinds of families began to make their appearance in higher numbers. Whereas Modell found that the ideal and quintessential cultural model of family-making in America, which her informants were alternately embracing and struggling against, was biological in nature, Janet Carsten (2004) wondered whether biology was ever the sole or principal guiding assumption about American kinship models. Regardless of whether it was, she argued that the more important task for anthropologists was to bring to light indigenous models of relatedness and what the construction and activation of relatedness meant to personhood in the context of people's practices and interactions. In her words, "[T]he important point here is that shared meals and living in one house go together, and these two processes progressively create kinship even when those who live together are not linked by ties of sexual procreation. Not surprisingly, there is also a strong moral value ascribed to these processes" (Carsten 2004: 40).

"Relatedness" and how it is constituted among families formed through adoption is central to this book (Carsten 2000).[3] Like Modell, I find that biology and "blood ties" continue to lurk as important ingredients in American family-making, including among adoptive parents and their children. However, many practices of creating relatedness as kin have emerged, leading to shifts in the social construction of "family" in American culture. It is not that American ideas about biologism are being supplanted or superseded, but, as Judith Modell documents, they are undergoing revision. As they undergo revision, they become catalysts for changes in how Americans think about family-making and, occasionally, for outright challenges to existing norms.

Private and Public Knowledge and Choices

American family-making is also situated and shaped by cultural notions of public and private, open and closed, and by whether, and how, lines are drawn between these constructs. Janet Carsten points out that these are similar questions to those that feminist scholarship began to ask once it became clear that classificatory models of sexual procreation, domains of private and public, domestic and political, and male-female bodies could no longer be taken as natural (Carsten 2004: 59; Lugo and Maurer 2000). Jane Collier and Sylvia Yanagisako (1989: 30, 36) led the way in arguing against creating a "conceptual impasse" between the "practical" and "symbolic" in approaches to feminist anthropology. This conceptual impasse, they observed, prevented anthropologists from grasping the myriad ways that consensus was achieved about dominant symbolic systems. It also mistakenly led anthropologists to assume that power was exercised in some spheres and not in others, and to create hierarchies of systems of meaning rather than recognizing that "all human practices are created by people living and acting within historically situated systems of meaning." Kath Weston (1991) developed this idea further, specifically with respect to family-making among gays and lesbians. She argued that to understand kinship we need to examine both those relationships that are intimate and very public, and those that are thought to occupy distinct domains.

Using a more historically based approach, Joan Scott (1988) and Bruno Latour (1993) also show that mixtures of nature-culture are socially constructed, and that we need to specify the networks and gatekeepers of networks that create hegemonic concepts and categories. The use of DNA testing is a good example that illustrates the intervention of nature-culture in contemporary family-making. It has become ever easier to rely on scientific technologies, especially DNA testing, to confirm blood ties, but at the same time, people are giving shape to "family" and arriving at practices that signify "family" bonds to them and others through ever more varied and creative cultural means and ideas (Ginsburg and Rapp 1995; Franklin and McKinnon 2001). The subtext of substantiating biological connections informs how these relationships are imagined, effected, and called into question, often as an uneasy counterpoint. Such connections include, for example, using DNA analysis to expose child trafficking or, increasingly, to confirm relationships between adoptees and birth parents, or birth siblings. Thus, even as bio-relatedness recedes as the taken-for-granted criterion for constituting a family, technologies based on biological connections, and such connections themselves, continue to play central roles in how parents and children imagine their positions and activities in families in America.

I also try to tease out what adoptive parents and adoptees think of as private and public in their family-making practices, the meanings they attribute to these domains, and how they are situated in contexts of power despite many adoptive parents' fervent claim that the decisions they make are based on individual choice. How do they feel about open or sealed birth records and active interaction with birth relatives? With whom do they share their adoption narratives and journeys, if they do? Is adoption something they want to keep hidden from public view or, in the case of adoptive parents, perhaps even from their children? What does the online explosion of adoption social movements and exchanges mean? Finally, in what ways are children who have been adopted transnationally and transracially attempting to shift the boundaries between these constructs and overturn the constructs themselves, as they grow up? These boundaries are culturally in flux but not easily overturned or moved.

Subjects and Statistics

The research I conducted took the form of interviews and interactions with thirty families with children adopted from China (CA), fifteen families with children adopted from Russia (RA), and twenty transracial families consisting of African American children adopted by white parents (AA). I selected these categories because at the time I conducted this research, China and Russia were among the top three "sending countries" of children for adoption in the United States.[4] According to the U.S. State Department (2011), between 1999 and 2010, of the 224,615 children adopted internationally in the United States, 64,043 children, most of whom were girls 2 years of age or under, were adopted from China, far more than from any other country. During the same period, 44,150 children were adopted from Russia, a roughly equally number of boys and girls, and a far higher number of children who were older. I included the adoptive families of African American children in my study because there are marked differences historically in how Americans think about "race" as an ingredient in family-making, in the context of domestic adoption and in reproductive policies in general (Solinger 1992, 2001). This history is pertinent because it bears directly on adoption practices: the availability of infants within the United States for adoption; how prospective parents view transracial adoption; and why they turn to transnational adoption.

Ricki Solinger (1992), Nancy Riley and Krista van Vleet (2012), and Ellen Herman (2002, 2008) have traced historically the sustained differences in how white and black women who became pregnant have been treated in the United States. These differences rest on the social construction of race and on class. Single, white, middle-class young women were whisked away to have their babies, who would subsequently be adopted by childless married couples. They were then encouraged to "get back on track" psychologically in order to conform to an ideal of womanhood that meant having children within a marriage. In the late 1960s and early 1970s, the onset of the civil rights movement, the women's movement, and the sexual revolution, along with the availability of birth control and abortion, led to more white women remaining single and keeping their babies. This change was a principal reason that fewer white infants became available domestically for adoption. In contrast, it was thought that black women "naturally" enjoyed their sexuality and that their friends and relatives would take care of their children. Yet they were also criticized for their behavior. The large number of "illegitimate" black births was used as support for the biological bases of black inferiority and public anti-black policies. Whereas white unwed mothers were viewed as a threat to the moral integrity of the family, black unwed mothers were viewed as an economic threat to white families (Solinger 1992: 41–42). The assumption also was that black people would "always take care of their own" (Solinger 1992: 190) and that therefore there was no need to provide them with adoption or foster services. When welfare policies were enacted and black women took advantage of them, the assumption became that they were having babies in order to use welfare services rather than because they were poor and lacked alternative economic opportunities. Solinger concludes that the "racially specific focus on illegitimate pregnancy and childbearing in the postwar decades and at the end of the twentieth century has made it very difficult for women of all races and classes to see what they have in common" (1992: 245).

I wanted to ascertain how adoptive parents themselves understood and thought about these racialized and class differences in the context of comparing and contrasting domestic transracial adoptions, represented by AA adoptive families, and transnational, transracial adoptions, represented by CA adoptive families. This seemed especially important given that Americans, in general, were adopting transracially and internationally in far greater numbers than they were adopting black children domestically. I also wanted to trace the reasons for their thinking and what effects it had on children themselves.

The differences in the paths that adopting parents were taking are also writ large in statistics on the different kinds of adoption. Although the interest of the general public in adoption has increased since the early 1990s, in 2011, U.S. adoption numbers were far from their highest. In 2010, approximately 125,000 children had been adopted annually in the United States since the late 1980s. In 2008, there were 463,000 children in foster care, 123,000 of them waiting to be adopted.[5] Ellen Herman (2008: 303), using data gathered from the U.S. Children's Bureau and the National Center for Social Statistics, notes that this is a sharp drop from the high point in adoptions—175,000 in 1970. Transnational adoptions, many of which are also transracial, more than tripled annually between 1990 and 2004, from 7,000 to almost 23,000 in 2004, accounting for about 12 percent of all adoptions by U.S. citizens (Kreider 2011a: 84).[6]

Domestic transracial adoptions have increased, but there are no reliable statistics, which is telling in itself. Ruth Kreider, who works with the U.S. Census Bureau (2011b: 97), notes that "there are few nationally representative data sources that can provide information about interracial adoptive families and how they might compare in basic demographic and socioeconomic characteristics with interracial families that were formed in other ways. Even estimates of the percentage of adopted children that are interracially adopted are very few."[7] Approximately 18,957 African American children were formally adopted in the United States through public agencies in 2002, but only approximately 1,000–2,000 African American children are adopted transracially each year by parents who do not consider themselves African Americans (Ly 2005).[8] Domestic adoption statistics are unreliable, and there are no accurate statistics on private adoptions. As Herman (2008: 303) observes, the symbolic significance of adoption is far greater than its statistical significance in the United States. In part, this is because of the high visibility of transracially constituted families.[9]

Inequality and Family-Making

Family-making through adoption is embedded in complex, contradictory, multilayered political and economic processes. These processes contribute to inequalities in how adoption unfolds across class, race, and national borders (Marre and Briggs 2009; Ortiz and Briggs 2003: 39–57). In making sense of how inequalities structure transnational and transracial adoption, I draw on a political-economy framework and on critical race theory. The policies and practices of states, international agencies, and many other kinds of institutions actively give rise to inequalities. It is well documented, for example, that children being adopted tend to move from poorer persons or "sending" regions to wealthier "receiving" ones (Coutin, Bibler, Maurer, and Yngvesson 2002).[10]

Adoption across national boundaries may also be used as a blunt weapon in confronting geopolitical tensions between countries. In 2013, the U.S. government, for example, passed a law (the Magnitsky Act) targeting Russians who had violated human rights. In retaliation, President Vladimir Putin, with strong support from the Russian congress, approved a law in January banning all U.S. adoptions of Russian children. Although it is indeed true and a serious concern that nineteen Russian children adopted by Americans have died (out of 60,000 adopted over twenty years), the ban was a convenient and powerful weapon that had very little to do with adoption itself or the rights of children.[11]

Informal and diffuse mechanisms also serve as means by which power is exerted and represented. These inequalities affect the choices adoptive parents make, the risks they take, and the categories and ideologies that are embedded in the stories they share about their adoption experiences.

The original underpinnings of critical race theory were oriented toward critiquing and transforming unjust legal policies and systems that purported to be founded on and operate with principles of neutrality. My goal here is less ambitious. It is to bring to light how race and racism work with and through gender, ethnicity, class, sexuality, and nation as systems of power, and to specify some of their more significant impacts on transnational and transracial adoption (Crenshaw 1991; hooks 1992). The exercise and circulation of power often stratifies or masks commonalities and interconnections among different social classes or sectors, resulting in identity politics. Just as problematically, the narratives and experiences of marginalized subjects may prevent those subjects from recognizing what unites them or how they might organize to contest the very forces and ideologies that fragment them (Nash 2008). By placing transnational adoptions, some of which are transracial, within the same frame as domestic transracial adoptions, the social construction of race at work leaps into view. For example, although adoptive parents use "heritage" with respect to transnational transracial adoptions, they tend to use "race" in the context of domestic transracial adoptions. The reasons for this make for very different choices and activities among families formed through adoption.[12] Crenshaw puts this well:

> To say that a category such as race or gender is socially constructed is not
> to say that the category has no significance in our world. On the contrary,
> one of the projects . . . is thinking about the way power has clustered around
> certain categories and is exercised against others . . . to unveil the processes of
> subordination and the various ways those processes are experienced by people
> who are subordinated and people who are privileged by them. . . . Categories
> have meanings and consequences. . . . This is not to deny that the process of
> categorization is itself an exercise of power, but the story is much more com-
> plicated and nuanced than that. . . . Clearly, there is unequal power, but there is
> nonetheless some degree of agency that people can and do exert in the politics
> of naming. (Crenshaw 1991: 1296–97)

The vectors of power through which adoptions unfold in the United States and how inequalities are confronted over time constitute complex dynamics and ethical conundrums. One frequently cited example addressed in the following pages concerns white adopting parents who have the luxury to choose between transnational and domestic adoption. Often they choose the former, adopting black children from abroad while there remains a need for permanent homes for black children in the United States. Yet even white parents who do choose to adopt black children from within the United States face criticism from blacks who are concerned that white families will not adequately equip black chil-dren to navigate America's racialized terrain.[13] Controversy also abounds over whether the inherent geopolitical inequalities between sending and receiving countries of transnational adoptees trump the ethical value of providing every child with a loving family (Bartholet 1993, 1996; Fogg-Davis 2002; Freundlich 2000; Hollingsworth 2003; and Marre and Briggs 2009).

Adoptive parents may embrace children's rights, regardless of race or nation, as an impulse for adoption, yet that same embrace may be compelled by senti-mental ideas about rescuing "poor and primitive" others and avoiding risks. In short, the ability to pursue adoptions across borders—racially, economically, or nationally—is the consequence of geopolitical inequalities that are themselves the result of particular histories and policies that the United States has helped create. Adult adoptees have articulated their own positions in these debates and have become increasingly active in making themselves heard, not an easy undertaking when they realize they must confront both the power and the love of multiple parents.

Transnational and transracial adoption practices in America, therefore, reflect how Americans conceptualize kinship and how family-making activities are embedded in ideas about race, class, and gender. Sexuality too is a factor, given the increase in single, gay, and lesbian parents and the battles they are waging for states to extend to them the same rights as heterosexual couples (Weston 1991; Carp 2004; Gailey 2006a; Lewin 2006; Horridge 2011). These ideas are converted into practices that carry meanings through which power circulates.

Ethnographic Approaches

Two major currents run through adoption research: therapeutic approaches, concentrating on the psychological and physical well-being of members of adoptive families; and sociologically or psychologically grounded quantitative studies that examine correlation or causality among variables such as race, income, and education (the data from these studies are abundantly available and I occasionally cite them). However, my intention here is not to arrive at broad generalizations. It is to vividly portray the lives of families who have chosen to make their families across lines of race, color, gender, class, or nation and to illuminate new understandings of adoption within a particular cultural and historical context.

The first decade of the twenty-first century saw an explosion of books, articles, movies, and memoirs about adoption in particular, and about families in general. This passionate attention to family in America might be a consequence of the long history of the centrality of families to labor regimes, state formation, gender relationships, religion, medical practices, and making a profit, especially via media accounts that pull at people's heartstrings or sensationalize family scandals and affairs. Without discounting this possibility, I would argue that the renewed attention to families and to family formation is indicative of cultural unrest about how families are perceived and understood, the practices associated with their formation, and how they actually work. This unrest is not due to a single cause but rather to a multiplicity of currents interacting in tension with existing discourses and structures of power.

An ethnographic perspective has the capacity to offer a nuanced account of why and how power is exercised and experienced among different groups of people, and the reasons for the seemingly sudden explosions of hatred or violent conflict around the world. It also allows people to reflect more on how their own assumptions and beliefs are channeled into their behavior and reactions. An ethnographic account can shake things up. Further, anthropologists themselves, whether "studying up" or "studying down," have become more explicit about defining their own subject positions (Nader 1972). What I most wanted to avoid in this ethnography was to *assume* that I already knew why and how participants in adoption felt and what guided them in what they did. Bruno Latour (2007: 53–58) lays out methodological requirements that he argues would permit social scientists to recognize "figuration"—how forces of power come to *be* and exert themselves—rather than taking them for granted and then drawing somewhat obvious conclusions from those assumptions. He also asks that sociologists, in particular, pay closer attention to the ideas that people have about what they are doing and what compels them to certain decisions and actions. In a similar but more anthropological vein, Jane Collier, Michelle Rosaldo, and Sylvia Yanagisako (1997) lay out why it is more theoretically productive and ethnographically meaningful to view family-making as dynamic, processual, relational, and taking place in more than one locale or institution. I have tried to heed emergent forces at work, tracing how they create connections, agency, breaks, and disruptions among people, and to take note of the metaphors people embrace and act upon.

All parents create narratives and a sense of origin or tangle of roots for their children (adoptive or not). Likewise, authors weave together a narrative, or sometimes more than one. There are intersections between the narratives I have built as a Euroamerican adoptive parent and the narratives that have emerged in my research. Hence, not least because I am very much both subject and engaged participant, I have erred on the side of restraint, striving to combine close analysis with tolerance and respect for the many voices and points of view that I listened to and reflected upon in the course of my research. I find myself in agreement with Alma Gottlieb who, reflecting on the problematic inequalities entailed in writing for or about "the Other," concluded:

> To live in a world in which we have given up on the dream of understanding the motivations for behaviors, feelings, and opinions of other human beings, or groups of human beings—whether each of those persons or groups comes from a different religious tradition, socioeconomic class, or language group from our own . . . or is our neighbor or child or spouse—this is a frightening thought. At an ideological level, such a world paves the way for war, with its assumption that the Other is epistemologically problematic and thus a legitimate candidate for annihilation. (Gottlieb 1994: xvi)

I hope this book adds to the stories being told among the communities of people with whom I did my research. I do not view it as conclusive but rather as part of the mix of voices and perspectives that has the possibility of reaching adoptees, their parents, a classroom of students, a lawyer or teacher, grandparents, or a friend in a chat room.

I spent two decades working in Latin America before beginning the research for this book. The analytical lenses used by some Latin Americanists have served me well in understanding adoption in the United States. In particular, I want to mention the work of Laura Nader and of Charles Hale. Hale (2006) spent years working in Guatemala, where a brutal and prolonged genocidal civil war pitted the Maya against military and paramilitary forces and the non-indigenous *ladino* population. In the aftermath, Hale has documented the tentative bridges that are emerging as ladinos reflect on their privileged position and the hegemonic racist ideology they took for granted for so many years, and the Maya experience an active cultural and political resurgence and florescence. His goal was to point toward emergent practices that did not reproduce the dualistic categories and ideologies that caused violent bloodshed. He admits that his may be a utopian undertaking, not least because the mapping of such a terrain could be used or seen by some as a rationalization for continuing prejudice and privilege. In short, it might be easier to return to the comfort of black and white critique. I found myself wrestling with the same concerns. At the same time that I have tried not to lose sight of the power of biology, "race," class, and nation at work in family-making, I have also strived not to reinscribe Manichaean dualisms and binary oppositions that may be easy to think with but that do not take account of the nuanced practices and sentiments associated with family formation through adoption.

To sketch out this terrain, it is important to try to "study up," as Laura Nader (1972) presciently argued. Anthropologists have overwhelmingly documented the cultural lives and the voices of marginalized or subordinated people, yet they have done so in different ways. Some have taken to heart Laura Nader's advice to give more attention to the lives of the powerful rather than relentlessly focusing on those who were powerless or colonized or living in poverty. By so doing, she argued, we would learn more about why poverty and inequalities existed, and would also find reason to reflect on the sedimentation and exercise of power within our own cultural and anthropological practices. In addition, we might incorporate sentiments, strong feelings we have about particular subjects, into systematic research on them. In order to study up, Nader was aware that anthropological methods would need to be revised. People in power did not necessarily welcome anthropologists' inquiries about them or their exercise of power, and anthropologists would experience challenges gaining access. Whether in their own country or elsewhere, anthropologists would also need to reflect more on the ethics of doing research on public and private aspects of everyday life; and anthropologists themselves might feel they were betraying those who were relatively powerless by studying people with substantial power.

In studying up and studying down the topic of transnational and transracial adoption in the United States, not only was I working within my own culture, crisscrossing between the celebratory embrace of adoption and the forces and institutions that structure it to favor powerful countries and upper-middle-class affluent families. I also had to wrestle with trying to penetrate the intimate domains of private family life and with my own position as an adoptive parent, which permitted me access to confidences that might not otherwise have been forthcoming (Seligmann 2012). I found myself simultaneously apprehending how people imagined what they were doing, the cultural logics that underpinned their behavior, and the forces that structured these logics. The power to imagine is integral to the capacity of people to catalyze social transformations in small ways (Graeber 2001). I thus illuminate the imaginative ways that people, in the context of adoption, have begun rethinking race and race relations, economic and political inequalities, and the relationships between biology and culture, explaining what I think they mean and what they might portend, without suggesting that individual shifts can be equated with social revolution.

Adoptees, especially transracial adoptees, as members of families both present and absent, are rarely members of like groups (used in a loose way)—unlike other kinds of immigrants to the United States. Many immigrants, when they arrive, form enclaves (Foner 1987; Hagan 1994; Portes and Rumbaut 1990; Stoller 2002). Adoptee immigrants, especially transracial adoptees, incorporated as individuals into adoptive families, harbor a sense of anomie, of not belonging, especially as they approach their teen years and young adulthood. Sometimes their bitterness and anger is potent indeed. Twenty years ago, it was rarely articulated or was kept well hidden. Since then, increasingly, they are voicing their sentiments in blogs, memoirs, and docufilms. In addition, multiple parenthood, the openness of some adoptive parents to cultural and racial differences, and the security of adoptees that they are loved have facilitated the ability of adoptees to voice their opinions. Many of them, then and now, feel that their adoptive parents have made few changes in their lifeways after adopting, that they have only paid lip service to transformations they should have undertaken in incorporating a child of another culture, race, class, and family into their own. They also view their adoptive parents' embrace of multiculturalism as evading the real impact of racism and poverty in America on them. Adoptees feel that the burden has fallen on them to undertake transformations. Yet, in another twist, the same powerful emotions and critiques by adoptees have led to the flourishing of adoptee groups and blogs (Kim 2010: 116–17). These groups, which meet both virtually and physically, are creating their own modes of belonging and community. The tensions that emerge in family-making through adoption in the United States are thus hardly binary oppositions, but rather a somewhat messy brew that is regularly stirred and disturbed.

Methods

I publicized my research project in a wide number of forums and on my own website, inviting individuals to participate in it. As people responded, I interviewed them. I was not seeking a representative sample, but as my research proceeded, I attempted to gain access to more single parents, fathers, and RA adoptive parents. I conducted intensive semi-structured interviews, lasting between one and three hours, with adoptive parents in each category. In one case, the interview lasted an exhausting six hours, and at midnight I had to put an end to it. I conducted the interviews primarily by phone, but if the families were local, I met them in person. The confidentiality I offered to those who let me interview them seemed to encourage openness. The floodgates, once opened, were difficult to close. Many were eager to share their family photos and blogs with me. This was of great help to me since phone interviews, despite the wealth of information and emotion that poured out over the line, still had a flatness to them. The photos and more informal postings provided needed dimensionality about my informants, as did sitting in their living rooms and kitchens with the television blaring in the background. In my daily life, I observed, in a more self-conscious fashion, interactions with families that had not been formed through adoption and listened to their narratives about families in general.[14]

A fascinating and ironic aspect of this research that distinguished it from my prior experiences doing participant-observation was that American families constructed private and public boundaries that prevented me from intruding on them on a day-to-day basis in their homes. In contrast, when I did field work in the Andes, I rarely felt discomfort spending hours in the kitchen and patio, where families conducted almost all their activities, including sleeping, playing, socializing, and ablutions (Seligmann 2012)! I surmise that they allowed me this access because of my status as an ignorant stranger, my perceived power, cultural differences in the sociospatial functions of the Quechua home, and Quechua people's more open and flexible practices of fostering and adoption (Bourdieu 1977; van Vleet 2008; Seligmann 2009). "At home" in America, there were simply some private spaces I had to content myself with not entering, but rather learning indirectly about them through narrative accounts and other means that I describe further below.

After conducting and transcribing the interviews from digital recordings, I coded the transcriptions. I listened to and read these exchanges repeatedly to apprehend context and subtle cues—key words, phrases, laughter, silences, and even the speed of the narrative. I pored over them with an eye to discerning the salient themes. This was not intended to be an exercise in systematic discourse or conversational analysis but rather a means to apprehend patterns and get a sense of when a point of saturation had been reached. Many adoptive parents' responses to my queries took the form of storytelling. Their stories offer a powerful window onto how adoptive parents and adoptees processed their experiences, and they are therefore integral to the chapters of this book. This is not a longitudinal study, yet even in the sideways slice of time covered by the research, telling patterns began to emerge. In some instances the stories reproduced dominant cultural understandings and representations, but they also reflected painstaking and tentative efforts to set out alternative maps and models. As I discuss below, the sharing and circulating of these narratives is one of the ways that adoptive parents and adoptees are changing the foundations of family-making.

The adoptive parents who participated in this project are located across the United States (the Appendix provides more detailed characteristics of all the adoptive families I interviewed). They live in Alabama, Alaska, California, Georgia, Idaho, Illinois, Kentucky, Maryland, Massachusetts, Michigan, Mississippi, Nebraska, New Jersey, New York, North Dakota, Oregon, Pennsylvania, South Carolina, Texas, Utah, Virginia, Washington, Wisconsin, and the District of Columbia. They lived in small towns of 2,500 and large metropolises of almost 3 million. Some are middle class; most are upper middle class. All of them are Euroamerican. Their household income at the time of adoption ranged from a low of $35,000 to a high of $400,000. Their average household income was approximately $120,000. The average household income of RA adoptive families was much higher than that of either CA or AA households ($205,800), and the average income of AA households ($92,000) was, on average, $18,000 less than that of CA households ($110,853).

Most of the families I followed were two-parent households. I talked to some fathers at length, but most of my interviews were conducted with mothers. The overrepresentation of mothers appears to result from two factors. Mothers continue to be the primary daily care-takers of their children in the United States. Heather Jacobson (2008), comparing adoptions from Eastern Europe with some adoptions from China, found that Euroamerican mothers have taken on the primary responsibility of "culture-keeping"—keeping alive their adopted children's heritage in various ways. Given that this is the case, it is not surprising that they would be more likely to want to speak about their experiences with adoption. Further, because I too had become a mother through adoption, they assumed we shared common experiences. It is worth noting that when I did become an adoptive mother, I became aware of a whole set of cultural practices and values concerning how Americans defined membership to family. Mothers were extraordinarily powerful in these activities. While I spoke and interacted with far fewer married fathers, those who already had children from an earlier marriage stated that one of the biggest differences they had experienced in adopting was in how much more involved they felt in parenting their adopted children.

Alma Gottlieb's (2004) research on the culture of infancy among the Beng in the Ivory Coast made her hyperaware of the cultural construction of infancy and parenthood when she became a mother. The sharp contrasts she initially drew between Beng and Euroamerican cultural constructions of infancy and parenthood were challenged over time as she did more fieldwork. She came to recognize heterogeneity in both Beng and Euroamerican parenting and how the Beng shaped her own childrearing practices; and like so many anthropologists, she had to learn to temper her initial romantic ideas about Beng child-rearing practices as she encountered child abuse and infant mortality. Although the focus of my research differs, the more I learned, the more my initial impressions of American family-making through adoption deepened and changed. Yet I always felt that a "double consciousness" guided my field work. For example, as mother to a daughter adopted from China, I knew that many CA adoptive mothers held at bay the idea that their children would be the target of racism they knew was leveled at African Americans. Instead, they thought of them as cute, exotic, and brilliant. When I attended cultural celebrations intended to keep alive a connection, however idealized, to Chinese culture, my daughter and I were also enveloped in these sentiments, and she, especially as a child, seemed to enjoy the events. I went along with them while simultaneously examining them with a critical eye.

In a different case, my interactions with RA adoptive parents quickly led me to conclude that both mothers and fathers were motivated to adopt from

Russia because they wanted "white" children, conforming to enduring American ideas about ideal family composition. For a long time I was blind to the ways that RA mothers, in particular, had formed unique caretaking networks, joining together to cope with the special needs of their children. These support groups were actually quite prevalent, but I had not noticed them because they were not part of my experiences of motherhood.

One percent of my interviews were conducted with single parents in each category and included both single mothers and single fathers. With five exceptions, parents were unwilling to tell me their sexual orientation. Therefore, it is impossible for me to know if some of the single mothers or fathers were lesbian or gay. This is partly because of legal constraints. Many parents present themselves as single rather than lesbian or gay because they fear they will be considered unacceptable by an agency, by birth parents, or by a country, not because they have not come out openly (Dorow and Swiffen 2009). For example, in 2007 China changed its regulations from tolerating lesbian and gay couples to prohibiting them from adopting.[15] Russia prohibits lesbian and gay adoption. However, one lesbian couple told me that although initially they represented themselves as a single mother and her close, supportive friend, the orphanage personnel they interacted with seemed comfortable with them as a couple, and they gradually relaxed their behavior during the ten days they were in Russia at the orphanage. A high number of adoption agencies that screen parents for domestic adoptions assume that birth parents or guardians would prefer heterosexual and young couples, though this is not necessarily the case (Horridge 2011). Similarly, in the case of transnational adoptions, the brokers and government agents in a child's birth country may informally or formally reject non-heterosexual applications. This bias has been internalized by adoptive parents who are gay.

Although many anthropologists have been doing participant-observation on questions about adoption, few have undertaken intensive interviews with adoptive parents and children (but see Gailey 2010; Jacobson 2008; Simon and Altstein 2002; Simon and Roorda 2000). I conducted interviews and gathered survey data from some of the children linked to the adoptive parents I interviewed. I also did more traditional participant-observation, attending playgroups, meetings, ritual events, religious services, focus groups, and adoption conferences, and talking with adoptive parents and children in a wide range of everyday settings. Many of the playgroups were monthly neighborhood affairs, announced via listservs (electronic email lists and discussion groups). Some of them included any kind of adoptive family; others were only for CA, RA, or transracial adoptive families. I did not find any specifically for AA adoptive families. I was always curious to see what kinds of groups the children formed as they played and the conversations that took place. It was helpful to have a child of my own participating. I attended ritual events dedicated to special festivals, such as the celebration of the Chinese Lunar New Year and Kwanzaa, citizenship and adoption ceremonies, and ceremonies to commemorate loss and healing. Some were intimate affairs that involved only family members; others included extended family, travel groups, or student associations; and others were hosted by official entities such as the National Immigration Service, the U.S. Congress, or the Chinese Embassy.

Because I appeared to be an adoptive parent, many other parents struck up conversations with me. They wanted to know the origins of our daughter and about our adoption experience. They freely offered their own views about adoption and assumed that I would be in agreement with them. This was not always true, but I refrained from confrontation or debate with them because of my role as an ethnographer. Instead, in the course of conversing, I sometimes offered alternative perspectives. I wanted to learn what the full range of discourse and perspectives was, rather than impose my own point of view, which I anticipated would put a stop to, or at least impede, the flow of the conversation. Again, this was a balancing act.[16]

When these conversations took place in the presence of their children, I wondered how they were processing the conversation; hence my growing interest in the children's perspectives. These conversations were far more frequent with CA and AA adoptive parents than with RA adoptive parents because the latter, often deliberately, were committed to "passing" as biogenetic families. However, through listservs, I was able to attend some of the RA playgroups and one conference sponsored by Families for Russian and the Ukrainian Adoption (FRUA). Gradually, RA adoptive parents contacted me directly to participate in this project.

I informally conducted participant-observation with non-adoptive families and adoption brokers, as well as observations in schools and religious establishments to gain a sense of how institutional settings shaped ideas and practices related to family formation. I traveled to China, visited one social welfare institute, and had the opportunity to interact with Chinese American adoptive families who had brought their children to China on heritage journeys. I also spent time with non-adoptive Chinese American women and students in the United States, who are playing a key role in structuring some of the novel experiences and practices of CA families.

To learn about the experiences of children who had been adopted, how they viewed their identities within their families, among their peers, and in society, and the ways they were processing loss, gaps in memory, difference, and racism, I relied on interviews, participant-observation, and online surveys. This is an area for further research. Gaining the perspectives of children about adoption and family formation is a challenge (Fine and Sandstrom 1988). When they are young (up until about age 8), they do not necessarily articulate their feelings and experiences surrounding adoption. At around age 12, they are more reflexive and able to express their views, but they often prefer not to, especially when they enter adolescence. This leaves but a small window that tends to yield unsatisfying results. Yet children, in general, have strong feelings about their membership in different kinds of families, and those who have been adopted, as they become older, have expressed those feelings through different media. To enrich what I learned from participant-observation, interviews, and surveys, and to get a better sense of their feelings and experiences over time and the agency they were exercising, I have pored over their memoirs, docufilms, blogs, and Web postings, and their stories and comments in magazines.[17]

The Internet is a powerful product and catalyst of globalization processes. Cartwright (2005) describes how the Internet and the centrality of commodification structure adoption "choices" at the inception of the adoption process. Here, while I trace how Internet use affected prospective parents' decisions, I focus more on their and their children's use of the Internet following adoption. For all three groups I gathered data from many different listservs, websites, and discussion groups in which both children and parents participated to get a sense of the discourse, representations, and dialogues surrounding transnational and transracial adoption practices.[18]

The Scaffolding

Excellent ethnographic accounts of transnational and transracial adoption have been published. I cite many of them that have influenced my thinking. Readers familiar with the institutional backdrop, regulatory environment, and ethical debates surrounding transnational and transracial adoptions may find the material in Chapter 1 familiar. For newcomers to the subject, however, I seek to explain their significant role in how all participants in family-making in America behave. According to a survey by the Evan B. Donaldson Institute (1997), almost 60 percent of Americans know someone who has been adopted, has adopted a child, or has relinquished a child for adoption (and surely the number has risen). Whether or not the metaphoric six degrees of separation accurately describes the impact that adoption has had on how Americans think about alternative forms of family-making, this research shows that there is a far greater embrace of *particular kinds* of adoption, which remain stratified by race, gender, place, and class and that are structured, sometimes in ways that are not immediately apparent, by laws and how they are implemented.

Chapter 1 thus addresses how power, circulating through the workings of laws, adoption brokers and intermediaries, and media outlets, contributes to the erection of social barriers. At the same time, participants in adoption have come to challenge some of those barriers because of their personal experiences, their efforts to organize among themselves, and their own use of media sources. This dialectical tension, in turn, shapes how family formation transpires and how people in America think about adoption. For example, beliefs about evolution, progress, salvation, and rescue in receiving countries clash with international laws that emphasize the rights of children in sending countries. Further, in each of those countries, government policies may not coincide with people's sentiments. Children and their circulation (from one family or institutional setting to another, and sometimes via illicit means such as trafficking) feed sentiments of nationalism, and nationalism itself structures how the circulation of children should take place (Fonseca 2009; E. Kim 2010; Leinaweaver 2008; Marre and Briggs 2009). Russia's ban in 2013 of U.S. adoptions from Russia illustrates how children can be used in geopolitical battles.

In this chapter, I use "institutional context" as a catch-all phrase to refer to institutions and ideologies that forcefully structure what is normative and what are considered aberrations or threats to existing norms. Institutions, of course, consist of people, and of values, ideas, and practices that circulate within society and create hurdles, boundaries, and pathways. People do recognize and challenge the technologies of control that produce institutional discourses, perspectives, and practices. We thus need to understand not only the mechanisms of social control, but also why and how people begin to resist them or reshape them, and the consequences of their actions and the tactics they deploy (Bourdieu 1977; Lamont and Molnár 2002; Latour 2007; and de Certeau 1984). The reactions of some adoptive parents to the guiding assumptions of adoption agency personnel, for example, shed light on some of the ways they are contesting these mechanisms of social control.

Faith, Design, and Choice

Popular religiosity plays a powerful role in motivating parents to adopt, and in justifying the choices they make—whether or not to pursue adoption and from where. This is a topic hardly addressed in the anthropological literature on adoption.[19] Institutionalized religion and faith have always intervened in the stances the general public takes with respect to the practice of adoption and abortion, but popular religiosity, as I discuss it in Chapter 2, is somewhat different.

Demographics are important in understanding the prevalence of "spirituality" or what I call "popular religiosity" among adoptive parents. Many of the parents who were born at the tail end of the boomer generation had no religious affiliation or did not practice their faith. But they thought of themselves as mystical or spiritual. Their expressions of destiny, fate, and mysticism are pervasive at a time when scientific rationality overdetermines reproductive choice. At one end of the spectrum of religious intervention in adoption practices and narratives lies an individualized mysticism or spirituality. At the other end, the same sentiment is expressed as emanating from the hand of God. More accurately, adoptive parents or prospective adoptive parents who embrace creationism or "intelligent design" view the genetic blueprint of human beings, adoption, and the race, sexuality, and even socialization of their child as choices that are made for them by a superior power. It has become their rationale not only for pursuing adoption and accepting its risks and unknown dimensions, but also for having adopted a specific child. A minority of parents I interviewed appeared to use this as a rationale for pursuing adoption in the face of infertility, placing higher value on families formed through biological connections, but invoking intelligent design to explain their decision to pursue adoption as an alternative. Their logic was partly propelled by the belief that creating a family was a major and even necessary ingredient of self-actualization. At the same time, some parents already had children and chose the path of adoption for religious reasons.

Dreams, symbols, signs, and coincidences also motivated parents to adopt and served as critical guides in deciding how to adopt and from where. This popular religiosity can be counterpoised to the religious metaphors that permeate adoption narratives and are appropriated deliberately by adoption brokers and agencies in encouraging prospective parents to adopt. Children waiting to be adopted are viewed as "angels"; adoptive parents as humanitarian "rescuers" and "saints." Through the embrace of these metaphors and religious beliefs, adoption becomes situated within the rescue efforts that Naomi Klein (2007) calls "disaster capitalism," thus highlighting how economic and political power may infuse the religious motivations of some to pursue adoption as a way to make a family. I discuss the ways in which parents felt and acted on their spirituality and suggest some of the reasons they viewed themselves as destined to pursue the path of adoption. I also address why participants in adoption are associated with salvation, rescue, and angelic behavior. The idea that a super-natural force intervenes in the adoption process may facilitate the embrace of adoption as a good way to make a family; but most acknowledge, politely and quietly, that biological reproduction remains preferable. In a more complicated fashion, expressions and examples of fate at work and uncanny coincidence appear to create significant building blocks of memory from which adoptive families form elaborate ties of relationality.

Making a Place

In Chapters 3, 4, and 5, I look at the how CA, RA, and AA adoptive parents, re-spectively, imbue places with meaning as they embark on the constitution or ex-pansion of "family." Forces of globalization and multiple legal frameworks shape their practices and ideas, and clear differences become apparent between how place-making unfolds in "far away" and "nearby" adoptions. Whether a child is black and adopted from within the United States, adopted from China, or adopted from Russia leads to different decisions and practices in place-making by adoptive families.

One would expect it to be far more challenging to incorporate Chinese cul-ture and a sense of heritage into a child's life in the United States than it would be to incorporate black culture and heritage. In fact, the ability to draw on an imaginary and the security of distance, in the case of China, is in some ways easier than dealing with the realities of segregation and the risks of crossing color and class lines in the United States, in the case of AA adoptions. Fur-ther, the avoidance of place-making altogether occurs to a much greater degree among parents with children from Russia (Jacobson 2008). The place-making activities of adoptive parents have consequences for the building of memories, ties, and interactions within their families, across borders at multiple levels, as well as for the general public.

Anthropologically, place-making may or may not be based on geography. A place is distinguished because of the values associated with it, its meaningful-ness, and the activities that transpire in and across a terrain (Green, Harvey, and Knox 2005; Gupta and Ferguson 1997a; Massey and Jess 1995; Seligmann 2009). Place-making has become ever more central as a subject of anthropo-logical interest exactly when time-space compression allows flows of people, objects, information bits, technology, and signifiers of ethnicity to occur at rapid speeds across great distances (Appadurai 1990; Harvey 1990). Perhaps less obviously, many people, particularly those who have experienced displace-ment, desire or seek a place to call their own, even if it sits precariously on a border (Stephen 2007). I argue that, in general, deterritorialization and reterritorialization feed each other in place-making activities, but not necessarily in ways that make people comfortable (Coutin et al. 2002; Gupta and Ferguson 1997b; E. Kim 2010; Malkki 1997).

Parents exert considerable authority in structuring their children's identity and their face as a family, at least until their children can begin to articulate their sentiments and act on them, sometimes embracing but more often rejecting their parents' perceptions of them. In this early process of identity-building, adoptive parents work to construct a sense of place for their children, struggling with how much adoption, race, and cultural heritage matter. Adoptees are initially fairly placid about these undertakings. It is not until they reach their teen years or enter young adulthood that they take matters into their own hands, as I show in the last chapter of the book. Just as place-making was important to how adoptive parents sought to incorporate links to their children's birthplace or birth family, it is also central to how adoptees are challenging that scaffolding.

Broken Links and Adoption Narratives

In Chapter 6, I discuss how ideas about biology and culture infuse and influence the rich and varied ways in which parents construct and share adoption narratives with their children. Recent work on adoption has examined the ways that adoptive families approach "kin-making" through means other than "blood ties" and biological metaphors (Howell 2006). The adoption narratives that parents have forged reveal patterns that follow well-established narrative structure. As parents tell these adoption narratives to their children, their children incorporate them into their identity-building. The structuring and fabrication of memory and cultural heritage are central to many of these tales, and adoptive parents complement them with shared activities that acknowledge their children's complex history and links to birth culture and families. The meanings of filiation, heredity, and alliance weave in and out of these narratives. Even as they contribute to both memory- and identity-building, adoptive children struggle with discontinuities, loss, exclusion, racism, and ghosts (Dorow 2006) that they sense in the narratives, either at the time or over time.

Paul Connerton (2009) contrasts the familiarity of place and its power in constituting memory with memorials, which signal significant moments or commemorations but carefully exclude much of the history surrounding the event or occasion that is commemorated. For adoptive parents, the structuring of "memories" for their children is awkwardly situated. On the one hand, they cobble together these memories from what they know or have learned about their children's birthplace, a place that is often unfamiliar to them. Their desire to commemorate unknown connections to birth families, and the periodic memorializing they engage in during their children's early life experiences, contribute to memory-making. These memories also materialize from their daily lives in the United States. All of these conditions affect how adoptive parents make and sustain connections to their children's birthplaces and birth relatives.

All families construct ties out of quotidian activities, intimate moments, and celebratory festivities. That is, the building of ties of relatedness and intimacy are selective, whether the family emerges through biological reproduction or adoption.[20] The principal difference is that there is often more to work with initially among non-adoptive family members, less initial loss, fewer gaps, and the geopolitical topography of inequalities that structure both domestic transracial and transnational adoptions is absent. In both transnational and transracial adoptions, cultural, class, and racial differences, and the tensions between biology and culture in American family-making intervene systematically. It is principally these aspects that distinguish the content and structure of adoption narratives.

Virtual Ties, Community-Building, and Learning Lessons

The adoption narratives parents share with their children begin to be called into question when their children move into the wider world. A key site where children began to reconsider their social selves was at school, unsurprisingly. Chapter 7 reviews how discourses of power that circulated at schools had a direct bearing on American ideas about family-making. Class composition, assignments, relationships between students and teachers, and interactions on the playground are examples of the push-and-pull between the lived experiences of children whose families diverged from the taken-for-granted model of the American family. This chapter also offers examples of the courageous and creative efforts of children (and sometimes their parents) to question or alter school assignments and to question ideologies of multiculturalism that are ineffective in practice.

In Chapter 8, I compare and contrast the discourse circulating among adoptive parents in virtual communities on the Worldwide Web. Adoptive parents are immersed in activities that shape their family-making practices and narratives, and they are also avid participants in computer-mediated or virtual communities. Virtual communities provide an outlet for adoptive parents to reevaluate ideas about their own practices. I discuss how and why virtual communities create grounds for building shared assumptions that are transformative. I also look at the ways that virtual communities sometimes simply reinforce the status quo.

Forging Links and Searching

The impact of the activities and attitudes of adoptees themselves on American cultural configurations of family is not well studied.[21] In Chapter 9, I follow CA, RA, and AA children as they reach their teen years and young adulthood, and begin to confront what I call the broken links in their adoptive parents' narrative chains. In trying to deal with these broken links, the children themselves served as catalysts for alternative modes of family-making. Almost all of them carried some ambivalence within (Goffman 1963) about who they were. The causes of their ambivalence changed over time as well. For example, at a young age, they were preoccupied by looking different from their parents and being singled out because of it. At an older age, some felt as if they did not belong fully to any group and wished they spoke Chinese or knew how to braid their hair. Or they felt angry that their adoptive parents had imposed a particular cultural identity on them. As much as they loved their adoptive parents, many wondered about their birth relatives, especially their birth mother, and entertained the idea of searching for them, sometimes with considerable anticipation and trepidation. The "ghosts" that motivated them to search were often introduced unwittingly by adoptive parents themselves through narratives that featured one-dimensional absent fathers; bereaved, alcoholic, or impoverished birth mothers; abandoned children on sidewalks or close to police stations; foster mothers and orphanage care-takers; other orphaned children or biological siblings; or even abstract monolithic state policies.

Yet the stigma of adoption that was prevalent in a previous generation is no longer as fundamental to American biogenetic classificatory systems of kinship and family. Adoptees themselves have challenged the stigma associated with adoption; and interestingly, most of them have expressed a commitment to form their families through adoption. A growing number are establishing far-flung and dynamic diasporic communities that are not confined to the virtual world, but are facilitated by local gatherings, niche magazines, films, and memoirs and edited volumes in which the voices of adoptees themselves predominate. Although these are more prominent among CA and AA adoptees, RA adoptees are also engaging in some of these activities to a lesser extent.

Eleana Kim's (2010) work on Korean adult adoptees and their searches for identity, moving between South Korea and the United States, is an important influence on this chapter. Kim found that when Korean adult adoptees returned to

South Korea, their "homecomings" made them feel disconnected, and "deterritorialized." At the same time, their shared experiences fostered a powerful collective identity among them that contested both a mythic nationalism and a fabricated folklore. The narratives of the CA children, together with the far greater number of narratives of Korean adoptees that have been published, emphasize how important return journeys and heritage camps are for them, partly to learn about their culture of origin, but more so to share among themselves the experience of knitting together their identities and living as divided selves; and they can relax because they are among others whose physical resemblance they share.

RA children, more infrequently, also participate in such journeys. And the "heritage journey" of AA adoptees often takes place in the United States, where their "coming home" is sometimes far more complex than those that happen in another country. All of these searching journeys share a view of identity formation as a process that incorporates heterogeneity and flexibility. I do not label adoptee identities as "hybrid." Rather, I show that they comprise multiple currents that are not always integrated, and I trace where these currents that create facets of identity come from, how they become shared, what makes identity formation and personhood dynamic rather than static for adoptees, and what causes particular aspects of personhood to become central rather than peripheral for them.

This ethnography seeks to capture subtle and complex dimensions of oscillation and change in family-making in the United States. Many transnational and transracial adoptees are actively building a range of identities through rituals, books, symbols, stories, and everyday encounters in schools, grocery stores, and religious institutions. In their bumpy searches and as they recognize the challenges to the effects of power that are inscribed on their bodies, they find anchors in memories and lessons learned, in challenging the narratives of their parents, in the exhilaration of discovery and the satisfaction of friendship. At the same time, they invest more energy than is usually acknowledged in dealing with silence, denial, and shame that are the consequence of stigma, and in arriving at their own building blocks, narratives, and networks. The glimmers of change, of improvisations that transform daily habitus, are apparent in their steps into the future. While Americans have not experienced a sea change in how they view adoption, this ethnography points to small steps of imaginative transformation that are under way on the part of adoptive parents and their children and shaping how Americans think about the ties that bind them into families.

1 Power and Institutions

Kimchee and grits, the Four Questions in Hindi, these are the fun, the joyous sides, of our diasporas and our ethnicity. We're right to celebrate them. But we mustn't forget to talk about power.

—Barbara Katz Rothman 2005: 171

To talk about power as it intervenes in adoption is to account for how it circulates in a society, giving rise to classification systems through which knowledge is organized, value judgments exercised, and laws passed and enforced. We must also consider how people come to challenge power and in what circumstances. This chapter looks at three key settings that structure the journeys of parents as they make their families through transnational and transracial adoption: (1) laws that govern adoption and that sometimes contradict one another; (2) the workings of adoption agencies and brokers; and (3) mainstream media outlets. It is intended as a general overview rather than an in-depth and exhaustive account. Schools and the Internet constitute two other major sites of power and are the subjects, respectively, of Chapters 7 and 8.

The economic and political conditions that structured transnational and transracial adoption were not immediately apparent to many adoptive parents. Even if they were able to articulate their concerns, they struggled to arrive at ethical practices in the face of state, national, and international laws that sometimes contradicted each other. Some laws tried to make the welfare of children a priority, yet what was in the best interest of children was a subject of ongoing debate. Other laws were a response to strong nationalist sentiments, yet remained rhetorical because countries did not have the resources to enforce them. Still other laws attempted to address identity issues but came up against entrenched educational and informal socialization practices.

An elaborate yet unpredictable legal scaffolding had to be climbed and maneuvered successfully in order to adopt a child in the United States. These laws had ramifications for how adopted children were socially and culturally defined. Some were intended to deal with the growing concern about child trafficking. A wealth of literature addresses the legal dimensions of adoption. What follows here is a discussion of two major laws—one international and one national—that structure the adoption process and have an impact on the status and identity formation of adoptees.

The Hague Convention

The most important law governing international adoption is the Hague Convention on Intercountry Adoption. The Hague Convention was preceded by the United Nations Convention on the Rights of the Child (CRC), passed in 1989, whose intent was to put a stop to "wrongful" adoptions.[1] In the wake of media accounts revealing the horrendous conditions of Romania's orphanages, where children were warehoused after the fall of Nicholas Ceausescu, also in 1989, together with the eagerness with which Westerners flocked to adopt them and entrepreneurs to capitalize on the situation, it became clear that the CRC was insufficient to enforce ethical adoption practices. In 1993, nations, including the United States, began crafting what became the Hague Convention in 1994. In order to become a signatory to the Convention, a nation had to commit itself to cooperate "to prevent the abduction, the sale of, or traffic in children" for international adoption. The United States signed the treaty in 1994, yet waited until 2000 to ratify it, and did not implement its requirements until April 1, 2008.[2] The Hague Convention includes a passage requiring that nations make every effort to keep children with their original family; that a Central Authority be charged with overseeing international adoptions; and that parents honor their child's cultural heritage.

The biggest problem with the Convention is that it allows signatories to the Convention to continue to transact adoptions with nations that either are not members (of about 195 countries, only 81 are members) or that have not yet signed the Convention. These include, for example, Ethiopia, Haiti, Korea, Nepal, Russia, Haiti, and Vietnam, from which many adoptions to the United States take place. Many "sending" regions also prohibit "receiving" countries from adopting from them if the latter have not ratified the Convention. This was true of the long period during which the United States had not ratified the Convention.

According to E. J. Graff, more than two-thirds of U.S. international adoptions come from non-Hague countries, where a significant number of adoption scandals have taken place. Graff (2010) lays out the loopholes and problems with the Hague Convention and with international adoptions involving non-Hague countries or those that have not yet ratified it, including the certification of adoption agencies as partners. Availability of resources, certification, the intervention of immigration offices and officials in non-Hague adoptions, training, and oversight of due process intervene in the effective implementation of the law and the prevention of corruption. In short, all participants in adoption processes are far more vulnerable to the violation of due process if both parties are not full members of the Convention, as the ban on Russian adoptions in 2013 demonstrated so well.

Weighing Social Justice: Ethics and Rights

Laws create the conditions for different kinds of rights to be either protected or ignored. Leslie Hollingsworth (2003) offers an analysis of what social justice means for the parties involved in transnational adoption, using three social justice frameworks—egalitarian, utilitarian, and libertarian. She argues that the differences in the frameworks rest on the interpretation of fairness, decency, and compassion. In an egalitarian framework, liberty, opportunity, income, wealth, and the bases of self-respect "should be distributed equally unless an unequal distribution is to the advantage of the least favored." In a utilitarian framework, the driving assumption is that the "distribution of resources is just when the parameters are directed to the greatest good for the greatest number." *Who* is the greatest number and *what* constitutes the greatest good are matters for interpretation rather than objective facts. Finally, a libertarian approach to social justice assumes that if individuals have "rightfully acquired the resources they possess, they have the freedom to decide how to dispose of them" and the government should not intervene in determining the distribution of resources (Hollingsworth 2003: 211).

Hollingsworth embraces the egalitarian framework but modifies it to recognize that in many circumstances, including adoption, the playing field is not level. Adopting families may benefit from existing inequalities such as poverty in sending countries; the condition of disenfranchised children; gender oppression and discrimination that select for the vulnerability of some children and not others; the lack of access of children to knowledge about and contact with their birth families; the "interruption" of the right of children to identify with their racial, ethnic, or national group; and the growing abduction, sale, and trafficking of children.

The United Nations Convention and the Hague Convention represent efforts to address these injustices. Nevertheless, Hollingsworth concludes that they have not had much impact because they are difficult to implement effectively. For example, a critical dimension of social justice linked to adoption processes is the need for social change in sending countries that would alleviate poverty and diminish the probability that children would be abandoned by their birth families or taken from their birth countries. That is, in the best of all possible worlds, children would be able to be raised by their natal families and in their culture of origin. Given that this is not the case, Hollingsworth argues that parents who adopt internationally should recognize the "losses incurred by internationally adopted children and their birth families" and they should "be aware of the importance of culture to children and of children to their culture" (Hollingsworth 2003: 216).

Only gradually are adoptive parents coming to recognize the losses that make adoption possible for them. In contrast, many adoptees themselves are pushing hard to open the general public's eyes to the conditions that led them to be adopted. In addition to wanting a greater voice in how adoption and practices associated with it are viewed ideologically, some are working to change economic conditions in their place of birth.

Adoptive parents I spoke with struggled with the binary oppositions and ethical dilemmas described above that went hand in hand with the laws that structured adoption, although they only recognized them as such after they had adopted. Almost all of them were uncomfortable with the fusion of monetary transactions and gifts in the adoption process, the unpredictability of regulations and their enforcement, the undercurrent of competition that structured how prospective adoptive parents were forced to present themselves as ideal parents, and the specter of child trafficking. CA and AA adoptive parents also found themselves confronting the complex issues surrounding the identity of their children, and the "plural and ambivalent" struggles they faced in the United States (Briggs 2006).

Some scholars who study the legal codes that underpin adoption argue that it should be viewed solely as an economic practice, a regulated "trading system." Their view is that the discourse of regulation has simply been moderated or replaced by terms more palatable to Americans for whom the cultural domain of family formation lies outside of commodity exchange. Deborah Spar (2006), for example, thinks that supply and demand must guide the laws that determine transactions and that the causes for supply and demand need not be addressed. As she explains,

> In purely economic terms, adoption is the most rational aspect of the baby trade. There is a vast unmet demand for children and a ready supply of them scattered across the world. By matching demand with supply, adoption would

appear to be the ideal solution to infertility, a match of immeasurable value on both sides of the transaction. . . . The "buyers" don't *really* want to purchase their babies. The *suppliers* don't want to sell. And governments around the world consistently condemn baby-selling as a crime akin to slavery. But still there are surplus children in the world, and would-be parents who want to adopt them. And so adoption has generated an ersatz market of sorts, a system of structured trades. . . . Money changes hands in this market-without-a-name, but the money is rarely buying children per se and the system is subject to a labyrinth of formal controls—far more, in fact, than exist in nearly any other sector of the baby business. (Spar 2006: 176)

Spar lays out the paradoxical situation in which a highly regulated "business" has historically operated in a "laissez-faire" manner with a hodge-podge of regulations and public and private agents and institutions, and in which humanitarianism is well mixed with the dynamics of consumerism. Concluding that it is impossible to separate economics from politics in the "baby business," she argues for more uniform and systematic regulations of adoption as a matter of "property rights" both inside the United States and internationally:

Embed this market in an appropriate political and regulatory context, to impose the rules that will enable the market to produce the goods we want—happy, healthy children—without encouraging the obvious risks. . . . If we can make the baby business work better—if we can match parents and children more consistently, at a lower cost, and with less uncertainty—then political support for the market is likely to grow. And if we clarify the politics, distinguishing what is acceptable from what is not, the market will inevitably work better. (Spar 2006: 197)

Spar relies on a neoclassical economic model. For her, the adoption market operates badly because of intractable political ideologies and uneven regulations, and her goal is to arrive at laws and enforcement mechanisms that make it work more smoothly. She does not address the *context* in which these ideologies arise and the baby business unfolds.

In contrast, a host of scholars, while they are concerned about the effectiveness of laws, argue that participants in adoption (and law-making) should recognize first and foremost that adoptions, especially transracial and transnational ones, are "neocolonial undertakings" that create impossible situations for adoptees (Briggs 2006; Marre and Briggs 2009). The very promotion of supply and demand as the best way to regulate adoption also reduces chil-

dren to objects of exchange. In the spirit of critical race theory and legal studies, they point to the economic and political ideologies that then set the stage
for facilitating particular kinds of transactions between sending and receiving countries and groups. They argue that while adoptive parents have become more aware of the geopolitical conditions that permitted them initially
to adopt, and of the need, once they adopt their children, to prepare them
for the consequences of racism in the United States, they are nevertheless in-
sufficiently cognizant of the painful conditions of identity formation among
adoptees and the myriad ways that the exertion of authority silences adoptees
and censures the knowledge to which they are privy. Tobias Hubinette lays out
his position along those lines:

> My main argument is that adopted Koreans have been fully acculturated and
> socialized into a self-identification as white. At the same time as having a
> Korean body, they are incessantly liable to a whole regime of Orientalist imagi-
> naries trying to fetishize them into an ethnic stereotype. Furthermore, being a
> non-white body, an ever-present discourse of Immigrantism wants to racialize
> them into an Asian and non-Western immigrant. Lastly as an ethnic Korean,
> nowadays they are also warmly interpellated by a Korean diaspora policy that
> essentializes them into and hails them as overseas Koreans. . . . I regard this
> acquisition of a white self-identification by adopted Koreans as a complete
> subordination to white hegemonic power, and as a magnificent symbol of the
> final triumph of the colonial project. (Hubinette 2007: 158)

Laura Briggs (2006: 345) expands on Hubinette's arguments, pointing to
the deleterious effects of media images, as well of child trafficking, but her
thinking is based on the experiences of Chinese adoptees rather than Korean
adoptees. She asks: "What burden does the "Chinese girl toddler" bear in com-
mercials, Olympic promotions, etc.? What does it really mean to depict her
in [the] context of the new 'American family'?" She finds that globalization,
while it has distributed wealth and information internationally, has created,
once again, dualisms, but ones that differ from those of the past. Rather than
presenting oppositions between pure/impure and white/racially mixed, the
dualisms now revolve around the contradictory notions that "internationally
adopted children can become the inheritors of their adoptive parents' national
culture and, on the other hand, understanding them as exilic, diasporic refugees whose inheritance is necessarily plural and ambivalent" (Briggs: 346).
Briggs also states that people in general, and adoptive parents in particular,
have "turned a blind eye to trafficking," yet "none of this is particularly new.

As Ann Stoler has continued to remind us, raising the 'orphans' of colonized people is a very familiar practice" (Briggs: 348).[3]

Thus, even as international law in the form of the Hague Convention attempts to address the heterogeneity of adoption practices and regulate them in order to protect child, birth parent, and adoptive parent, the law itself is enforced on a playing field that is already deeply saturated with histories of colonialism, economic inequalities, racial ideologies, and national reproductive policies. These conditions create unevenness within and between both sending and receiving regions that cannot be addressed by laws alone.

Multiethnic Placement Act/Interethnic Adoption Provisions

A second law that has played a major role in structuring adoption practices, especially AA adoptions within the United States, is the Multiethnic Placement Act/Interethnic Adoption Provisions (MEPA/IEP). In 1994, the U.S. Congress passed MEPA in light of the high number of African American children in the state welfare system without adoptive families. The law was intended to prevent the matching of children and to increase transracial adoptions. In 1996, Congress passed IEP (the Interethnic Adoption Provisions), more stringently enforced legislation that was part of welfare reform.[4] MEPA, at a minimum, converted into law the notion that racial matching and, by extension, cultural commonalities, should be irrelevant in adoption.

The passage of MEPA was a direct rebuttal to the position taken by the National Association of Black Social Workers (NABSW). In 1972, the NABSW issued a statement that transracial domestic adoption was equivalent to cultural genocide for African Americans.[5] The NABSW saw domestic AA transracial adoptions as leading to an absolute loss of black culture. They argued that because black children adopted into white families would adopt white culture, black culture would be further marginalized. They also believed that white parents, in their privileged position, were not equipped to teach African American children how to use the tools of racial navigation they would need in U.S. society, especially as they grew older. In 1984 and then again in 2003, the NABSW reiterated its position. MEPA/IEP has generated great controversy. The account given by AA parent Amber of her adoption process, which described the power of state agency workers in interpreting and implementing MEPA/IEP, was the norm:

> I never decided to adopt a black baby. I just decided that I would be open to
> it. And I think once you say that at these agencies, they're going to give you a
> black kid or Hispanic. I think it's their kind of diplomatic language that they

have to use—if you're open to it. All these other people who want white only, it's unlikely that you're going to get a white kid. There are so few takers for the others. So as soon as you say you're open to it, it's kind of clear to me that you're going to get one. (AA5)[6]

In practice, MEPA/IEP's tenets contradict the Hague Convention's emphasis on cultural commonalities and heritage, which are aimed at international adoptions (Ishizawa 2006: 1209–10). Smith et al. (2008) found that MEPA and IEP have made no difference in increasing the number of transracial adoptions from the welfare system (see also Evan B. Donaldson Adoption Institute 2008). Negatively sanctioning racial matching in an effort to encourage transracial adoption from the state welfare system has not worked. Deeper structural inequalities, demographics, and cultural practices may explain better why African American children are not being adopted in higher numbers out of the child welfare system. For example, among African Americans, informal kinship care is more highly valued than adoption (Stack 1974). For African Americans, adoption of African American children with a price tag attached to them also evokes a market model that existed all too recently under slavery; and many do not have as much familiarity with adoption as Euroamericans since they were excluded for many years as potential adoptive parents.

Infant adoption and adoption out of foster care have also too often been conflated. Children in foster care tend to be older and have more problems, regardless of their race, although it is true that African American children are disproportionately represented (Dept. of Health and Human Services 2004; Freundlich 2000: 30). Infants of all races are far more readily adopted than children in foster care, and African American children in foster care may already be enmeshed in a fairly stable and permanent network of kinship ties (Freundlich 2000: 2–26). In assessing MEPA/IEP, Twila Perry, a specialist in family law, remarked,

> Studies have consistently shown that entry into foster care is closely associated with poverty, inadequate housing, and parental substance abuse, issues which transracial adoption policy in no way addresses. Despite the symbolic significance of transracial adoption . . . in the end, it does not provide a solution to the many problems that the vast majority of Black children in this society face. (Perry 1993/94: 107)

Class standing also helps explain why MEPA/IEP has not been successful. The income range of both African American and non-African American prospective parents who adopt African American children is lower than that of parents who adopt internationally. The key here is that the correlation between income and race creates greater choices for white, heterosexual prospective parents who are middle- and upper middle class (Horridge 2011).

Two related trends highlight tensions surrounding the adoption of African American children in the United States. Americans are adopting black children in increasing numbers, not from within the United States, but from Ethiopia, which figured among the top three countries from which Americans adopted children in 2009 and 2010, and has been among the top ten since 2004.[7] Concomitant with this trend is another. Davenport reported that "African-American babies are going to parents overseas even as U.S. couples adopt children from other countries. The United States is now the fourth largest 'supplier' of babies for adoption to Canada, most of whom are African American." One Canadian working with an adoption agency in British Columbia remarked, "Most of our families just want a baby as young as possible and the United States is the best place to go for a newborn. We are not ignoring the race issues, but we don't think, like the Americans, that the less black the better." And another woman noted, "The families from abroad do not think of black babies as being second best, babies that they'll 'settle' for because white babies are hard to find."[8]

In domestic transracial adoptions, the passage and enforcement of MEPA and IEP, ironically, have brought race and culture in through the back door of the adoption process, fostering some pathological practices. Because social workers are not permitted to openly discuss whether parents are willing to accept children of color prior to the finalization of adoption, social workers report comments such as, "yes, but I didn't expect a child *that* black." Consequently, they are spending inordinate amounts of time in post-adoption sessions, negatively sanctioning parents who do not properly expose their transracial children to the part of their heritage and culture that is not white. These kinds of socialization or training could not be broached *before* adoption because states run the risk of losing their federal funding if they raise the issue of race. And states have been fined hefty amounts by the federal government. Thus, in the name of anti-racism, racism is reinscribed.

Agencies and Brokers

Adoption agencies and the brokers who work with them are of paramount importance to how adoptions unfold. Their ideas and actions are constrained by laws that operate at multiple levels, but their choices are also motivated by their life histories and aspirations (Leinaweaver 2008). They may be selective in pressuring prospective parents toward one kind of adoption rather than another. Agencies also have the right to demand that prospective parents become informed, whether they want to or not, about issues of race and culture that could play a role in their child's identity formation. This does not necessarily mean parents follow through, but the information conveyed to them, often in the form of workshops, alerts parents to what they can expect and encourages them to seek out further information in the future when and if they need it.

Adoption agencies dedicated to international adoptions have long been in the forefront of proffering information about race, culture, and heritage. They are also supposed to provide participants in adoption with social support services before, during, and after the adoption. They are responsible for ensuring that parent-child welfare is being properly attended to after an adoption takes place, with social workers conducting between two and four visits to the newly constituted family. Many culture camps and heritage journeys have also been established by these same agencies or by individuals who worked in them at one time. They are money-making ventures, but the individuals who promote them also view them as vital to the welfare of adoptive families.

Nongovernmental organizations (NGOs) have become brokers themselves, but in a more indirect fashion. They have established cooperative relationships with adoption agencies or with governments themselves to provide services to orphanages. These services help to create better living conditions at orphanages and become conduits through which adoptive families maintain communication and gift exchanges with orphanages following their return to the United States.

In transnational adoptions, brokers who work closely with adoption agencies are often from the country of origin itself. They are familiar with individuals who can facilitate or obstruct the adoption process, they know how to navigate bureaucratic hurdles, they have forged networks among themselves, and they are eager to make a living and satisfy their clients. These brokers are critical to the adoption process, giving the impression that all is going smoothly, closing or opening crucial gates, and withholding or offering up information to prospective adoptive parents. Many transfer their aspirations for upward mobility to prospective adoptees, assuming their lives will be far better elsewhere (Leinaweaver 2008). As Leinaweaver makes clear, the positive view of adoption and of foreign adoption held by brokers is not necessarily shared by their fellow citizens. Helena's depiction of a broker who intervened on her family's behalf when they were adopting a child from Russia characterized the mediating position and practices of many international adoption brokers like this:

> Irena lived in Moscow with her mother and was an only child, and she had learned English in school and then essentially became fairly proficient on her own to the point where she came across this job working for this agency that we used, which was International Family Services. And we were lucky enough to meet her after she had done this kind of work for a few years, so she had quite a lot of experience already dealing with Americans who were in the process of adopting. So she seemed to know what to say and when to say it and was very good about helping us to understand the Russian point of view on adoption, the important role that Americans were playing in helping these children have a better life, but also the ambiguities and the difficulties that Russians faced knowing that they couldn't care for their own children sufficiently and that they had to resort to strategies such as this. (RA9)

In Russia, adopting parents were expected to make two visits. During the first visit, prospective parents would meet the child and determine whether they wanted to proceed. Once the birth parents' rights were terminated officially, a second visit was arranged. At first, the child selected for Helena and Bessie was extremely withdrawn. Helena worked assiduously to get him to respond to her over a period of a week. She described what happened and how it affected due process:

> At one point I picked Giorgi up, held him up above me, and then he looked right into my eyes and from that point on, it was like, he woke up . . . and became this entirely different person than he was. And it must have been a pretty big deal because when I went to court the following month, that was all the doctor kept talking about, and the doctor kept telling the judge how disturbed Giorgi was and then he woke up when I got there and as soon as I left he went back to sitting in the corner doing nothing, and [he told] the judge [that he] had to waive the waiting period and give him to me today, and the judge waived the waiting period and gave him to me that day. It was not normally waived. . . . We were home for only two weeks. (RA15)

Helena found that most of the brokers she encountered—interpreters, doctors, and judges primarily— advocated to get children into homes and out of the orphanages.

One sensational case in the United States drove home some of the sobering and contradictory effects of the regulatory environment on transnational adoption. In 2010 a single mother from Tennessee sent her 7-year-old adopted son back to Moscow with a note to the Russian Ministry of Education stating she "no longer wanted to parent this child" because she could not cope with his psychotic and violent behavior. She wrote that the Russian adoption personnel and the orphanage director had blatantly lied to her about the child's mental stability.[9] The case raised issues about legal responsibility. Since the boy had been legally adopted in the United States, when there were problems agency workers in the United States should have been alerted to them and the parents should have sought help. This appeared not to have happened. Nationalism intervened as well because, despite most Russians' negative view of domestic adoption, after the boy was returned, several Russian families offered to adopt him. Yet, as noted, he had already been legally adopted in the United States.

The Russian case was somewhat unusual, but precisely for that reason it called attention to the effects of laws and practices and the power of brokers that were normally hidden from view (Coutin et al. 2002). Less extreme cases abounded in the narratives I collected from parents, such as this one, involving a lawyer. Tamar and her husband eventually adopted from China rather than Eastern Europe:

> We had some problems with a lawyer . . . we were working with, Jim Sherman, up in Maryland. He was into a lot of international adoptions. He was flying in these girls from Russia over to Texas (he was in cahoots with another attorney down in Texas). The women would come over here and have their babies and the babies would be citizens of the United States, and then he would fly the mothers back to Russia. So he was getting people to buy people [babies] from them. Well, anyway, they got found out. 'Cause he went out to West Virginia, it was in the paper, we were shocked when we saw this—what he did was that he went out and told this mother that she had to give her baby up and he had a gun. (CA 21)

While I was writing this book, Russia had shut down adoptions to the United States and, despite the unsettling experiences described above, U.S. prospective parents were waging their own battles to reopen adoption.

China, as well, has had to confront the reality that its adoption process is less than transparent. Until 2008 it was considered a desirable country from which to adopt for many reasons, one of which was that the process was well established and prospective parents knew what to expect. China had also ratified the Hague Convention. Many more stories of child trafficking for profit and the involvement of petty bureaucratic officials in these activities have come to light, forcing adoptive parents to reflect uneasily on the adoption process.[10] CA adoptive parents noted with distress the growing number of individuals who expected monetary "gifts" in the adoption process and who reduced adoption to a money-making proposition. The semblance of standardization and the smoothness of the process masked the lack of attention to the status and life conditions of individual children and birth family members, and limited adoptive parents' ability to know more about them. Adoptive parent Sally commented,

> Well, I can speak for myself. I think in our particular agency they did not address attachment, and it's a big piece of the puzzle when you adopt a child.[11] Regardless of from where, whether it's a country outside of the United States or inside, attachment is an issue, and some attach better than others, and we don't always know what that looks like. So that's definitely an area where it needs attention. They were more concerned about us getting over there and getting the child than they were with us being prepared for whatever we were going to have to deal with. (CA18)

Her husband, Chris, added, "What I learned was it's a paper mill and it's an industry, and they try to make money. So they want to get you over there. They don't want to tell you about all the problems the kids might have" (CA18). Tamar's perspective was similar:

> I mean, everybody wants a piece of the pie; we paid everybody . . . the State Department, ...the Chinese Embassy, if you want an expedited review. . . . And that is before you send in your dossier. And there's a couple down in Woodbridge, and all they do is carry documents in every day. . . . So we paid them their money. Then we went to the Great Wall and . . . then we came back and we got on the plane and flew to the Province. Got to the hotel and we weren't there more than ten minutes and they brought the children in. It was the worst thing to do. . . . They were rushing us through because they had another group. . . . It was just insane. . . . We got Kristy that night. They brought her to our room, and so every time you came back to your room, the child would cry. . . . I don't want to go through it ever again because the poor kid . . . didn't know what was going on, caretaker people were crying, and somebody videotaped it, and I keep the videotape out of spite. . . . It's very sad. And everybody had to get a gift for the orphanage director, for the caretaker. (CA21)

Individuals and agencies that perform brokerage functions almost always engage in wheeling and dealing; hence the phrase "It is "hard to find an honest broker" is especially apt. Satisfying the parties involved in transnational adoption meant weighing speed, efficiency, and economic returns upon completion of a successful transaction against due process that involved the protection of the rights of participants. Contradictions were also apparent among adoptive parents and their agencies, which then exerted pressure on in-country brokers. Tamar and Chris were taken aback by the undue haste with which adoption proceedings were taking place in China and by the numerous monetary transactions that accompanied each step. On the other hand, their agency, and adoptive parents in particular, wanted to have a predictable process in place, and they also wanted to complete their adoption as rapidly as possible. It is not surprising that the process left room for bribery and a lack of full disclosure.

The concerns of the AA adoptive parents I interviewed revolved more around the non-uniform regulations governing adoption within state agencies and among states (interstate compacts), the intensely competitive nature of presenting oneself as an ideal adopter, the possibility that adoptions would not proceed because of changes of heart on the part of birth parents and their relatives (especially if money had changed hands in order to support the birth mother during her pregnancy), and the sentiment among some agency workers that white parents should not be adopting black children. Some adoptive parents voiced all of these concerns at once. Alexa emphasized the lack of uniformity in the process:

> So, I'd love to see federal adoption laws standardized. Who has rights, this is what you need in a home study, and maybe not quite to that level of nitty-gritty but to the extent that, like now, a wedding, a marriage in one state is valid in another usually, gay marriage aside. So why can't adoption in one state be valid in another state? Why do we have to have such huge differences? ... If you go to Texas [to adopt] and you live in California, you should be able to bring the baby back to California. It's all one country, so why do we have such wide variances? And then of course there's adopting through the state, and there has been a lot of research that says that people that try to adopt through the state and try to inquire just never get their phone calls returned, and they are taking so long and it's probably because social workers are so overworked ... so they give up or they just do something that is more efficient or private. (AA3)

Betsy and Allen, like other AA adoptive parents, spoke to me about the portfolios and albums they had to prepare for birth families who would select among them. The structure, content, and preparation of portfolios and how they were received deserves its own analysis (Horridge 2011). Adoption agency personnel play a central role in counseling prospective adoptive parents about what they should include and exclude in such albums. Betsy explained:

> Today, almost everywhere, you have to put together an album that depicts who you are, and it's actually for some people a very disturbing undertaking. There's competition in order to be accepted. It's the market, so people spend money. . . . One person who did this found she was an expert, and so she's now planning to start a business to assist people in preparing this. (AA8)

Brandy, a street-savvy woman who had lived in Chicago for many years and worked with foster children in an elementary school, thought that after she and her husband had two children they would adopt three or four more. She was critical of the child welfare system, arguing that they were more concerned about racial matching than about the welfare of children. She and Roy were open to adopting mixed-race children and non-infants. They agreed that if they adopted one African American child, then they wanted their other children to be African American as well. They worked through the public welfare system and fostered their son, Lance, before adopting him. Since he was African American, they then decided after a short time to try to adopt a sibling group of two girls and their brother, Joni, Kayla, and Jessie. Brandy described with bitterness what happened, an experience similar to others reported to me by adoptive parents of African American children, and that demonstrated the power adoption agencies and brokers can exercise in structuring family formation.

> Our original case workers were very good. They were very sensitive to the . . . fear, you know, what if we are never chosen? What if we get the kids and something goes wrong and we have to give them back? How do you live through that? You know, grief, 'cause every stage, you reprocess your grief, their grief, just the whole thing that life isn't a storybook and that things don't always happen the way you think they are going to happen when you are 12. Then they brought in a new supervisor—luckily our adoptions were almost finished, because I think that had they not been so far along in the court case she would have tried to block them. The new case worker was very much of the opinion that black children should be in black homes and not white. You know, people were like, well, what is the reality? You have, I forget how many it was, like

two hundred black children on this agency's caseload alone and you have four black families. Do you want to put fifty kids in a home?

Linda: Was she herself African American?

Brandy: She herself was African American. She was involved in the lovely decision to split my daughters away from my son because it would be easier to get the girls adopted out, and then they [the state welfare system] could get the money for them. So she never had the children's best interest at heart because when they split the girls away from their brother and placed them in ... African American homes [at] the house that my girls were placed in, um, they beat my daughter. So, yeah, okay, they were in a black home but at what price? You know? She got hit! But she [the case worker] was mad when she found out that the girls had been given to us to adopt because why not place them in a home with a good black mother? And I'm like, "She hit her. She hit the kids!" And the case worker answers, "So, maybe they were bad." And I'm like, "You can't just place them with whoever just because they're black. You've got to look at the whole, what's best for the kids." And she basically told us, "Don't even bother trying to adopt anymore because I'm not going to let you." And her only reason was that we were white and the kids were black. . . . I know several other families filed similar complaints against her, but she kept denying it . . . so we were never able to get her out from the agency. . . . I know a couple of the other families switched agencies to get away from her. I just actually heard over the summer that she had left the agency, and who knows where she is now. (AA10)

Brandy was frustrated by the experiences with matching that her agency (or at least this particular social worker) engaged in and its consequences for her children. At the same time, she was apprehensive about how African Americans would view her family because of the cultural genocide policy that the NABSW had laid out.

Brokers also intervened in the production of official and unofficial documents. Paper trails (and their lack) powerfully affect children in how they construct memories about who they are and who they will be, as they grow up (Yngvesson and Coutin 2006). Adopted children use documents that are culturally viewed as foundational guideposts in lifelines—the names of progenitors, birth time and date, medical records, and landmarks (birth location)—to create their paths to the future. The paths they create are "crab-like," as they embrace the documents, return to their birthplace and/or birth parents to substantively recuperate their past, challenge and reinterpret the documents themselves, and hence reconstruct their initial narratives (Yngvesson and Coutin 2006: 183).

Adoption agencies and the intermediaries who work in them thus directly affect "given" family models, which then intervene in adoptees' identity formation. The actions they take have legal implications as well. Becky, a single mother of two African American children, told me of her confrontation with a social worker about the ownership of photographs that she felt were rightfully her son's and that validated his relationship with his birth mother and foster mother. Becky had already worked hard to gather as much factual information about Jerrick as possible—his age, health, and the moves he had made. Mary May, the social worker, visited Becky at home:

> She had brought a photo album . . . very lovingly prepared by Jerrick's most recent foster mother. Mary May was flipping through the photos and I got to see it. It was really nice. There were pictures of Jerrick when he was, 3, 4, and 5. One of them was a picture of Beulah, Jerrick's first [birth] mom. And the social worker takes a look and says, "What's this? Oh. This shouldn't be in here!" She takes it out. But this was Jerrick's book! And it took six months for me to persuade her to get it out of her file cabinet . . . because it wasn't her property. It wasn't her legacy. It was his! And so the first family member I met—who gave birth to Jerrick—is through a photo. And that was removed, but I'm very proud of the fact that I got it back. And as time went on, I made copies, made it bigger. I think that was an important part because there was this instant reaction of "Well, that's not right!" (AA6)

These trails and traces follow a stereotypical pattern. In foreign adoptions, documents many times appear to be fabricated by bureaucrats acting as brokers who are involved in adoptions at different stages and for different reasons. Yet found places, abandonment decrees, medical records, visas, passports, notarial documents, birth certificates, birth certificates issued in the country of origin, birth certificates reissued in the United States, and so forth, are viewed as creating truth, access, and in short, a particular reality. Adoptive parents, focused on successfully completing an adoption, have only recently begun contesting their lack of access to and the veracity of some of these documents.

Sylvia, a single mother who adopted two children from China, openly described her attempts to penetrate the smokescreen created by a fabricated paperwork trail for the sake of her daughter, Yvonne. An older woman had found Yvonne as an infant after she was abandoned, and Yvonne had lived with her for five years. The woman, who was 65, was a retired obstetrician and already had three adult children. She opened a savings account for Yvonne, but when the time came for her to go to school she could not enroll her because she had no birth certificate. The only way she could go to school was if the woman sent her to the orphanage, which is what she did when Yvonne was 5 and a half. Sylvia explained:

> It was heartbreaking because Yvonne said that her "grandmother" [the older woman who had taken her in]—she called her Nai-nai—came to visit her a few times, but they would just both cry, and so after a while she quit coming. I went to get Yvonne one year later, so she was 6 and a half when I got her, and we found the police report, 'cause I guess she took her to the police station and the police took her to the orphanage, and we went and found the police station, and they knew her [the "grandmother"] and said she lived around the corner, and we went and found her house and she had moved. And they didn't know where she went. I think they said that she had gone to live with her daughter in Beijing. And I said, "Where? Don't you have an address, a phone number?" Nothing. So we came back to the States and as it turned out a lady at my church, a Chinese American woman, was from the same city, and she had family there and she called up her brother and her brother had connections[and they had connections] . . . and they found this woman because you have to register when you move. . . . You can't just live wherever you want, you have to register with the local police station and they keep track of the population that way. And they found her in Beijing, living with her daughter and son-in-law and grandkids. And we went and visited them. And so when Yvonne was 8, I guess she had been here for two years, we went to Beijing for a week and she got to spend time with her grandmother, who is a wonderful woman, as you can imagine. (CA20)

In most cases when adoptive parents are prevented from accessing documents, or when documents are either missing or fabricated, things do not end so well. The documents serve as barriers, dividing families from one another. Had they had more information about their children's earlier connections, then adoptive parents, birth relatives, foster parents, and caretakers might have had more interactions with one another. Family preferences will differ, but increasingly, adoptive parents and adoptees express a desire to have these kinds of connections and have tried to establish them, despite legal constraints.

Questions of access and openness, as well as the fabrication of documents, confronted the domestic and transnational adoptive families I studied in different ways. In AA adoptions, birth parents had the option, in conjunction with adoptive parents, of choosing the degree of openness in their relationships with their children, even if they officially severed rights to them. These agreements usually began as written contracts, crafted carefully by attorneys and regulated by adoption agencies, but over time, participants informally altered them. The violation of official legal restrictions is far more common than is reported because adoption workers themselves sometimes collaborate in facilitating contacts by leaving confidential records open on desks when they leave the room or by providing knowledge about the whereabouts of a birth relative.

Secrecy and sealed birth records are intended to protect birth parents. Adoptive parents generally welcome the practice as a symbolic reflection of full relinquishment. However, growing numbers of adoptees have advocated for open adoption and argue that keeping information from the children about their own backgrounds violates their rights. The following example was ubiquitous among domestic adoptees, transracial or not.

As an adult, Kevin Hoffman decided to search for his birth mother. He described his reaction to the case worker who denied him access to his papers:

> She tells me that my birth mother did not sign a consent form. . . . My access is denied. . . . This frustrates me because technically my birth mother did not say I could *not* see the information. She never said either way, but since this one piece of paper is not in the file, my birth mother's right to privacy trumps my right to my own information. . . . This thought plays over and over in my head. I am sitting at my desk in the corner of my dorm room and I am talking to a woman in Detroit. She, who has no connection to me, knows more about me than I do. The name of my birth parents, and their social security numbers, are all on a desk in Detroit and I can't see it. I sit at college powerless. There is no arguing this, and it appears my search has ended before it begins. As a consolation, the woman informs me that she can send me my "non-identifying information." . . . I want to scream and yell and chew this woman's head off. She is only doing her job. (Hoffman 2010: 133)

One contrast between domestic transracial and transnational adoptions was that more AA adoptive parents were not averse to, and some eagerly sought, open contact with birth relatives and depended on agency personnel and attorneys to facilitate these contacts. Almost all of them reported, however, that birth relatives were more tentative about these contacts. Barbara Melosh (2002) offers a careful account of the complexity of legislating openness between birth and adoptive family members and the struggles to balance the rights of adoptees and birth family members in particular.

Sometimes AA adoptive parents sought greater openness for their children's sake, as Brandy did; others wanted enough openness so that they could have access to medical records. Most CA and RA adoptive parents, in contrast, initially pursued transnational adoption because they opposed the idea of maintaining ongoing connections with birth relatives and wanted a "clean break," a "new family." Over time, CA and RA adoptive parents began to regret that more information and connections were not available to them.

Information about how birth relatives and caretakers in transnational adoptions feel about openness is scarce. When CA adoptive families have returned to visit the orphanages from which they adopted their children, the response has been positive and caretakers have been eager to receive photos and regular updates about the children who were in their care. The few cases where reconnections have been made with birth parents or foster parents have also been reported in a positive light, but the numbers are small.

Media Portrayals: "All in the Family"

Four broad trends characterize media representations of adoption and, indirectly, families in America. The first trend, most notable in children's feature films and children's literature, is the long tradition of portraying orphans as living in horrendous and inhumane conditions in orphanages and as eventually being saved by better-off families and living happily ever after. This portrayal has had an enormous impact on how adoption is viewed in America.[12]

A second trend is the depiction of adoptees' search for and eventual reconnection with their birth families. The scenario presented is that, after a series of trials and tribulations, adoptees are eventually reunited with their birth families. One example is the television series *Find My Family*. And there are others. Internationally, they have an additional dimension to them that Eleana Kim (2010) has documented. She argues that in the case of Korean adoptees, the reunion of children with birth parents is a way of reincorporating adoptees into their nation of origin.

A third trend is to publicize the numerous children in foster care who are seeking permanent families, as represented by the television program *Wednesday's Child*. Publicizing these children may lead occasionally to foster-to-adoption happy endings, but the program producers rarely level with the public about the children's biographical details or the economic circumstances and social assumptions that have created such a burden on the child welfare system.

The fourth trend focuses on the underbelly of transnational adoption, especially child trafficking and the institutional conditions of children in different parts of the world. The excerpts below provide an overview of how adoptive parents have responded to media representations of adoption:

> Going international is more as a result of the domestic process being so different in every state, and everybody knows the horror stories because that's what *Dateline* shows. . . . Apparently, like a week ago or something, they had this "birth mother" who had scammed like seven different couples into adopting a nonexistent baby. . . . I mean it's news, yeah, but at the same time, could you present the other side? . . . I don't know if you've ever seen the *Baby Dance*, but that was my nightmare. It's with Stockard Channing and Laura Dern. . . . Anyways, at the end Laura Dern has this baby, but the cord gets wrapped around the baby's neck, so the husband of Stockard Channing doesn't want to adopt the baby and the baby ends up being essentially abandoned at the hospital and that's the end of that. And I am like, "Oh I am so glad that I spent my time watching that movie." This was way before . . . so the other thing about domestic adoption is you see this couple and you've seen them give them thousands and thousands of dollars and then they end up not adopting the baby. (AA3)

> Because all you ever hear on the media is the bad. All the ones that don't work out and all the ones that kill their adopted moms. You never hear about the good adoptions and the good families that are formed. Especially watching just regular television, there were a couple of adoption storylines on some TV shows that made me really cringe. They were so negative about adoptive parents and adoptive parents being baby stealers, that sort of thing, but I think that it's just the way media works. They pick the most sensational story, and a sensational story is not a happy, normal, cohesive family that just happens to have adopted an African American child. (AA11)

> The sensational story is the negative effect of adoption. And that's all brought on by what we've seen in the media. . . . It's just how everyone keeps spinning it. (AA14)

Most television media portrayals presented adoption in sharply black-and-white terms, whether to celebrate or decry adoption practices. Adoptive families felt as if they had little clout in combating these representations, especially as they affected their children. Marge, whose daughter was adopted from China, in the face of these kinds of portrayals of adoption, was trying to communicate her own reasoning to convey to people that nothing is black and white in adoption:

It's a very convenient, pretty way to come out and say, "Oh, wasn't that a nice thing that you did!" I think sometimes people say these things because they want to come off as if they are okay with this whole crazy adoption thing that you did. I think the media definitely portrays it, especially if you look at what's going on with Madonna right now. This whole thing is about saving your Madonna and blah, blah, blah and doing it all, and granted she's gotten a lot of backlash, but she's even sort of fallen into that whole stereotype herself just talking about—now granted, I know she does a lot of charity work there but really, a child is not a charity case. . . . I want her [Marge's daughter, Tess] to understand that wherever you came from you still need to make your way in life and that's really important. I'm feeling that it's so important to me that people understand that what she has is what she has now, but it's not neces-sarily better. It's not better in the American sense, like an American looking at an American saying, "Wow, she got a real upgrade!" I look at it in the sense of what I've seen of the people and the experiences that I had in China and knowing what Tess has lost culturally, and knowing those things, I look at it differently. You will drive yourself crazy if you say it's better or worse. It's not something that is quantitative. So I try to reframe it like that. . . . I'm not big on the whole, sort of, cultural co-opting I guess you can say, that the media and people do. Do you know what I mean? (CA8)

In absorbing the discourse and representations of adoption circulating through the media, the general public tend to think about adoption as a high-risk good deed. They are also dazzled and inspired by the reports of celebri-ties who have adopted children. They view families who defined themselves as adoptive or who "look" as if they might be, with a voyeuristic curiosity. For families formed through adoption, these attitudes translated for them into an objectification, a search for privacy, and often frustration and anger. Amber bluntly stated: "You know, I'm told a lot of times how brave I am and how lucky Ashley is. 'Wow, that's so brave of you.' And part of that is because I'm single, I'm brave and how lucky I am, but I certainly doubt that white adoptees get that as much" (AA5).

Ethan, the father of one of the first children adopted from China, was the subject of a front-page story in the *New York Times* accompanied by his daugh-ter's photo. She (and her father supported her in this) most resented that she was singled out as a spokesperson, partly because she was "the spearhead" (a pioneer "riding the first wave" as one of the first adoptees from China in the United States), but also because she represented exoticism. "She's been spokes-kid for an anti-bullying campaign, and she got that because she's Asian. They needed an Asian face. . . . She doesn't want to be just an image. There's more to her being than that" (CA10).

The RA adoptive parents in my study were the most likely to embrace their own adoption experiences as rescue missions, but they viewed adoption in a positive rather than negative light, in contrast to media representations. Emily and Michael had adopted two children from Russia, one of whom was autistic. Emily shared with me her views of the media:

> I think that initially [the media] approached adoption in a bad way . . . [with] sensationalized stories. They wanted to report the bad things. But I think . . . it's forced us to be more open with saying, "It's great, it's wonderful, it's nor-mal." Get our stories out there. We've made more of an effort to get the good stories out there. So I think we're learning to use the media in that respect. For me, it's what I owe the children that were left behind when we adopted. I think that's what I can do for them. If I can get one other family to go and adopt children from Russia then that's amazing. (RA4)

Some adoptive parents were countering the media portrayals that have shaped public perceptions of adoption. They were participating in Internet forums and discussion groups and had also started newsletters, magazines, and catalog com-panies that offered a broader range of views and images of adoption, as well as adoption resources. Many documentaries and docufilms have also begun to circulate, some of which are made by or in collaboration with adult adoptees. The major narrative thread of these powerful films is usually crafted by adoptees themselves, but also includes other voices and perspectives, such as those of birth and adoptive siblings and parents, people in their neighborhoods, and adoption agency and school personnel. Films such as *Off and Running*, the story of Avery Klein Cloud, an African American woman who was adopted by a white lesbian couple and who searches for her birth mother; *First Person Plural*, the story of an adult Korean adoptee who returns to Korea and brings her birth and adop-tive families together; *Somewhere Between*, which focuses on the coming-of-age stories of four girls adopted from China; Phil Bertelsen's *Outsiders Looking In: Transracial Adoption in America*, which explores Phil's search for black identity; and Barb Lee's documentary comparing the experiences of a Korean adoptive and Chinese adoptive family in *Adopted: When Love Is Not Enough*, are just some depictions of adoption that talk back to sensationalist and romanticized portraits of family-making through adoption. They especially emphasize the challenges facing adoptees and their families in the context of identity formation. (See Opper 2009; Liem 2000; Knowlton 2011; Bertelsen 2001; Lee 2008.)

Adoptive parents have also become more sensitive to the kind of discourse circulating through the media. Debate has raged, for example, among them about the television program *Modern Family*, in which a gay couple, discussing their decision to adopt another child, announced, "We're buying domestic." Adoptive parents reacted. They appreciated the depiction of different kinds of families in the show, yet they raised many questions and points about the connections the show made between adoption and purchase. They pointed out that parents who could not cover all the costs of childbirth would not be prevented from keeping their child, whereas the opposite would be true in adoption; that if birth parents could afford it, they would likely keep their children rather than make an adoption plan or be forced to make one; that it was exceedingly important to acknowledge the ways that money shaped family formation in order to increase awareness of how it intervened in trafficking and corruption; and finally, that the discourse of "buying" was problematic in constructing a narrative for adoptees.[13] *Modern Family* is an example of a type of show that may become more common in the future, one that brings into the open the many ways of making families and the controversies and opinions that Americans have about them. Nevertheless, current media representations reinforced public perceptions of adoption as a high-risk win-or-lose game. These perceptions structure how Americans understand family formation through transnational and transracial adoption and are reflected in their daily discourse and social actions.

Discussion

Laws that broadly govern adoption, adoption agency workers and brokers, and mainstream media sources powerfully structure the initial paths that adoptive parents took and their subsequent decision-making. The assumptions that underpinned these sites of power influence and reinforce the general public's understanding and views of adoption: the clash of ideas about matching; the emphasis on culture and heritage; aspirations of adoption personnel to provide children with a "better life"; the mainstream media; and stories of search and reunion by adoptees and their birth families. .

At the same time, changes were taking place that called into question these very ideologies, representations, and practices that have been taken for granted. While dominant ideologies and their concomitant practices cannot be escaped or revolutionized wholesale, daily improvisations may be used to challenge the status quo and lead to transformations in how people think and what they do (Bourdieu 1977). Michèle Lamont and Virág Molnár (2002: 168–69) distinguish between "social boundaries" and "symbolic boundaries." Social boundaries are "objectified forms of social differences manifested in unequal access to and unequal distribution of resources (material and nonmaterial)," while symbolic boundaries are "conceptual distinctions made by social actors to categorize objects, peoples, practices, and even time and space. They are tools by which individuals and groups struggle over and come to agree upon definitions of reality. . . . [They] also separate people into groups and generate feelings of similarity and group membership." In constituting symbolic boundaries, people draw on "interpretive strategies and cultural traditions that they deploy in creating, maintaining, contesting, and dissolving institutionalized social differences (e.g., class, gender, race, territorial inequality)."

Thus, even as social boundaries coalesce and take on normative proportions as structuring mechanisms, the line between symbolic and social boundaries can be permeable. This permeability matters because it helps to explain how social boundaries become erected *and* how they may undergo change. When enough people challenge, for example, the embrace of particular ethical or legal assumptions, or the rationale for, or the meaningfulness of, unequal access based on class, race, gendered identity, or monetary wealth, then social boundaries themselves may be called into question. Usually, this process takes place gradually and somewhat haphazardly, although occasionally it may take more dramatic turns. The push-and-pull of improvisation, and the investment of symbols and symbolic systems with new meanings in contention with the reinscription of norms, is reflected in some of the experiments adoptive parents and children have embarked upon in how they forge family and community. The following chapters show how family-making through transnational and transracial adoption is situated within dynamic tensions created by social structures and by the less obvious circulation of power through the production of knowledge and symbolic systems.

2 Fate and Faith

Adoption and Popular Religiosity

When Madison was teaching English in China, she had visited a local temple in a small city and received a "sign" that she would adopt a child from China in the future:

> We went to a temple for the city god. . . . I was kind of drawn to it and found out that it was the god that people pray to, to have children. It was kind of odd that I kept being drawn there, and I just had the realization at that point that I would probably be adopting a child from there one day. It was a couple years later when I did that. (CA7)

Linda, who had a medical condition and knew she and her husband would not have biological children, also received spiritual direction in their adoption decision: "I wouldn't say that I'm an overly religious person by nature, but it just kept seeming that we were getting hints from God almost because everything just seemed to be heading toward China" (CA5). Likewise, Christine, a member of the Latter Day Saints, told me how her recurring dream foreshadowed her adoption of Marisha:

> Okay. I had had actually a dream about this little girl, and in my dream she had olive skin and black curly hair and black eyes, and every time I woke up from the dream, I knew I was to adopt her. . . . For a long time I kept this to myself because I thought, "Oh, this is kind of crazy. And then a couple of months later I just told Pierce, "Gosh, I've been having this repeated dream, and I think we're supposed to adopt this little girl and, you know, she's got darker skin, and dark hair and dark eyes. And I don't know why but I think she's supposed to be our first little girl." It was such an impression . . . that I

just knew I had to do it. There was no other experience that motivated that decision [to adopt an African American child] other than that. (AA12)

Adoptive parents often alluded to the intervention of supernatural forces in explaining how they came to adopt a child from one place rather than another. Along with specifying a particular locale in their initial narratives, they stated that a mysterious spiritual energy connected them to the place from which they should adopt and the particular child they should adopt. The invoking of supernatural forces by parents well before an actual adoption took place contributed to the transubstantiation process that lies at the heart of kin-work among adoptive families (Howell 2006). In short, religiosity played a powerful role in structuring family formation among American adoptive families, a topic rarely addressed in the anthropological literature on adoption (but see Jacobson 2008 and Rush 2000).

Religious beliefs have always shaped ethical debates about adoption, especially in light of moral positions espoused by religious institutions. At its most inflammatory, the debate has centered on the morality of adoption as an alternative to abortion. Religion has also driven policies and practices of the American welfare system with respect to adoption, such as a commitment by religious institutions and governments to assist single mothers who face ostracism or impoverishment if they dare to keep their children, the more unique role of the Black church, or the efforts of adoption agencies and the social welfare system to "match" the religion of child and prospective parents (Herman 2002, 2008). Barbara Katz Rothman (2005: 256), for example, among others, notes that the overrepresentation of Jewish parents who have adopted children of color is due, historically, to the reluctance of adoption agencies to place children of Christian women with Jewish couples.

Popular religiosity has also always been important in child welfare, but has received little anthropological attention in understanding the choices that prospective parents make about family formation through transnational and transracial adoption. Many Americans view the adoption of a child as an absolute good because they consider it a form of rescue and salvation. The changing value attributed to children in America such that they have become "priceless" and their lives therefore "sacralized" also contributes to the centrality of religiosity in adoption.[1] A far-from-clear division exists between adoptive parents' participation in activities directly connected to religious institutions, on the one hand, and what I call here "popular religiosity," on the other. Popular religiosity, comprising more individually tailored beliefs in mysticism, faith, fate, and spirituality, places less emphasis on prescriptive institutional practices, experiences, and beliefs. For Peter Williams (1989: xi), popular religiosity requires the convergence of at least two of the following criteria: "(1) found outside formal church structures, (2) transmitted outside the established channels of religious instruction and communication employed by these structures, and (3) preoccupied with concrete manifestations of the supernatural in the midst of the secular world."

In the United States, there has been a steady progression, from one generation to the next, away from institutionalized religion to more informal modes of spirituality, as well as a growing openness to mixing religious faiths.[2] Winnie's description of her religiosity resembled what I heard from many adoptive parents:

> I was raised Catholic. I had disagreements with the Catholic Church in the first grade. I just didn't believe that given that you were on Earth for two seconds, that you were then forever and ever to be judged and that was the end of it. There were things that just didn't make sense, and that's just my spirit. I have a skeptical, rebellious streak obviously. A single mother with four kids, something going on there. But the moral system and the values, at least some of them, are very embedded in here, so my kids are taught a mixture of Catholicism or Christianity, and I've studied Buddhism on my own for many, many years. Zen philosophy is all part of it too. Some pieces may overlap and other pieces are radically different. . . . My mother is still very involved in the Catholic Church, so the kids, if they're over at my mother's, do go to church, and if we're . . . up there, we go. It's a Jesuit-run church. It's quite nice. We've been to other churches with whoever goes to church. It doesn't really make a difference to me, the denomination. I would say I'm spiritual, but I don't go for the dogma, you know, the absolute. (CA29)

In this chapter, I discuss how popular religiosity figured in the ways adoptive parents came to adoption, in their adoption narratives, and in their interactions with the general public. I also briefly examine the participation of adoptive parents in more institutionalized religious settings. Surveys conducted by the Pew Forum found that when people from different faiths marry each other, their religious behavior is complex. While they may not participate in institutionalized religious settings as regularly as non-mixed couples, they experiment with and incorporate more different kinds of religious practices into their daily lives.[3] My more inductive research findings with adoptive families revealed the same pattern. And if one adds race to the mix, religious behavior includes increasingly greater doses of non-institutionalized religious faith and practices, together with more radical changes in behavior with respect to which kind of religious service or faith to embrace.

Some of the religious practices among adoptive families were directed to cultivating and extending familial ties across entrenched racial and class lines and geopolitical ties. At the same time, adoptive parents embraced traditional religious belief systems and notions of faith as a way of justifying how they had formed their families. Popular religiosity manifested itself in a faith in "intelligent design," in the "hand of God" at work, and in the mystical belief that children who had been adopted were "special" and that their adoptions were "meant to be." These beliefs supported adoptive parents' incorporation of children into families that diverged from the American model of heterosexual parents and children united by blood ties. They self-consciously saw themselves as pioneers, entering into unknown territory.

Popular religiosity even supported their invention of new rituals to symbolize the fusion of families that diverged from the norm. The Mitchells, AA adoptive parents of infant twins, held a "wedding" in Eugene, Oregon, with their children's birth mother to signify that the two families were now one. The hospital chaplain "united the families." Amanda Lucart, the twins' birth mother, explained, "I wouldn't have been able to do this [give her children up for adoption] if I hadn't been able to see my children." Jennifer Mitchell and her husband were equally committed to an open adoption. Jennifer's view was that Ms. Lucart would be "Mom Mandy" because the twins "need to know their mom. This just means more people to love them." The agreement between Lucart and the Mitchells was that the twins would spend time with Lucart once a month.[4]

Beryl described the rituals she had developed to include her three adopted AA children's birth relatives (she and her husband also had two biological children). Although none of these practices were "religious," they were ceremonies of heightened significance for the participants:

> We celebrate their birthdays . . . they actually last for a week in our house. . . .
> With the three younger babies . . . the day of their birthday I send flowers to
> the birth mom; I've done that every time. And the day of their party, or the day
> of their birthday, is their day. They are king or queen of the day. They have to
> go to school, . . . [but] they get to have whatever they want for breakfast, they
> get to have whatever they want for lunch, and then we go to Chuck E. Cheese
> for dinner. That is tradition. . . . And then that is the day they get some of their

presents. Sometimes we will have some family or some friends will come. And then the weekend after their birthday, we have their birthday party. That is when all the family and friends come. And depending on the child, the birth family might come too. With Karina, her birth mom and her aunt and her grandma come for her birthday party. They celebrate with everybody. If it's Cecilia, we usually try to go visit her birth mom and birth family around her birthday. And with Rich, we go over to them because we celebrate with Rich and his sister, D., who is a year older than him. So it lasts the whole week long. You know that they are part of the family. Other holidays are usually spent the same way. (AA7)

Karen Berman took her cue from a children's book to begin celebrating the ties between her family's children as siblings and the formation of their own kind of family. Her two children were adopted on separate occasions from Russia:

My opinion has always been that family secrets are dangerous. . . . Keiko Kasza's (1992) *A Mother for Choco* is about a mother bear that raises several different kinds of animals as her own children. Stories are a wonderful way to introduce and explain the concept of adoption. . . . May 19 has become a very special day in our home. It is the day we celebrate "Brother/Sister Day," the anniversary of becoming a family. We honor this day by spending time together having family fun and, of course, a homemade cake. (Berman 2003: 175)

The emphasis for the Bermans was not on reinforcing ties between adoptive parents and children, but rather on the creation of links between the siblings. In another instance, Clare and Philip told me they had celebrated the finalization of Chaz's adoption by having a small party. They asked that people not give presents but rather "make a donation to Lydia House, which is where he had come from" (AA13).

These ritual practices, in big and small ways, signified new kinds of connections and models that families were developing, and, through them, adoptive parents acknowledged both their children's prior connections and their new ones. Simultaneously, they emphasized the individuated, unique, and exceptional nature of their children, holding at a distance their embeddedness in multiple social units and cultures. These two strands, I argue, were sustained in tension with each other in many domains of American culture, if not with exactly the same particulars. Faith and creative kinds of rituals and spiritual beliefs allowed adoptive parents to live with these tensions without being overwhelmed by contradictions, thus sustaining cognitive dissonance in everyday life. Further, and not surprisingly, such faith- and spiritually based beliefs and practices offered comfortable narratives for parents to invoke when they tried to explain what was awkward, unknown, or outside their control.

Intelligent Design

One philosophical strand that exemplifies a more conservative aspect of popular religiosity was the embrace by parents and their extended families members of the role intelligent design played in adoption and family formation. Physical anthropologist Eugenie Scott (2004) explains that "proponents of intelligent design posit that the universe, or at least components of it, has been designed by an 'intelligence.' They also claim that they can empirically distinguish intelligent design from that produced through natural processes (such as natural selection). The origins of life as well as a number of other biological conditions are "categorically unexplainable" by natural causes (Scott 2004: 116–17).

There is a superficial similarity between "intelligent design" and "creationism," especially in how people think and speak about them in their everyday conversations, yet their respective tenets diverge. Creationists do not think there is any need for empirical evidence to support their position. Those who are willing to entertain the existence of "intelligent design" think that whatever "super-intelligence" is responsible for the extraordinary patterned complexity of nature should be discoverable empirically. If evidence for it does not exist, then it should be rejected as nonscientific or at least regarded with great skepticism. "Creationists," in contrast, embrace a theistic explanation of evolution and view the Bible as direct evidence of that abbreviated evolution. Evolutionary biologist Richard Dawkins argues, however, that intelligent design and creationism should be subjected to the same scientific scrutiny:

> The presence or absence of a creative super-intelligence is unequivocally a scientific question, even if it is not in practice—or not yet—a decided one. So also is the truth or falsehood of every one of the miracle stories that religions rely upon to impress multitudes of the faithful. Did Jesus have a human father, or was his mother a virgin at the time of his birth? Whether or not there is enough surviving evidence to decide it, this is still a strictly scientific question with a definite answer in principle: yes or no. Did Jesus raise Lazarus from the dead? Did he himself come alive again, three days after being crucified? There is an answer to every such question, whether or not we can discover it in practice, and it is a strictly scientific answer. The methods we should use to settle

the matter, in the unlikely event that relevant evidence ever became available, would be purely and entirely scientific methods (Dawkins 2006: 56).

The idea that genes account for a wide range of human behavior and temperamental dispositions has grown in popularity in the United States. Genes do exist, of course, but parents involved in transnational and transracial adoption who invoked "intelligent design" were convinced that the genetic blueprint of human beings—their race, their sexuality, and even their temperament—was the product of design proffered by a supernatural entity (not necessarily God), rather than the product of natural selection and evolution. They fervently believed that something far greater than their own powers guided and explained who their children were, and their formation as a family. Parents who were infertile and chose to adopt internationally or across racial lines often framed their experiences and choices as destiny. They conceptualized the matching of a child with them as parents in the context of a hidden and uncertain process as intelligent design. "God had a plan in store" was an affirmative statement, a reassuring comment in the face of disappointment or, alternatively, of success, that I heard adoptive parents make again and again.

Although they did not appear to be conscious of it, adoptive parents used intelligent design as the rationale not only to pursue adoption, but also to pursue the adoption of a specific child. A minority of parents I interviewed appeared to use intelligent design as a rationale for pursuing adoption in the face of infertility. They placed a higher value on families formed through biological connections, but invoked intelligent design to explain their decision to pursue adoption as a culturally and socially acceptable alternative. Some adoptive parents (in all three subcategories) referred specifically to the Bible to explain their actions.[5] Betty, who adopted her first African American child from Birmingham, Alabama, the same area where her own grandmother lived, had to confront and examine her own feelings of racism. She subsequently adopted a second African American child. Her view, which she shared both with me and on her public blog, was the following:

As many of you know, the subject of adoption is very near and dear to us. Our family was created as God blessed us with two precious girls from another woman's womb. We feel most privileged to call them our daughters. The four of us are living proof that you don't even have to look alike to be joined together by God as a family! Did you know that the concept of adoption is one inspired by God? In love He (God) predestined all of us to be adopted as His sons through Jesus Christ. He chose to adopt you (let that sink in), just as He did me. There's not one person that God doesn't want to adopt! Better yet, there was nothing that we did to make God desire to adopt us. He wants to adopt us into His family simply because He loves you and wants a relationship with you. Have you accepted God's invitation to become part of his family? (AA9)[6]

Closely linked to Betty's rationale were the allusions to mystical or fateful coincidence that so many adoptive parents reported. Many "New Age" spiritual faiths, rather than centering on the social good or a single path to salvation or an explicit set of moral percepts equated with faith, were more focused on the "primacy of the self" in the process of spiritual striving (Heelas 1996: 21; Kent 2003: 86). The desire of prospective adoptive parents to create a family as powerful and positive proof of self-actualization, expressed through the medium of mysticism and fate, was strikingly evident in their comments.

Not all adoptive parents followed this line of reasoning. A minority already had children and chose the path of adoption for religious reasons. For them, adoption was a path that "God" had chosen for them, but they delinked it from the drive or social pressure to form a family. In other cases, older parents in a second marriage wanted more children; in a few cases, they were suffering (especially mothers) from empty-nest syndrome; and in two cases in my interviews, they had suffered the tragic death of a child. The invocation of intelligent design or sometimes "the hand of God" also subsumed biology within the purview of a supernatural power and fate. Penny talked about her experiences adopting from China in conditions of uncertainty. She compared the adoption and birth processes, and her husband, Dewey, laughed about what he called "the matching room":

Well, we were doing our paperwork when China adoptions were closed in '93 . . . for sort of a reorganization. So we were one of the few first families who were actually allowed to adopt again as soon as they opened, but it was all quite mystical. . . . It's such a unique experience and I've never had any other kind of experience like it. I suppose it would be like if a group of people went through a divorce, in a certain sense. It . . . is a shared trauma. . . . There's something very grueling about waiting for an undetermined amount of time. If you're pregnant . . . you know that around this time period you're going to have a baby, but when you do the adoption process, it's very nebulous. It could be five months. It could be two years. They give you a ballpark time now, but you don't really ever know. . . . We laugh about the matching room. Everybody talks about the matching room.

L: What's that?

My husband called it the "Big Swivel." He sees this big room with a box on one side and box on the other in China and the guy's in a swivel chair and he picks up a card from one side [*prospective parents*] and he picks up a card from the other side [*children in orphanages*] and he matches them. But we think that God does the matching. We've always told the girls that, "God chose us for you and you for us." (CA14)

Amy Eldridge, who had visited the "Big Swivel," that is, the Central Chinese Adoption Authority (CCAA), explained that children were not matched with parents "by chance":

It is not random . . . as in "baby 1 in stack with parent 1 in stack." There are eight lovely young women in the matching room who DO look at your condensed info on the computer screen and then look through about five to six baby files to see which one is the best fit. You are most definitely matched. It can be from appearance on those passport photos . . . it can be by hobby (baby who loves music being matched to a woman who loves piano), it can be by meaning of the baby's name (baby whose name means "flower" being matched to a family who runs a nursery), or many other factors. . . . Sometimes it has to do with age. . . . for instance, if there is an agency group with six families and then six babies, and one parent is 60 while another is 31. . . . They might put the youngest child with the youngest couple. But not always! And that is because another feature might have jumped out to why a match needed to be made. Baby files are on one side, color coded by province and orphanage, and parents' files are also color coded by agency. Of course they try to keep agency groups together if possible, so if it is a huge group of families, they will pull an orphanage who sends more children. That is why every so often you will see an agency with twelve referrals from Hunan and one lone referral from Guangdong. They tried to keep them all together, but there weren't enough babies from that orphanage that month.[7]

Most adopting parents were pragmatic, weighing carefully considerations of race and age, the choice between domestic and transnational adoption, and financial costs. The ability to choose permeated their decisions even though they felt they were constrained in the options available to them. It is easy to understand how prospective parents would construe this bureaucratic and culturally specific process—taking into account *certain* criteria—physical features, age, avocation, or occupation—as mystical because of a lack of control. They had little knowledge of the culture or background of the country from which they were adopting; they were located thousands of miles away from their child-to-be in the case of transnational adoption, and they might be aware of, but not very knowledgeable about, the hurdles they could face in pursuing domestic transracial adoption. An embrace of some preordained design or fate seemed to mimic the mysterious origins of the child and the mystery that accompanied childbirth. It simultaneously served to assuage the anxieties of prospective adoptive parents.

The belief that the uncertainty and mystery of adoption were preordained, while it provided reassurance to most parents, also created heart-wrenching ethical dilemmas. Parents who encountered their child for the first time only to find out that the child they thought was chosen for them was extremely sick, had special needs, or did not bond with them were then faced with excruciating choices.

Prospective parents could choose to reject a referral if the conditions were apparent before adoption, or they could decide to proceed. Those who chose the latter option often did so fervently believing that the child's condition was "a sign from God." And some parents deliberately embraced the adoption of a child with special needs as a God-driven good deed. The embrace of intelligent design, fate, or creationism created curious paradoxes, especially if a child did not bond with adoptive parents. Parents thought they could change the child's condition through their own parenting and actions. Some of them could, but many of them found that despite their religious faith, they could not.

There were consequences to whichever path adoptive parents took. Kyle, an Episcopalian, who decided to reject the referral of a child, felt as if he and his wife were "playing God": "On a more fundamental level . . . I personally felt that if these kids had been born to us and they were both blind or they had no limbs or whatever, we would have dealt with it. . . . but when you're playing God and can consciously choose, it's very hard. A person who hasn't been through that doesn't have any idea" (RA6). The second course of action—especially common in the case of children adopted from Eastern Europe—was when parents took on more than they could handle and subsequently had to disrupt their adoption (see Chapter 4). In the most extreme cases, despite their belief in intelligent design or in "the work of God," adoptive parents who were unable to control their prolonged frustration abused, injured, or killed their children.[8]

Parents openly acknowledged harboring a range of negative emotions about adopting a mixed-race or black child and worrying about racism among members of their extended families. Some of those did not proceed with adoptions, but others decided to go ahead in spite of their concerns. When they found that race did not impede bonding and their love for their child, they came to see their participation in adoption as the result of supernatural intervention that was transformative for them. Denise, who pursued a domestic transracial adoption, simultaneously called attention to her concerns about race and to her conviction that God would make it all right: "Ceci is chocolate—Cadbury chocolate—which I love, and I tell people, 'she is like that because that is how God made her and wanted her. She lives with me because I always had her in my heart and God wanted her with me'" (AA16).

AA parents also invoked religiosity to protect their children from racism. Parents whose faith aligned well with creationism struggled with whether to send their children to public school or homeschool them, as they had initially intended. They viewed homeschooling as a way of instilling in their children faith in God and correct moral values and feared exposing them to unacceptable behaviors in the public schools and to knowledge that they considered false, especially related to evolution. At the same time, they wanted to provide their children with an ability to cope with racism.

Most of these discussions took place on the Internet, and I present one typical exchange here. Despite the concern she had voiced about racism and how she could help her children deal with it, one mother ultimately concluded that God meant for her family to adopt their African American children and would therefore show them how to teach their sons to handle the racism they were likely to encounter. Anisia began the online exchange because her husband did not want her to homeschool her child. She ruminated:

> Did I make a mistake? I love my boys and can't imagine not having them. Will they grow up and hate me because I am not their race? Can white people really raise well- adjusted non-white kids? Oh, please pray for me! I love my kids and want to do what is best for them. . . . raise them according to God's word. . . .
> I have heard so many negative adoption stories lately. I do understand that the media, Internet included, is full of more negative stories than positive. There's bound to be positive ones, too, right? Or are all of us going to be the first positive ones? I am in the process of reading *Inside Transracial Adoption* but haven't finished it yet."[9]

She received a response from Kelly, who homeschooled her children:

> Thank you for being so open to expressing the same thoughts that I have had in the past . . . but haven't always had the courage to admit to myself much less someone else. Our children, to me, seem to start out life with so much to have to deal with (loss, abandonment) and then to add to that being in an all

white family . . . and all that entails in the public eye . . . therefore all our fears. . . . I homeschool my oldest, which is adopted and white. Several months ago, I realized that my reasons for homeschooling my youngest (age three), who is African American, were completely different than my reasons for my oldest. I was thinking about homeschooling my youngest to protect him from all that society dished out. In my weakest moment, I actually thought about not taking him in stores so to protect him from prejudice. Then I realized that by doing that I would be crippling him. I needed to prepare him to face the world and all its ugliness. But how do I do that since I have never experienced what he will experience? My brain can take over and say "I'll read books. I'll seek help from the African community, counseling, etc. . . . I am paralyzed by fear sometimes. . . . But, where would our children be if we had not adopted them? . . . God gave these boys to you because He knows that you have all that it takes to raise them to be stable, loving, kind, strong, gentle, wonderful African American men. It is a challenge for me, for all of us, to give our children all that they need to face this world . . . but we will do it. And with God's help (which He will give us because He made our family what it is), we all will not only make it but do so abundantly. In spite of all my flaws . . . somehow, God is going to use that to strengthen my boys. God made you, your husband, and your boys a family for a reason. . . . You did not make a mistake. God made your family, Abigail. He led your heart and directed your path. He will give you/me the strength and courage to love, educate, and grow our little boys to be GREAT MEN that will in turn do the same with their children.[10]

The intervention of God in adoption choices was most forcefully expressed by AA adoptive parents in reaction to fears they had about how they, and especially their children, would be treated as members of transracial families. The currents of racism in the United States interacted with two different religious beliefs they held—one that emphasized Americans as do-gooders in the world, the other that expected that if people followed a proper moral path God would intervene. Especially AA adoptive parents believed that even if trials and tribulations accompanied the formation of their family, God would view it as "right" and would provide them with the fortitude and ability to face those trials. These beliefs did not extend to all AA adoptive families, but they constituted a major force that stressed the transformation of the individual rather than of society. Claudia, who went through with a transracial domestic adoption, admitted:

It is a challenge for me, for all of us, to give our children all that they need to face this world . . . but, we will do it with God's help, which He will give us because He made our family what it is. . . . In spite of all my flaws, and as a mom I have so many, somehow, God is going to use that to strengthen my boys. God made you, your husband, and your boys a family for a reason. (AA14)

It is this rationale, saturated with faith, that angers many opponents of transracial adoption. They feel that it is akin to wearing blinders and badly serves AA adoptees, who need more than God's help to deal with the racism they are bound to encounter in their daily lives.

At the same time that a belief in God helped allay adoptive parents' concerns about lack of control and their anxieties about how racism in America would affect their future as families, it also dovetailed with the idea of doing good through practicing adoption and thereby preventing women from seeking abortion as an alternative to giving birth. Few parents explicitly stated this, but instead told me they used the curious and invasive queries of others as an opportunity to tell them what a wonderful gift from God adoption was. Abigail and Betty thought that the questions strangers asked were rude but quickly reframed them as an opportunity to proselytize in behalf of adoption and the work of God. I asked Abigail why she had decided to adopt a child:

Our first son's birth mother called us when she found out she was pregnant to see if we would consider adopting her baby. I grew up with her, and she knew we could not have biological children. We talked about it a lot and prayed about it and decided that if she called us, then God must want us to have children after all. . . . Our sons are a year and a day apart in age, and they are both blessings. Our first son is Caucasian/African American, and our second son is Caucasian/African American/American Indian. Sometimes I choose not to respond to people's comments, but if they are truly interested in adoption then I will usually take the time to stop and chat with them about our wonderful blessings from God [her two sons]. (AA2)

Betty, who was so torn about pursuing transracial adoption initially, was passionate about using it as a means to proselytize. I asked her what her school plans were for Melanie, her daughter. She had initially thought about homeschooling but decided against it because:

What I think the Devil meant for evil—you're going to stand out, you're going to look like a sore thumb, whatever—God has just made good because it is our perfect opportunity to talk about adoption because people come up to us. . . . I'm a talker! I don't give them the entire life story like I'm giving you now, but I do use the way that we look different to talk about adoption. Number one, just adoption in general, and number two, I try to use it as an opportunity to evangelize. God has taken that and turned it into something good. (AA9)

This statement was striking because Betty associated "standing out" with the devil, but concluded that because adoption was a good thing and she had adopted an AA child, then standing out was transmogrified into a good. Religion became a justification for her to challenge what she understood to be the American normative model of a white heterosexual nuclear family.

The Protestant ethic of doing good deeds and a more general abiding commitment to "rescue" others drove the formation of some adoptive families and the growing positive view of international adoption. Jae Ran Kim (2006: 151–66) offers an excellent analysis of the relationship between the dynamics of international adoption and the Protestant ethic, in the context of faith-based organizations like Holt and their deep involvement in Korean adoption.[11] The cost of pursuing an international adoption is high, at least $30,000. Religious ideology as expressed by adoption agencies—specifically the idea and discourse of sacrifice—served as an incentive for people to adopt. The indignant reaction of Gretchen, who adopted a children from Russia, illustrates her exasperation with those who criticize international adoption and her own justification of it as a mode of rescue, partly motivated by religious faith:

> American parents don't abandon their children in huge numbers to be abused and neglected in state housing. It's rather disgusting how American families are so lambasted . . . about how we raise our children. Perhaps the Russian children are told that if they don't behave they will face the gulag (oops, I mean orphanage). At least we are coming to rescue some of the Russian children. (RA8)

In some instances, entire churches were adopting children, or congregations were donating funds so that a single family could adopt a child internationally as an indirect mode of proselytizing and as a means to pursue a mission they believed to be God-sent. This has been true of initiatives pursued by the organization Focus on the Family, which encourages churches to sponsor orphans in Liberia, for example, in order both to facilitate their adoption and to encourage them to "come to Christ."[12]

Linda explained to me that she and her family attended a small rural church with their daughter Jenny.

> The first day we went I thought we were a spectacle maybe because of us looking so different, but I come to find out from the minister that we weren't

so different. It was because we were a new family that was new blood. Because most of the people seem to be older in the church, they were just excited that somebody with a child came. . . . They are just all over Jenny. I think everybody loves her to death. . . . I approached the foundation group. We had gotten a small grant from them. I sent in a letter to the minister of our small church. She was going to bring it before their mission's committee as a possible fund-raising activity to help someone adopt internationally. (CA5)

In addition to sponsoring adopting families, church-linked organizations such as the Russian Orphan Lighthouse Project were active in bringing Russian "orphans" to the United States for summer "stays" with families in hopes that some of the host families would decide to adopt them. Some of these organizations had no religious affiliation, but others were explicit that theirs was a Christian mission.[13]

One adoptive parent cut through the mysticism and religious fervor surrounding the rightness of adoption as rescue to point to the underlying economic and political conditions that had allowed her and her husband to adopt their child:

Many adoptive parents describe their connection with their children as something that was destined by a larger force. "God brought us to each other," they'll say. "We were meant to be a family." I understand why we want to think that, but the reality is, Flora is my child because something went wrong. To believe otherwise would mean that God intended for Beatríz to suffer because she couldn't afford to raise her child, that we were meant to have the option of adding a girl to our family because we could afford the price. (Larsen 2007: 59)

Larsen's re-evaluation of adoption as rescue, good deeds, or predestiny was echoed by Ken, who reflected, "It is a mean and vengeful god that would place a child in a terrible situation when he knows that child will endure horrible conditions before she can be placed with her 'predestined' mother." He felt that the rationale was disrespectful to all participants in adoption (RA7).

Both of these adoptive parents observed that arguments condoning the conditions—economic, cultural, political, and personal—that compelled birth parents to make an adoption plan for their children were flawed. They felt it was important to recognize the inequalities that made commodification part of the adoption process. In short, their statements, which diverged from the views expressed by many other adoptive parents, called attention to hidden structural conditions that played a big role in how adoptions unfolded across borders and they challenged using "God" as a rationale.

Eleanor had pursued a domestic transracial adoption with trepidation because of her anxieties about criticism from African Americans. Her experience is an example of border crossings—between birth and adoptive mother and between black and white—that did not often occur in transnational adoptions.

> One woman came up to us in a grocery store. . . . It turned out she had given up her baby for adoption and the baby was adopted by white parents, and she said, "I have to tell you. This is just one of the most emotional things I have ever experienced." First, she said, "That baby sure is happy, isn't she?" I said, "She IS a happy baby." She said, "She's lucky." And I said, "I'm the lucky one." And then she just paused, and said, "I have to tell you. I gave up my baby as a teenager and I don't know where she is. I hope my baby is as happy as you two are." And I was, "Oh my god." I got out in the parking lot and just started weeping. It was very powerful. She felt like an angel to me. And she said she felt like it was a spiritual experience to have run into us because it was an affirmation for her that she had made the right decision and it was all okay. (AA5)

Eleanor viewed this exchange as a powerful spiritual moment. Yet in my interpretation of it, it seems that although the woman in the grocery store expressed her satisfaction that Eleanor's child was "happy," she also communicated her distress and sadness to Eleanor that she knew nothing about the baby she had given up. It was a moment of transference in which Eleanor interpreted the exchange as a validation of her own decision to form a transracial family, and a sign for the woman she encountered that she had done the "right thing" by giving up her child.

Angels

Children waiting to be adopted, as well as prospective adoptive parents themselves, were often referred to as "angels" by adoption agencies and media. They used the word "angel" when referring to children who had not yet been adopted—as if they were already or almost dead, and as if to give them an otherworldly purity.

I wondered why children were seen as angels, already in heaven, just because they were waiting to be adopted? It seemed to be a way of obscuring the reality of tangled ties in which these children were situated. It presented the children as blank slates that parents could, by adopting them, inscribe with their own value systems and practices, and it served as a way to appeal to prospective parents who were religiously minded.

Families who had adopted from Russia almost always invoked God to explain the process by which their children came to them. When I asked Emily how she explained adoption to her daughter, Mandy, she told me,

> Mandy's version right now is that she's my heart baby. She knows, biologically, that a lot of people carry babies in their tummies and give birth. . . . She'll tell you that she was an angel in heaven. The baby angel sent her to Russia and that's where she was born. Her mommy and daddy didn't live in Russia, so we flew over there in an airplane and we met her and we loved her and we brought her home and she's our daughter. She was in my heart. (RA4)

For some adoptive parents, how a particular child became part of a particular family was explained in terms of a Christian ethos, which took precedence over the uneasiness and concern they harbored about racial issues, and served to successfully obscure the terrain of geopolitics on which such sentiments and practices unfolded. John Thrall and his wife, Cayce, who had adopted fourteen children "of diverse races," put it this way:

> It does not take long to love adopted children the same way a parent would love its biological children. . . . Replace every fear with an act of faith. Knowing what we know about where we all come from and who we are gives us an eternal perspective to the importance of families. We're all different on the outside but we all have the same basic needs in life that a loving family can help to provide. As those needs are met our love for those around us increases greatly. Just trust in the guidance of Lord and blessings will come to you and to your family. Your family will help positively change the lives of these beautiful children forever. (Waters 2008)

To an even greater extent than adoptive parents, their extended family members found solace in the notion of rescue as a way to explain family formation through adoption. When I asked Clare about the reactions of her family to her decision to adopt transracially, she wryly explained:

> It's my dad who's . . . almost 80 years old. I think this is just so different for him, not that he doesn't wanna be open to it. Mostly when we got Melea his reaction was kinda like, "You're doing this 'cause you're Christian" kinda thing. "You're saving somebody," and I was like, "No, Dad. That's not why

we're doing it," and then he really struggles with the whole open adoption thing. (AA13)

The idea of salvation remains a powerful lens through which Americans view adoption, a perception that parents like Hilda, a single mother who had adopted two older children from Russia, bridled against. One of Hilda's daughters, Larisa, at 15, had taken to challenging her mother's authority and using her adoption against her. I commented to Hilda that she was one "tough Mama" and she responded:

> I am, but it's even like, in school, the teachers gave them a little leeway with grades because they were the poor orphans from Russia. I would tell the teachers, "Treat them like you treat anybody else. Do not make them special because they're not." Once they hit middle school, you know, they're on their own. In the beginning in elementary school, the teachers, I really do think it was just because "they were the poor little ones". . . . That's what they said to me in Russia. "I'm an angel." And people here would say, "Oh, you are blessed." And I'm thinking, "No, I'm not. I did this for purely selfish reasons. I wasn't out to save anybody." I don't tell them that. I don't think I'm a hero. Or an angel for doing it. (RA10)

Hilda viewed her adoption of Larisa with a healthy dose of realism, recognizing that as human beings, she and Larisa were fallible and responsible for their mistakes. Whatever sacrifices might have been entailed in her actions as an adopting and adoptive mother, they did not take precedence over the everyday struggles Hilda and Larisa, like any other parent or child, faced. They were not "angels."

Fate and Mysticism

Mysticism, spirituality, fate, and rebirth were widespread concepts that situated family-making through adoption. The emphasis on fate and mysticism, on the one hand, and the individual choice to take the "right" path and do good deeds through adoption and "rescue," on the other, is intriguing in light of the growing ability of prospective parents to choose different modes of reproduction (grounded in scientific rationality and the use of sophisticated technology), juxtaposed with a generalized embrace of spirituality among parents who adopt internationally and confront a high degree of risk and lack of knowledge (Ginsburg and Rapp 1995; Čepaitienė 2009). Parents' belief that a supernatural being or spiritual force intervened to make possible the adoption of a specific child by specific parents created emotional issues that children subsequently struggled with, a point I discuss in Chapter 6. When I asked Sally and Chris whether they had chatted with Jim about being adopted and how he was faring with his peers, they chimed in together:

> Sally: No.
>
> Chris: No. I don't think he thinks about it much, to be honest with you, from what he says.
>
> Sally: I mean, we've had a couple of kids call him "China boy" or asking in line, "How come your eyes are so skinny?" or whatever, but . . .
>
> Chris: It's supposed to bother him. He doesn't take offense.
>
> Sally: He doesn't at this point take offense, and we've just made him feel very special that God made him special, and he's just special to us, special to God, and so at this point, he's just happy to be so special. (CA18)

Parents viewed their adoption process and the narratives they structured within a mystical framework. Fred, for example, was convinced that supernatural forces (in this case, God) were responsible for his adoption of Shannon. He was also sure that good friends of his who became pregnant the night before their departure to adopt a child from China would not have adopted the child they were supposed to if the wife had gotten pregnant at a different time. Hence the adoption was meant to be. Fred, a social worker, was married to Lisa, an elementary school teacher, and they already had two daughters, ages 14 and 12, before they decided to adopt Shannon. Fred explained,

> Lisa was very anxious throughout the whole process. I was not. . . . I said, "Well, we're meant to have a particular daughter. We'll get our daughter when we're supposed to get her, not one day later, not one day sooner." That's kind of the role I played. We went to China, we adopted. Through a mutual friend, we met another couple who were going to China and . . . we started to get together. . . . It turns out they got the referral and she got pregnant that night. And I always say, "Because you were meant to have Sarah. Sarah was meant to be your daughter and if you were to have Yonnie, you wouldn't have gone to China. You were meant to. (CA6)

I asked Fred if he had a story he shared with Shannon about her adoption:

> We put it in a religious context. That we were praying to God for a child and that God didn't send us a child, and finally God said one day, "I have you a baby, I found you a baby but you have to go to China." While you were in

China the *ayes* [amahs] were taking care of you, and so when I got there, you know, I found you, they brought you to me, and you cried and she'll tell you the whole story of what happened, she goes through the whole thing. Shannon seems focused on the *ayes*. (CA6)

Allen, who had a dry sense of humor and tended to be incisive and analytical in his worldview, was surprised by his own embrace of mysticism when he and Betsy were in the midst of adopting their daughter Maia:

The interesting thing was that I dreamt about it beforehand. . . . The night before [we got the call] or the two nights before, I'd had this nightmare . . . in which the president or director of the adoption agency had called me up, and she said, "We have this little black girl and she's been put up for adoption and we're bringing her around and we'll leave her on your doorstep. That sums it up. And I woke up screaming and lo and behold, the next day or the day after, she called and. . . . She almost repeated what I had heard in the dream, but she wasn't going to leave Maia on the doorstep. I was literally speechless, and all I could say was uugh bugh what oi. . . . We thought we had nine months and now we're going to have two weeks. I went out to buy a copy of *Dr. Spock* to remind me how to change a goddamn diaper. That was the important thing. (AA8)

Helena and Bessie had already adopted Giorgi from Russia. Helena told me what happened one day when she went to pick him up from daycare:

One of [the] other moms looked at me—she was adopting a little girl from Russia. . . . She saw me . . . and said, "Yesterday this kid came in and they left him at the airport and they're looking for parents, and I thought of you immediately because you said you wanted more kids, so if you are interested, here's who you should call." It was so bizarre. I went home and we looked at each other and like, it just feels like we're supposed to call. It was really strange. We ended up calling and two weeks later they dropped him off. The second time, we weren't even thinking about adoption. (RA15)

Subsequently, they also adopted a little girl from Vietnam, and again she saw this as having been long in the making:

From the time I was 7—I have four brothers—I thought my parents should adopt a girl. They were completely unreliable at having girl babies. So that was not going to be a way for me to get a sister. At that time was the Vietnam Baby Lift, and I thought they should adopt one and they said no. So I said, fine, then when I grow up, I'm gonna. And I ended up doing it. It's not that it was intentional, but it was always in my mind that I was going to adopt a baby girl from Vietnam from the time I was 7, and I did it when I was 47. (RA15)

Emily and Michael had already adopted Richard from Russia. She told me about her experience with supernatural coincidence:

Michael came home from work that evening and I said, "I got this from the hospital. This is how much is in my IRA. He said, "Well, what do you want to do with it? You want to leave it there? Move it? I said, "I'd really like to cash it out and go over to Russia and adopt a girl.

Linda: So it was in the back of your mind?

Emily: Not really, until I got the letter from the hospital that day. Lightning struck. I said, "You know, I really want to go back and get a little girl." He kind of stood there a moment and said, "Are you serious?" I said, "I really am serious." He walked to the phone, called our agency, and said, "What do we need to do it again?" This is what's so weird. When we sent our application to our agency for Richard, it was February 3, 1999, which was the day he was born. Only later, looking back through our stuff . . . and I was doing our income taxes, I realized the two dates were the same. It was the same week that Mandy was born that I got this letter, and we called our agency to do it again. Looking back, we realized there's something at work larger than us in this. (RA4)

All cultures have milestones that also serve as guideposts for reconstructing memories. In the case of adoptions, those same markers, such as documents with a birth date, became the basis for constructing initial memories and, as Michael and Emily articulate, became imbued with a mystical power. In part, they acquired that power because they were a bridge between the known and unknown in building a child's (and a family's) life history and identity. More subtly, the attribution of fate or design to family-making was also one way that adoptive parents either could justify choices they made or abdicate responsibility for them.

Being Special

The specialness with which adopted children are viewed has created challenges for children and their adoptive parents. Many adoptive parents try to educate people not to single out their children as "conspicuous," and children themselves have become a vocal force in fighting back against this tendency. Earlier generations of parents did the opposite—refusing to recognize that their children who looked different from them stood out. Among those I interviewed, some are working hard to find a middle ground—protecting their children from being objectified as "special" yet giving them coping mechanisms to confront racism and inappropriate curiosity that is an invasion of their privacy. Yet many of these same parents do consider their children to be "special gifts" that were made theirs through a religious or mystical act.

The parents' belief that the children themselves may be a medium for creating fertility also contributed to the specialness with which they imbued their adopted children. This is a dimension of adoption that has never been well understood, either by doctors or by parents. Nevertheless, there appears to be a long-established pattern of parents adopting children and subsequently, after years of unsuccessful infertility treatment, becoming pregnant. Though the proportion of parents who have this experience may be quite small, the power and mystery of the phenomenon is not lost on the general society. When it happens, the act of adoption itself comes to carry a degree of magic that is conveyed by the adopted child.

Institutionalized Religion

Black Church-Going

The wide range of practices and attitudes among adoptive families with respect to institutionalized religious participation resembles that of a broad swath of Americans. More unusual, however, were the practices of AA adoptive families and Jewish adoptive families. Denise, for example, was raised Roman Catholic but did not practice. She thought of her family as Unitarian, and was considering attending an African Catholic Gospel Church:

> We [she and her husband] were both raised Roman Catholic, and we probably consider ourselves Unitarian now. The kids have been asking us to go to church, so I guess we're gonna be. . . . There is a African Catholic Gospel Church which is a very interesting combination. What I have found is that while I have the main core real deep friendships and a few that I have added of other moms I've met, and we're on the same page with things or enjoy the same things, there's more of a satellite where we meet with a group for a specific reason, and that's not saying that I'm using these people. It's just that you know it provides this outlet for the kids. You know what I mean? (AA16)

In seeking out a religious institution to attend on a regular basis, adoptive parents weighed how comfortable they would feel in that setting against its importance to their family. One AA family had been members of an Episcopalian congregation where the husband was a deacon. While the congregation welcomed adoption, many of its members were so racist that the family eventually joined another congregation that was more receptive to mixed families but far more conservative politically.

When their children did not look like them, adoptive parents put the comfort level of their children before their own, especially AA parents who decided to attend black churches.[14] Christine and her husband have since moved to Europe, but when they lived in Chicago in Morgan Park, they regularly attended a black church with their African American daughters. Christine had a positive view of those occasions: "The support of the church was outstanding. Never did we feel uncomfortable about our family composition. We were completely embraced, and our two daughters had the privilege of starting their lives in a great example of what a church should be: caring, supporting, and nurturing" (AA12). There were not many other AA adoptive families in the congregation that Christine's family joined, but there were many transracial couples who attended. They had become close friends with two of the families and got together with them twice a month. She continued her description of the church they attended:

> This church is not at all a place that we would prefer to worship. It's just not our style. It's very traditional. . . . We're pretty contemporary. . . . We joined this church, the pastor was white and her husband was black. . . . Now our pastor's Asian and her husband's white, and that is just absolute true testament to what the church is. There's a lot of black families. A lot of white families. And a lot of integrated families. And we just think it's so perfect for our family and letting Marisha see others in a situation like hers. (AA12)

Eleanor also wanted her family to attend a black church, but her husband rejected the idea: "I thought about it a little bit. I know there's actually a great black church in Newton, but we're not really church-goers. I said to Harry, 'Well maybe we should just go.' And he's like, 'I'm not goin' to church for the wrong reasons'" (AA18). Eleanor resigned herself to "networking" through other means, such as playgroups or music classes, but was skeptical they would lead her to meet and socialize with other families of color.

Brenda and Richard lived in a rural area in Colorado and had adopted two AA sons. They too made the decision to attend a black church:

> My friend in Michigan actually suggested that I read the book *Inside Transracial Adoption: Adoptees Tell their Own Stories*. And I read that, and my husband and I both felt very strongly that we both needed to do something

to make sure that our boys were around positive role models that looked like them, and so you have to understand northern Colorado is very Caucasian. What we ended up doing was I just walked into the office of black student services here at Colorado State University and said, "What can I do?" The lady was very kind and she said, "Oh, we go to church in Greeley which is only about 15 miles from us. . . . It's a nice church and we'd love to have you, and so we ended up going there, and we've been there about two years now. . . . It's a community Baptist Church and it is probably . . . not very big, probably 60 to 70 people right now . . . but I would say it's probably 60 to 70 percent black, 20 percent Hispanic . . . then the rest Caucasian. (AA11)

Brenda told me they were the only mixed adopted family there, but they had been received "with open arms and love. I think they all applaud what we're doing and what we're trying to do and how we're trying to raise our children." They had made friends with the pastor and his wife and two sons, and with a mixed-race family, with whom they socialized regularly outside of the church setting (AA11).

It was difficult for adoptive parents to explain what they felt when they attended black churches. In general, they wanted their children to witness and participate in a setting where African Americans were worshipping and actively socializing in high numbers. Their hope was that the heterogeneity of African American people at the church from all walks of life would be helpful to them and their children. They also hoped to find acceptance in such churches. They found that, as Denise noted, "In the mainly black churches I feel we are welcomed, no questions asked. In the churches that have been all-white we have had to field some questions about where our girls are from" (AA16). The many functions of black churches have been explored extensively. One, of relevance here, is that they act as an extended family, offering support, nurturing, and advice. This too appealed to AA adoptive families.

Being Jewish and Adopted

Betsy and Allen were the adoptive parents of Maia, their African American daughter. They lived in Washington, D.C. Betsy was Jewish, and Allen was agnostic. Both were professors. According to Allen, after they adopted Maia, they temporarily became religious, celebrating the Jewish holidays with greater fervor and frequency than they had ever done before, and they even converted Maia to Judaism. Although they had agreed to send her to Hebrew school, they did not follow through. Maia was invited to attend Sunday School as well as a christening ceremony at a Baptist church by their African American neighbors, which Betsy reluctantly agreed to allow Maia to do. However, both Betsy and Allen agreed with Betsy's sense that "When Maia has to choose among the various identities at her disposal, the society has already chosen which identities are the most important" (AA8). They talked about the power of Christmas in U.S. culture and how hard it was to resist. According to Allen, Betsy considers "Santa Claus a total aberration." He explained, "In the past when Maia and I had conversations about Santa Claus, we just excluded Betsy because she says it doesn't exist, it's all a lie. And we said, "Who is this woman?" Guess who hung up a stocking last Christmas?" Betsy responded, "Well, because Maia wanted one. But I'm not doing any Christmas stuff anymore." Betsy and Allen, who relish a good argument, agreed that Jews who adopted black children faced unique challenges, given the centrality of the church in black social life and the long history of racial and class tensions between Jews and blacks in the United States.

Out of the total U.S. population, a disproportionate number of CA adoptive parents are Jewish. In the 2003 National Jewish Population Study, just over 5 percent of Jewish households with children reported an adopted child residing in the home, a total of approximately 35,000 children.[15] According to the U.S. Census of 2000, the first U.S. Census to include "adopted son/daughter" as a category of relationship to the householder, adopted children made up 2.5 percent of all children of all ages (U.S. Census Bureau 2003). This means that the rate of adoption in the Jewish community is about double that of the American population at large. Two reasons for the higher rate of adoption among Jews are the lower fertility rate of Jews in comparison with that of the general population, and the central role adoption is thought to occupy in Judaism, beginning with the story of Moses. The high number of CA adoptive parents is also due to the value that Jews place on intelligence and learning, and the projection of this stereotype onto Chinese children. In his research on Jewish CA adoptive families, David Straub found that the highest number were in New York City, but they were found across the country and had even formed their own nationwide subsidiary of Families with Children from China, called Jewish Families with Children from China. The group's Yahoo forum had 340 members in 2011 (Straub 2008: 230).

Jews have always embraced adoption, but they have simultaneously emphasized bloodlines and lineage, thus leading to an ambivalent attitude toward adoptive families (see endnote 5, which expands on this observation). Transracial Jewish adoptive parents struggled with acknowledging their child's Jewish and Chinese roots, and with trying to find a balance and the time to give their child regular exposure to things Chinese and Jewish. Adoption is given legitimacy in the Talmud—"Whoever brings up an orphan in his home is regarded, according to Scripture, as though the child had been born to him" (Sanhedrin 19b, Talmud). Nevertheless, Straub found that Jewish CA and AA adoptive parents experienced anti-Semitism from outside as well as prejudice from within the Jewish community itself (Straub 2008: 233). Depending on the congregation in question, it could be more or less flexible and welcoming to adoptive families. Some required that adopted children be converted to Judaism, but others did not. The same assumptions that guided different perceptions of transracial AA and CA adoptive families, respectively, played a role in how guidelines developed with respect to performance of Jewish ceremonies. For AA adoptive families, their identity was filtered through "race," whereas with CA adoptive families, it was filtered through "culture." Some rabbis have counseled that in bat mitzvahs for CA children, elements of Chinese culture, such as their Chinese name or a Chinese story, should be included (Straub 2008: 234):

> There are plenty of American Jews, of course, who do not "look Jewish." And grappling with identity is something all adopted children do, not just Chinese Jews. But seldom is the juxtaposition of homeland and new home, of faith and background, so stark. And nothing brings out the contrasts like a *bat mitzvah*, as formal a declaration of identity as any 13-year-old can be called upon to make. The contradictions show up in ways both playful—yin-and-yang *yarmulkes*, *kiddush* cups disguised as papier-maché dragons, kosher *lo mein* and veal ribs at the buffet—and profound. Yet for Cece, as everyone calls Cecelia, and for many of the girls like her, the odd thing about the whole experience is that it's not much odder than it is for any 13-year-old. "I knew that when I came to this age I was going to have to do it, so it was sort of natural," she said a few days before the ceremony at Congregation Rodeph Sholom, a Reform synagogue on West 83rd Street where she has been a familiar face since her days in the Little Twos program. Besides, she said with a shrug, "Most of my Chinese friends are Jewish."[16]

According to Merri Rosenberg's research, Jewish mothers of Chinese daughters struggle with how much to infuse their lives with Chinese culture, and how much with Jewish tradition. She spoke with one woman, Joan Story, mother of a 7-year-old, who complained:

> I got a lot of grief for sending her to a Jewish day school from the general Chinese adoption community. They felt she wouldn't be around a lot of other Asians. She would have been in a New York private school anyway, with only a

few Asian children in each class. There are some adopted Asian children in her school, just not in her class.

When Story attempted to introduce Alexa to a Chinese dance class, Alexa refused to go back. As Story concedes, "She's very identified with the Jewish community. She told me that 'we can't leave this building. It's special, because this building celebrates Christmas and Hanukkah. Other buildings are just Christian'" (Rosenberg 2006: 27).

Tolerance for transracial Jewish adoptive families appears to be on the rise, although CA adoptees inside the Jewish community may be more welcomed inside of Jewish temples and Sunday schools than they are outside, where they are viewed as "Asian" (Rosenberg 2006). David Straub has noted that transnational adoption may actually increase the Jewish population in the United States because the majority of adoptees are girls (2008: 234).

Two interesting observations in this regard concern the children rather than their adoptive parents. One 11-year-old Jewish CA adoptee relished that she had "choice," again perpetuating this very American cultural value, explaining, "When you're adopted, you get to choose whether you are Jewish or not. At my bat-mitzvah, I'm going to say I'm choosing to be Jewish" (Rosenberg 2006: 27). On the other hand, another 12-year old Jewish CA adoptee reflected that what she most appreciated about being Jewish was that "no one could see it from the outside." Ceci, who was bat mizvah-ed at age 13, chose for her speech a discussion of caring for strangers: "This long journey to becoming a bat mitzvah today has provided me with so many ways of learning," she said. "The part that will always stay closest to me is the importance of caring for strangers. Just like Jews were once strangers in the land of Egypt, we have all been, or will be strangers at some point in our lives," an apt reflection on her experience of family-making" (Newman 2007).

RA adoptive families were least perturbed by the choices they made regarding their participation in institutionalized religious settings. They also exhibited the most continuity in their religious practices. For them, the community of the church was also more central in their lives than for CA adoptive families. It played a prominent role in the adoption process itself, as many churches hosted contingents of children from Russia who might spend a summer with a family in the United States in the hope that they would then be adopted. Finally, AA adoptive families made the most dramatic changes in their religious practices, attempting to create new paths of socialization, interaction, and possibilities for value formation for their children.

Discussion

Religion. God doesn't see people in terms of race or color. God is focused on loving your neighbor as yourself, and He is the main true judge. He created us and has the power to destroy us at any time. That's my one answer.

Simon and Rhoorda 2000: 80

Whatever else religion does, it relates a view of the ultimate nature of reality to a set of ideas of how man is well advised, even obligated to live. . . . In religious belief and practice a people's style of life, what Clyde Kluckhohn called their design for living, is rendered intellectually reasonable, it is shown to represent a way of life ideally adapted to the world "as it 'really' ('fundamentally,' 'ultimately') is." At the same time, the supposed basic structure of reality is rendered emotionally convincing because it is presented as an actual state of affairs uniquely accommodated to such a way of life and permitting it to flourish.

Geertz 1972: 406

Religiosity came into play among adoptive families in many different ways. It is commonplace to acknowledge that religion helps to explain the unknown and provides solace in the face of what cannot be controlled. Some of the religious practices and expressions of faith described above may appear unremarkably traditional. Yet they took on potency because they signified both how people were going against the grain and what they thought the costs were of creating mixed families through adoption.

Recognizing that they were now a mixed family led adoptive parents to change their practices, often relaxing their personal embrace of religious orthodoxy or dogma. Parents who went to Baptist churches rather than Jewish synagogues for the sake of their children, despite their own uneasiness, is but one example. Religious discourse and practices also illuminated more explicitly values that many Americans embraced enthusiastically, such as doing good works and rescuing others, in the course of which they created "angels" out of adoptive parents and orphans. The sentiment that adoptive parents had performed a good deed by adopting a child was bound up with a Protestant ethic and with paradigms of modernization, development, and charity. However unconsciously, it situated "rescuers" in a superior position in relation to those who were being rescued. The metaphor of being "an angel," associated with children who had been adopted, may have been intended as a positive and endearing descriptor. Nevertheless, the metaphor also registered a semiotic domain that encompassed being vulnerable, possibly close to death, and unearthly. While adoptive parents were pioneers in family formation—across racial and national lines, in particular—these belief systems could not help but reinscribe American sociocultural norms that took for granted the unequal geopolitical and social inequalities that structured adoption.

Almost a third of Americans surveyed in a 2009 poll conducted by the Pew Research Center in conjunction with the American Association for the Advancement of Science stated that they did not believe in evolution.[17] It hardly comes as a surprise, then, that intelligent design and creationism were comfortable and comforting explanations for how families came to be, given the trials and tribulations adoptive parents encountered in adoption processes. Such beliefs were also a way to rationalize their decision to pursue forming a family through transracial or transnational adoption. The faith they placed in fate or intelligent design, as I have described above and as adoptive parents themselves articulated, allowed adoptive parents to take as a given, existing social hierarchies and inequalities, as well as a prized American cultural value, individuality. Adoptive parents embraced faith, mystery, and fate to assuage their anxiety—about the racism they and their children might experience, about forming families through nontraditional means, and about the lack of control they had over aspects of family formation through adoption, such as when and if they would actually become a family, or if they would bond at all. The sophisticated scientific technologies that today accompany reproductive processes, such as sonograms that provide visual images of a fetus as it develops, made it all the more compelling for parents to counterbalance their lack of access to this kind of knowledge and control in the adoption process with an embrace of faith and fate.

In adopting a child from a background and place with which they were unfamiliar, they took a path that, despite all the legal procedural requirements in place, was often highly risky and uncertain. Religiosity also became a way of ratifying adoption, which is not yet unmarked in American society. That an adoption was "meant to be" was a powerful response to the ambivalence adoptive parents experienced from family members and the general public. It also channeled their own reluctance to take the plunge in figuring out how to more actively battle racism and its structural roots as mixed families.

3 China

Culture and Place in Imaginaries of Exoticism

Our identities are forged without genealogical patterns, without biological histories beyond our embodied selves. By their very absence, these mysteries of heritage construct our selves as much as our known families do, for the sense of being without a "true" family history and identity—in a society that defines familial "truth" through biology—shapes our vision of our selves and our place in our families and in society. For while we may at times seem to belong in our families or our social groups, we know that we are different, that we came from somewhere else. We lives our lives at the margins of difference—perpetually crossing borders, we are both insiders and outsiders, both natives and foreigners.
—Sandra Patton, *Birthmarks* (2000: 6–7)

My husband and I love to travel. . . . That part of foreign adoption appealed to us . . . the prospect of going to a country we had never been to. The whole thing, once we started looking at international, was just exciting and very positive. We didn't have any fears, didn't read anything that was fearful to us.
—Kimberly, RA4

It . . . felt so "meant to be" with China on all levels. . . . I wouldn't say that I'm an overly religious person by nature, but it just kept seeming that we were getting hints from God almost because everything just seemed to be heading toward China. . . . I suspect that our girls . . . are going to have a lot of questions that us as moms and dads probably are not going to be able answer. . . . What am I doing here? Where do I belong? Where do I fit in? And you know, there may not be good answers for that, but at least there will be somebody else in the same boat
—Lola, CA4

Place and Culture in Transnational and Transracial Adoption

The ease of traversing physical distances and traveling to and from multiple locations—what some have called "space-time compression" (Harvey 1990)—has led anthropologists to focus increasingly on "place" and the meanings associated with places. In their introduction to *A Place in the World?* Doreen Massey and Pat Jess (1995: 1) note:

If a common notion of place, and perhaps especially of small-scale places, is often bound up with settledness, coherence and continuity, then any current talk of *dis*placement, most particularly through migration, depends likewise on a prior notion of cultures as embedded in place. Yet in today's world, this is either less and less true or . . . it must be thought about in a different way. The simple relation between local place and local culture is not one which can be assumed. Perhaps the notion of local *culture*, too, must be re-thought.

Given these global interconnections, what might "local" culture mean in the context of transnational and transracial adoption practices? While the local is partly defined by familiar everyday activities in a particular space and time, it is also saturated by all sorts of associations, symbols, and material artifacts, and active engagement with very distant places. Liisa Malkki (1997: 72) makes the point well when she observes that "to plot only places of birth and degrees of nativeness is to blind oneself to the multiplicity of attachments that people form to places through living in, remembering, and imagining them." Places are also embedded in political and economic processes that simultaneously facilitate connections between people and reinscribe or even exacerbate differences in power between them (Gupta and Ferguson 1997a; Green, Harvey, and Knox 2005). These processes are channeled through bureaucratic structures, institutions, the media, and the images they project, as well as the flow of particular kinds of commodities.

The "production of locality" by adoptive parents thus fuses material anchors and associations with symbolic qualities that then have the potential to be embraced as "real" and to have tangible impacts (Appadurai 1996). The associations adoptive parents have with China or Russia, for example, bear on their decisions and behavior. How and what they imagine about these locales, as well as their experiences within them, serve as catalysts that compel them, as prospective parents, to select them as locations from which to adopt a child. The ways that adoptive parents initially think about a place, including why they choose one place rather than another from which to adopt, becomes integral to how their children begin to build a sense of who they are.

In this and the following two chapters, we look at the ways that adoptive parents took account of place in making their families, beginning with their decision about where they should adopt from. We untangle where these connections and associations came from in the first place and trace how they shape adoption practices. There are many influences—including artifacts—that have an impact on what prospective adoptive parents envisioned about a country called China or Russia, or about the Windy City of Chicago. What interests us here, especially, are the ways the associations that prospective adoptive parents had with particular places became channeled into the choices they made, how the associations circulated, and their influence on how adoptive parents thought about the family ties they were creating.

Associations with places and their meaning[s] are hardly new. People have always left places that they associate with particular sentiments—loss, comfort, nostalgia, excitement, joy, relief, indifference, liberation, hatred, and longing. What is new today is the ease with which many people are able to return to places they have left, their movements back and forth among distant sites on a regular basis, and equally common, to not associate any place with something familiar except the act of moving between points (Appadurai 1996; Hannerz 1996). Despite this general ease of movement, culture, class, gender, and race make it easier for some than for others to move between places. For these reasons, Lynn Stephen (2007) proposes that we employ the concept of "transborder crossings" to emphasize what happens when people traverse not only national or geographic borders, but also cultural, racial, and class borders.

As is true of moving between places, attachment to a place is not a case of "free-floating hybridity," despite the ease of transport and communication today (Schein 1998). The participants in my research were anchored to particular physical locations, and it is hard to imagine that identity formation would take place for them in a vacuum without a specific context. Yet the associations they made with places were infused with social and cultural metaphors; they were affected by global capital, state policies, and national identities, and they were inflected at times by transnational communication circuits and social practices (Smith 2001: 3). The imaginary of birthplaces, the ghosts of unknown birth parents and foster parents, the undercurrents of racial ideologies, the power of having U.S. citizenship, class inequalities, and the massive amount of paperwork that underlay physical movements between adoptive home and birth country provide just some of the context for how place-making unfolded among adoptive families (Dorow 2006; Yngvesson 2005). Especially for AA adoptive families, the proximity of birth relatives and the contrast between being black yet living in white, upper-middle-class, weakly diverse neighborhoods was integral to how place-making unfolded for them (Gailey 2010; Hoffman 2010; Rothman 2005).

In general, places acquired heightened and even exaggerated importance in the context of American adoption practices because they substituted for other kinds of rootedness. Fascinating comparisons can be made between how secrets and private knowledge affect family dynamics. Families formed through biological "blood ties" also come with the "baggage" of family secrets, sometimes resulting in searches that resemble those of families formed through adoption, in which place is central. In CA and AA adoptions, in particular, many activities and ideas that replaced blood played a paramount role in structuring children's identities and their building of kin ties. In short, when adoptive parents crossed racial and class lines, as well as national borders, the ways that they created and communicated meanings associated with particular places to their children fused the intimacy of making kinship with the idiosyncrasy of biography and the politics and culture of transnational and transracial adoption.

Making Memories

The structuring of memory was central to the associations that adoptive parents made with places. Paul Connerton (2009: 51) shows how places act as "carriers of cultural memory." For Connerton, the building blocks of memory result from acts of reciprocity that create "memory chains of obligation," bonds of trust that generate "cultural memory," routinized movements that create specific spatial contours, and "familiarity or deep knowledge associated with everyday places." Connerton also asks, "Why, by what means, in what sense, do subjects acting together in labour processes, invest places, financially and emotionally, with that degree of permanence which causes them to become the locus of institutionalized power and culturally specific perception?" He introduces these ideas in order to argue that particular conditions in today's world make it harder to generate memories than it used to be. We are living in a "culture of forgetting" (53). Digital media, the superabundance of information, and the "dominance of pathways over settlements" that create "spaces of flow" rather than "spaces of place" (110–11) encourage "cultural amnesia." One question here, then, is whether, through place-making, adoptive parents engage this "cultural amnesia" (99), and if so, how?

Anthropologist Johannes Fabian (2007), in a series of essays, scrutinizes how memory and forgetting transpire selectively among anthropologists and their informants in ethnographic inquiries. His observations are applicable and relevant to the ways that place-making happens in adoptive families. Arguing that the "work of memory" is a dialectical process involving active communication and shared experience, like Connerton, he reminds us that remembering and the creation of memory between self and other is not natural but rather an act of "re-cognition." As such, forgetting, then, is not simply omission but rather "a social act of commission"; it is "forgetting with a purpose/reason/motive" (Fabian 2007: 88). Taking this yet one step further, Fabian also does not see forgetting and remembering (memory-making) as separate from each other but as acts that need to be studied together, with an eye to uncovering their tensions and contradictions, their contributions to collective memory, and as simultaneously interpersonal and political (Fabian 2007: 79, 82, 96; Blassnigg 2009).

The dialectical interaction between self and other as a primary mechanism of socialization and self-identity-building, as laid out by Leo Vygotsky (2004) and George Mead (1967), underpins the approach I take here. Many of the associations with place that children initially have are filtered through interactions with their parents. For transnationally and transracially adopted children, these associations were explicit and made from a young age. Some of this kin-work involved travel, communication, social interactions, and events that took adoptive family members far away from their familiar coordinates and that led some of them, gradually, to create new defining coordinates. Given these challenges, how did adoptive parents in this study invest places with meaning? What did they exclude, and how did they contribute to the creation of children's memories into the future where few existed in the past or where they were deliberately erased?

For children adopted at a young age, it was their adoptive parents who construed who they were and what their life experiences were in their birthplaces. Psychological research suggests that [all] children "forget" early memories until they are about 2 years of age. However, many of their memories, including those linked to place, are created and mediated by their adoptive parents. Subsequently, their children might come to challenge or supplant the images and narratives conveyed to them by their adoptive parents; this is a phenomenon that cognitive psychologist Jerome Bruner (1968) points out in his work on how children remember and learn. This dynamic lies at the very core of identity-building among transracial and transnational adoptees, especially when they begin to imagine "traveling toward home" (Schein 1998: 292) as young adults.

Decisions: From Where?

Immediate experience of the local, long prized by common sense as the only experience worth having is, for people in certain class positions, no longer a trustworthy guide to practical life in the modern world. . . . We must examine how the age-old link of locality and truth has been made strange for us, if not topsy-turvy.

Peters 1997: 83

With rare exceptions, most families with children adopted from China had little direct knowledge of China as a country—its geography, history, or culture—when they chose China as the country from which to adopt their children. Their choice was based more on their understanding of the plight of girls in China and their availability, their age as prospective parents, the perception of Chinese Americans in the United States today as a model minority, and stereotypical images they had of children adopted from China as "bright," "beautiful," and "caring." Ethan confided to me that this was indeed the case: "It's a significant factor. I think that, in all honesty, part of it was, you think, "Oh Asian. They must be smart. . . . It's absolutely stupid, but I think that was part of it" (CA10).

Pragmatically, they embraced the orderliness and predictability of the adoption process, including the lack of claims by birth parents. Ethan also commented on this:

> We had the experience of a friend whose adoption fell through, and we felt that this one would not fall through in any way. There was a highly publicized case, as I recall. We felt that some mother in China was a lot less likely to come back and claim her child. Most of it was totally irrational, but it worked for us. (CA 10)

Nora spoke to me in similar terms about the difficulty of deciding from where to adopt:

> It's a hard call because there's a piece of knowing that there's a need for domestic adoption, but for me, it was the thought that, okay, if somebody is going to come back in ten years and say, "I want my daughter back." I think you hear those sorts of things that go to court. It's a whole other ball of wax. . . . I have two friends who have adopted from the U.S. One of them has developed a relationship with the birth mother. . . . there are pros and cons with both but, for me, it was not the route I wanted to go. (CA11)

Whereas more families adopting black children within the United States had embraced open adoption, few transnational adoptive parents initially considered links to a child's birth parents to be positive. Paul emphasized the risk of domestic adoption:

> Domestic? Not domestic because I was afraid of not having it be sure enough. I almost liked the fact of not dealing with the birth mother and birth father. Yeah. Too scary. What if something goes wrong? What if they changed their mind? And what if you go through the whole process and at the last minute they back out? That kind of stuff happens, you know. (CA6)

Carmen reflected on the change in her views *after* adopting a child from China:

> And domestic adoption? It was interesting. Before I read a whole lot about adoption, I thought it best for both parents [meaning birth and adoptive parents] not to be involved [with each other]. It is more challenging in the U.S.,

but then my conclusions changed. I decided it was very selfish after reading more, and now I don't think it's a bad idea. I decided that maybe that's not such a wise thing to not want a third parent involved. (CA4)

Alexa, who had adopted an African American child with her husband, Max, thought that race remained very important in the ways Americans formed their families:

I think everybody knows somebody who adopted a baby from China at this point. I think that sometimes, frankly, Guatemalans and kids from Kazakhstan, and certainly even kids who are from China and Asian, are closer to white, so I do think there is a race issue there. I think that it's like, "If we want a child to look like us kind of who could be our child biologically, then we have to go international because you can't find a Caucasian baby here and we really want a baby as close as possible to our skin type." And I think, again, Asian is seen as being safe because of the stereotype that Asians are smarter and all those kinds of things, and I think that's an issue. (AA3)

A minority of parents stated that they had been open to adopting children across the color line in the United States. They assumed that whether the child was of Chinese or African American origin, she would be categorized as "non-white." However, when they pursued domestic adoption, they had lost precious time because they were not selected by birth parents. Usually the mother or birth parents had turned them down at the last hour. Sarah and Chester described their agonizing experiences. The first time the agency itself put a stop to the prospective adoption; the second, the birth mother decided to keep her children:

Our agency was beginning to do adoptions in Texas. They asked us if we were open to biracial or black kids. I said, "Well, my husband is extremely white and I am extremely Hispanic. So I think that would be okay. . . . The next day, they actually had a referral for us, and then they called back and said, "I'm sorry. It doesn't meet your criteria," because we had basically said "healthy" and they learned within the course of the twenty-four hours that the particular girl was a drug baby. So even if we would've said yes, because of our home study and those sorts of stipulations, they wouldn't readily allow us to adopt it. Then they said, "But how open are you?" And we go, "Well, tell us." So they had twin boys, African American, that had just been born, and I says, "Wait, let me cry," because twins was—to me—the ultimate. There's so many twins in my family. That would be just wonderful. Well, we had to wait a course of twenty-four hours for the mother to sign off. The mother, she was only 21, had two children living with her and had adopted two previous out, and these twin boys, she did not want them to go into the state welfare system, the foster care system. So she was insistent that we go out so she could meet us, and the agency would not allow us to come and spend the time going and money going until she sent a release form. Because of that, it was a tumultuous week. Long story short, she kept the children. They couldn't even find her. She discharged from the hospital. It was a little bit messy. . . . So, having one fall through, then another, we took a break for about a month or so, and then made our decision to go to China. (CA19)

CA adopting parents found it uncomfortable to be sorted and preferred to be in better control of sorting themselves. Rachel acknowledged that the widespread notion that many birth parents rejected adoptive parents at the last minute in the United States was partly due to sensationalism in the media. She and her husband decided on China, not because of fears of rejection by birth parents, open adoption, or racism, but because of the lack of control they felt they could exercise over how they were picked by a prospective birth mother and the time it might take:

> Those are the stories that the media picks up on [being reclaimed by birth mothers]. . . . It's very rare that that happens. . . . That was not an issue for us. The main reason why we decided not to adopt domestically was because we didn't want to wait five years. We knew also it could be five months. . . . It was just too stressful. . . . We had thought that we would go through an agency and . . . do the scrapbook thing and hope that a birth mother would be interested in us and be shown the scrapbook, and it seemed so emotionally draining.
>   Linda: Okay. I see, and would you have considered—if you did consider domestic adoption—would you consider adopting transracially?
>   Rachel: Yeah. I mean, I don't think that would've been a huge issue for us because we went to China. (CA15)

Older adopting parents, gay and lesbian parents, and single parents, to a lesser extent, encountered similar frustrations in sorting. Scrapbooks were a principal mediating artifact of sorting in AA adoptions, especially in the case of non-state adoptions that were private or mediated by private agencies. Prospective parents had to carefully frame who they were or reframe who they were in the best possible light for birth mothers. Agency personnel or attorneys intervened and assisted with this, using specific criteria.[1] Sally and Chris wanted to pursue an AA adoption but adopted from China instead. They explained what happened:

> We went to a domestic seminar and we were pretty much told that when a birth mother who was approximately at that time 21 to 23 years old would look in these three-ring binders and pick a parent for their kid, when they saw our age, they would discount us because we would almost be the age of the birth mother's parents. So it would be like the baby being raised by a grandmother of the birth mother's kid, and they just said, "They won't pick you." (CA 18)

The information on the Internet (see Anagnost 2004: 139–67; Cartwright 2005: 185–212), the proliferation of voluntary associations such as Families with Children from China (FCC), the active pursuit of prospective adoptive parents by adoption agency brokers, and the actual number of families with children adopted from China, including single and gay parents, also fueled its own replication through networks. Chris and Sally described the fortuitous yet typical way that some prospective parents decided to adopt from China:

> Chris: Somebody actually got up and advertised a big adoption seminar at our church on a Saturday, and we went there, and there was like over 100 parents, and they didn't really spend a lot of time on the how to's of adoption. They got up and talked about the purpose of adoption and why they did it, and then they brought—they really used the sucker mode. They brought all the parents with the little babies up. Of course, so that hooked everyone, and then they had a phenomenal Chinese dinner afterwards, and they . . . all got up and gave their stories, and they were real tearjerkers, let me tell you.
>
> Sally: And these cute little girls, walking around with their Buster Brown haircuts, and it was just like . . .
>
> Chris: It was like, "We want one of those."
>
> Sally: The reason we liked China was because of my job. I have known families, have met families that have adopted from other countries, and they just didn't have the smooth sailing as China does with adoptions, and so that was another thing. I didn't want to make two trips to Russia, plus I was not a fan of alcohol fetal syndrome babies, not that they don't need loving homes as well, and then Guatemala had all these issues with lawyers and padding pockets. (CA18)

Two mothers I interviewed had had some direct experience in China prior to adoption. One had "fallen in love" with China when she had visited the country as a college student. Mary, a single mother, had dedicated her summers to service projects and had worked in orphanages and taught English in China.

Many prospective parents made their decision based on positive associations with exoticism and, specifically, beautiful Chinese girls. The idea of China as exotic and Chinese girls as beautiful and talented can be juxtaposed with the long history of mistreatment of Chinese people in the United States, and with the allure of what is not easily fathomable or understood. Chinese children, who were mostly under the age of 1 at time of adoption, were classified in a distinctive category that fused allure with exoticism. Silvia made this clear to me when she explained why she had picked China. She herself was Latina:

> Well, of course, most people don't consider international adoptions first, but when I finally decided that was a better option for me. . . . I think early on I heard that China was available and that settled it for me. As soon as I heard "China," I thought, "Wow, that's it" because I'd been to Japan before when I was in the Navy, and the thing I remember the most about Japan was those children were beautiful, the most precious. . . . And I thought, "Wow, I could have an Asian child, I think they're gorgeous and China is such a cool country and it has such a long history, such an amazing culture!" So I thought that's it. To get a cute baby from a great country like China, that's a cool place to adopt from. I mean, I was considering Latin America because I'm from New Mexico, my dad's Hispanic, so a Spanish-speaking child would have been convenient, but I always go for exotic things. China was just more exotic. There is something completely different. Back then, there weren't many adoptions from China. (CA20)

Vivienne and Alex were firmly committed to adopting from China. They had thought through all the variables discussed above. Viv explained to me that their choice took account of their age, their desire for a healthy infant, their fears of domestic transracial adoption, and their image of China:

> Somebody's going to have to pick you, and we were older. I didn't really want to go through that whole thing Alex's brother had. They were decided on by three people and had lost three babies that way. No way we're going there. And Alex had lived in Japan for a year and really liked Asian culture and Asian people. China really appealed to him, and as we investigated, it seemed to be one of the more stable programs. We know a lot of people in our community who have kids from China, and Alex had been impressed that they were generally healthy and smart and happy. (CA26)

These comments provide a glimpse of the different ways prospective parents envisioned China. They imbued the country with the attributes of pragmatic efficiency and orderliness—and with images of "cute, bright, and gorgeous" Chinese girls whose heritage would be steeped in centuries of civilization. Adopting parents who had had positive life experiences in Japan or China did not make distinctions between them but rather conflated them using the descriptors above. As I subsequently learned from my conversations with non-adopted Chinese Americans, they were always taken aback by this conflation, given the horrors of the Rape of Nanking massacre in China in 1937 and the prolonged war between China and Japan (1937–1945).

Adoptive parents I spoke with also expressed their anxieties about adopting from within the United States owing to the immediacy of institutionalized racial discrimination against African Americans, with which they were all too familiar, and the unpredictability of "matching," which included taking account of their age, given that many of those who adopted from China were older parents. Some of them feared or had already had the painful experience of birth parents or relatives changing their minds about following through with an adoption. This fear was intensified by the geographic proximity of birth family members, in contrast to a "far away" Chinese birth mother. Although CA adopting parents stressed their uneasiness about "matching," they too were required to prepare a scrapbook of photos that was then sent by the adoption agency to China's Central Adoption Authority. The *distance*, culturally and physically, that this entailed seemed to make them less uncomfortable. As we have seen, most of them had no idea what Chinese authorities might look for in a series of photographs in "matching" them with a child.

Naming

Only by understanding . . . names as bundles of relationships, and by placing them back into the field from which they were abstracted, can we hope to avoid misleading inferences and increase our share of understanding.

Eric Wolf 1982: 3

Names are the manifestation or outcome of bundles of social relationships and processes and an investigation of the ways they are bestowed on children who are adopted, how children themselves view these naming practices, and how the society "reads" or makes sense of names gives us insight into the broader cultural context in which adoption unfolds and how it is linked to place-making.[2] For adoptive parents, naming created links between themselves and the child that were a first step toward incorporation into the family unit. This was hardly a simple process, however. The choices revealed contradictions and paradoxes between incorporation into a new family unit through adoption, recognition of birth family members or culture and the child's already existing links to it, and the intervention of political institutions such as the state.

Elizabeth Olson writes of how "babies move from being an 'object' or a slate with physical characteristics to having names.[3] In this narrative, love with the physical entity and its features leads to naming and a sense of relatedness." In American culture, naming is used to identify people as unique individuals and as members of a group who are part of the social fabric. Naming also reflects the parents' aspirations for a child's future identity and individuality and creates explicit links between the present and the past. In the case of children who have been adopted, names may create connections to an unknown past in their birth country, sustain continuity with birth family members, or fabricate originary ties to their adoptive family. The weight of the state in structuring kinship and its intervention in intimate domains also makes itself felt, silently and not so silently, through the naming process. Sealed, destroyed, or modified documents with critical naming information may legally prevent children who have been adopted, for example, from tracing their connections to others who have nurturing or biological connections to them. As adults, however, they may have the legal right to modify the names on their birth certificate.

Naming required decisions about belonging, connection, and identity for all of the adoptive family members I interviewed. Indeed, while names in American culture are always subject to change, in the case of adoption, especially transnational adoption, naming was an unusually active terrain of potential transformation and conflict that served to contest normative ideas about family formation. Most CA adoptive parents retained their child's Chinese given name as his or her American middle name. Even if they knew almost no Chinese, they spent many hours and time on the Worldwide Web attempting to determine the full meaning of their child's Chinese name. In a survey done on a major listserv, of 141 who responded, 74 percent said they kept a part of their child's Chinese name, 14 percent discarded it completely, and 16 percent kept all of it.[4]

Parents acknowledged their child's connection to China by focusing on his or her Chinese name. They also read into their child's name individual qualities about who she was that they believed might have been ascertained by the child's birth mother. Anthropologists have noted that in many cultures the name given to a child is thought to shape the child's personality. CA adoptive parents invested time, energy, and skill in creating life histories that demonstrated their daughter's "group" affiliation and individuated personality before adoption. Jeanne Marie Laskas wrote about her own deliberations:

> Right away I tried to figure out what her Chinese name meant: Hi Jong Bin. At first I got: Lucky Red Kneecap. Then I got: Lucky Roasted Hair on Temples. Hmm. Translating Chinese into English is something of a fine art. . . . I was able to get a good match on Ji and Hong. Lucky and Red. Bin was giving me a lot of trouble. Lucky Red Riverbank? Lucky Red High-Quality Iron? Eventually, I found it. A character with every last squiggle accounted for. So here was my daughter: Lucky Red Equally-Fine-in-External Accomplishments-and-Internal-Qualities. It seemed a big name for such a little girl. But I liked the meaning. The notion of balance. The notion of luck. What a wonderful wish to place upon a six-pound baby lying in a paperbox. (Laskas 2006: 40)

Laskas's tone is light, yet her focus on the symbolism of a name and what it might portend was as much about the mystery and lack of control entailed in adoption as it was about American individualism and the establishment of a specific name for a specific being, independently of her adoptive parents' traits. Laskas also points to how adoptive parents read into their child's Chinese name qualities that were stereotypically associated with "the Orient," such as balance, achievement, and being artistic.

Most children from China who were in orphanages were given the last (family) name of the director of the orphanage at the time, or the director of the orphanage sometimes arbitrarily picked a last name. In one case, the last name the orphanage director gave to the children in her care was "She," which simply means "socialism." Although one might think that through these last names it would be possible to trace all of the children who came from a particular orphanage in China, the directors frequently changed, and therefore so did the last names, and more than one orphanage director gave children the last name "She." CA adoptive parents simply eliminated that name, but parents were alerted to the significance of the name if they participated in orphanage site groups online. All children with the original last name "Peng" were adopted from a specific orphanage at a specific time. If a new director took over, the last names would change to "Zhang," for example. One mother was vehemently opposed to this practice:

> I would also like to make some suggestions while visiting with the orphanage directors. I would like to see them name the children with real family names. I met some adopted children whose last names are not official Chinese

surnames, based on the "Hundred Family Name Handbook." These adopted children could feel ambivalent at a grown-up age, when they find out that one of the few Chinese identities they have is fake.[5]

While CA adoptive parents placed inordinate emphasis on a child's more distinctive Chinese first name, it was unclear whether those names were given to the children by their birth mothers or by the director of the orphanage. CA adoptive parents nevertheless always assumed that it was given to their child by her birth mother, constituting an originary link. They attempted to provide their children with evidence of their connections to a culture and to individuals before being adopted, but the American cultural and bureaucratic norm of taking the last name of adoptive parents prevailed. Hence, these connections were "in name only" as parents offered clues to their children of how social ties were made biological (through acquiring, (usually) the patronymic last name of their adoptive parent(s)), and biological ties were made social through the retention of an originary middle name. First names were up for grabs, although they partly depended on the age of the child at the time of adoption or the preference of the birth parents.

Images, Artifacts, and Lifebooks

Once prospective parents traveled to China for the adoption process itself, some of them engaged in limited and structured sightseeing, but most remained in their hotels, except when shuttled to and from notary offices, the U.S. consulate, and sometimes, the social welfare institutes (SWIs), what orphanages are called in China.[6] Yet the structuring of place as part of their child's identity had already begun. Because of the Internet and the extensive circulation of information, many adopting parents, before their arrival, had already thought carefully about how they would make memory books for their children. While they were in China, they selectively took photographs and collected materials to that end. Prominent subject matter for photographs included tourist sites, the social welfare institutes (if adoptive families were permitted to visit them), and the handing of the child from the child's Chinese caretaker or from the director of the welfare institute to the adoptive parents. These photos or videos included other children in the orphanage, the child's caretakers, sometimes the director, and the grounds of the orphanage. The iconic photo of the newly adopted children in the adoption group, sitting on a sofa in the White Swan Hotel in Guangzhou, was also essential. Guangzhou is where the U.S. Consulate is located and where parents were granted the U.S. visa that permitted them to bring their child into the United States with a Chinese passport.[7] Many prospective parents stayed in the luxurious White Swan Hotel. The process of converting a Chinese baby into an American citizen had already begun—captured through documents and representations—but the focus on the child and the routine of transfer helped to make the bureaucratic and social conditions and the state regulations almost invisible. And the "symbolic coding" that set the process in motion helped maintain the momentum.

The symbolic coding that structured China as "a place" was conducted in part through consumption practices. Parents shopped for items that symbolized their child's connections to China—Chinese pajamas, silk embroidery, tennis shoes that honked, chopsticks, jade bracelets, calligraphy sets, chops (name stamps) engraved with their child's name and astrological sign—and interacted, however briefly and superficially, with Chinese people they encountered while they were there. Some adoptive parents I interviewed had received guidance before their journeys, either from participants in virtual media discussion groups or from social workers, regarding the most meaningful and appropriate keepsakes to purchase for their children in China. Buying these items from China provided a pathway that was intended to substitute for the lack of routes to birth parents or even information about them or their relatives. Adoptive parents carefully saved whatever items of clothing the child was wearing and any tattered pieces of paper that were pinned to the child when she was found.

Norma told me an extraordinary story about her daughter Madeleine's origins. It all boiled down to a brown coat:

> Madeleine was in pretty bad shape when they found her, very small. Jane [the adoption agency representative] said, according to the paperwork, she weighed three or four pounds. . . . I have several friends here who work in a neonatal care unit, they look at Madeleine and they can still tell she was a preemie. She was wrapped in rags but she was also wrapped in a big brown man's coat. Jane said that was a huge clue . . . that in China people who have brown clothes have good jobs, the other people wear dark or black. To have a brown coat, someone in Madeleine's family, probably the father, had a government job, and probably Madeleine's mother was his mistress. And by Madeleine's facial features, she said she's not from around here. . . . The other local little girls here are all real heavy-featured and -faced and Madeleine's were not. She looked like the people in Guangzhou, really fine-boned people. She did not look like the people in Hubei. So she speculated that . . . they abandoned her out in the

country because they didn't want her traced. And he obviously had enough money to abandon her in the coat. And that was another huge clue. He was wealthy, he could give her the coat. And they found her right on the orphanage steps, and they probably just drove out there and asked where the nearest orphanage was and just left her there. And you know, I kind of thought, how did all that information come from one coat? (CA12)

Each artifact adopting parents found or acquired carried with it the potential for creating stories and became the scaffolding for what Appadurai (1986) called the "social life of things." These "things" became fused with the social life of adopted children as they moved from China to the United States and from their Chinese caretakers to their American parents.

Many adoptive parents spoke about the lifebooks, also known as memory books, they prepared for their children. Lifebooks constituted powerful schema and narratives that encouraged commonalities in how children structured memories of their early years. What parents chose to chronicle and emphasize in lifebooks as key moments in the adoption process and in their children's life history were then incorporated as components of dynamic memory-building. As the practice of making lifebooks has become increasingly popular among adoptive parents, it has also become a cottage industry with specified categories and content.[8] The structure of the lifebooks adoptive parents purchased, together with ideas other adoptive parents had about what were the most significant categories to include, contributed to how adoptive parents crafted their children's early memories.

CA adoptive parents viewed lifebooks as an important part of family-making and place-making. It was one way to address broken links and to process what would always be unknown, as well as to acknowledge and make explicit the loss, sadness, and anger their children might feel over time. Over the years, adoptive parents and their children would revisit different concerns or themes through their lifebooks, or would feel differently about images and texts they had already seen.[9] While each lifebook was unique, all of them included the journey to China, key sightseeing spots, the orphanage, along with the caretakers at the orphanage, if they were permitted to visit, the moment of transition of child from Chinese caretakers to adoptive parents, the sites where paperwork was conducted, photos of other adoptive families and their children, and the journey home. Subsequently, lifebooks went in multiple directions. Some adoptive parents were assiduous about accompanying the photos or videos with detailed narratives.

Ruth and Dan had been talking to Bella about being adopted since she was 18 months of age. They did it using the vehicle of her lifebook:

> We made a little photo book of our trip and of her orphanage—we sent a camera before we went—and so that's her adoption book. We read it and talk about the whole process. Up until recently, I haven't said anything about a birth mother, but we're starting to kind of weave that in because developmentally, she's just right at the moment where she's very interested in babies and where they come from, but she knows she's adopted, and she knows she was born in China. (CA17)

Marge's view of the utility of her daughter Tess's lifebook was to allow Tess to own her story and not to censor it. This approach was an interesting exception to the deliberate exclusion of specific language or images by many adoptive parents because they thought they might be too painful or raise too many questions for their children initially. Marge explained:

> One of the bigger things that I really want to teach her is that her story is hers and she never has to edit her story or her feelings about it for my benefit. I think it's really important that she processes it the way she needs to. . . . I don't necessarily want to make it into a neat and tidy little package. I think it's really important that she draws her own conclusions. Obviously I'll help guide Tess, but if she feels angry one day I want her to be able to say that to me. If she feels like she really misses her birth mom one day I don't want her to feel afraid to say that. I want her to be able to say, "You know I really wish I knew who my biological mother was." I want her to . . . always be aware that there is nothing you can say to me that is going to make me love you less or is going to make me wish that you weren't mine or any of those things. If I can give her that safe place to work that stuff out, then . . . I'll feel like I've done the best that I could for her. . . . When I wrote her lifebook . . . I thought long and hard about the type of language I was going to use, and I've seen a lot of lifebooks that were very pretty and were very neatly packaged stories, and I just decided not to do that because I thought . . . it's for her, it's not for me. . . . It was cathartic for me to write it all out, but this book was essentially for her and there aren't tidy little edges about it. I just wanted to present it as neutrally as I could and to not make it too—you know, the Red Thread book thing;[10] that's all well and good, but it's not reality. There is certain terminology that she will have to accept, and so I used that terminology because it's all over her paperwork. I'm not going to throw it in her face, but it's just part of her story, and I'd rather

that she hear those words in a safe environment where we can help her to reframe them and understand them . . . before she goes out into the world and has some ignorant person say that to her. (CA8)

CA adoptees did, in fact, return time and again to their lifebooks, reviewing and asking questions about their early years, and as they approached adolescence, what was there and what was not in the images and narratives became major catalysts for adoptees themselves to reconstruct their lifebooks and their connections to China.

Imagining China

The imaginary adopting parents constructed—what I call the process of Chineseifying—fueled demand for a particular kind of "China," now being produced as a robust industry within a defined touristic space within China (Traver 2007). Sara Dorow (2006: 113–62), who accompanied families on their adoption journeys to China, offers a detailed account of this stage of building relationships through connections with China as a narrowly construed place and culture. In the roughly two weeks that adopting parents remain in China, they become "clients" of the Chinese government and economy through their purchasing power; the child who is to be adopted becomes a "gift" from the Chinese; and both adopting parents and their child become unofficial "ambassadors" who will communicate the positive dimensions of Chinese culture.

The structuring of place in the initial adoption journey is the result of how participants in the process sought to imagine China; it is also, in part, the result of the assiduous surveillance of all foreign visitors to China such that they are exposed to what Chinese government officials considered appropriate for them to see and experience, and what they wanted them to buy.

In my own experiences as an adopting parent, while I was aware that this was happening, I could not escape its strictures. My husband and I were taken to small stores selling items for adopting parents, such as embroidery, stylized paintings for children, silk pajamas, chops, and scrolls. We visited the jade market where we could purchase carvings and jewelry; we strolled along the riverwalk across the street from the hotel; and we went to a museum. With some trepidation, twice we struck out on our own. Once we took a taxi to a huge department store. I left our daughter with my husband while I went to look for diapers. When I returned, he was surrounded by a group of older women who, with avid interest, were reading our daughter's palm. Another time, with our daughter in tow, we left the compound, crossed a bridge, and, descending the stairs on the other side, found ourselves entering a completely different world, an open-air market that seemed to sprawl for several miles. The vendors, selling things we had never seen for sale before, stared at us with intense curiosity. When we adopted our daughter, we were not permitted to travel to the welfare institute, for reasons we never found out, but instead stayed in a large city about an hour and a half from the orphanage.

Culture, Heritage, Politics, and Place

Like the Hague Convention governing international adoption, the Chinese government explicitly desires that children who are adopted by foreigners learn about and take pride in their cultural heritage. Whenever the Chinese government issued paperwork and an adoption certificate with a photo, officially transferring a child being adopted, the notary made a speech to the parents stressing that, now, they were "members of a Chinese family." Norma described this moment to me:

> I'll never forget what the notary said at Madeleine's ceremony that they translated for us, that we now are Chinese also by adopting Madeleine, a member of a Chinese family. Not only did they want us to bring her back someday and visit with our new family, but they expected it. Oh, my gosh. (CA12)

Winnie's different, and more sobering, experience led her to reflect deeply about what her incorporation into China as a family meant when she adopted her daughter Camille. I had asked her about naming Camille and why she had decided to keep Camille's Chinese name as her middle name. She told me:

> I knew I would keep her Chinese name. I really had kind of a thought, should I go by her Chinese name with her heritage? At that time, I did try hard to make a connection with the assistant director of Camille's orphanage. It [the orphanage] was very, very poor, and that's all I knew about it. They remained very proud people, and the orphanage director rejected my offer to help. . . . I had wanted so much to retain communication with them, and to be able to send pictures, and just have that connection for Camille. And the orphanage director's point of view—what was said to me through the translator—was "Why would you want to maintain a connection to an orphanage? Just teach her China. China's too big, you know. She needs a point of origin." That was our exchange. I cried. It was in some very deep way terribly unsettling. . . . I see it differently now, of course, but she did not want to retain some connection to this child. I thought it was a rejection of this child, and maybe in some way really it was. (CA29)

Winnie had thought about Camille's "place"—her links to China—as being intertwined with her caretaking in the orphanage, but the orphanage director was a bureaucrat, performing a state function. Her vision of "connection" for Camille was to China as a country, and it had almost nothing to do with family-making.

Returning "home," Chinese American adoptive parents took different approaches to integrating China as a place into their children's personal history. As Toby Volkman (2005b) and Sara Dorow (2006), among others, have noted, China as a place and connections to it are carefully imagined, and much is excluded. The place-building CA adoptive parents pursued upon their return to the United States told its own story. Many dressed their children (even their non-adopted children), and sometimes themselves, in Chinese outfits, made efforts to learn to cook Chinese food, attended Chinese ritual festivities, sent their children to Chinese dance classes, and strived to expose their children to Chinese through language classes. Some took these activities very seriously. Their children attended Chinese school for three or four hours each weekend. Occasionally, adoptive parents participated as well. Ruth explained her focus on things Chinese for her daughter in the following way:

> I want her to have some kind of knowledge about her place of origin. . . . It will never be the knowledge that she would have or the relationship that she would have if she stayed there, but I want her to have something because I don't want her to feel like she's just sort of floating in space and not rooted in any way. And family, I don't know what she's ever going to have to know about that, but I'm carefully filing away every piece of information that I have about her life before she met us so that she can have . . . as much of that information as she can. (CA17)

A few adoptive parents found these efforts frustrating and useless. Take, for example, the experience recounted by Jeanne Marie Laskas to expose her children to "all things Chinese" through Chinese lessons, which they rejected vehemently. Laskas reassured herself that the most important thing was that they were a family:

> Oh well. . . . So we bond over our shared stupidity. It's still "*bonding.*" I don't want to apologize to my girls for taking them out of China, a homeland that was not, in the end, a home. I don't want them to grow up apologizing for leaving, as if that crowded country gave them any choice. A lot of people seem to want to romanticize this situation, dressing their girls in Chinese silks and

taking them to the mall for professional photographs to hand out. Maybe that's good. I don't know. Maybe that's better than just walking around as a woman who finds herself awakening in fits and starts with a stubborn rage. *How dare you leave these girls to fend for themselves, even for a second. How dare you! What is the matter with you people.. . . . .* Look: "My girls are fine. My girls are home. My girls are part of a family. We are Mom and Dad and Kikki and Et. . . . We have our reasons." (Laskas 2006: 121)

Laskas placed more emphasis on the right of children to safety, shelter, and affection and to a particular kind of childhood. Other adoptive parents, in the face of social criticism of China's trade policy or population control policies, reluctantly became defenders of China expressly for the sake of their children. Garrett, a father who had never before traveled outside the United States, commented:

> We find ourselves defending China a great deal. . . . People would talk about our trade debts or they'll talk about the one-child policy, and you just have to be an international policy expert because these people come at you with every angle there is. That's a factor that I could not relate to giving birth that I had with Jenny [That is, Garrett could find no analogy between the questions and comments people made about his adoption of a child from China and those comments people made about biologically giving birth to a child.] (CA5)

More personally, Lisa equivocated about the negative impressions of China held by many Americans and concluded that she "owed" the Chinese a great deal: "I've kind of made my peace with it. First of all, I feel a bond with China, with the Chinese people. . . . This is the land that gave birth to my daughter, who I love and cherish above all, so there's a bond" (CA6). As a result of incorporating a child from China into their respective families, Garrett and Lisa began to challenge preconceptions both they and their fellow Americans held about China. Their child catalyzed and mediated a kind of biosentimentality about China as a "sending region" (Sharp 2006).

While many children seemed to enjoy this initial phase of place-building (*pace* Laskas), as they became older [they] recognized that where they lived and how they were situated in it did not include connections to their biological parents, or even any specific information about who their birth parents were, such as their names, what they looked like, and where they were born. Also, they began to wonder what, precisely, about Chinese policies, had caused them to be separated from their birth family and then transplanted elsewhere. These unknowns led them to ruminate about the meaning of their adoption in quite a different way, in relation to place. At this juncture, the "imagined" roots their adoptive parents had worked so hard to create began to take on greater significance for them. The imaginary China collided with questions that could not be answered and a desire for more knowledge on the part of children themselves.

Later, children became ambivalent about these forays into place-making and culture building, as we discuss in greater detail in Chapter 9. Families located in dense urban areas, such as Boston or the Upper West Side of Manhattan, where the number of adoptive Chinese families was high, were more likely to embrace place-making practices because they had friends and peers pursuing the same kinds of activities. Both density and absolute numbers mattered enormously. In smaller communities where the proportion of children adopted from China was high and there were regular gatherings among adoptive families, novel kinds of place-making, as emergent cultural practices, were becoming regularized and familiar. Even so, as children grew into adolescence, they began to question these connections, either rejecting them altogether or commenting extensively on them.

Many CA adoptive parents wrote of their children's indifference to or rejection of their efforts to celebrate Chinese culture and to make Chinese cultural materials available to them once they reached about age 7 or 8. They had strived to incorporate heritage journeys, Chinese language instruction, and role models such as Chinese university students into their lives, but these efforts were often unsuccessful. Julie wrote:

> We went back to China in about second grade, and even though we have tried to suggest more trips to China, she would much rather travel the U.S. and Europe (not that we travel too much anymore). We live in a predominately Asian town and she fits in pretty well. . . . She is pretty resistant to anything related to adoption or events for Asian adoptees (like FCC events), but she has joined a few organizations set up for Asian kids on her own over the last couple of years, so we know she is finding her own way.[11]

Emily also worked hard to integrate aspects of Chinese culture into her daughters' daily activities, such as Chinese playgroups, and hired a Chinese university student who taught the whole family Chinese. The daughters rejected all her efforts, although they still enjoyed looking at their photo albums. One of her daughters professed to prefer Japanese, but when her teacher told her that the written form [of Japanese] was Chinese [characters], she refused to believe her teacher.

Because of their desire to avoid the possibility of U.S. birth parents changing their mind about giving up a child for adoption, parents adopted internationally from places like China and then went to extreme lengths to make sure that their children were Chinesified. In this way, although parents appeared to separate having biological ties to their children from building a heritage linked to their birthplace for them, they fused race and ethnicity, desiring to construct a culture that accorded with the child's appearance and truncated roots. By "race," I mean the physical perception of their children as Chinese. By "ethnicity" I mean the practices and symbols—including language, artifacts, dress, festivals, and food—that adoptive parents associated with "being Chinese" and that they were attempting to teach their children. Barbara Lal points out that while "ethnic identity" is often understood in terms of descent—where one is from—it is "primarily a matter of learned culture. Culture is not inherited; rather it consists of learned symbols, stories, rituals and world-views" (Lal 2001: 159).

One reason CA parents embarked on the difficult undertaking of learning about and embracing Chinese traditions, either punctuating their daily practices with them or interweaving them in a more intricate pattern, was to enact reciprocity—gestures of gratefulness—to unknown birth parents and to the Chinese government. Abel, a single father (he married several years after adopting Belinda), mused about the journey he had taken thus far and why he was so intent on communicating anything he could about Chinese culture to his daughter:

> Two countries allowed single males to adopt—the United States and China. . . .
> Bottom line, I think it was destiny. . . . I actually dreamed about my daughter
> before I met her. . . . Everything seemed to point to China. . . . I took a Chinese
> history class in college. It was wonderful and very interesting. . . . My mom
> is really into Chinese history and stuff. . . . There were wall hangings around,
> books, and whatnot. Clearly, she communicated her utter respect for the history and culture, and I think that was passed on to me. The bottom line was
> that they were opening their country to me. I think nothing really trumps that,
> the fact that they had faith in me. I could go on gushing. . . . I haven't taken
> Belinda back to visit, and I think that is important. . . . I'm so grateful to so
> many people. (CA28)

When I asked Abel whether Belinda was learning Chinese, he told me that he himself had been studying it because he felt "it's really important. . . . A certain degree of me feels I need to prove . . . that I'm a good father. And being a good father means that I recognize that she's also China's daughter. She's my responsibility because she's my daughter, but I also feel like it's bigger than that." Toward the end of our conversation, I asked Abel if there was anything else he wanted to share with me. He was thinking about all the different ways he had tried to show Belinda how proud he was of Chinese culture, but he really did not know what kind of impact it was having on her:

> I guess the only part is the stuff I don't know, which is what's truly going on in her head . . . I can read the outside of her self-concept, but I don't know what's going on inside, and I don't know what's going to happen. I've heard stories from a lot of people, [that] a lot of girls, mainly, turn their back on their culture, everything else, when they get into middle school. But then, I guess, some start to come back too. (CA28)

Abel was very intense about his efforts to instill a pride in Chinese culture and language in Belinda, but he nevertheless communicated what many other CA adoptive parents felt. At the same time, his perceptive awareness that Belinda might eventually question what he was trying to convey, and that he really did not know how she was processing what he was doing, were somewhat unusual.

Chinese Americans

Many non-adopted Chinese American citizens in the United States were eager to ensure that children adopted from China learn Chinese and appreciate Chinese culture. Yet they themselves were astonished at the passion of adoptive parents. More than a few confided to me that they were learning about their own culture through the practices of families who had adopted their children from China. This, of course, is not unlike the generational dynamics of enculturation among immigrant families or of interfaith marriages requiring conversion. The person who converts is often far more religious than the spouse. Sue sheepishly confessed:

> I'm from a small town in Washington state, certainly not from the big city, and our support group is smaller as well. About three years ago, our group . . . made a big effort to invite the Asian community to our Lunar New Year celebration. They all came. However, most of them haven't been back. Most of the white adults huddled together and talked adoption stuff, and the Asian adults sat together and talked more generally about life. Some of them talked in Mandarin or Korean. All the children played together. It seems that most whites only care about talking China when it's about travel or orphanages or purchasing Chinese goods. There wasn't much effort at getting to know each

other from either group. My friends, Chinese and Korean, and I laughed about it later. They told me that most of the Asian adults don't have the patience to sit through adoption and travel talk. They're busy talking about their businesses, real estate purchases, immigration issues, etc.—you get the idea. Most white adoptive families, in our town, are only interested in playing "tourist" when it comes to China.[12]

Passion for an imaginary China differed from the reality of China or the reality of Chinese Americans living their lives in the United States. Adoptive parents tended to erase the more muddy aspects of being Chinese in sharing their daughters' "original culture" with them, though they struggled with their own choices. In attempting to honor the wishes of the Chinese government and in trying to heed the challenges they expected their children would encounter as both American and Chinese, these early years of place-making hardly resembled everyday life in China. Even so, it took a lot of work to make these kinds of connections materialize. However exotic and distorted these tokens of Chinese culture and history were, they were what was accessible to parents who had few other means of learning rapidly about China.

Non-adopted Chinese Americans were ambivalent about the racism, patriarchal ideology, and one-child policy that existed within China. At the same time they saw commonalities between themselves and CA adoptees, "the politics of native roots" among Chinese Americans intervened, as anthropologist Helen Siu (1994: 32) explains. They associated the physical appearance of being Chinese with China and with being Han. Chinese themselves considered Han Chinese to be an ideal type. As an ethnic group, they constituted the overwhelming majority of China's population. Yet a substantial number of children adopted from China hailed from minority groups, mixed backgrounds, and from rural rather than urban areas in China; they were girls; and their presence in the United States was the consequence, in part, of China's population policies. Hence, while having roots in China might unite adopted and non-adopted Chinese Americans, there were points of stress and divisions between them. Some non-adopted Chinese Americans found it discomfiting that parents of adoptive Chinese children did not seem to partake of the same ranking system and that they held up to them a mirror of exactly what was disturbing yet still meaningful to them in their country of origin. Others, mostly of an older generation, were resentful of the advantages that accrued to Chinese children adopted by Americans. In addition, Chinese Americans simply did not think that Americans were capable of teaching their adopted children Chinese culture and believed that Chinese children should not be "exported" but rather raised within China. These perceptions, partly grounded in nationalism, confronted some CA adoptive parents, who told me about their experiences, although many were oblivious to these sentiments.

Fred was so deeply distressed by two different negative reactions of Chinese Americans to his family's adoption of a daughter from China that he could hardly talk. His family was eating at a Chinese restaurant. The server was initially enthusiastic that they were going to visit China, but became appalled when he heard why they were going. His gregarious behavior abruptly changed. He did not speak to the family again, only returning to bring them their check. In the second incident, after the adoption, a Chinese American co-worker asked Fred what he was doing culturally for his daughter. Fred narrated the conversation to me:

She continued: "I don't mean to offend you," and I've since learned that when people say that to me I will stop them and say, "it sounds like you are going to offend me so why don't we end the conversation now," but I didn't say that and then she goes, "I really think that Chinese children should not be raised by white people." And I was just flabbergasted but I didn't know what to say. And she went on and on and on and on.

She said that they should be raised in China . . . by Chinese people, that we don't understand the culture and that they are losing their identity, and she kind of made it sound as if all these girls were born to under-age mothers. . . . I was in shock. She's a social worker, and I think social workers should be a little more open to people and different experiences and that type of thing. . . . I didn't say anything, and as the day went on, I was still in such anger, especially when I put my daughter to bed that night [*Fred began weeping*]. I put her to bed that night and I'm laying with her and I'm saying to myself, "She should be sitting in an orphanage now because J. has a problem with her being in a house, and I'm loving her and she should be sitting in an orphanage because J. has a problem with white people raising Chinese?" No, you know, I don't think so. That makes no sense whatsoever. (CA6)

More CA adoptive parents gradually became conscious of the double bind in which they found themselves, as the somewhat anguished words of one mother revealed:

Sometimes I feel really inadequate on being the teacher of a foreign culture (to me) for my children. One of the best things I think I have done in order to learn more about Chinese culture is to start taking Mandarin lessons from my tutor C. . . . As we have deepened our acquaintance, I have also been introduced to some of her views about transracial adoption and white parents adopting from China. C. is very polite and very, shall we say, ambiguous in how she states certain opinions (a virtue in China, she says) but as she has become more comfortable with me, she has also felt very comfortable telling me how she does not understand why white people go to China to adopt "rejected" children. I have found this to be a fairly common viewpoint from a lot of Chinese (born in Mainland China) and Chinese-Americans that we have relationships with. It has made me realize that my daughter will have two handicaps going into her journey to build a Chinese-American identity: White parents; and the perception by many in the Chinese American community that will look at her as "damaged/thrown-away goods."[13]

Chinese Americans reached out to CA adoptive families, but the process was fraught. CA children were discovering that they had much in common with Chinese Americans *ethnically* and that they shared important yet subtle historical experiences along gendered lines with Chinese American women. Many Chinese American women had fled the constraints of patriarchy in China. Unlike an older generation of Chinese immigrants, they were educated, and many were independent professionals who moved between the American and Chinese cultures. They spoke fluent English but they also continued to speak Chinese. They got together with their Chinese friends, they learned to line dance, and they watched soap operas. They were circulating in both worlds. They sometimes also came up against their own identity contradictions and confusions.

One woman I came to know well, Jenny, was a divorced, very independent, Chinese American woman who had managed to make her way to the United States in 1972 during the Cultural Revolution. She was well educated, with a degree in chemistry, fluent in English and Chinese, and worked as a librarian at a university. She emphasized that she was "CBA" (Chinese-born American) rather than "ABC" (American-born Chinese) and would berate her Chinese American women friends for criticizing conditions in the United States, exclaiming, "I always ask them, if you don't like it here, why don't you go back? Why did you come here then?" Yet Jenny also confided in me her displeasure with American men who approached her with the expectation that she would conform to their stereotypical idea of a docile Chinese woman or "China doll." She was committed to working with families with children from China, teaching them Chinese, and introducing them to Chinese culture, partly for the income, partly because she thought it was important for them to have the strength to maneuver, as girls, in a society where they were always going to be "in between" and needed to defend themselves. Jenny knew well the reality of patriarchy and surveillance in China, and had also struggled to counter the image of the China doll in the United States.

Some Chinese American women who resembled Jenny (though who were perhaps not quite as intense or independent)were making concerted efforts to interact with Chinese American adoptees, in collaboration with FCC. The heritage camp movement (See Chapter 9) also offered opportunities for cooperation with Chinese Americans. In the Washington metropolitan area, Chinese American women have made it a practice to hold events throughout the year for Chinese American adoptees and their families. I attended several of these events, mostly overseen by older Chinese American women who were sometimes accompanied by their husbands. They prepared Chinese food, oversaw crafts for the children, put on dance performances, taught them to play with Chinese yo-yo's, and not surprisingly, took advantage of the occasion to sell all sorts of books, apparel, music, and hairpieces. Pride in Chinese culture, their own experiences of racism, and gender stereotyping in the United States motivated these women, who simultaneously remained critical (to varying degrees) of China as a political regime and its patriarchal ideology. They too were actively contributing to building a sense of place for CA adoptive families.

Discussion

CA adoptive parents struggled to make connections with cultural practices and an ethos that they could not incorporate easily or meaningfully into their everyday lives. In the course of place-making, they confronted tensions between love for their children and their children's right to survival and a minimum level of comfort, on one hand, and their right to embrace their heritage and to be members of "their culture," on the other. The question of children's rights to their culture and heritage has been articulated most forcefully by black adoptees who believe that their adoption was a form of abduction, and by the National Association of Black Social Workers (NABSW) (see Chapter 1). Many adoptees argue that the position of the NABSW is applicable to all transracial and transnational adoptees.

For Tobias Hubinette, abduction or forced uprooting is the dark shadow of the place-making attempted by most transracial and transnational adoptive parents. Adoptees who argue that they were abducted point to how little most adoptive parents care about the underlying geopolitics that fuel transnational adoption or about the cultures of Korea or China, for example.[14] Hubinette makes the forceful claim that when transracial adopted children grow up they bear the brunt of racism, like many immigrants to Europe or the United States: "When the adoptee leaves the adoptive family to become an adult, the immigrant identity is waiting. From a privileged adopted child with adoptive parents who fight to make their adopted children believe that they are "special," not immigrants, the adult adoptee becomes just one of many other non-white immigrants. That is the African-American's strongest opinion against interracial adoption: white parents can never teach their non-white children strategies how to survive in a racist society."[15]

The positions I have outlined in this chapter have had a major impact on the investment of CA adoptive parents in place-building for their children. Many of them have taken to heart that they must teach their children about their cultural heritage. However, as we have seen, and as Hubinette claims, their initial place-making activities for their children, especially their daughters, tended to exclude what it might mean for their children to occupy a place in between as non-white, usually upper middle class, Chinese immigrants whose truncated "blood ties" and positioning were papered over with a celebration of Chinese culture. Their place-making practices and narratives emerged out of transnational and globalizing processes and imaginaries, as well as the tensions in American culture between nature and nurture, market models and moral models, and the interests of different stakeholders. In the early stages, place-making among CA adopting and adoptive parents was situated simultaneously in the ideas that they had about China, their experiences there, the important ways that the Chinese and Chinese Americans themselves help to structure these experiences (both in China and later in the United States), the sentiments that Chinese things evoked for them; the lifebooks they made, and last but not least, the ways that their children, in the course of exchange and transfer, mediated these place-building activities. The children themselves created the reasons for pathways to begin to take shape. They also facilitated monetary, cultural, and emotional transactions.

Place-making is anchored to children's life stages and cognitive development. Increased openness in adoption in the United States, ironically, is accompanied by the reality that "the circumstances of the child's abandonment are profoundly hidden, unknowable, for example, in China" where "abandonments, which are illegal, take place in secrecy" (Volkman 2005b: 86). Children adopted from China and elsewhere, at different points in their life deeply felt that gap, the inability to fill in memories, to *ever* make connections. Chinese New Year celebrations, Moon Festivals, books, and dances acquired a different kind of emphasis and meaning at those points. Children began to question the celebratory aspects of place-building when they found they could not substitute for more detailed and specific knowledge about the place and persons from which they had originated. Whatever knowledge they did have, as recounted through and by their adoptive parents, began to seem suspect to them. Their losses raised a host of questions, intimate and geopolitical in nature, that compelled families, particularly those whose children knew they were from another country and who "looked different," to return to their place of origin.

Few parents I interacted with explicitly conveyed to their young children that a regime of population control and one-party political control had created the availability of their daughters for adoption. This would have required a move away from an essentialized depiction and transmission of Chinese culture and place to a more nuanced acknowledgment of the complexity of Chinese culture and political economic practices; many adoptive parents believed that, developmentally, their children would be unable to process such an explanation.[16]

On the other hand, the children themselves, on their "return" journeys, step by step, created links between fragile documents, tenuous roots, former foster parents and caretakers at orphanages, and permanently unknowable blood relatives. The latter prompted children to begin to recognize the complex terrain that constituted their understanding of sentimentality and place-making. Sonia, one CA adoptee who was 8 when I chatted with her, wondered, "Why is it that my mother had to abandon me? Why couldn't any of her relatives take care of me? Why didn't anyone see when I was left? Why do the Chinese have to watch everyone?" When such questions arose, CA children came face to face with a more concrete understanding of the reasons for the trajectory their lifeline had taken. Their "starting point and place" were the very reason they did not have one (Yngvesson and Coutin 2006: 183–84).

CA adoptees reassessed the Chinese world their adoptive parents had crafted. In addition, children and parents alike experienced a growing and sobering awareness that how *they* saw themselves clashed with how the broader public saw them. This awareness surged forth most commonly when CA adoptees were in high school, and it set into motion the hard work of structuring an identity grounded in color and culture. As they took account of the power of race and racial discrimination in America, they began to push against the kinds of places their adoptive parents had struggled to erect for them. These included their attachment to white cultural values and middle- and upper-middle class parents, and their simultaneous connections to China in the form of food, language, aesthetics, tattered documents, and baby clothes that acknowledged their Chinese origins.

4 White Russians

All Americans are immigrants. It's just a question of how far back you look. (Even Native Americans are thought to have arrived here across a prehistoric land bridge.) One of the many strengths of this country is our ability to absorb, blend, and celebrate the cultures of origin of all our different peoples. Each one of us is an American, and each one of us has both our shared national culture and our cultures of origin to celebrate. That's another reason I celebrate my son's birth culture. By doing so, I honor his role as a new American and our country's history of bringing many cultures together.

And I still believe that if you love your child (as I know we all do), and your child is Russian (or Ukrainian, African, Armenian, Kazakh, or anything else), then you love a part of their birth culture too.

—**Adoptive parent of Russian child**

Our trips to Russia were, without a doubt, some of the most exciting travel we have ever done. Having grown up during the Cold War, it was an incredible moment for me to stand on Red Square or to see Lenin entombed. So, just as I bought souvenirs when I went to Honduras or England, I bought souvenirs when I went to Russia. Artwork for the walls, matrushka [sic] dolls, jewelry, birch bark boxes, all sorts of stuff. This stuff is on display not so much for the sake of my children as it is for me, to remind me of the journey of a lifetime I took twice.

—**Adoptive parent of Russian child**[1]

How does place-making among RA adoptive families compare with that of CA adoptive families? The most obvious difference was that many RA adoptive parents did not view integrating a sense of place into their children's identity formation as problematic because most of the children adopted from Russia looked "Caucasian."[2] As Kyle pointed out:

I don't perceive the international dimension to be significant at all. . . . If you adopted an African kid or a Chinese kid . . . I can imagine there are issues. . . . In our case . . . you can't physically tell, at least at quick notice, unless you study our kids, [that] they are not biologically related to us. If you walk into a restaurant, nobody is going to turn heads because we look different. . . . I assert there is still a bit of stigma in society. . . . If I am totally honest, even me, as a father of adopted kids, when I see other families or know about families that have adopted kids, the thought crosses my mind, how cohesive is that family? I'm civilized enough to suppress my thoughts in terms of any behavior . . . but when I think about my own family, I honestly have forgotten that our kids are adopted. (RA6)

Matching and Claiming

Eighty percent of the parents I spoke with selected Russia or the Ukraine as the place they wanted to adopt from because they thought their children would blend in in the United States. Billy did not want his family to be "a walking-around advertisement for adoption, as you have with children from China" (RA4). RA adoptive parents had concerns about the racism they knew they would encounter among their extended family members, even if they themselves did not share those sentiments. These concerns were mingled with anxiety that their family would not sufficiently resemble the ideal American family model, characterized by general physical similarities, grounded in blood ties. Gretchen and Keith were adamant about not pursuing transracial adoption for those reasons:

> Gretchen: We originally looked domestically. . . . When we looked at all the kids available for adoption, what we found was black, and Keith comes from a family of unabashed bigots, and he said he could not put a child through being exposed to it, a black child, whereas my family would not have cared. Keith very, very strongly did not want China. He wanted Russia. Partly because of his family, I think, wanting a child who looked like us.
>
> Keith: It doesn't bother me personally but my family would have been very cruel.
>
> Gretchen: His extended family.
>
> Keith: I have a couple hundred cousins back up in Michigan, and whenever we went back up there it would have been hostile. (RA8)

Adopting parents, motivated by concerns about race and blending in, also thought it would be easier and often less costly to adopt a white infant from Russia than to adopt a white child from within the United States. Political economic, ideological, and cultural reasons explain why this is so (see "Introduction). The combination of the sexual revolution, birth control, the availability of abortion, and changing mores about single parenthood beginning in the 1970s meant that the demand for infants, in general, and even more so for white infants, exceeded supply (Solinger 1992). In addition, the long history of racialized policies with respect to control of reproduction in the United States contributed to the greater availability of mixed or black children than white infants. The transaction fees for private adoptions of white infants ranged from $30,000 upward; the fees were lower for adoption of mixed or black infants or children, either publicly or privately.[3]

Grey Markets

The differences in what adoptive parents were willing to spend on different kinds of adoption illuminated the paradox in American culture between children as "priceless"—invaluable to the constitution and completion of family and defined without reference to the value they potentially represent within an economic sphere—and the reality of children as partial "commodities" in the transactions that transpired in family-making practices through adoption, as well as other reproductive technologies (Zelizer 1985, 2005). Viviana Zelizer, in her groundbreaking book *Pricing the Priceless Child: The Changing Social Value of Children*, traces the historical emergence of children as "priceless" in America between 1917 and the 1930s, when "the emergence of this economically 'worthless' but emotionally 'priceless' child created an essential condition of contemporary childhood" (1985: 3). This transformation took place in the context of the shifts in the boundaries between "public" and "private" spheres and the emergence of the "domestic" domain of the family. She notes:

> Pricing the priceless child therefore became a complex task, creating confusion in legal thought and practice, controversy in the insurance business, and uncertainty in the "exchange" of adoptive children. Children were viewed to exist in a cultural domain *outside* commodification in the United States. At the same time, however, they became the focus of household consumption among upper-middle-class families, in particular. (Zelizer 1985: 210)

Judith Modell (1994) wryly observes that, in this "grey market" shaped by capitalism, it would indeed seem an oddity to at least some persons if children had no economic value attached to them, given the value they generally attach to what they purchase: "People do value what they have invested in, and payments can be 'legitimized as symbolic expressions of sentimental concern' by adoptive parents" (Zelizer 1985: 207). Those who are about to relinquish a baby may also appreciate the sense of value implied by a transfer of money. Willingness to pay indicates a commitment to care for that which is acquired at cost; such commitment is not, of course, antithetical to adoption principles. Simultaneously, and paradoxically, ... referring to a market ... reminds a reader that babies are not "products" but human beings, not to be bought and sold or distributed according to a cold calculation of worth. (Modell 1994: 54)

This grey market in which children became the locus of intimate desire intertwined with commodification and in which value itself was calculated in light of class, race, and, sometimes, gender characterized adoption practices, not only in the United States but in many other places and contexts as well.

The measure of a child was no longer according to "an economic yardstick," but rather, as Zelizer (1985: 193) observes, "judged by new criteria; its physical appeal and personality." RA adopting parents were aware of the sliding scale of transaction costs described above. Some of them were distressed by it, but most of them viewed it as a matter of pragmatics, especially if they were intent on adopting a white child.

If RA adopting parents already had biological children, they also thought their family's adjustment would be easier if their children were not distinguished by race and therefore subjected to greater social scrutiny and invasion of privacy. "Matching" of siblings occurred, not only among some white families seeking to adopt white children internationally, but also among CA parents, who decided to adopt from China a second time, or among AA parents so that their two children would look like each other and would be able to share how they felt about being adopted, not looking like their adoptive parents, or their experiences of racism.

RA adoptive parents, like some CA adoptive parents, also expressed a preference for adopting children from *outside* the United States because of fears about birth mother claims. A worry that I heard expressed, more by fathers than by mothers, was the possible discomfort and psychological turmoil that open adoption could incite. They felt it would be confusing for a child to have "two mothers." Especially with the adoption of Russian children, in which great efforts were taken to match each child with adoptive parent(s), a furtive biological model made itself felt at the very inception of identity building through place in which place and race were closely linked.

Personal Histories and Cultural DNA

This is not to say that all RA adoptive parents ignored connections with Russia, as the quotes with which we began this chapter illustrate, but these connections existed *before* adoption rather than subsequently. At least one-third of the parents I interviewed selected Russia because they themselves had Eastern European ancestry, they had visited Russia, or they or their extended family members had studied Russian history or literature. Fran, Kyle's wife, explained:

> My mother had her Ph.D. in Eastern European history, and she's studied the Russian language and inevitably done a lot of Russian history and literature as a part of her course. I studied Russian in college for a year and a half or so and went on a trip there in 1982. So I was also fascinated with the place. Then

my older sister is married to an Englishman and lives in London, and he is a Russian scholar. He almost finished his Ph.D. on Russian history, speaks fluent Russian, and has a business that has a Russian office. He travels there a lot and one of his clients—he is a literary agent—was Boris Yeltsin. (RA6)

Mandy made the choice to adopt from Russia for similar reasons:

I have a number of Russian friends and studied Russian in college, and have always liked Russian music and literature, and that was one of the reasons that adopting in Russia seemed good to me. I have read in postings and writings by adult adoptees how important it was to have their birth cultures respected and acknowledged, and how important it was that it be part of the fabric of their lives, and it seemed to me that as I already had Russian things in my life, it would be easier to do that than if I had to learn a new culture in connection with my adoption.

Mandy wanted to instill in her son a positive sense of connection with Russia as a culture and place, not simply because that was where they were from but so that they would be proud of who they were and of their adoptions. Implicitly, her statement was also a commentary on her concerns about how transnational adoption and Russia might be viewed in the United States:

I intend to try getting Roger to study Russian with me and my mother when he is securely rooted in English. . . . I don't feel that I've stayed as connected as I should, although my good friend from Russia has honored my son on every Russian holiday and has acted as a sort of Russian godmother to him. I may be rationalizing, but in the end, I think the most important thing is your attitude—that you like and respect the culture and the country, even if there are things with which you disagree. If you are going to give your children a strong sense of self, I think you have to show them the good in their country and culture of origin, and make sure to make clear that any flaws or failures are a result of being human, like Americans, not of being Russian. I also think that at least having some elements of the material culture around (e.g., art, books, *matrushkas*, etc.) for kids to see and connect with as they begin to absorb the whole story may be helpful. I will let my child understand the whole story as he grows up, but I want his first taste of his birth culture to be one of the beautiful parts. I already had a matrushka collection, as I've had a tradition of buying one matrushka each time I visit Russia. . . . We brought home some beautiful things . . . that are now part of our daily life. My son loves to hear

about them, and . . . where they came from and where he was born. It clearly
makes him happy, so I think it has worked out well so far. (RA14)

Grace and Joel had adopted three children from Russia. Initially, they had
been adamant about not revealing that their children were adopted in order to
ensure their privacy. By the time of the adoption of their third child, however,
Grace had dramatically shifted her view, though Joel was less enthusiastic about
embracing openness:

> We went to some adoption seminars. . . . We read some of the books. . . . There
> is a feeling that you want to give the children some sense of their culture and
> . . . to do that . . . you had to have some bond or affinity to the culture that
> you were adopting from. So, for me that eliminated China . . . because I really
> never had any interest in Chinese history. . . . I . . . began focusing on regions of
> the world that I was interested in. . . . My family is from Russia and Poland, but
> the other factor . . . is that I felt that adoption should be a very private matter,
> which it hasn't turned out to be . . . especially when the kids are teenagers. I
> just thought it's such a personal thing. . . . People are so unbelievably rude.
> I've seen situations of people walking down the street with a mixed-race child
> and people say, "Oh! Is that child adopted?" And I just thought, what if the kid
> doesn't want to talk about that? I didn't know which way our kids were going
> to go, but just in case I thought it might be better if we adopted kids of same
> race. So that was another thing that drove me towards Europe was that we
> could get Caucasian children. . . . Now our third child is actually mixed race
> because by the time we went to adopt David I had decided—we were being so
> open about the adoption anyways that I became less concerned about it. (RA7)

Grace and Joel's experience reflected the ambivalence that adoptive parents (and their children) wrestled with. On the one hand, they wanted to protect their children's privacy. On the other, they recognized it was important
to give their children the resources to feel connected to their birthplace. Over
time, Grace and Joel tried to accommodate both, in part because their third
child was obviously not white and they were forced to be more open about
adoption. The public reaction to their mixed family, itself an indication that
transracial adoption was still marked socially, ironically encouraged them to
acknowledge that all of their children were adopted, a first step toward rejecting "passing." In Grace and Joel's case, it did not seem that a biological
model of family determined their choices but rather the right to privacy of
their children (and the family as a whole). Their open acknowledgment that

they had adopted nevertheless began to call into question the social value they had attributed to passing as an "as if" family. It called into question cultural assumptions about the normative model of family grounded in "blood ties" and the possible stigma attached to racially mixed families, even though that may not have been Grace and Joel's intention.

Patricia, who had adopted from Russia because she had studied there in college and loved it, made a remarkable connection between place-making and personhood on the one hand, and genetic links on the other:

> I wanted a child from St. Petersburg, where I had studied. Since the child would not have my DNA, I wanted her to be from a city that I loved and was attached to. Russia itself was a DNA substitute. . . . When I adopted a second time, I chose Russia again, because I wanted my children to share an ancestry.[4]

Patricia chose a mode of creating her family in which sentiment and attachment to a place substituted for sharing genetic material linking parent to child. Along with matching through color, this attachment to place became a link between siblings themselves. RA adoptive parents also made connections between their autobiographical timelines and places. This work of place-making, in which personal histories and those of relatives and ancestors (with links to Russia or Eastern Europe) became ingredients in kin-building between them and their adopted children was also one way that they constructed their past as a family. The connective tissue that bound their family members to one another was created for them, not through links of DNA but rather through links to a place that frequently already figured in their immigrant histories or biographies.

Incorporating: Names and Lifebooks

The ways that people think about naming and the activities associated with naming are cultural indicators of how people also think about and distinguish between different kinds of relationship and connections. Adoptive parents used the naming of their children to create particular kinds of relationships with their children as kin. The naming practices of RA adoptive parents stressed prior connections of children not only with their birth families, but also with the Russian state. Interestingly, it was in naming that RA adoptive parents were most open about acknowledging their children's losses, particularly if they were adopting older children.

Jamila Bargach (2002) observes that names are associated with a whole backdrop of connections—but when names are assigned to a child who is adopted in order that he or she may be incorporated into one family unit or society rather than another, the relationships that led to that name are frequently truncated. This is particularly true of prior natal connections. Hence, in the United States, children who have been adopted receive or keep names that suggest natal connections when few if any such connections may be traceable, while their last names serve to convey that they have legally become members of an American family. Ilena Gershon (2003: 442–45) finds that, through naming, the epistemological principles that govern the circulation of different kinds of knowledge become apparent. That is, bureaucratic ways of knowing—what the state, for example, might ascertain from names on such documents as passports and birth certificates—may be based on different principles than those that underlie what adoptive parents, for example, might see reflected in the names they attach to their children (see also Bowker and Star 1999; Herzfeld 1992). Naming condenses these different ways of knowing and becomes a part of people's identity, which is culturally grounded and almost always has political implications as well.

Gretchen and Keith commented on these processes at work. They intimated that they had endeared themselves to the Russian authorities and their sense of nationalism because they had kept their daughter's Russian first name. At the same time, they also strongly felt that Nadia's name was part of her identity and conveyed to Nadia herself her connections prior to becoming a part of Gretchen and Keith's family:

Gretchen: We asked, "What is her name?" and her birth daddy was Finnish so she was Nadia Rajala. We knew we wanted to keep the Nadia, we knew we couldn't keep the Rajala.

Keith: We wanted to keep Nadia because she'd already lost everything and she already knew her name.

Gretchen: We were taking away her whole world. There is no way ethically we could take away her name. I know that is a hot button for a lot of parents. We could not do it. Parents feel they need to give their children American names, or name them to claim them or whatever. Not a factor for us. We absolutely wanted to keep her name.

Keith: Which I think also was a big deal to the Russians.

Gretchen: We knew were weren't going to hyphenate, but we knew one of her middle names was going to be H., which is my last name, and it was just one of those, you know, flashes of intuition at 2 a.m. sort of things where I knew her [other] middle name was going to be Nicole named after St. Nicholas, patron saint of travelers. So she is Nadia Nicole. (RA8)

Hilda echoed Gretchen and Joel's view that that their children's first names were all they had to carry with them into the future. She said she had never thought about changing Larisa's or Gena's names because "there was stuff that I had been reading that suggested that for older adoptees the name is the only thing that they have from their past. . . . The only thing that was changed was she had no middle name, so I had to give her a middle name and of course the last name." (RA10)

Names are considered to be almost mystical vehicles that create social life and identity, as Ellen and Neal made clear in explaining how they arrived at their daughter's name:

> We were convinced that her name would be Sophie, and it was. When the social worker in St. Petersburg told us what her name was, Neal and I looked at each other and we said, "Of course it is. This is who we are supposed to get. It was really bizarre." And we named her, we kept her first name, Sofia, and we gave her a middle name, which was my great grandmother's, Leonore, because Kurt [their biological son] has a family name too for his middle name, and then we realized that my great grandmother's middle name was Sophie. (RA2)

Naming dynamics thus were yet another means that adoptive parents used to situate their children, in relationship to themselves, to extended family members, to birth families, and to political entities, such as the Russian state. Like a talisman, names wielded powers that went beyond serving to signify or identify because they carried within them bundles of relationships, past and present.

Few RA adoptive parents made deliberate efforts to create lifebooks for their children, although a movement has been under way, in conjunction with the trend toward openness in adoption, to encourage RA adoptive parents to construct albums and narratives for their children about their earliest years. Sierra, an active member of FRUA (Families for Russian and Ukrainian Adoption) posted her own advice, counseling other adopting parents about how they should make lifebooks and their importance:

> Talk about the things you took to your son. Describe the room where you first saw him and how you felt the first time you laid eyes on him. Go through the photos one by one, talking about each. On the anniversary of our adoption, we always break out the photos and video and we go out to dinner and retell the story. They always laugh and I always end up crying at some point and get some good-natured teasing from my husband and the kids for doing so. Throughout the rest of the year, we keep the pictures out where the kids have

access to them. . . . We made our two their own photo albums with copies of all the original photos. Repeated viewings have left them with pages falling out and a few pictures bent. Whenever something happens that reminds me of some part of their adoption story, I tell about it. It is usually something very fun or funny. It's always upbeat. When we drive by a nearby church, I tell the kids about walking to the orphanage one morning when an old woman approached my husband yelling at him in incessant Russian about her food stall. Overwhelmed and before he knew it, my husband was lugging around a huge watermelon, which he detests, along the street, into stores and to a restaurant—a very funny sight. He finally took the melon to the orphanage where the older kids devoured it. The kids eat up (pun intended) these kinds of stories. The kids' interest in their adoption comes in waves. They go for months without mentioning it and then all of a sudden there is a question, a photo, or the mention of a memory. We ALWAYS stop whatever we are doing to give them [our] full attention at these times. For example, just the other day my daughter, now eight, said that when she grew up she was going to grow up and adopt two girls. I told her how wonderful I thought that would be, and that I would help her if the time ever came.[5]

Sierra's narrative about making a lifebook emphasized the roots that her children had to people and places in Russia that were meaningful to them. She also connected those people and places to herself and her husband, through events in which they had participated directly.

Holly had done lifebooks for each of her children—a photo album with their stories written in detail, attached to their pictures, and photos of the entire trip. She told me she had recently shown Alisa's lifebook to her, that she "loved to hear little stories about her adoption," and that this last time, looking at her lifebook had led Alisa to ask openly about her birth mother for the first time (RA11). The dynamic nature of lifebooks meant that the past filtered into the present and future as children thought about their origins. Sierra's child, reviewing her own origins, exclaimed that she wanted to adopt children, and Alisa reflected on her birth mother openly for the first time.

Emily's experience with making a lifebook for her RA son, Richard, took a surprising turn when she came back to Russia to adopt her daughter, Mandy:

I had to take in a photo album of pictures and things of Richard from when we adopted him up to the present. The judge asked us a zillion questions in court about Richard because . . . she hadn't had that many families come back that had recently adopted and she could ask questions about the other child.

. . . She was ga-ga over everything. Most of that court date was more about Richard than it was about Mandy. (RA4)

In CA and RA adoptions, aspects of lifebooks were intertwined with an awareness on the part of adoptive parents of how the Chinese or Russian state might view these books. That might not have been their intent, but adoption officials—judges in the case of Russia and sometimes caretakers—wanted evidence that the children were being taken good care of and that they had experienced upward mobility, moving from an impoverished condition to a higher standard of living. Hence, making a book of photos, accompanied by a narrative, was not only for the eyes of adoptive parents and their children, but also for multiple publics.

Multiculturalism

While RA adoptive parents were sensitive to sustaining a connection with Russia and to protecting their family's privacy, overwhelmingly they felt that the most comfortable and best way to nurture their children's sense of belonging was by promoting the discourse and practices of multiculturalism, with less emphasis on heritage, "racial" mixing, or origin of their adoptive children than on their own hyphenated ancestry—Irish-American, Canadian-American, French-American, German-American, or some other "ethnic mix." Shannon viewed place-making as an important, additive undertaking and adoption as simply a form of immigration:

> If we did nothing to honor our own heritage, if I didn't ever refer to myself as a Norske or my husband as a bohunk or black Irish, then maybe I would have felt different. But because heritage was already a part of our family, it was important for us to broaden our scope to include our newest members.[6]

Shannon had a positive view of immigrants and saw her child as an extension of hyphenated immigrant identity. It is likely, though not certain, that most RA adoptive parents already felt comfortable with an ideology of multiculturalism before they adopted their children. Helen, who lives in Texas, explained that her contribution to her child's identity would be to build in him a strong openness to the importance of culture, rather than a specific culture, and that she luckily had the tools to help him with that. When I asked if she intended to offer her son Emil the option of learning Russian, she responded:

> Learn Russian? As you know, the best time to learn a language is as an infant. And he's past that. And we're not going to pull that off. I can't get into the

Russian right now. . . . I'm an anthropologist and that's my contribution to his self-identity. I can talk to him about culture. We do cultural stuff, in terms of vacations, friends. We took Emil and Anna [her daughter] to see the Moscow ballet in the "Nutcracker". . . . That to me is a reasonable response, given my lack of knowledge about Russian culture and language. We do what we can to expose them to various world cultures. Last spring vacation we went to Arizona, and the highlight of the trip was going up to Hopi with a former Hopi chairman, and he showed us everything from A to Z, store, *piki* bread, pottery, dry-farming, an amazing day and these kids couldn't believe it. That's our cultural substitute. And I don't think it's a bad substitute. (RA9)

These comments and practices highlight the complexity of U.S. multiculturalism as a process that is neither "good" nor "bad," as Daniel Segal and Richard Handler (1995: 392–93) have pointed out, but may allow parents to sidestep more difficult challenges concerning how to approach their children's roots and connections. Multicultural rhetoric and representations have ambiguous motivations and consequences. They may constitute a strategic marketing move by corporations; a comfortable political stance, voiced and enacted by individuals and institutions, which does not require major social upheaval and even unknowingly "masks power relations"; and the discourse of multiculturalism may contribute to the reification of identity-groupings in the United States (Gupta and Ferguson 1997a). On the other hand, multiculturalism may indeed give minority groups greater possibilities for social and political enfranchisement.

The few parents who adopted biracial children from Russia had markedly different experiences of place-making. Some, while they were still in Russia, came to understand that their children were unwanted and rejected within Russia because they were biracial or had "bad genes." Lilia Khabibullina documents the negative sentiments that Russians themselves harbor about adoption in general, and about international adoption in particular. Russians placed heavy emphasis on the transmission of genes from mother to child. They also expressed a nationalist anxiety about losing "genofund" because of the transnational adoption of Russian children. According to Khabibullina (2009: 183–84), genofund does not have a fixed definition. It refers not only to Russian DNA, but also to Russian surnames and physiognomy. While Russians viewed the transmission of Russian genes within Russia as a good thing, they simultaneously frowned on the transmission of "bad genes" or "bad inheritance" within Russia through adoption. RA adoptive parents, aware of these views, were ambivalent about celebrating their ties to Russia, and they were also more sensitive to racism in the United States:

> We . . . have adopted a child of Eurasian descent. The prevailing attitude from those Russians we spoke with in-country was that we were doing a "wonderful" thing to adopt such an "undesirable" child (THEIR words, not ours!!). We do not know the nationality of the birth father, so Russian culture is the only one we will be able to explore with her. I have no problem with the basics (place, holidays, saint she was named after, etc.) but also need to teach or prepare her for the cultural bias a mixed-race person will face (both here in the United States and in Russia). As far as actually visiting Russia, I will leave that up to her. I would want her to be old enough to withstand any unkind statements or behaviors she might face, but then again, at what age are any of us old enough for unkind treatment by others?[7]

Sissy, who had adopted both a white and a mixed-race child from Russia, was dismayed when Russians responded in markedly different manners to them. She mingled her dismay at their contempt with her strong belief that America was a "melting pot":

> My daughter met a Russian family who enrolled their children at our elementary school, and they had a look of visible distaste on their faces when I told them my daughter was Russian. "Is she Uzbeck?" they asked. Then they looked right past her, went over, and kissed the top of my also-adopted son's head (he is Caucasian). . . . Someday, my daughter is going to have to learn that she was rejected by her entire maternal birth family for being biracial and that both countries of her birth heritage (Russia and China/or Korea) hold mixed-race children in contempt. She will also face racism from some Americans particularly when it comes to her dating their sons. This will be SO difficult for me too. . . . to grit my teeth. Nonetheless, the best place in the world she could be is in America, for the opportunities to be whoever she has the will and grace to be.[8]

Mary, also an RA mother, wrote about the model of "family" that her biracial child created. It diverged from the prototypical model of "family" in the United States. Rather than being radial or bilinear, she saw it as a dispersed model. Her mother described it as one in which kinship and geography were intimately fused:

> My Eurasian daughter (age 7 and home 3 years) is very sensitive to her appearance and to her birth past. Someone must have asked her or assumed she was

adopted from China because we had an ongoing discussion during the school year. . . . She kept insisting [that] when she was a baby she was in China, and I kept assuring her that she was born in Russia but that, possibly (and we do not know and may never know), her birth father is in China. In my mind I wonder if he might be Korean or even one of the Mongol-indigenous Russian groups, like Chuvashi. . . . So many unknowns. . . . She wished she had a "rewind button" . . . so she could go back in her life and see what she looked like when she was a baby. This week in a movie theater she drew a world map on a napkin and showed it to me. She had divided the Eurasian landmass and drawn figures labeled "My Father" on the left and "My Mother" on the right . . . then there was a big space (ocean), then she wrote "my family" with all of us on another big piece of land. So I KNOW she is really thinking about this, and I got her a globe so we could discuss geography and all these concepts. . . . All I can say from my experience is that each child is different in their reaction to "biculturalism." . . . I guess for now we are just "winging it" with all the other issues we are dealing with. Talking about it (Russia and Russian culture) but not going out and looking for it.[9]

RA adoptive parents, despite attacks by Russians and Americans on their families for having adopted a child with "bad genes" or for being open to racial differences within their family unit, clung to a multicultural framework, but were beginning to entertain the possibility that such a framework might not be sufficient to the task of helping their children build their identities. Mary's daughter, for example, was creating a remarkably innovative and complex family model that was fused with geographic connections and divisions.

Living in Russian Orphanages: Special Needs and Challenges in Place-Making

Few RA adoptive parents spoke much about their interactions with people or tourist sites in Russia, aside from their encounters at the orphanage or in courts. Helena, however, told me a story about one of her few experiences with Russians in another setting, a positive interaction that she has never forgotten. She and Bessie [her partner] were visiting a small museum with Giorgi, whose adoption they had just finalized. Giorgi had never been outside the orphanage before and had serious special needs:

I was trying to get to know Giorgi [and] at the same time I was trying to keep him safe. . . . We went to a small museum. Giorgi touched something. A woman yelled at him in Russian. It sounded very harsh to us, although I don't think it sounded very harsh to him. Giorgi lay on the floor and started crying. I took him outside and tried to put his coat on, since everyone else was bundled up in snowsuits. It did not go over well. Giorgi was crying, screaming. . . . This old woman, a grandmother, comes over, touches my arm, takes the coat, and starts talking to Giorgi. . . . And he got up and put the coat on for her. She handed him to me. He and I are both crying at this point. She put her hand on me and then walked off. It was just very sweet, unexpected, but a very much appreciated hand. I don't think our interpreter would have been able to do that. Something about her mannerisms, age, he was very, very responsive to. (RA 15)

This brief interlude humanized and tempered the adoption experiences that most RA adoptive parents reported. It was such experiences that children found most important when, much later, they began to rethink where they were from and who they were in light of their origins. For the most part, however, RA adoptive parents had negative reactions to the harsh living conditions in Russia and found the bureaucratic hurdles in the course of adoption, which usually required two journeys to Russia of unpredictable length, daunting. Keith and Gretchen explained:

Keith: There's different kinds of cottage industries. A cottage industry that says I'm going to help and we'll loan you the translator that we have, who was there and no doubt well paid for his efforts, to help us translate and help us fathom our way through their system, and get us in and out of our hotel and make sure we've got meals and all that stuff; being our personal tour guide. Okay, fine. I understand he has the right to be paid adequately for his services. . . . But we're also instructed when we go to visit the orphanages to take along gifts for the orphanage. We took about four suitcases full of clothes and boots, shoes. . . .

Gretchen: We took what they said they needed . . . paper supplies, markers, art supplies, and boots for teenagers.

Keith: And we never figured out just why they needed paper supplies in a town with a paper mill.

Gretchen: It's Russia. But you know, on the Internet boards I see example after example after example where that stuff goes and it never gets near the children it's brought for.

Keith: The orphanage takes it and sells it to get other resources.

Gretchen: For whatever.

Keith: Or for their own personal profits. So one way or another, you know, somebody is making money off your needs, your desires. (RA8)

RA adoptive parents found that Russians seemed perplexed by why people in the United States would want to adopt children, and their impressions of conditions in Russia and the orphanage personnel were mainly negative. Gradually, they have become more informed about conditions in Russian orphanages and the way that orphans are stigmatized within Russia. In orphanages, children were rarely held or spoken to, and a culture of dominance and subordination among the children prevailed from a young age.

With the surge in adoptions from Eastern Europe, the signs of FAS—fetal alcohol syndrome—have also been more systematically specified. Birth mothers' exposure of their children to alcohol while pregnant means that a disproportionate number of children adopted from Russia have FAS and suffer from a spectrum of neurological disorders (Landgren et al. 2010). The International Adoption Medicine Program at the University of Minnesota has done extensive research on fetal alcohol syndrome among children adopted from Eastern Europe in Minnesota. In a study of 483 children seen at their international adoption clinic in 2003–04, only children from Eastern Europe and the countries of the former Soviet Union were diagnosed with fetal alcohol spectrum disorder (FASD), and of those, Russia alone accounted for 79 percent of the children and 85 percent of the FASD.[10]

Nevertheless, most RA adopting parents believed that because they were acting with good will to rescue the children they were adopting, they would be able to transform their lives by moving them out of orphanages and into stable homes in the United States. While they might have the good fortune to adopt an infant or much younger child, the darker side was that it was impossible to recognize many indicators of FAS. Helena and Bessie, who had both worked in health care professions, had adopted Giorgi when he was a toddler. Helena described their reaction to videos they watched at an adoption workshop before they went to Russia:

> Both Bessie and I had spent a lot of years in health care and working with developmental disabilities. We thought we would be able to identify things we couldn't handle. In the end, everyone thinks they want a baby. In class, we saw videos of babies and we thought, "Oh, My God. You can't tell anything. The babies were just blobs." At ten months old, they were not sitting up, moving, not doing anything. No babies for us from Russia. We had the opposite reaction than most parents. . . . The videos were eye-opening, but it is a double-edged sword to adopt an older child as far as socialization and language acquisition. (RA15)

RA adoptive parents, describing what they were going through with their children, confirmed Helena's impression that it was a tremendous shock for children to move from the stark orphanage conditions to the "overstimulation of America. It was really like a deer in the headlights" (RA 15). It was terrifying, unfathomable, and, often, intolerable for the children. What was comforting to American children was unbearable to Russian adoptees who found new textures and sensations, including being held, overwhelming. Rachael Stryker also found that many RA adoptive parents, especially at the beginning, were unaware of the cultural and historical context for what has been diagnosed as reactive attachment disorder (RAD) syndrome:

> It is described in the *Diagnostic and Statistical Manual of Mental Disorders* (DSM-IV, 1994) as an inability to bond with a parental (most often maternal) figure, owing to early separation from a primary attachment figure (Richters et al. 1994). A child's symptoms include being superficially charming, forming indiscriminate attachments or being overly friendly to strangers, lying, stealing, needing to be in control at all times, poor cause-and-effect thinking and an inability to feel guilt, remorse, or compassion (Stryker 2000: 79).

Rachael Stryker has been a pioneer in promoting workshops that expose RA prospective or adopting parents to the cultural dimensions of RAD so that they understand what they must grapple with if they pursue adoption from Russia. She does not oppose such adoptions, but rather argues that parents need to be fully informed about cultural and historical conditions in Russia and the life experiences of children in orphanages:

> These sessions, called "Adopt a Child, Adopt a Culture," use ethnographic data to familiarize parents with the societies their children are coming from, and include an in-depth discussion on the culture of child rearing in which the children have been brought up. This aids prospective parents to be more realistic about the needs of their adoptive children and their own needs as new parents. (Stryker 2000: 82)

Helena and Bessie had adopted two children from Russia and a girl from Vietnam. Giorgi was 2½ years old when they adopted him; they adopted Sacha, at age 6½, after his first adoptive parents decided they could not cope with an older child and left him at Dulles Airport with social workers upon returning from Russia. Shuttled from one foster family to another, two days at a time, and then a week with a third foster family, Sacha finally connected with Helena and Bessie. He joined them as a foster child and they then adopted him. Helena and Bessie dedicated most of their waking hours when they were not working to taking care of Giorgi and Sacha's needs. Giorgi suffered from a wide spectrum of problems, including FAS, but most dire was his aversion to food. When Helena and Bessie decided to take in Sacha, they were already old pros. I asked Helena whether she and Bessie were going to have their kids learn Russian or integrate other aspects of Russian culture, such as rituals, foods, or festivities, into their socialization. Helena put it bluntly:

> You know, in the U.S., when Giorgi is spoken to in Russian, he goes to a cor-
> ner, sinks down, buries his face in his hands, and puts his face in the wall. He
> does not want to hear the language at all. Before they came, we had idealistic
> ideas, but they are now real people that moved in with us. Oh, for crying out
> loud, if one more person asks us if they are going to keep their Russian, we're
> trying to keep them alive! Everyone always talks about the health benefits of
> having family dinners. Family dinners are not that pleasant for us. They are
> about forcing Giorgi to eat, not about conversation; they are about whether
> or not we get calories in him. We have a lot of great family time together, but I
> wouldn't say any of it surrounds food.

Helena expanded on the views she and Bessie held about cultivating their family's connections with Russia and celebrating Russian culture and heritage:

> Do we think about going back to Russia? We do, but I think one of the issues
> that we face that others don't is that Sacha was adopted by another family, and
> we don't know how Russians would view that we have him [instead of his first
> family]. No way that before he's 18 we would entertain the thought of going
> back. . . . They love that they are from Russia. They tell the world. If they see a
> picture of St. Basil Cathedral, they will say that it is in Russia and that they are
> Russian. They love their story. . . . We do not do anything particularly Russian,
> no festivities or rituals. Nothing Russian. . . . We talk about that they are Rus-
> sian, that there are holidays. . . . It is still a lot for me to stay on top of things
> so that they can be successful where they need to be. I have to catch things
> quickly enough so they do not spiral downward. My friends on Facebook—
> they talk about celebrating the Chinese or Vietnamese New Year. My response
> is, "Great, you made dragon cakes, I like it," and I post that on Facebook, that's
> as far as I get. (RA 15)

Helena and Bessie were tireless advocates for their children. For them, place-making was about the bottom line, survival, and when I spoke with Helena, although Giorgi still struggled with eating issues, both he and Sacha were at grade level, doing well in school, and secure in their relationships with their siblings and adoptive parents.

RA adoptive parents were willing to take great risks, viewing their children's physical and mental health as individual conditions that could be transformed rather than the consequence of serious social and structural conditions that would be hard, if not impossible, to undo. I was struck by the frequency with which RA adopting parents who were aware of problems, such as serious health issues, and who had the option not to accept a child, went ahead and did so anyway. Helena and Bessie, who went in with their eyes open, were an exception in this respect. The reasons they ignored such indicators varied, but the most common was they did not want to return to or stay any longer in Russia. They believed they could transform the situation they were confronted with into something else. One systematic study confirmed this (see Ishizawa et al. 2006: 1207). The researchers found that well-educated white parents thought they had the status to deal with risk factors and racial issues. RA adoptive parents also believed that the choice of a particular child for them was ordained by a higher being, usually God, and that sacrifice was to be expected. In *Kinning with Foreigners*, Signe Howell (2006) employs the idea of "transubstantiation" to describe how relationships are established and built in a wide range of ways in adoptive families and between members of adoptive families and the larger society. RA adoptive parents frequently commented to me that it was clear the child was "intelligent" and that the availability of data about the child was comforting, even if the data themselves revealed that the child had serious problems:

> Damn rosy glasses. . . . It's not going to be you. Your kid will be the one in a million who is unscathed. I think from my perspective it was that having so much data made it feel like, okay, I can handle this. I understand this. I don't think we realized it was just the tip of the iceberg. (Keith, RA8)

The undercurrent of exceptionalism Keith expressed was also linked to a faith in Western science. Both Keith and his wife, Gretchen, worked in areas of engineering. More generally, many parents underwent challenges and hardships even to get to the orphanages; and they were faced with obstructions from adoption personnel, who then insisted that if they did not make a decision right away they would no longer have a chance to make a decision.

After they returned to the United States, RA adoptive parents tended to cultivate associations with Russia in a narrow virtual domain, especially if they were struggling with issues of attachment, prolonged institutionalization, and the consequences of FAS among their children. Like Helena and Bessie, they had to track down resources, find therapists, work toward diagnoses, engage in frustrating battles with the public school system to obtain special education for their children, and in the course of these undertakings, try to create a "family life."

The Internet and the use of social media and blogging became a haven, a place of solace, a significant means of building an empathetic community for many of them. Emily explained,

> I have a blog because on these adoption sites I was answering the same questions over and over. You tend to talk more about the child that has issues than the child that doesn't. I said, "You know what? This is the new age. I'm going to start a blog and talk about our adoption. I've only had it for about a month and have gotten hundreds and hundreds of hits. I've been quite shocked at emails from people who say, "Thanks for writing it," . . . or "How great it is to have a child with issues. It's no big deal." (RA4)

Few RA adoptive parents interacted regularly with other RA adoptive families, whether through in-person gatherings or Internet communications and networking. However, if their children faced special needs, they joined electronic mailing lists (listservs) focused on special needs issues. Helena had become extremely active in a special needs group in her neighborhood. Only two RA children were taking Russian language classes. Emily made a joke about this when I asked her, "Are they going to learn Russian?" She said, "My daughter Mandy talks more southern—Scarlett O'Hara. My son, Richard, we laugh, it's funny because especially when he was younger and going to speech [therapy], they'd say, "We didn't know Richard was bilingual." He can speak English and some Spanish" (RA4).

Two sets of RA adoptive parents made efforts to find a Russian-speaking au pair for their son, and more thought that they would make a return journey to Russia at some point. Grace and Ken felt strongly that it made more sense to interact with people who were from Russia than with other adoptive families of Russian children if they wanted to instill a sense of identification with Russia in their child:

> Ken: I'd say we made a weak effort. There are these adoption organizations, FRUA (Families for Russian and Ukrainian Adoption) is one, they have a local chapter and we've gone to one or two events, but I don't know how many people you can hang out with. . . . I guess we don't feel that the experience has

necessarily kind of connected us with anyone just because they had the same experience.

Grace: Yeah, we'd rather be connected directly to the Ukraine through some of these people like our babysitter, who I love. She talks to us about the Ukraine and has told us things. My cousin is married to a man from the Ukraine, so we get his stories and his family, who we see. (RA7)

At the same time, Grace and Ken made extraordinary efforts to keep their daughter, Sonia, in contact with another little girl adopted from Russia because the two children had created a special "fictive" kinship tie between them, as Ken explained:

We do see a fair amount of Sam and Ava. When we went over to the Ukraine we traveled with another couple and they, it turned out, are from Westchester, which is 45 minutes away and they adopted a girl a little bit older . . . from Sonia's orphanage. So we see them fairly often, and the girls talk and they say that they are god-sisters and that they are the oldest friends and they pretend that they remember each other from the orphanage.

Grace: Which they didn't 'cause they were in different rooms. But anyways, so they have that, they kind of create a connection.(RA7)

RA adoptive parents were less likely than CA adoptive parents to share adoption narratives in any kind of detail with their children, a subject we will discuss at greater length in Chapter 6. In part, this was because they thought it less necessary, given the lack of racial differences in the majority of cases. However, other factors were at work as well. Most of them ignored that their children had already been integrated into a social web in their birth country. For them, their child had been reborn as an individual, a blank slate ready to be connected to a fresh family, unencumbered by birth entanglements. Emily's views resonated with how many RA adoptive parents conceptualized their relationship to Russia:

I think when it's all said and done, you're just a regular plain-old family. Adoption can be as big an issue or as small an issue as you make it. I think that sometimes adoptive parents, in their quest to be such an adoption advocate for their child or so up front . . . making it seem so all right to be adopted that sometimes they are more hung up on it than the children. . . . Once you're home you're just pretty much like everybody else. I think that's the way that we approach it. . . . I just think, you can choose to make your child always think of themselves as adopted or not. I don't understand why, for some families, it's such a hard decision to move from infertility to adoption. I hope that things like your study, the research, and whatever is put out about it, hopefully it helps families on the fence, that want to know that once you're home with your child they're fine, they're normal, they're like every other kid, you feel the same about them as you would had you given birth to 'em, and that you're just a regular, normal family like your next-door neighbors. (RA4)

RA adoptive parents who did not feel any particular attachment to Russia expressed annoyance that within the "adoption community" parents who had adopted children of color thought they were racist for having adopted a white child from Russia. Adoptive parents like Emily and Michael explained their views:

Emily: The people who are most negative or rude about adopting from Russia are families that have adopted from China or Guatemala or a very ethnically different child. They, I think, are [more] prejudiced about our choice of going to Russia than anybody else.
Linda: In what way?
Michael: Because they think because we have two blond-haired, blue-eyed children, that we're trying to hide adoption, or we were choosing the easy way. . . . If you're thinking about adopting from Russia, then adopt a child with a mixed heritage. It's like the darker-skinned, dark-haired child has more of a right to be adopted than the blond-haired, blue-eyed one. It's really within the adoption community that there's more prejudice about it. (RA4)

Emily and Michael's position was that adoption should be understood within a framework of children's rights—whether children were white or of color mattered, not because, in the end, they had not been motivated by considerations of race. While their position was shared by some RA adoptive parents, many had chosen to adopt their children from Russia in order to pass as a traditional, white, American family.

Discussion

For RA adoptive parents, the centrality of place-making across borders resided in a combination of racial considerations, ease of blending in as an "as if" American family, privacy issues, transaction costs, and a commitment to rescue and "doing good." Less frequently, the sexuality of adopting parents also played a role, as was true for two lesbian couples I interviewed. Both had been turned away from the U.S. state welfare system because they were same-sex couples.

For RA adoptive parents, advocating for their children's special needs also left them little time (or patience) to dedicate to pursuing or celebrating Russian culture and connections.

In short, RA adoptive parents preferred to emphasize the idea of America as a melting pot of immigrants in which "America" was most central to who they are. For them, there remained room to acknowledge Russian, Italian, or Irish roots, but they felt it best to regard Russia as a heritage that could be traced as one among many strands, almost as a "thing," rather than as a living culture with social dimensions and relationships of importance to their children that they could actively build upon. More than other parents who pursued transnational and transracial adoption, they embraced a folk model of a "traditional family" underpinned by racial sameness.

Figure 1. Miles being handed adoption papers at Cook County courthouse.

The author wishes to thank those she interviewed who shared photos with her, and to graciously acknowledge the permission she received from them and from their family members to use the photos in this book. To protect their privacy, pseudonyms are used in the captions.

Figure 2. Esther, with Casey and Mason, both adopted.

Figure 3. Emily sharing a treasure hunt gift she made for her adoptive father, Thomas, for Father's Day.

Figure 4. Celina hugging her birth uncle.

Figure 5. Brianna, with her adopted son's birth mother and his birth sister.

Figure 6. Brianna and Sam's adopted and birth children and their adopted children's birth siblings running together.

Figure 7. Jenny and Priscilla with daughters of family friends adopted from the same orphanage. They consider themselves "siblings."

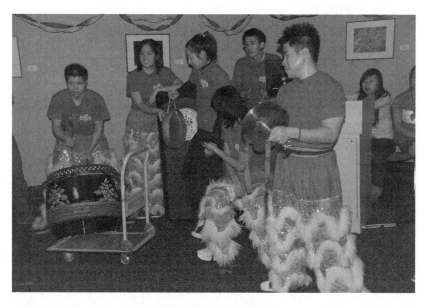

Figure 8. Chinese American students in small town that sponsored Lunar New Year celebration for Chinese adoptive families. Photo taken by author.

Figure 9. Woman teaching children on a heritage journey to China how to prepare dumplings. She made lunch for everyone in her house. Photo taken by author.

Figure 10. Nannies and caretakers at orphanage looking at photo booklet that one family brought to share with them when they returned to visit. Photo taken by author.

Figure 11. Kristen and Kevin with their three children, Sophia, Jason, and David, all adopted from Russia.

Figure 12. Mary and Jack, with Leo (front), their son adopted from Russia, Alisa, their birth daughter, and Anthony, Jack's son and Mary's stepson.

5 Black and White Crossings

*My husband, Ryan, said, "I've really been thinking about this. We were pre-
pared to parent a child with the social stigma of HIV. Why are we not willing
to parent a black child?" . . . I remember saying, "No!" I was so mad. "No, I'm
not doing this." . . . Maybe I would do a biracial child, but not . . . full African
American." And so we went home and we talked more and we prayed more
and . . . I just had this war going on . . . inside me. I can just hear, "You are
going to be a public spectacle. Everywhere you go, people are going to look at
you." You know what my dad ended up echoing? 'People are going to think you
slept with a black man.' . . . Here's the kicker part of it. When the lady called
me and she said, "We have this little girl." I said, "Well, where's the child now?"
She said, "Are you familiar with Birmingham, Alabama?" I was like, choke,
"Yes!" She said, "Well, the little girl was born in Birmingham." I said, "Well,
what hospital is she in?" She tells me the hospital, and that's like a quarter mile
away from Ryan's grandmother's house. So here's this baby born in the city
that my husband and I grew up in.*

—Betty, AA9

*Every day, parents look into the face of their child and they see a different race
and a different ethnicity. And yet, they compartmentalize that truth and deem
it unimportant. Why aren't the movie stars talking about the birth parents
of their kids and modeling the opportunity to do it right? And while many
adoptees won't want to meet their birth families, virtually all would like basic
information about their background. We grow up in environments where it is
so much about your DNA, it's quite natural for adopted people to feel excluded
because we don't have that basic human right.*

—Elizabeth Larsen 2007: 54

*"Where do you come from?" he [June's beau, Neil] asked me. This is the
number one most-asked question in all of South Carolina. We want to know if
you are one of us, if your cousin knows our cousin, if your little sister went to
school with our big brother, if you go to the same Baptist church as our ex-boss.
We are looking for ways our stories fit together. It was rare, though, for Negroes
to ask white people where they're from, because there was nothing much to be
gained from it, as their stories weren't that likely to link up.*

—Susan Monk, *The Secret Life of Bees* (2002: 105)

The activities AA adoptive parents engaged in to make a place for themselves as
a family were framed by three key dimensions: openness, risk, and race. Above,
we see that Betty, adoring adoptive mother of Melanie, initially was more receptive to adopting a child with HIV than to adopting a black child. AA adoptive parents confronted obstacles of place-making for their children every day.
More than CA and RA adoptive parents, they worked at maintaining construc-

tive openness with birth family members. Their risk of being rejected before an adoption was finalized, even though rejection occurred in a minority of cases, seemed greater to AA adopting parents because they often had a chance to meet their prospective child, and interact with the birth mother, sometimes over weeks or months. Some AA adoptive parents were taking steps to learn about and incorporate black culture into their lives despite their own discomfort and internalization of racism. Inequalities frequently created both the conditions for adoptions to happen, as well as chasms between adoptive and birth families, as was also true of CA and RA adoptions.

Open Adoption

AA adopting parents were more willing to take the risk of birth parents repeatedly changing their minds about the adoption plan for their children (and consequently lengthening the adoption process and causing emotional turmoil) than parents who adopted transnationally. One unexpected finding of this research was the high number of AA adoptive parents who opted for domestic transracial adoption because of their personal life histories. Brenda had worked with foster kids and had seen the kind of trauma they experienced (AA11); Christine's mother had taken in foster children when she was growing up (AA12); Deborah, a single mother herself, had not lived with her own parents but with a single, lesbian mother who had adopted Deborah's distant cousin (AA15); Denise's husband, Noel, worked at United Way and had decided he wanted to pursue domestic adoption. After visiting him at work, Denise agreed that it was a good idea (AA16); and Becky's parents had fostered a child in Tanzania who then returned to his family, and her current supervisor was fostering a child from Sierra Leone (AA6). A few of the AA adopting parents opted for domestic transracial adoption because it cost less than an international adoption, because they thought it was God's will, or because they thought they would be able to adopt a younger child and be able to bond more easily as a family. Finally, many AA adopting parents thought, like Betsy and Allen, that there was a strong need to adopt children from within the United States (AA8).

In the course of finalizing an adoption, the birth and adoptive parents had to agree on the degree of openness that would prevail between the parties. These discussions were usually mediated, in the case of agency adoptions, by the agency. Many times, the formal agreements became less formal and more flexible as the relationships between birth and adoptive families evolved. Judith Modell describes how openness in domestic transracial adoption, ambivalent and fraught as it can be, can also be an important step toward challenging cultural assumptions about American family models:

> Open adoption does create an alternative model for chosen parenthood.... Supporters of open adoption use the word "gift" to describe the transaction: a child, freely given and received, who creates a bond between the adults. Once more there is ambiguity: in one respect, this reaches back to traditional modes of child exchange; in another respect, a gift model radically restructures American adoption. In forming a bond, a gift eliminates the distance between giver and taker; they are united by the "item of value" they share. Behind a vocabulary of love and generosity, then, the linchpin of American adoption is pulled out.... The move toward open adoption is more subversive than even its opponents claim, constituting an "unselfconscious resistance" to ideologies of the family, parenthood, and gender that adoption has upheld for over a century. Eliminating the separation between giver and taker of a child, distributing the components of motherhood over several individuals, and attaching a child in different ways to different parents represent substantial revisions of familiar custom. (Modell 1994: 234–35)

Modell emphasizes the sobering enormity of what it means to birth parents and their children when adoptive parents are not willing to pursue openness: "What finally condemned adoptive parents in the birth parent's eyes was the rejection of their "own" child's natural parent. As one said, 'I was good enough [for them] to take my baby but not good enough to acknowledge.'" (Modell 1994: 89)

The trend of closed adoptions has shifted. AA adoptive parents in my study were questioning the American model of family grounded in blood ties and the stigma attached to mixed-race families. Some of them wrestled with their internalization of racism and were coming to recognize how the systemic nature of white privilege would shape their lives as a mixed-race family. In short, they were trying to figure out how to deal with the racialization of American society in light of their children's welfare. A high number of parents who adopted African American children had embraced open adoptions because they were convinced of the "dysfunctionality," as one parent put it to me, of closed adoptions or truncated relationships with birth parents (AA1). Some still found open adoptions threatening and problematic, but more of them thought that it was better for their children.

These differences are not surprising given that RA and CA adoptive parents decided to take the international route, precisely because they did not want to face these risks. RA adoptive parents such as Kyle alluded to the social stigma of adoption itself; in contrast, AA adoptive parents, such as Betty, emphasized the stigma of race. While some of these same parents felt that the choice other parents made to adopt internationally rather than domestically was motivated partly by racism,[1] others were nonjudgmental and welcomed the range of options available to prospective parents. However, in their own case, they felt strongly that having knowledge about their child's birth parents and relatives was important in their own decision:

> We have friends who have adopted internationally. It's a different kind of calling. . . . We wanted . . . the possibility that if the children wanted to someday meet their birth parents they could. In international adoption, that's nearly impossible. . . . It kind of felt like it was a door we would be closing if we did an international adoption. (AA10)

AA adoptive parents engaged in open adoption practices that included birth parents, grandparents, and their adopted child's siblings as members of their immediate family. Sometimes these were mainly symbolic gestures, such as sending a birthday card to a birth aunt or uncle. At other times they were more extensive, involving regular interactions with birth relatives across considerable distances through gatherings, letter-writing, shared baby-sitting, and phone calls. In homes I visited, adoptive parents had created photo galleries that included pictures of their child's birth relatives. Betty explained her views of open adoption this way:

> I am super intense about keeping that relationship open and going. . . .
> I cherish it. . . . Ester [the birth mother] does not realize that all our family lived there [Birmingham]. . . . I can be all things to Melanie, but I can never be black, period, end of story. If I don't keep as much openness with Ester as possible—I don't want it to be like my friend Michelle who didn't know who her parents were or what had happened or what had happened to the siblings. I want to keep it as open as possible for all those questions Melanie's going to have. (AA9)

Alise and her husband, Thomas, had formed a complex blended family comprising eight children, including Thomas's three children from two prior marriages, Alise's three children from a prior marriage, and Alise and Thomas's two African American children, one whose adoption had been formalized, the other whom they expected to adopt but were currently fostering. Alise had acquired experience and insight as a member of a blended family before embarking on adoption. While divorce and remarriage have increased the number of step-families in the United States, how incorporation happens in step-families and the way they function is hardly unproblematic, as David Jacobson spells out:

> [Middle–class Americans] subscribe to a set of beliefs that constitute what might be called the "standard model" of families and households. In the model, it is expected that marriage will be monogamous, that the family will be nuclear, neolocal, and co-residential, and that the members of the family household are entitled to one another's attention and affection. The effort to create viable stepfamilies is constrained by these ideas and beliefs. (Jacobson 2003: 31)

How boundaries are set, assumptions about where family members reside, the terms used to specify family members, and not least, the "blending" together of unlike cultural values and belief systems are some of the dynamics that also characterize the formation of families through transracial adoption, and especially transracial adoption within the United States. I was impressed by how much time and energy Alise dedicated to making her blended family work—criss-crossing the country with her children when they were younger, then trusting them to visit their relatives on their own. As we see below, with her newest additions, Alise had gone to great lengths to keep open channels with their respective birth families. She explained her philosophy to me:

> More and more people have blends of families and they mix them up lots of different ways. . . . Once you adopt you've got to understand that you're sharing right off the bat. All that possessiveness that comes into it when you have a child in your family, all that ego as an adoptive mother. . . . "Oh this is my child." You've got to realize this child has a whole other part of them that comes from someone else, and you've got to acknowledge that from the get-go because then it's easier for the child to grow into it. (AA4)

Alise went on to explain that being part of a blended family as an adult and having a clear-eyed understanding of the importance of "family" even if it was not an ideal one—which was the case when she had been a child—had made a huge difference in her desire to encourage openness for her adopted/fostered children:

> My concern with my new one right now is that she doesn't have much contact with her mother, but she's been in the system sixteen months with once-a-week contact with her mother, who cares for her very much, for two

hours a week. A child needs her mother more than two hours a week. But, on the other hand, perhaps her mother can work things out where she can have her back. In the meantime, of course, she's supposed to get attached. The child needs attachment in order to be healthy. That's just a compromise you make with yourself in order for the child to be healthy. You know someday it might be like severing an arm from yourself, and that's just what it's going to be. (AA4)

With Zenialisa, her older daughter, whom Alise and Thomas adopted after she was abandoned in a hospital, she explained:

We discovered she had grandparents in the area who had come forward, on and off, but never . . . expressed interest in the agency to possibly adopt her. . . . It would be just a phone call here and there a couple times a year. Later on we learned that they had their hands full. Her grandmother was ill and she had the older daughter, I mean older sister, just by a year or so. . . . I think her sister is eighteen months older than she is . . . so that to me would present a huge challenge for her grandparents, and to take on another young child who was as ill as Zenialisa was. But we have established some contact, and I feel like I have potentially some connection to Zenialisa's biological family, and I feel very lucky for that.

She also felt that her embrace of open adoption was partly the result of her own upbringing:

I think because I grew up in a home situation—my parents were not entirely healthy—I do know what it's like to be a child who, at all costs . . . no matter how unhealthy my father and mother may have been, they were my father and mother. I couldn't imagine another father and mother. I wanted my father and mother to be healthy. I wanted them to care for me and do well, but just because they weren't doing it right shouldn't mean I want a different one. Does that make sense? I think little kids want to be loved by their parents or their family or they want some connection. They need to look like somebody, they need to understand that they belong to some bigger part of something, and I think adoptions will change that. There are definitely going to be questions with my girls, and there's going to be all kinds of issues that come up. If I can have any connection with family to help answer some of those questions or make them feel like it's okay to be a part of two families, then I think that would be better for their health in the long run. (AA4)

Penelope and Morgan had an open relationship with their daughter Danielle's birth parents and were encouraging other AA adoptive parents to do the same:

> Danielle's birth mother has access to our family blog where she can see pictures of what we're doing. She has probably seen Danielle seven or eight times over the last three years. She talks to Danielle on her birthdays, Christmas. . . . We just felt like for Danielle to be a healthy individual it would be better for her to just have everything out in the open from the very beginning, so that was just our choice. . . . Well, our openness with Danielle has had effects on other adoptive couples that we have met. . . . We have a couple that we've really become close to. They adopted. Their first daughter is biracial, and she is a year older than Danielle, and then they adopted their second son, who is full African American. And about a year ago they received a letter from the adoption agency from their daughter's birth mother asking for more openness. They had first had a closed adoption, and then the birth mother asked for some openness, and so, you know, there was a period of about two months where C. would call me and say, "Penelope, what do I do?" and I just said, "Open it up." You know. You know, use your judgment, but open it up because it's only going to help her, the birth mother . . . and only help, you know, A. [their daughter] too. And so they did. They opened it right up and it's been a really neat experience. And her birth mother has just like grown leaps and bounds emotionally because she can now see how her daughter is doing and all of those kinds of things, so I think our experience, our willingness to be open, has probably helped more than just our adoption experience itself. (AA20)

Amber was clear-eyed about the sharp differences between her lifestyle and class status and that of her child's birth mother:

> At that very first meeting, I said to her, "I want Ashley [her daughter] to have contact with you, and I would really like to always be in touch." And she said, "Yes, me too." We talk . . . maybe every six weeks on the phone. . . . It's kind of become a little bit of a mentoring relationship. She really doesn't have anybody else in her life. Her parents are . . . still addicted to drugs and she has no support whatsoever coming from them, and she's really totally on her own, so I've become kind of her cheerleader and her advisor. So I think she sees me more as her big sister, really.
>
> Linda: Do you send her photos and stuff?

> Amber: We get together every three months and she sees Ashley. We go out
> to eat. I've had her to the house with her other kids. (AA5)

The conditions of openness Amber mediated between Ashley and her birth mother were difficult. AA adoptive parents came to understand such conditions as *socially* structured, created by a combination of lack of education, poverty, discrimination, and diminished opportunities.

Denise told me how indignant she felt when one of her neighbors had asked in a critical tone, "How could Ceci's mother have given her up?" She did not tell her neighbor, however, what she told me:

> I have fond feelings for our birth mom, so it insults me when people assume
> they know something about her. It bugs me when people assume the birth
> mom is uncaring or unloving. Maybe some birth mothers are that way, but
> ours is not at all like that. She wept for hours on the day she had to sign the
> papers. I know because we had to sit in the waiting room for about seven
> hours. She told me flat out that she decided this because she loves Ceci so
> much. Her point was clear: if she didn't love Ceci so much she would have just
> limped along as an unwed teen mother. She wanted more for her. (AA16)

Amber and Denise interacted regularly with their children's birth mothers, but many AA adoptive parents struggled with what limits to place on relationships between them, their adopted children, and their adopted children's birth relatives.[2]

Naming and Lifebooks

Not surprisingly, the naming practices of AA parents differed from those of CA and RA adoptive parents because of the greater openness that prevailed in AA adoptions. Many adoptive parents knew their children's birth parents and something of their children's family history. More often, they respected birth parents' (usually the birth mother's) decision about all or part of the name to give their child. However, adoptive parents sometimes found ways to connect a child's given name to values, events, or individuals who were already important in the lives of adoptive families, as Deborah explained:

> His birth name was Aaron. His legal adopted name is Elliot Aaron and we
> call him Aaron Trey. And I had a boy's name picked out that was gonna be
> Elliot Joseph. And at that moment when Selena [Aaron's birth mother] told
> me "Aaron," I said, "I'm keeping that name." And what I've always found very
> kind of mystical in this whole thing . . . very spiritual. . . . I realized when I

said that to Selena and then put it in some paperwork I had to fill out through the agency—it had boxes where I had to write my name, full legal name, and then his full legal name—and immediately, it was like, wow. Our names are identical, same letters . . . which was not at all what we had planned. . . . It was supposed to be Elliot Joseph. If Selena had told me, "No, I'm not going to share the name," it would have been Elliot Joseph. One more letter [in his name than in mine]. So, and then the fact that I always saw myself with an African American or child of color. . . . It is so powerful to me. (AA15)

AA adoptive parents also bestowed on their children the names of individuals who were highly respected for their contributions to black history, culture, and civil rights struggles. Abby and Zach named their daughter Ella for Ella Fitzgerald, and Abby also exclaimed proudly that her Ella was born on Maya Angelou's birth date. She told me confidently, "Ella's going to sing 'A tisket a tasket.'" Amber, who lived in Chicago, witnessed firsthand racial segregation and the inception of busing, and after she adopted her daughter she volunteered for a mentoring program for children, most of whom were black. The story of how she named her child was closely connected to her own philosophical and activist position. She was committed to creating a daily life in which she and her daughter would feel as if they had a connection to both black and white culture without falling into what she called "double jeopardy," where they would feel comfortable in neither world. When she named her daughter, she created a connection to her own ancestors who, even though they were white, struggled for social justice:

It was mostly my mother [who] was *über* [extremely] Liberal Progressive. My grandmother, who Ashley is really named after, was, I'm sitting here looking at her "Membership in the NAACP" plaque that I took when she died. My grandmother was a big civil rights proponent, so I grew up knowing and believing and being taught that everybody was equal, etc. (AA5)

There was also an ongoing discussion among AA adoptive parents concerning their conflicted feelings about "traditional" names "of dubious pronunciation" given by birth parents that affirmed their children's connection to them and "white bread" names that did not so readily identify their children as black.

Many AA adoptive parents relied heavily on lifebooks and photos to accompany adoption narratives they shared with their children. Deborah, the single adoptive mother of Aaron (whose name we discussed above) lived in

Westchester, New York. Deborah herself had moved in with a foster family at the age of 12 after suffering domestic abuse by her father that caused her mother, a longtime teacher, to gradually deteriorate into mental illness. She had also been close to an older cousin who was adopted by a lesbian mother. In her words, "they lived a lie," a public secret that was tolerated in the neighborhood because "they just loved children." She told me she had always thought she would adopt a child: "I didn't even belabor it. My vision was always me and a child of color, a black child of color." Her commitment to open adoption was such that the photos of Aaron's birth relatives were seamlessly interwoven into her lifebook: "And we have pictures that are right in the sequence of our family photo album. If you were to look at our family photo albums, from when we met, and two months later when we visited, and they're like right in our family photo albums" (AA15).

Lisa Wittorff and her husband had adopted three African American children. She created what she called "pre-adoption books" for each of her children. The books included "descriptions of their house, neighborhood, friends, relatives, and important people in their lives." The lifebook she made for one of her sons included photos of the foster families who had cared for him before he was adopted, as well as their names, addresses, and any other information she could obtain. Curiously, in her case, the lifebooks of her children ended when their adoptions were finalized. For her, the purpose of the pre-adoption books was to acknowledge and legitimate her children's lives prior to adoption, but her decision that their lifebooks should end at that point inadvertently seemed to punctuate discontinuity. It is hard to know yet what her children make of this approach, since the oldest was only 9 (Alperson 2001: 8–10).

When I asked Claudia whether she was sharing any kind of adoption narrative with her daughter, Elsie May, she immediately explained that she was making her a lifebook:

> I'm into scrapbooking, so we've created a bit of a lifebook. It's not totally hashed out completely, but we do have a couple of pages of her birth mom and the picture we have of her and her birth mom, and I wrote out her story: what her birth mom told us and when we got to meet her birth mom, and why she chose to place her. We don't really have a lot about her birth father. I'm hoping we can get a little bit more. (AA14)

AA adoptive parents seemed fairly comfortable about providing information to their children about their birth families, even when that information might be difficult for children to understand initially or painful for them to absorb. Almost all of them thought that it was in the interest of their children to recognize those connections, although some of them were less committed to sustaining those interwoven connections through lifebooks over time.

Race and Place

Openness in AA adoptions was inevitably entangled with racial issues. On the one hand, openness allowed children who had been adopted to know about all their family members; it was about more than exchanging photos; it was also about having relationships with birth relatives. Carol Stack (1974) has shown that among African American families, "kin care" is a project undertaken by multiple members, especially multiple mothers—sisters, grandmothers, and aunts—for the well-being of the child.[3] Hence the idea that adoptive family members might want to arrive at some kind of "sharing" arrangement with birth relatives might not seem so unusual, yet it was a recent phenomenon.

AA adoptive parents also realized that they, as white mothers of black children, were not particularly competent in dealing with issues of race and racism in America. Abigail commented, "I think, unfortunately, racism is alive everywhere, and some people don't even think they are racist until they are faced with a white family becoming a nonwhite family" (AA2). As a whole, AA adoptive parents had mixed responses to these issues. They were conscious of the impact of racism on them as a mixed family and on their child as the target of racism—simply because of his or her physical appearance—but many of them remained wedded to more superficial ways of incorporating black culture into their lives.

Stigma

Erving Goffman (1963: 3–4), discussing the dynamics of stigma, argued that an awareness of the attribution of social stigma within a group—in this case, within a family—results in differing responses, but in all cases, people make efforts to manage it. By stigma, he means "attributes that are deeply discreditable" but only in the context of the "language of relationships." Stigmas may take the form of physical differences, undesirable character traits, or what he calls "tribal stigmas"—race, nation, or religion—that diverge from what is deemed "normal." He adds that tribal stigmas can be "transmitted through lineages and equally contaminate all members of a family." However, an attribute in and of itself is "neither creditable nor discreditable as a thing in itself" but rather emerges out of social interactions.[4] Goffman observes that one form of managing stigma is the "capacity of family . . . to constitute itself a protective capsule for its young. A stigmatized child can be carefully sustained by means of information control, which leads the child to see himself as a fully qualified ordinary being, of normal identity." Yet this "bubble" does not last for long, and Goffman notes that there is a "point at which the domestic circle can no longer protect him," giving rise to "a moral experience when it occurs" (1963: 32–33).

Some AA adoptive parents, from the first stages of place-making, attempted to enter a world of daily practices where the barriers to entry were high and where the issue of race was central. If they entered, how could they avoid reproducing the politics of whiteness? Parents might make great efforts to move to more racially diverse neighborhoods, schools, and religious institutions but, as Barbara Katz Rothman (2005: 170–71) observes, neither color-blindness nor ethnic liberalism eases the structuring of personhood for AA children brought up by white, Euroamerican parents.

AA adoptive parents faced racism from other Euroamericans, and they faced criticism from African Americans. African Americans were concerned about what it meant for black children to be detached from the black community, and they were equally disturbed by the seeming ease with which white parents could adopt black children, whereas the adoption of white children by black parents, to put it in the starkest terms, was rare. Claudia Castañeda (2002: 91) critiques the position laid out by Elizabeth Bartholet, a prominent scholar involved in issues surrounding transracial and transnational adoption. Castañeda finds untenable Bartholet's argument that children's "racial make-up" does not prevent them from being "entirely mobile," able to travel from one "racial community" to another. For Castañeda and the NABSW (National Association of Black Social Workers), "when a white family adopts a black child" the child's movement from one community to another is not "unproblematic" because the child is "attached to its community by virtue of its shared raciality and the unequal position of that raciality within the broader society." In other words, for Castañeda, race is not simply skin deep but entails existing social relationships and structural inequalities. By highlighting race as "purely physical and surface characteristics," AA adoptive parents too often ignore "the histories and politics of culture, geography, and nation that race "might otherwise signify."

While some may argue that these views simply emphasize and reinscribe "race" and racism where it does not exist, Barbara Katz Rothman, who herself adopted an African American child, remarks that it is in the course of raising a black child that non-African Americans like herself become aware that race is not difference but marked. As she put it, "Raise a black child and you lose whiteness: you are not and never will again be white, not white in that raceless, taken-for-granted way you used to be. . . . It changes your understanding of whiteness when you raise a black child." She quotes Maureen Reddy, a white woman married to a black man, mother of black children: "I *look* white, but that white skin conceals my inner life. This feeling of being costumed in one's own skin, of 'masquerading' as white in public, may be the only thing white partners of black people, and especially white parents of black children, share regardless of the other differences among us" (Rothman 2005: 157–58).

Twila Perry further argues that this journey is also undergirded by questions that few ask about white privilege, linked not only to race but also to class and to family-making: "Would anyone suggest that white children are being discriminated against because they do not have the same opportunity to be adopted out of race as children of color? Because of the great need for the adoption of children waiting in foster care, the question is avoided, yet it remains an issue of symbolic importance . . . to the African American community" (Perry 1993/94: 103). Noting the profound discrepancy in how adoptive resources are viewed for white and black children, Perry concludes, "They affirm a system based not on colorblindness but on racial choice. Race can still be used to match white families with their choice of the valuable commodity of a white baby. White families are, of course, free to select Black children for adoption. The problem, however, is that this principle operates only one way. Choosing across racial lines is reserved for whites" (1993: 104). For Perry, this raises questions about the role of race and culture in adoption and about a system of choice at work that "differentially vests power based on the race of adopters, despite the ostensible commitment to "colorblindness" (Freundlich 2000: 47–49, citing Twila Perry).[5]

My interviews abounded with examples of Euroamerican racial prejudice against African Americans in general, and mixed families in particular; and of African American concern and uneasiness about what would happen to African American children taken out of their cultural environment.[6] Judy Stigger, director of international adoption at "The Cradle," a private nonprofit adoption agency in Illinois, participated in a National Public Radio special entitled "A Family Tree's Special Routes." She commented that "people are curious and do ask how much the baby cost and whether or not that's one of those crack babies . . ." Stigger added that in discussing whether to adopt an African American child, "We [she and her husband] had a conversation that said, 'If we do this, this means we will only live in certain kinds of neighborhoods...It would color, to use the verb, friends that we would have. We understood it had some implications'" (NPR 2007). Alise described to me many of her interactions with African Americans, including the experience of their criticism directed at her:

> Some people really believe they have the right, the church ones too, to ask me every question they can imagine about her birth family. They can't seem to get the focus on, or get the fix on, that I've been her mother for two years. They want to know what do I know about her birth family? So where does she come from exactly? What were the issues? There's a lot of shame involved with it too. The child doesn't go into the foster system unless this child isn't supported somehow by the black community. Does that mean you're not supporting your own children? Or do you want to divide yourself from that and say those are the black people that aren't making it and I am. I know that that's their curiosity. They don't mean to be rude or anything. What they're saying to me is, "Are you sure you understand the implications of what you've done here?" You've taken a child out of our culture, and their culture is much stronger than what I consider our general white culture to be. They have history, which isn't all that far back either, that bonds them that I don't [have] with my other Caucasian friends. I came from European parents too. I wasn't a very American child growing up anyway, so I understand some of it. Some of the expressions and "we have to stick together" kind of thing, I understand that. (AA4)

AA mixed families highlighted historical signs of stigma in American society, such as hair and skin color. At the same time, the very incorporation of black children into white families also compelled many African Americans and AA adoptive parents to acknowledge these "signs" publicly and do something about them.

Race: Proximity and Propinquity

To transracialize, we adoptive parents must make decisions that may disrupt the plans we previously envisioned for our families: homes in comfortable suburbs, homogenous private schools, etc. Instead, we must put ourselves into the environments that are most likely to welcome our children and give them the cultural, racial and ethnic support we can't provide. . . . Many of us consider identity something we possess, a static condition inherited or passed on from person to person. But when you think of it as a verb— something we do—the connection between our actions and their effect on our children's sense of self becomes much clearer.[7]

Racialization in America profoundly affected the attitudes of AA adoptive parents and their place-making practices. Their embrace of open adoption practices could be interpreted as the pursuit of connections with African American birth family members, so that the children they had adopted could find peace in knowing their roots. Yet some AA adoptive parents I spoke with went far beyond a narrow understanding of a connection with African Americans and their everyday lives. They were struggling to educate themselves about black culture and racism in America and its history through reading books, watching films, and taking bigger steps, not just to move into more integrated neighborhoods or schools, but also to make black friends in those neighborhoods and confront racism in the schools. They began to recognize that the discourse of multiculturalism masked serious social inequalities, reflected in the distribution of resources, which could not be resolved by the act of embracing multiculturalism.

Celebrating Kwanzaa, buying black dolls for their children, and cooking greens were just a small part of the efforts they needed to invest in contributing to their child's sense of identity through attachment to African Americans and black culture and building pride in themselves. When I asked Alise about her connections with black culture, she contrasted celebrating a holiday with a more realistic understanding of daily life among African Americans:

> I know all about Kwanzaa. We mix it up. And someday she may choose something that she does want to celebrate, but hopefully she'll have a heads up enough about what it is to celebrate. But I don't know if that's what makes you black. [(AA4)]

Agnes and Drew had adopted three African American children. Joshua, their son, was already 16, Brittany was 13, and Aamina 10 when I spoke to Agnes. She was glad that she had done as much as possible from the start to educate herself and move beyond what came naturally to her:

> I read tons of literature about adopting transracially, and I was very prepared for someone African American to feel it was inappropriate that we had taken a child out of his culture. . . . I have a good friend who's African American, and she's a single mom and has two kids; and our sons are good friends; and she and I have often talked about how difficult it is, even for her, to have good African American male role models. I mean she says she has brothers and a father, but she can't imagine, you know, to go beyond the family in the community, it is very, very difficult to find good African American role models and how important it was to her that our sons remain friends because they need to have each other and stuff like that. So she has the same concerns, even though her child is a biological child. (AA19)

Alise sought out weapons and tools of racial navigation, and was also philosophical. She thought that she had an obligation to do as much as possible to
do make her children proud of their identity—focusing on their connections
with their birth families, their hair, and relationships with other African Americans—in order that not only they as a family would feel secure, but also African
Americans would feel more secure. She placed a premium on

> allowing people to feel more strength in being an individual so that they
> aren't threatened by the diversity in someone else. If your kids feel strong and
> secure—It's only the kids on the playground . . . that aren't feeling great about
> themselves that bully. I find that in adults too. The adults that are most fearful
> about this mix aren't sure of where they stand. They're afraid that something is
> going to be taken from them. . . . When other black people approach us about
> hair I remember, yes, it's a deeper issue than that. If I conquer the hair thing,
> they feel more secure. . . . I was in a store not long ago. A black woman walks
> over to me [and] I'm already ready. She's going to come up to me and go,
> "What you doing with that one's hair?" 'Cause Ebony didn't have the greatest
> head of hair that day . . . We're still trying to figure that head of hair out. How
> often to do it and what to do with it. She walks over to my Zenialisa and goes,
> "Where do you get her hair done? It's adorable." I looked at her and held my
> breath and said, "I did her hair." She goes, "Awww, you're kidding. It's beautiful.
> Can I look a little closer?" She was so sweet and so polite about it. Then she
> tells me she's got four girls, and she knows exactly how much time it takes to
> do hair, especially my daughter's hair that's so heavily textured. And so we're
> standing there in the parking lot having this conversation with this strange
> black woman for a half-hour about hair care, about girls, about where they go
> to school, what they like to play with. Do you know what we finished talk-
> ing about? [She said,]"You know what, I've often thought I'd do foster care. I
> had often thought we'd adopt a boy. I have all girls. I've talked to my husband
> about it. Is it hard to do? How do you start?" To me, that's just so cool. . . .
> For me this was part of the bigger picture, and it wasn't hurting my daughter
> to sit there and look at her little kid and goof around in the carts together.
> But maybe that's the beginning of something else. My daughter sees, she's
> just almost 3, she sees me talking with a black woman about something nice.
> Somewhere that gets in her head. She may not actually understand it but . . .
> Does that make sense? (AA4)

This exchange had many levels. All the uneasiness about crossing racial lines
coursed through the conversation. Alise thought the woman who approached

her was concerned about how unkempt Ebony's hair looked (and Alise told me that, as the woman walked toward her, she already knew that was why she was approaching her), yet she observed that Zenialisa's hair was well-done. Although never stated, it might have been that she was also uncomfortable with Alise's mixed family. However, the exchange itself, the social interaction, transformed these assumptions when the woman learned that Alise had taken on the responsibility of learning how to do her children's hair. The woman, in turn, had the courage to confide to Alise that she, too, wanted to foster and possibly adopt a child, and welcomed any information she could share with her. At the same time, their children were interacting with each other across their respective shopping carts. And Zenialisa, Alise hoped, might remember that moment—the woman, the child, the exchange.

Shortly after adopting Zenialisa, Alise tried to extend her social networks into the black community:

> It started off where I would call the Yellow Pages looking for black churches or anything like that where I could find some people who were black. . . . I found a black hairdresser in a black neighborhood. . . . I have other white girlfriends . . . and I remember they said to me, "You know, you're there all day. . . . The funny part for me is now I've learned that it's okay therapy to sit around and talk with some other women, to talk about your kids and what's going on. . . . It can be very nurturing. . . . I've met other black people through them. It's so funny the connections I made. . . . I'm a music teacher who holds events in other larger communities. Of course, I show up with my black child and there might be a black family there. In some way, you've got to work that much harder coming outside of yourself. You're so conspicuous anyway, you might as well start something up . . . [I] start[ed] up a conversation with a young father whose wife wasn't there. . . . Few weeks later, I find out her daughter is on a soccer team that's playing my daughter in a whole other community. They are all an hour apart. But you've got to work at it. It's a lot of driving, it's a lot of talking to people that maybe you don't feel like talking to people every day. We go to a Christian community church in Decadia which is very large and very open to transracial families. And that fits a certain need. And we also go to another church that is almost exclusively African American, but also very open to helping support adoptive families. So we're the minority there and that's good for us. (AA4)[8]

Trying to find where black people worked, worshipped, and socialized by looking through the Yellow Pages might seem almost laughable, but it was a place to start, and in Alise's case it did lead to some genuine milieus of sociability. For girls and boys alike, hair was a topic with which to begin building connections. Deborah told me how she learned to do Aaron Trey's hair:

> Trey has dreadlocks that we've been working on since January. It was really an outgrowth of him getting *Sports Illustrated* magazine for kids and seeing the football players. And he says, "Mom, what kind of hairstyle is that?" And I said, "Oh, those are dreadlocks." "I kind of like that, Mom. I'd like to have my hair like that." And so he has like four inch dreads. So Mr. G.'s daughter, who's the stylist at this barber shop, helped me initially, and now has taught me, and I maintain his dreads, and I feel very proud of myself. (AA15)

Dolly, like Alise, found a quiet peace and sociability when she took Pearson, her son, to get his hair cut:

> Well, one thing we've done since Pearson was small is that I've taken him to a black barber shop. This was even before we moved to Omaha so that he could get his hair cut by a stylist who understood his kind of hair. And just being surrounded by the social atmosphere at the barber shop, which is like a community, is hugely important and they know me there. When I come in there, they're not like "Oh, who's this white lady?" It's like, "Oh, hi, how are you and how's it going?" And Philip is accepted. (AA17)

The efforts of AA adoptive parents to "connect" might appear, at first glance, to be superficial acts, yet small symbolic acts, as Alise knew, could have unpredictable and substantial impacts. What began as arduous and somewhat troublesome or anxious undertakings sometimes became new grounds for familiar practice over time. In these early years, as the personal biographies of children were unfolding, they might find ways to intertwine their multiple selves, of which they were already becoming aware, even if the strands were loose and prone to coming undone. And a small number of AA adoptive parents faced the reality that they were no longer a Euroamerican family or a multicultural family. Instead, they were bicultural and black, and would have to figure out what that meant.

AA adoptive parents were conscious of how actively engaged they were in trying to deal with racism. Before they adopted their children, evidence of racism in their lives was mostly intangible, unreal, and invisible to them. They were not very aware of white privilege and what it meant. After completing their adoption, they recognized it but felt uncomfortable about how to deal with it, without *using* others who were far more skilled at wielding the weapons of racial navigation in the United States. Amber, in rethinking her own assumptions about culture, emphasized the importance of building a sense of shared norms, cultural values, practices, and schemas:

> For me personally, if I had had to describe "American" culture it would have been some low-key amalgam of the secularized version of various holidays. . . . I think culture goes way beyond this though. It's what we live and breathe and absorb in the going about of living our lives. I don't think you can "teach" culture—it has to be lived, experienced. That doesn't mean we should give up on it though. It just means we have to try harder, and make an effort to provide connections for our children to people who are living the culture we want them to learn. For most of us this means stepping outside of our comfort zones and making a real effort at outreach to people and places we never thought of or connected with before. The challenge for me personally has been getting over the false feeling of this. I don't yet know how to get over the feeling that someone will think I only want to be friends with them because of their race or culture, and working through the uncomfortable feelings of getting to know someone new, which is something I wrestle with often as a relatively shy person (AA5).

Shannon found herself stymied in figuring out how to explain to her children the paradox that institutionalized racism in the United States also partly accounted for the privileged conditions that allowed her to adopt her children. In thinking about how to talk to her children about racism, "the sheer absurdity of it" increasingly struck her because she could no longer "separate the political from the personal." Her power derived from her authority as a parent but, also, because she was white, she experienced first-hand better treatment in many social venues than they did, and she was aware that many people viewed her children as "poor starving orphans" and her as "their savior." Although she did not view herself in that light, she realized that was what she represented. In her words, "simply, I am the wealthy white person who could afford to pay to care for them while their rightful parents couldn't." Even as she recognized the realities of power at work and struggled against them, it fell to her to "teach my black kids about racism! My son said the other day that our family is "equal" because we have two black kids and two white parents. How can I begin to explain the truth to him?[9]

Kelly took her understanding of racism one step further, coming to recognize how much she needed to change her own behavior:

> Our children need to see us interacting with people of their race on a regular basis so that they will be comfortable with people of their own race and see

that you are comfortable and accepting of people of their race. . . . People in our community that is predominately white are totally accepting of our cute three-year old right now. But what will happen when Ben knocks on their door to take their little girl on a date? Or, if they find out that their son is dating our African American daughter? Right now, we are actively looking for jobs in a much more diverse community where we can attend church with African Americans, have African American doctors, live in an African American neighborhood, etcetera. It is also not always really easy because there is a large group in the African American community that is against white parents adopting African American children. Now, of course this isn't everyone but it is out there.[10]

AA adoptive parents discussed at length the issues Shannon and Kelly raised, which acquired greater urgency and importance as their children got older and interacted outside family settings.

Another key practice that a minority of AA adoptive parents began to pursue was attendance at black churches. Brandy, the Euroamerican mother of four African American children, three of whom are biological siblings, traveled far outside her neighborhood in New Lenox, Illinois, in order to attend a church that had the largest black population of any church in their county—30 percent black, with a total of 175 families. While making an effort to introduce their children to black culture and role models, she and her husband also did not sugarcoat the struggles of black families in communities across the United States, including the struggles of their children's birth parents. Brandy also jokingly told me a funny story about her sustained efforts to introduce black culture and role models to her children:

They get exposed to a lot more black art and black books written by blacks and written about blacks, and blacks on television. We've got a friend who grew up black. I mean, his mother is biracial and his father is black, and he identifies himself as black, and he laughs because he said that if somebody came into our house at Christmas and his mother's house at Christmas they would think they were the white family and we were the black family. At their house, when he was little, all their angels and all their Santas, everything was white, and he's like, "It didn't matter that they were black, and clearly for your kids it's beneficial to have that." (AA10)

Betty, who lived in South Carolina, unlike Brandy or Alise knew almost nobody who was black. For her, the Internet was a critical way to obtain knowledge about the experiences of other AA families. She described her efforts to connect with people within a black community setting:

> We don't know a lot of black people. . . . My husband works with a huge variety of people because of the business that he's in . . . and so for him, it wasn't such a big deal, but for me, I didn't see any African American people except for when I went through the drive-thru at Wendy's or when we were in a store or in the mall. . . . But he had a friend at work who had invited us to come to their church Easter service, and the guy was black and I asked Ryan, "Is this going to be an all-black church? And he said, "I don't know." . . . We walked in and we were the only white people in that church. . . . You know what my first reaction was. . . . I had set down my purse beside me and Melanie was still in her car seat and a young black man and woman walked up and sat down beside me and you know what my first response was? I looked for my purse and that was the biggest letdown because at that point, I had started to work through some of those—I called it "unpacking my baggage." I listed out in a notebook the things I was fearful of and then just started finding Bible verses that addressed them. . . . Racism is not in the Bible. . . . I had a lot of unpacking of my bags to do. (AA9)

AA adoptive parents tried to disrupt informal segregation in small and big ways and had begun to realize how deeply rooted and distorted their assumptions about race were. Some were, as Vicki Múñiz (1998: 24) states, moving from "proximity" to "propinquity," tentatively calling into question the conditions of "intimate segregation" that characterized many neighborhood and institutional settings. These settings—schools, eating establishments, places of entertainment, and urban neighborhoods—appeared diverse. Yet it is almost a truism in America to state that diversity is not equivalent to interaction between different groups. For AA adoptive families to move from proximity to propinquity required going beyond the visibility and celebration of difference among people, however difference was defined. It entailed cultivating growing familiarity and ease with other African Americans through regular exposure and interaction on the part of the entire family.

AA adoptive families experienced what it was like to be a minority, to feel both marginalized and conspicuous when they visited predominantly black churches or neighborhoods. These interactions created heightened anxiety for AA adoptive families even as they constituted opportunities for them to figure out how to be a bicultural, biracial family in America. When they began to socialize in each other's homes, have extended conversations, exchange good-natured jibes, sometimes with an edge, seek each other's advice, and make a range of experiences part of their everyday lives, parents and children alike could confront more openly the social stigma of race in open conversations and develop deeper relationships that went beyond the color of their skin. These spaces of propinquity were exceedingly important, and children took note of them, allowing them to distinguish between superficial interactions with people they considered "strangers" and more organic relationships with those who were familiar to them.

Becky, mother to Jerrick, age 12, and Kadema, age 6, had strong feelings about her interactions with other AA adoptive families and with nonadoptive African Americans. She wanted her sons to feel comfortable with other people of color *and* she wanted them to have a peer group with whom they could share their feelings and experiences of adoption. Becky confided to me,

> Lately I hate going to transracial adoptive parent support groups. I get a sick-to-the-stomach feeling when I see fifteen white moms with twenty-five black children in the same room. Then I get really sick to my stomach when I realize I am one of them. . . . I remember when I sent an email to a group of adoptive parents who attended the Pact 2004 Camp for Adoptive Families of Color. I encouraged parents to participate in their local Juneteenth festival. . . . During previous years, I invited African American neighbors to Juneteenth.[11] My sons seemed comfortable being in a group of their African American peers with only one white chaperone, me, nearby. I was relieved when it turned out that only one set of white parents with one black daughter traveled down to celebrate Juneteenth with my family. I'd made an effort to help my sons feel like they fit in at Juneteenth, and I didn't want to undermine this by increasing the likelihood that we would be conspicuous by having a bigger group of white parents with black children. I realized that I have to seek out different settings for different purposes. It's hard to provide opportunities for my sons to participate in activities that connect with their culture of origin in a way that their difference as kids who joined an adoptive family through foster care, doesn't stand out as much. And I also participate in social and educational events for multicultural adoptive families so that my sons gain friendships with adoptive friends of color. I think adoptive peers are very important. That unsettled feeling in my stomach was also related to the messages that I thought my sons would receive about adoption and their culture of origin when being in social situations with only white adoptive parents and black adopted children. (AA6)

Becky had invested a great deal of energy in organizing and taking her children to activities and events in which African Americans were also directly involved, and she sustained this energy over many years. She and Alise, in particular, had committed themselves to building a foundation for creating a different sense of place from that which existed before they adopted their children and became a transracial family. It was only because of the growing consciousness of what whiteness connoted that AA adoptive parents could challenge taken-for-granted discourse and practices. Brandy was able to do this when Gina, her first-grader, came home from school, upset because her friend would no longer play with her. Brandy told me what happened:

> Gina had one little girl in first grade tell her, "I can't play with you. My Mom doesn't want me to play with kids with dirty skin. . . . Gina came home crying: "She won't play with me because she thinks I'm dirty. I need to take a bath and wash this off." I said, "Well, honey, it doesn't wash off. . . . It's how it is." I took Gina and we marched down to the little girl's house and I said to her mom, "You know that Gina said your daughter can't play with her because she's too dirty," and the Mom just looked at me horrified, looked at her daughter and said, "Where did you get that?" And she goes, "Well, Mom, you said I'm not allowed to play in the mud and be dirty." And she says, "Honey, she's not dirty. That's the color that she is." And she goes, "Oh, so I can play with her?" Her Mom is like, "Yeah." And she's like, "Okay, let's go!" and that was it. The little girl had gotten it all mixed up in her head. That little girl basically lived at our house the next three summers until they moved away. (AA10).

Children, through social and linguistic cues and interactions, build their understanding of race and color. Goffman (1963: 67–68) called this process "cognitive recognition," the perceptual act of "placing" an individual, whether with a particular social identity or personal identity. He observed that "the range of status and identity pegs that are discernible results in particular kinds of recognition and treatment," a dynamic as true among children as among adults. In the story of Gina and her friend, the friend's mother's analogies between purity and pollution, and white and black, for example, were clear even though the stigma associated with being black was not openly acknowledged by Gina's mother or her friend's mother. At the age of 5 or 6, their children's cognitive understanding was concrete and literal. While the interaction described above between the children is not surprising, given their stage of cognitive development—associating dirt with dark skin—the example, nevertheless, points to how attitudes about race may, literally, be inscribed on the body (Goffman

1963; Rush 2000). The body is, as Mary Douglas (1966) has shown so well, a most convenient vehicle for communicating and transmitting desirable and undesirable social values and practices, which are "coded" systemically as "signs" and symbols. Children began to read these signs and decode them from an early age—as soon as they were interacting in social situations. Hence, the kind of place-making work that AA adoptive mothers such as Alise, Amber, Brandy, and Becky were doing was notable and differed from what most AA adoptive mothers did a generation ago.

Race and Class in Place-Making

Almost all the AA adoptive parents I spoke with considered race of far more urgent concern than adoption, unlike most parents who had adopted children from either China or Russia. Brandy explained,

> Race is probably more important in our lives because adoption essentially is an event. They were adopted on March 29, 2001. It happened. It's something that happened to them in the past, whereas race, they are always black. They wake up today, they are black; they wake up tomorrow, they are black. I guess they always have been adopted, but my kids are pretty quick to tell you when someone says, "Oh, are you adopted?" They'll say, "Yes, I was. I was adopted years ago, this is my family." So, I think race, plus when they are out in public without us, or only with me or my husband, it means you are never sure. Maybe the spouse is black? You know, the adoption isn't always as in your face as race is. (AA10)

Implicit in Brandy's observation above was the idea that kin-work transforms the "event" of adoption into the process of living in a family day to day. Being black does not change, however, and *where* one lives, *who* one interacts with, and *how* one socializes matter greatly.

Betsy and Allen, a well-educated couple who lived in Washington, D.C., were thinking aloud about how to describe to me the way they thought about their daughter's identity-building in light of her African American roots. They ventured that their own Jewish and Scottish backgrounds contributed to Maia's sense of family history, but that it was from her situatedness as a black person growing up with white parents that she was constructing who she was. Allen wryly described what happened when he took Maia to get her hair done: "It was an all-black business run by a woman from the Islands. . . . One particular woman would do Maia's hair who really couldn't stand whites. It was very funny. I would go over to pick her up at this place. I mean, I would drop her off, they did an excellent job. This woman wouldn't give me the time of day. And Maia finally said, "Listen, Dad. You have to realize something. She doesn't like you 'cause you're white. Just accept it" (AA8).[12]

In a similar vein, Denise told me what happened when she made an appointment for her daughter Rachelle at a black hair salon for the first time:

> Nobody would help me. And I stood up after about 15 minutes sittin' there, getting really ticked off . . . and I said, "Excuse me, I have an appointment." Well, a gentleman came over and he said, "Who do you have an appointment with?" and I told him, he said, "She'll be here in a few minutes," I said, "Fine." So after more getting looks, looks, looks, finally she showed up and she sat Rachelle down in the chair, she looked at me, without barely sayin' hello. She looked at me, said, "She adopted?" And I said, "Yeah." And she's like, "Well, alright then." A total attitude change. All the women were comin' over, I was like their best friend, whatever. I came home and I called my black girlfriend and asked, "What was that about?" And she said they prob'ly have issues, think you might've married a you know . . . and I said, "Wow! I didn't even think of that one." (AA16)

Class differences also intervened in how the production of locality figured in the identity formation of AA children. While the average income of AA adoptive parents was lower than that of RA and CA adoptive families, it was usually higher than that of their adopted child's birth parents or relatives. This was also the case for RA and CA adoptive families, but the difference was that AA adoptive parents were in touch with birth relatives more regularly, so class differences played out in visible and consequential ways, as some of the examples above illustrate. AA adoptive parents struggled to make sense of the effect of poverty on birth relatives and on their adopted child and their family. Although these effects were not as apparent in my research because most of the children were still young, Christine Ward Gailey (2010) found that AA adoptive parents did not usually hold birth parents responsible for the impoverished conditions their children had experienced. Yet these conditions made it difficult for AA adoptive parents to figure out how to interact with birth relatives, and it meant that the choices they made for their children were very much informed by class standing and aspirations.

Discussion

In general, parents in America understand in an abstract way that whether or not their children are biologically related to them, they will not necessarily look or act like them. While this is obvious, it indirectly de-essentializes biological family configurations and privileges other modes of relatedness that are not biogenetic. It may well be that because of the cascade effect of the expansion of networks due to interactions among transracial families, the general public, and especially children, the next generation will accept a broader range of family configurations.[13] Nevertheless, institutionalized settings such as schools and places of worship, and the media, play a huge role in the cues children absorb as they build their assumptions about family formation in the United States. Sharon Rush (2000: 135) muses in *Loving across the Color Line,* "I wonder if I would have been moved beyond my own white Liberalism if I had not become the mother of a little black girl and fallen in love with her. . . . Racism is here to stay if White people of goodwill are going to move from their comfortable position *only* if they fall in love with a person of color."

The efforts of AA adoptive parents to challenge prevailing and contradictory structures of race and power were ambitious as well as ambivalent. Few AA adoptive parents had gone so far as to engage in political activism, attempting to combat directly the causes of racism in their neighborhoods or on their streets, but more of them were doing battle in the schools. Carol, a librarian, was mobilizing public libraries to carry a wider range of books for children of color, and Brandy and Roy had decided to join Barack Obama's grassroots community campaign for the presidency, arguing that it was important to get "their kids involved in understanding that here's someone just like you, black, in Illinois, and look at what he's doing. Whether he gets elected or not, look at the change that he's really working for" (AA10).

Among CA, RA, and AA Euroamerican adoptive parents, racial issues were far more critical than adoption itself for AA adoptive parents, because of the persistence and tangibility of racial segregation, the emergence of open adoption practices, the history of institutionalized racism, and in some but not all cases, the economic inequalities and hardships that gave rise to the possibility for adoption. CA and RA adoptive parents were more able to pursue placemaking by forging novel networks connecting distant worlds and cultures to one another. Inauthentic as they might be, these flows created imaginaries that they could act on, enrich, challenge, and integrate into their idea of themselves as a family and into their children's identity-building.

For AA adoptive parents, it was more difficult to pursue such imaginaries. Their safety bubble burst when, as a family, they interacted socially—whether in intimate spaces or more public ones. They confronted their whiteness and the effects of racism in the United States on their family. While they could celebrate black culture by bringing African American artifacts, food, and festivals into their lives, place-making was a more uncomfortable and more delicate undertaking for them. If they took a misstep, they could also be "caught out" by African Americans, as the many stories about "hair care" showed. A growing number of AA adoptive parents realized that an alternative to passing was to recognize that they needed to invest much greater effort in a more sustained and genuine integration of black people and culture into their lives, including their children's birth relatives.

The production of locality that adoptive parents undertook for their children in their early years and pre-adoption entailed attributing meaningfulness to foundational places, cultures, and people that then played significant roles in their children's identity formation. Adoptive parents, through naming and media such as lifebooks, created cultural representations that were also power-laden. These representations projected symbolic and social meanings of family, nature, nurture, race, culture, heritage, and gender. Their children, in the course of pursuing their searches for self in the world, reflected on and challenged these representations. Place, rather than constituting "a space of order and agreed-on meaning" was an important site for struggles over meaning that, in turn, structured and defined place dynamically. In these struggles over meaning, culture itself became both "a site of difference and contestation" as well as "ground and stake of. . . . cultural-political practices" (Gupta and Ferguson 1997b: 5).

Parents who had adopted transracially and transnationally wrestled with, sculpted, and sometimes struggled to transform dominant cultural forms. At times, they ventured across borders and experimented with new ways of interacting and creating a sense of belonging to a family. Nevertheless, the combination of individualism, the deeply grounded cultural values of American voluntarism and exceptionalism, and the broader canvas on which sociopolitical inequalities unfolded in transnational and transracial adoptions help explain why it was so difficult for adoptive parents to know how to make these crossings. It was unknown territory despite the long history of adoption in the United States.

6 Broken Links and Adoption Narratives

The Power of Storytelling

Experience is messy. Searching for patterns in behavior, a consistency of at-
titudes, the meaning in casual conversation, is what anthropologists do, and
they are nearly always dependent on a ragtag collection of facts and fantasies
of an often small sample of the population from a fragment of historical time.
—**Margery Wolf (1992: 129)**

Randolph Severson, in the foreword to *Ethics in Adoption* (Babb 1999) wrote that narratives about adoption, especially those written by psychologists and personal accounts, tended at that time to be either unduly detached or "almost compulsive." Comparing them to "the Ancient Mariner in Coleridge's famous poem, condemned to repeat his tale again and again to anyone within hearing," he thought there was a need to bring together "mind and heart, intellect and emotion" in order to arrive at the formulation of a "new myth."

> The field divided into two categories of expression just as, I guessed, adop-
> tees themselves were sundered. I wondered if the literature and, through the
> literature, the profession itself was becoming isomorphic with the subject of
> its study and perhaps was even in some profound sense responsible for the
> adoptee's self-division. How could adoptees ever find healing and dignity if
> the chief theories in the field and the practices built upon those theories could
> never seem to integrate heart and head in their language and approach? If
> ideas have consequences, then maybe the failure to develop a truly integrated
> vision of the meaning of adoption produced the old closed adoption system,
> which then, through its policies, practices, and procedures, afflicted adoptees
> with the selfsame split. . . . Much of the important work done in adoption
> during the last two decades can be understood in terms of this formulation of
> a new myth. My hope is this: change the adoption myth, change the adoption
> culture. Change adoption culture, change adoption policy, procedures, and
> practice. Change practice, change lives for the better. (Babb 1999: xviii)

New myths about adoption that might mobilize shifts in the culture and practices of adoption seem to be in the making. In the 2009 film *Adopted: When*

Love Is Not Enough, Barb Lee contrasts the journey of Jennifer Fero, a struggling Korean American woman, then 32, who was adopted in 1979 by a white, working-class family in Maine, with that of Min Xinpei, adopted from China in 2004 by John and Jacqueline Trainer, who then renamed her "Roma." There were sharp differences in how the respective parents viewed and prepared for their adoptions and the subsequent practices they incorporated into their lives. Jenny mourns that she is "lost" and has never experienced "self-actualization." "Fitting nowhere—I'm adopted but I'm not. I'm American but I'm not. I'm Korean but I'm not"—Jenny bitterly concludes, "Parents adopt, adoptees adapt," and "adoption is celebrated, but abandonment is ignored."

Jenny's adoptive father had completely ignored Korean culture as integral to their family. Instead, he spent years researching his genealogy back to the American Revolution and was angry when Jenny took him to Chinatown and begged him to meet her halfway on her journey toward self-actualization by trying Korean food and understanding what it feels like to be surrounded by Koreans but not be a part of them.

In contrast, Roma was adopted a full twenty-five years later. Her adoptive parents acknowledge that Roma's initial dramatic grieving is because she was wrenched from her foster mother. They spend a little time interacting with her weeping foster mother. Subsequently, Roma and her adoptive parents embark on learning Chinese together. Jacqueline actively builds a new and more diverse friendship network that she hopes "will help her raise their child"; and John quietly comments that he is looking forward to the three of them learning about their heritage as Chinese Americans. (Lee 2008)

This chapter examines the narratives adoptive parents crafted for their children before their children reached adolescence and their children's reactions and responses to them. The narratives contained new ideas about family-making yet also incorporated traces of well-established assumptions about the face and formation of American families. While each story had unique qualities, many adoptive parents, almost unconsciously, drew on particular narrative themes and sequencing. I have selected narratives that give readers an idea of the structure and content adoptive parents thought most critical to include in creating a story that told how their children became part of their family through adoption. I also selected narratives with an eye to highlighting differences and similarities in the narratives of CA, RA, and AA adoptive parents.

Overwhelmingly, the production of these narratives was gendered. Adoptive mothers rather than fathers took primary responsibility for contributing to structuring particular kinds of affective bonds and cultural connections for their children through the narratives. Heather Jacobson (2008) describes a similar pattern in her ethnography of international adoption practices. In part, this may be because children from a young age intuitively understood links between mothers and biological reproduction, but it may also have been because more adoptive mothers than adoptive fathers participated in virtual community discussions about how to make and tell adoption narratives.

Memory-Building and Storytelling

The anthropology of storytelling and life stories offers important insights into how to analyze these narratives. Most of this research has focused on autobiographical accounts, shared as "life stories" with anthropologists, or interactive accounts between teller and listener.[1] The narratives below differ. They constitute bits and pieces of "life stories" adoptive parents shared with their children and conveyed to me as anthropologist. Hence, a secondary mediation transpired that bears on the narratives themselves. Adoptive parents, while they told me the narratives they told their children, also confided in me what they would *not* share with their children. The narratives were thus fluid autobiographical familial accounts, constructed in light of myriad variables that could change over time. "Partial representations and evocations of the world," these stories were "versions of reality" rather than simply a reflection of reality (Ochs and Capps 1996: 22). Their construction and telling had "the power to structure perceptual experience, to organize memory, to segment and purpose-build the very events of a life" (Bruner 2004: 674). Place-making and the making of life-lines thus went hand-in-hand. Especially true of adoption narratives because they provided the "ground" out of which family grew and self was constructed, "every telling provides narrators and listeners . . . with an opportunity for fragmented self-understanding. . . . Narratives have the potential to generate a multiplicity of partial selves" (Ochs and Capps 1996: 22).

These adoption narratives took place in an interactive context, the stuff of parents' memories and sense of self; and they were filtered through the "formulation of beliefs, values, and ideas that were basic to a particular cultural tradition" (Peacock and Holland 1993: 373). The narrative structure itself—the story of the birth of a child and her subsequent adoption in the United States, and the emphasis on immediate bonding between child and adoptive parents—had a fairy-tale quality that went from difficult beginnings to happy endings. The prototypical example of such a tale that is often cited in adoption circles is "The Ugly Duckling." In reality, this was rarely how adoptions unfolded. Adoptive parents, faced with gaps they could not fill in about their children's past, and with information they deemed unpleasant or confusing to explain (especially in light of an American cultural context and morality), anguished over how to construct and relate narratives to their children. The stories had a deliberate quality to them, and some adoptive parents told me they had practiced them over and over again before sharing them with their children. They also used the lifebooks they had created to complement and cue their narratives and to check their own memories as "the time of adoption" receded.

Stories have multiple purposes. They tell a family about itself, and they tell a particular child about herself—she becomes "storied." They convey social and cultural values and communicate intentionally and unconsciously all sorts of things to a public or imagined public listening to the story being told. They establish connections between past, present, and future, creating links, filling in the blanks, and smoothing over contradictions, what Wills (2007) calls "broken lines." They have a mythical quality to them, which made it difficult to distinguish archetypical social truths from historical truths.[2] Further, as the renowned anthropologist Claude Lévi-Strauss (1962) suggested, the stories themselves constituted efforts to mediate and transform life contradictions. They also had the power to shift the ground on which Americans and adoptive families themselves understood and then acted on adoption because, as Jerome Bruner wisely noted, "Any story one may tell about anything is better understood by considering other possible ways in which it can be told" (Bruner 2004: 709).

The narratives collected here revolve around contradictions: being part of a family and having been relinquished by or truncated from another family; being bound by love whose value is immeasurable but which simultaneously exists in the form of children exchanged for gifts and money, who have already suffered and experienced loss. Another theme is the image of children as recipients of nurturing ties, as would be true in any "ideal" American family, but also as recipients within a family to which they are not linked by blood. The narratives offered children one sense of their past and their future; they could thus "impose order on otherwise disconnected experiences" (Ochs and Capps 1996: 24); and they exerted power by evoking emotions that were associated with significant places in their lives (Ochs and Capps 1996).

To give but one example, I had to wonder about the uncanny similarities in the stories adoptive parents shared with me about their children's birth parents. It is not an exaggeration to view these stories as myths in the making. In the narratives that RA adoptive parents shared about why their child was available for adoption, I was told that the birth parents had died, been murdered, or drunk themselves to death or to the point where they were neglectful of their children—first the father, then the mother—and that grandparents or a sister had agreed to terminate rights. In the case of CA adoptive parents, the story was built around the one-child policy, the discrimination against girls, and a birth mother's love that led her to abandon her child. The stories told by AA adoptive parents varied more, partly because it was easier to gather together bits and pieces about birth parents' (especially birth mothers') situation. Relinquishment was framed by poverty, drug use, abandonment by the birth father, and the birth mother's decision that both she and her child would benefit from adoption.

All of these stories likely contain more than a grain of truth. Yet many pertinent details were missing, especially from the transnational birth parent stories. Deep inequalities, personal tragedies, and the reality of child trafficking were erased. Adoption brokers, as a matter of convenience in the context of following procedures to facilitate adoption, created general explanations for prospective parents of why children were available for adoption. These became the basis for shared narratives that circulated among adoptive families. Filtered through cultural assumptions, they emerged from what adoptive parents were told during the adoption process, what they learned from their own research and information sources, and their adoption experiences. The stories had a mythical quality because the structures behind the myths often remained hidden. On the other hand, even these narratives of convenience were difficult to share with children.

We all have stories, and we all have family secrets, so what makes the stories and secrets of adoptive families any different from those of other families? Milan Kundera (cited in Ochs and Capps 1996: 21) has dedicated his writing to the "paradoxical relationship between remembering and forgetting" and the "struggle of memory against forgetting." Adoptive parents viewed the narratives they shared with their children as "private." They rarely retold them outside narrow family circles. Unless children could identify and communicate with birth relatives or intermediaries who had known them before or during their adoption process, there was no one for them to turn to for alternative accounts about their origins or to contest the narratives they were told. It was thus difficult initially for children to consider other perspectives or narratives or even to understand that their narratives might be incomplete. In short, adoptive parents exercised considerable power—what Ochs and Capps (1996: 36) call "narrative asymmetries"—in their storytelling.

Alison Landsberg (2004) and Sarah Sweetman (2013) conceptualize storytelling as a way of creating "prosthetic" memories.[3] These memories are grafted onto an adoptee's biographical timeline and spun out of a fascinating array of materials. All familial stories have a "selective character" (Youngblood 2001: 64). The stories CA, RA, and AA adoptive parents told to adoptees, the stories adoptees told to themselves, and the stories they eventually would tell to each other and the world at large have generated "a politics of memory" that shapes the present and propels them into the future (Boyarin 1994: 22; Bruner 2004; Van Vleet 2008).

Kristin Peterson (2001: 249), writing about the "generative force of oral history" and its evocative powers in family stories, notes that the telling and retelling of stories "can be a haunting experience" in which the emphasis on "what may count as family" conjures up simultaneously the silence surrounding those who do not count as "relatives." The silences that become apparent in repeated tellings of a narrative lead listeners to wonder more about them. Eventually, listeners may come to reflect much more on where and how they should look for meaning in narratives and how they relate to the narratives and to the storytellers. She concludes that "mostly it is the repeatability of stories about people whom I never knew or met that remains with me. For in speaking, ghosts are conjured up and something new may emerge. Silence may actually get brave and start saying something. Haunting may have its own tactics and agenda, and belonging may find new meanings."

Storytelling serves as an avenue for the creation of individual self-understanding, but even more important, for children to socially construct "the self." Children may create "jointly constructed narratives" that serve as "a repository of the group's experience." Through "matching claims" and "parallel experiences"—a kind of interweaving of narratives—"personhood" could thus extend "beyond the skin" even if experiences were not temporally, spatially, or cognitively accessible to the individual child (Miller et al. 1990: 303–6).

Although adoptees did not accept wholesale their adoptive parents' stories about who they were and how they came to be a family, it was hard for them to achieve the kind of co-ownership described above in their earlier years, given the private nature of adoption narratives (see Zerubavel 2006). Nevertheless, hearing their stories was an important first step for them. The existence of the narratives meant that they could use them to begin a process of evaluation, to reflect on gaps and silences, and for some, to eventually contest and resist them.[4] Co-ownership blossomed when adoptees embarked on searches, interacted with one another, and began to publicly construct alternative narratives to the dominant ones that had prevailed when they were children.

From America to China to America

For children adopted from China who had only the sketchiest information about their earliest years, their adoptive parents' narratives emphasized cultural heritage. The parents explained to their children (almost always daughters) from an early age that they had wanted a child and could not have one (for various reasons); that there was a mother in China who could not take care of her child; that the mother therefore left the child in a safe place where she would be found and taken care of—in front of an orphanage, at a public place, or at the police station; that the mother had pinned a note on her (sometimes with a few instructions), a birth date, and maybe a name; and that the waiting adoptive parents were then matched with the child; that they went all the way to China to get her; and that then she came to join her "forever" family. The narrative constituted a private story about a public abandonment that was "safe" but secret; it emphasized movement from "here" (the United States) to "there" (China) and back again, and from uncertainty to permanence.

While each narrative had unique aspects, as adoptive parents considered how to fill in missing links they emphasized a lack of information, a general plan on the part of birth mothers (and in one case, the birth father), the precarious condition of the child prior to adoption, waiting adoptive parents, mediation with the Chinese government in order to adopt the child; and fear and sadness on the part of the child at the moment of transition, followed by happiness on the part of adoptive parents at the moment of incorporation. The birth mother was portrayed as strong but helpless before the power of the Chinese state, yet a love of China was also communicated in the narrative; and some narratives mentioned, in a positive light, nannies, caretakers, and foster mothers and their sadness when they bade farewell to the child at the moment of transition.

The excerpts below are representative of the patterns that prevailed in CA adoptive parents' narratives. Norma and Elliott lived in Boise, Idaho. She worked for a small business and he was a teacher. They already had one biological daughter, age 11, and Elliott had helped to raise Norma's daughter from a prior marriage. Madeleine was 5 when Norma told me the story she shared with her.

> We've told Madeleine that she was born in China. For some reason, we don't know, her birth mother could not keep her, but she put her in a place where she would have been found right away...... They don't think she was outside in the cold morning air more than twenty minutes, but she probably wouldn't

have lasted if she had been out an hour. She was physically not in good shape because she hadn't been fed. That bothers me. Why wasn't she fed? To keep the baby that long and not feed it? So, I'll never share that with her, that's not information she needs. And basically, that's what we've told her. And Madeleine stayed in that safe warm place with her nannies until they found a mommy and daddy for her. And the mommy and daddy in America were so wanting a child that we wrote a letter to the Chinese government and asked, "Please, could we adopt one of your little girls that doesn't have a mommy or daddy. And they said yes. And they put us in touch with some really wonderful ladies that work in the place that puts mommies and daddies and babies together and found us for each other, and we went all the way to China to get you and we flew back. And we love China and we're going to take you back. I'm not trying to put, you know, "your mommy loved you" cause I don't know that. I'm not going to tell her that. (CA12)

Parents like Norma told me things that they censored from the narratives they shared with their children. They did this because they found particular practices or possibilities horrifying based on their own autobiographical experiences and an American cultural and moral model—a mother not feeding a child or leaving it in the cold, for example; they also did not want to portray their children's birth parents, especially the birth mother, in a harsh light. They found it a relief to share their distress with me. I was older, an adoptive mother myself, and they placed me in the category of researcher who wanted full documentation.

All of the adoptive parents used some type of self-censorship. Some strived to create dynamic narratives. For example, Jan, a single mother, had been in her mid-40s when she read about another single mother who had adopted a child from China because China did not exclude single parents from adopting. Jan decided to follow suit and had adopted two children. She did not think her narrative had closure but rather that she and her two daughters would have to figure out how to build it together:

The older one [Miranda], I've talked about it with her some, and I made her a lifebook to look at with pictures and stuff. They don't say much at first, but then recently Miranda asked me, "Why couldn't my birth mother take care of me?" Then you think you're going to have a good answer, but then when they really ask you, you go, "Ah, I don't know." The truth is you don't know. You don't really know anything except that they were found and where they were found and where they were taken, so that's kind of been the extent of the conversation so far, and I know that's something that's going to be kind of on-going and they'll circle around and revisit it probably their whole lives. (CA23)

More rarely, adoptive parents like Leslie tried to personalize their narratives, highlighting relationships their children were part of before they came to the United States:

I do tell Virginia her adoption story, and she very much likes to hear it, in very simple language. We sit in the rocking chair before she goes to bed and I say, "Do you want to hear the story about how we became a family and how you became our daughter?" Mom and Dad decided they wanted a little girl for their very own, and they wrote a letter to China and asked, "Do you have any little girls?" and China said, "yes, we have a little girl named Sha Yun and she needs a mom and dad, and she's a wonderful little girl and you'll love her very much." So we got on a plane with Tina, your godmother, and we flew over to China. And we talk about the first day we got Virginia and she was a little scared and that's about it. It's very interesting to me how much she likes the story, and it seems to give her great comfort. There seems to be a lot of pro-cessing. She must have some memories, it starts quite young. (CA4)

In Leslie's narrative, emplacement was important—being in the rocking chair together before bedtime created a sense of security and comfort. Leslie also incorporated Virginia's Chinese name into her story. She did not take for granted the referential terms "family" and "daughter." Instead, she validated the vulnerability she imagined Sha Yun must feel *now* hearing about why and how she left China—she imagined Sha Yun must have felt scared—and she also stressed how Tina, her godmother, and Sha Yun/Virginia were linked by non-biogenetic connections to Leslie and George. She attributed memory-making and personhood to Sha Yun/Virginia from a young age in a respectful way that infused her narrative.

Marge and Frank were a young couple who lived in Madison, Wisconsin. Tess was ten months old when Marge and Frank adopted her, and she was 2 when I spoke with them. Both she and Frank were divorced from their first spouses, they had stepparents and stepchildren in their respective families, and they had close friends who had adopted children from Korea. Marge was open about her experiences in China and more adventurous than other parents I spoke with. She relied heavily on a lifebook she had created with maps and photos of China and of the city Tess had been adopted from, and when she shared her narrative with Tess she told me she made sure to include "what the day that she was born might have been like from the birth mother's perspective. It just kind of throws some questions out there for her." She had also created a lifebox that she, together with Tess, filled with things she had brought back: "I plan fully to have her participate with me in a lifebox: "These are the shoes that you wore when I picked you up" and things like that. "These are the soybeans that this person gave me . . . and who knows, she might grow up and she couldn't care less? But maybe those things will mean a lot to her?" (CA8)

The story of the soybeans, described below, was central to the narrative Marge created for Tess and the connection she felt to China. She knew more than most adoptive parents about Tess's early history, including contact information for Tess's foster mother, and felt that she was lucky to have gotten a sense of daily life in China rather than the "adoption Disneyland" that she felt Guangzhou represented:

> I think the only real accurate portrayal was when we were in the home province and we were able to travel a little bit throughout the province and kind of see how people really live. It just galvanized my desire to teach my child about the land of her birth and to show her the strength of character and the work ethic of the people that she comes from. One of the more amazing experiences that I had when I was there . . . was when we were coming out of the gates of the orphanage. . . . Just to the right of the gate was this woman in a little clay shack, and she was harvesting soybeans and she motioned for me to come over. . . . I walked over to her . . . she was nodding and smiling and I think she was saying, "Xie xie" which is thank you. . . . I was trying to talk to her, and of course she didn't understand but it was like we understood each other. . . . She had taken my hands and she opened them up and she just put this handful of soybeans in my hands and she just closed them up and she just nodded and smiled and sort of sent me on my way. . . .
>
> Those are the kinds of moments I really want to remember and tell Tess about and just help her to understand that, yes, China has its faults, a Communist government, and there are things about that that are pretty scary, but you know, I love my country but there are some things about our government too. It's just about the people. It's about where you came from, about the type of people that were around you and nurtured you and cared for you. When I look at the pictures Tess's first foster mother took of her—we sent cameras over beforehand—she's just beamingly happy. . . . I didn't meet her foster mother, but I know from looking at those pictures that she was loved and

loved back, and I am so grateful for that. I just have felt such a deep connection and just such gratitude for her love. (CA8)

Marge's story was replete with narrative mechanisms that facilitated Tess's ability to identify with it. She used documents, photos, videos, and mementos to complement her words. She gave ample room to Tess's birth mother and father; she included her affection for Tess's foster mother; and she conveyed that Tess had already experienced the joy of reciprocal love before she was adopted. The photos of Tess with her foster mother documented those ties. She told Tess about China and the city where she was living; she looked forward to learning about "the land of her birth" with her; and she placed the governments of the United States and China within the same frame, an unusual thing for adoptive parents to do. The mementos in Marge's lifebox were linked to Tess's past; and Marge's exchange with the older woman outside the orphanage had a kindly tone with details that made it seem concrete and realistic.

CA adoptive parents told *me* about particularly difficult times in the adoption process—problems related to attachment (prior attachments their children had to caretakers, foster families, and children in the orphanage), the health conditions they and their children were struggling with, and the panic and grief their children initially experienced. They also contemplated why their children had become available for adoption. Nevertheless, these details were almost always left out of the narratives they shared with their children (Tess was an exception). Sara Dorow (2007: 169, 170) shows how narrative formation is social, evolving, and historical; the teller strives to provide coherence to identity through a retelling of the past in order to make sense of the present and future, observing that "because [the trauma of adoption] cannot be remembered, it must be narrated." CA adoptees, by the time they were around 8 years of age, began to pay close attention to the broken links in the stories they were told. They noted that figures were initially present, only to go missing; or they wondered how it was that they had at one time been part of a family, but that no family members or relatives had seen them go missing when they were deposited at the front of an orphanage, on a sidewalk, or at the corner police station.

Abandonment trauma and a reification of China as a "collection of things" (Traver 2007; Wills 2007: 240) and of "ancient culture" wove in and out of their adoption narratives. Wills (2007: 240) tells the story of two adoptees who were chatting with each other. One commented to her friend that her adoptive parents were "Asian-philes"—collectors of all things Asian—and then she added that she herself was part of the collection.

Many adoptees began daydreaming of an abstract "mother" or relative who looked like them or shared their skills. Tracy shared the following with me: "When Sabrina was little, she said, "I want to have blue eyes." It immediately went to my head: "Oh my gosh! This means she is not adjusting." Finally, I say, "Oh, but your eyes are beautiful" and "Why do you want blue eyes?" Sabrina says, "Because I want to see what you see!" (CA24). Tracy assumed that her daughter's comments reflected the importance placed on physical resemblance among family members in the "normative" model of an American family. In fact, it had occurred to her daughter that seeing through blue rather than brown eyes would give her a view of the world like her mother's. Not so metaphorically, she was right! The desire among children to find commonalities in personality traits as well as physical characteristics with parents, adoptive or not, was widespread.

In reflecting on the narratives parents shared with them, pre-adolescent CA adoptees mentioned that they appreciated the perspectives they gained from "being different" but knew that "different" was equated with distinction and with being in the public eye where not all distinctions were viewed in the same way. They pinpointed what was most difficult for them: "People ask a lot of questions"; "Having to deal with explaining to people why I don't look like my family or how I'm not a foster child." Some were aware of the one-child policy in China but did not understand why it existed. Their partial understanding reflected both their cognitive development and the narratives their adoptive parents had shared with them.

Until they approached adolescence, the facts about reproduction were somewhat mysterious to them. When I was talking to Sabrina, age 9, she told me, "I know about China, the place, but not about the people." Mariel, a thoughtful 11-year-old, spoke of her adoption narrative in the context of her favorite books. She explained that in *Jeremy Fink and the Meaning of Life*, a boy and girl try to work together to find the meaning of life, which is supposedly in a box given to Jeremy by his deceased father. In the end, "Jeremy finds that the meaning of life is actually a billion things stringed [sic] together." Muriel liked her other favorite book, *Maniac Magee*, because "Maniac is a guy that doesn't see the difference between black and white people. He doesn't realize that there is a West End (white) and an East End." In parsing Mariel's comment, what I found interesting was that Mariel most liked that Maniac did not focus on difference in skin color and, therefore, was not reinscribing racialization as a primary mode of stratification and boundary marking. Mariel told me what she had learned from her parents' narratives about China: "What the people looked like, how they liked me, the place was beautiful, polluted, fun, very cultural." She concluded, "It gets very hard to remember certain things that happened to me in China because I only lived there until I was 3, so I get sort of nervous and quiet when I am asked questions about how life was like when I was in the orphanage in China."

Of course, most 3-year-olds don't remember being that age, but friends and family members likely have provided them with cues. Eleven-year-old Gail was exceptional among CA adoptees in telling me that she considered her sisters, her adoptive mom and dad, *and* her birth mom and dad to be her family. No other pre-adolescent CA adoptee I spoke with included their birth parents explicitly in their family.[5] She was most perturbed by "people who don't really understand adoption" and who ask questions like, "Do you know who your 'real parents' are? They say *real parents* like my adoptive parents are fake! It makes me mad." Gail felt "strong and proud to have gone through these kinds of transitions from country to country," but she found it hard "not knowing why I was adopted, my health history, my genes. I just wanna know!!" She concluded by confiding to me that she would rather be "Chinese than American," but that for whatever reason, when she thinks about couples, "I want to be with an American."

These comments challenged the coherent narratives that adoptive parents had worked to craft. Adoptees observed that some of their experiential knowledge differed from or failed to resonate with their adoptive parents' narratives. They were already sensitized to distinctions that people drew between different modes of family formation; they did not like being conspicuous, yet they did not reject being Chinese or adopted; they were working hard to "string a billion things" from the box of life into a meaningful sense of self; they were frustrated by gaps and the lack of information about their early years or their medical history; and they were concerned that their early memories might fade away altogether. Few of them expressed anger at their adoptive parents, but they wondered, in an increasingly open fashion over time, about the idealized view of adoption and China conveyed by the fairy-tale like quality of their adoptive parents' narratives.

From Russia with Love:
Blending Families and Facing Special Needs

The narratives told by RA adoptive parents in their early years differed from those of CA and AA adoptive parents. Because they had internalized adoption as a marked category, they did not develop or only weakly developed adoption narratives to share with their children, and felt no compulsion to replace broken links with cultural heritage and material culture. Some who crafted narratives were trying to figure out if and how they should acknowledge their children's connections to Russia through them. Many RA adoptive parents who wanted to share adoption narratives with their children could not because their children had special needs that prevented them from really understanding them, or their children were terrified by the stories themselves. They associated the stories with "being returned" to the orphanage.

I wanted to find out how young RA adoptees themselves felt about the adoption narratives their parents had told them, but this was hard information to gather. The adoptive parents revealed little in interviews, and children were even less forthcoming, precisely because they had received less information than the other adoptees in the form of structured narratives. To be clear, it was not that the narratives RA children heard were true or false, but that they were sparse. The excerpts below are representative of the stories the RA adoptive parents told. I also include some of their children's reactions to them, in the few cases I was able to tease them out.

Fran and Kyle were well educated, and Kyle was an economic consultant on emerging global markets. They had lived for a long time outside the United States in Asia. Fran had always thought she might adopt a child but had been reluctant to pursue adoption as a single mother. She married late, and she and Kyle immediately began to look into adoption. Kyle's father wanted them to have a traditional family through pregnancy in order to transmit Kyle's genes. When they announced that they planned to adopt, Kyle's father asked if they would be adopting "a slanty-eyed kid." They decided to adopt two boys from Russia because Fran felt that adopting girls would lead to even more identity issues than were usual between mother and daughter and because Kyle's mother had connections to Russia.

One of their children, Nicholas, has serious physical and mental challenges that have been difficult for everyone to accept, especially Kyle's family. Kyle and Fran repeatedly alluded to the premium that Kyle's family placed on intelligence and how "they intellectualized" everything. When I asked whether Kyle's father's views had changed over time, Fran, somewhat acidly, offered the following response: "Mikhail has talent. That is something that Kyle's father can relate to and value. I think also, his dad values the fact that Mikhail is so attractive and is very popular with the girls, so again, that's something that men kind of view in a very positive light."(RA6)

Fran was grappling with many issues after they formed their family through adoption—the ambivalence of Kyle's family toward adoption and the stigma they associated with Nicholas's learning difficulties. I asked Fran and Kyle if they had shared any kind of adoption narratives with their two sons. Fran said:

> I think the whole question of how much you highlight for them their own ancestry and cultural background . . . is very important to do in theory, but in reality we haven't done a lot of it, which bothers me but not enough to make me do it. . . . We've certainly in the past tried to highlight things that we saw or read about Russia and . . . they are definitely not interested. Nicholas is not interested at all . . . although I think in England when he was in first grade the boys got into a fight over who was on the Allied Forces and who was fighting with the Nazis. They told him that the Russians were fighting on the Nazi side and he was very upset, and I assured him that that was not the case. (RA6)

I asked Fran and Kyle if the children grasped that they were adopted. Kyle responded:

> In the World Cup, Nicholas is supporting the Russian team, although he also supported the Italian team and the Japanese team and the English team, so there's a bit of it that comes out that he's Russian, but it's actually less than you would expect. I kind of get Russia-proud in those moments because I think, "We've got Russian kids," and then Russia does well in an international sporting event and that's something we should feel a connection to. I don't think Mikhail really feels much of that at all.(RA6)

Kyle felt that his children did not particularly care about their connection to Russia, but he too was ambivalent—about adoption and about their relationship to Russia. Fran had created an adoption narrative for each of her children, a "little story about this little boy named Mikhail and a couple called Kyle and Fran, and I'd fill in all the things and he just loved it. He'd be so attentive and want to hear more and more. Whereas Nicholas, I don't know if it was ADHD or the learning disabilities but I think it's partly his personality; he could care less." Kyle chimed in that, despite their having created a narrative, "Mikhail has no desire to hear it anymore either." The tension between Fran and Kyle escalated as I was speaking with them to the point that Fran responded to Kyle in some exasperation, exclaiming, "I am, much more so than Kyle, very open about the fact that they are adopted, and talk to other people about it in front of them." She also told me that, despite Kyle's assumption that the children did not care, Mikhail's teacher had reported back that he did:

> His teacher in the second grade said to me, "He's really very open about his adoption." And he told this other kid he was adopted. . . . And the other thing that was really nice was this year in school on "Back to School Night" the teacher made the kids in Mikhail's class write a letter to their parents, and the last three things had to be something they were grateful to their parents about, and Mikhail said, "One, for sending me to the school." Two, I can't remember what he said, and the third one was "for adopting me." That hadn't been discussed before.(RA6)

Kyle again returned to the question of an adoption narrative when I asked Fran and Kyle whether they planned to return to Russia:

> Yeah, that's funny 'cause I was going to mention this when you were talking about whether the boys have had any sort of consciousness about their being adopted. The one and only time that Mikhail was sort of sensitive about being adopted, and it was not really about being adopted, it was when he was about 3 or 4. . . . We were laying in the bed and we were just talking, and I said, "Someday we're gonna take you back to Russia," and what I meant was we'll go to visit, and he started crying because he thought we meant we were going to take him back and leave him there. Of course then I felt awful, and the story has obviously stuck in my memory because it was so awful but . . . I'm trying to figure out what age is the right sweet spot to go back so that they are old enough to appreciate it. . . . We haven't forced them to do Russian language or anything like that. (RA6)

Fran and Kyle continued arguing throughout the interview about how central adoption should be both in their lives and wondering how much it might matter to their children to know they had a blood relative:

> Fran: 'Cause you know, one of the things that I just feel strongly that Kyle and I came together as a couple to start a family. . . . we're a different set of genes. . . . we're all individuals but together we make up a family. Adoption is only part of the story. It became a more important part of the story at the beginning of Mikhail's life, but as he ages and has all these different experiences it'll just be one part, and it's who he is and it's who I am that I wasn't able to have children. It doesn't mean it's a bad thing, it's just part of our story.
>
> Kyle: Just one other comment because I'm not sure what I think of it, . . . my aunt . . . who has the two adopted boys said to me . . . that when her son,

the younger boy, had a biological child with his wife, that she felt good for him because he now had a blood relative. It struck me because I had never thought that that would have been an issue for her or for him. For her it was obviously significant that there was now somebody on the planet that was definitely blood related to him. Most of the rest of us have definitively, but these kids don't and our kids don't, knowingly. (RA6)

Fran and Kyle expressed very openly sentiments that many RA adoptive parents harbored. Their view of family, reflected in the fragments of their narratives, was more sharply defined by the biological grounding of kinship ties than the narratives of either AA or CA families. Passing as if they were a biologically formed white family nevertheless did not occur as easily as many of them had thought it would. Learning challenges, differences between couples about whether and how to acknowledge adoption, and the lack of shared and patterned adoption narratives among RA adoptive parents, in general, created difficulties for them. Their anxieties about these difficulties were embedded in their narratives or the lack thereof.

Emily, like other RA adoptive parents, told me Richard could not process the adoption narrative she had created because of his special needs. She did not think there was anything shameful about her son having "issues," living in an orphanage, and being adopted, but she explained,

> "Richard will say, "I was born in Russia." I think part of it is his language delay. . . . We will look through his books—we have his scrapbooks and all his things about his adoption—but he's just not interested. . . . We have talked to him about it since day one. . . . Because of his issues. . . . I've found out there's a lot of adoptive parents of children with issues. They do not want anyone to know they were adopted in an orphanage and [to infer] any relationship between the two. I've just never felt that way. . . . He spent a year in an orphanage, had very low stimulus, he was very underweight. (RA4)

When I talked to Richard, age 9, it nevertheless seemed he wanted to hear about his own behavior and life in the orphanage, regardless of what it meant exactly, and that he appreciated his adoption narrative. I was struck by how much he was working to put himself in his story and to bring together into the same temporal frame events and connections that defined his past, a period of transition, and his emergence into the present as a "heart baby" to Emily and Michael. He told me, "There were some things I did not understand about adoption. I talk to my parents about what I liked to do as a baby, what Russian food I ate, the plane ride back, when I first saw my mother, and how I am glad I was a heart baby instead of a tummy baby." Richard liked to "look at the pictures of me in Russia when I was a baby in my lifebook." He especially "liked to see the pictures of the big party I had at the airport when I arrived here, and I liked to see all the pictures of the first time I did stuff." When I asked how he felt when people asked him about adoption, he said:

> No one has ever asked me any questions about being adopted. Most people do not know because I have been here since I was a baby and I look like my parents. So does my sister [also adopted from the same orphanage]. I was placed at birth and my birth mother was 29 and I was the fifth child. The town I was born in was very poor. My grandmother worked at the hospital. She was very happy that my mom and dad came for me and that I would be very happy. (RA4)

He concluded that the best thing about being adopted was having "My mom and dad and sister" and that "it is neat to tell people that I was born in Russia. I like that our family did something different."

When I asked whether Gretchen and Keith had shared an adoption narrative with their daughter Nadia, their response was similar to Emily's but more dramatic:

> Gretchen: We can't. The last time her book came out of the story of the trip, the airplane ticket, of the pictures of her with the caregivers at the orphanage, she was a basket case for days.. . . . It was emotional overload. For a long time we made the mistake of showing her the video of her in the orphanage. . . .
> Gretchen: She knows she was not in my tummy.
> Keith: She knows she is from Russia.
> Gretchen: She is very proud that she is from Russia.
> Keith: And we have lots of Russian knick-knacks and stuff. I even have an old Soviet flag around here. I can say, "Here is the Russian flag."
> Gretchen: Yeah, she has her flag on her bed. She knows that we went on airplanes. She knows, her term is that she was at "a school" before she came to us. School of hard knocks. That is her framework. And she says, "the boys were mean at night." She was able to verbalize it along with the setting where the cribs were. Why she didn't want to go to bed was because "boys were mean."
> Keith: I'm not going to disabuse her of that. Let her keep that thought until she's 30 or 35.
> Gretchen: We don't talk about it like you hear other families talking about it.
> Keith: We don't avoid it. We just don't bring it up. (RA8)

Nadia had severe emotional problems and fetal alcohol syndrome. Gretchen and Keith gave a nod to cultural heritage (the flag) when they told me their adoption narrative. The narrative had a subtext explaining Nadia's horror of the orphanage—that, likely, she was sexually abused there. For me, hearing this exchange was painful because Nadia's father, while he did not gloss over his daughter's probable abuse, hoped Nadia would remember it in order to defend herself from future abuse from young men as she grew up, even though he refused to talk about it with her.

More than other parents who have adopted transnationally, RA adoptive parents have had to do battle with demons of imperfection. While upper-middle-class Americans have embraced the cultural value that children are priceless, the costs of struggling with fetal alcohol syndrome and with reactive attachment disorder are high indeed. And by cost, I do not mean solely the economic cost of providing the services and therapy these children need. I also mean the emotional and social cost for parents like Fran and Kyle, Gretchen and Keith, and many others. Whether adoptive parents viewed their family configuration as preordained by God, as an outcome of intelligent design, or as a voluntary choice they made with unexpected consequences, these conditions created additional scrutiny and self-reflection for them. Some RA adoptive parents I interviewed openly told me that they were coping with marital stress as a result of the adoption of their children. These conditions contributed to the ambivalence with which they viewed adoption as a form of family formation, which only increased *after* they adopted.

One of the most unusual aspects of the narratives of RA adoptive parents was how they wove into them their children's life experiences prior to their adoption. Many more RA children than CA or AA children were adopted at an older age and had memories of being part of other families, friends, and places. For those who were older, their narratives played a different role. They knew where they had been and what had happened. When I asked parents who had adopted older children about their narratives, they mentioned scrapbooks and videos. Rather than telling me a story, instead they told me directly about their children's prior experiences and connections in Russia. They also omitted particularly unsavory dimensions of their children's past when speaking with their children. For a few, the stories they shared with their children provoked them to make special efforts to rekindle or maintain connections between their children and friends in the orphanage.

Hilda, a single mother with degrees in nursing and psychology, and who worked as a registered nurse in a hospital in Texas, went so far as to adopt her daughter's best friend. She first adopted Larisa at age 5 and subsequently adopted Gena at age 6 because Larisa missed her so much and said she wanted Gena "for a sister." The two girls were now 15 and 16. When I asked Hilda if she shared any kind of adoption narrative with Larisa or Gena, instead she told me about their links to relatives and caretakers:

> They know their history, siblings, parents, grandparents. Larisa has an older brother who was in the orphanage, which she did not even know about it. He was there before she was born. She was removed from the family, [from] her mother, because of neglect at nine months. She had been in the orphanage ever since. Her mother never went to see her. Her father went to see her once. The mother was in and out of jail. That's pretty much about it. The same thing with Gena's paperwork. . . . Her mother was drinking. . . . There were siblings. Gena says she met her brother once. What she remembers is her grandparents. She was living with her grandparents. . . . I didn't really construct a story about adopting them. We were very open about they were adopted. As far as the parents and why they put them up for adoption, I made it sound not as ugly as it was . . . that the parents couldn't take care of them. They had no money. . . . As they got older, I added in the alcohol. And they've always had access to the papers. So once they started reading and were more interested, then they took out their albums and read them periodically. (RA10)

When I asked if Larisa or Gena had expressed interest in learning more about Russia, Hilda said,

> Not really, because I have all of this Russian stuff I purchased for them and made attempts for them to really be proud of their heritage and they kind of pooh-pooh it. As far as learning Russian, not really. I have a big desire to learn Russian. They don't have a big desire to learn much about it at all, which really surprised me. (RA10)

Hilda told me that Gena had become very attached to Solveg, one of the caretakers at the orphanage, who kept in close touch with her and told her about her friends there:

> Gena knows what's happened to the kids she grew up with. Oh, actually both of them. Larisa keeps saying she wants to go back to Russia and adopt. . . . They both want to go back. . . . They have mentioned finding their parents. I told them, that's fine you know."(RA10)

Gena told me she appreciated "having a better future and a family that can take care of me" but that "I miss my friends and teachers that I grew up with in the orphanage." What comes through in these reflections is a sense of intense vulnerability on the part of children who felt that they had managed to escape a dreary future or fate, and they had to bear up under the loss of their early connections. Hilda recognized this and was trying to ensure that Gena could act on some of her longings for people she cared about in Russia.

Elsie and Mitch had also nurtured their son's desire to maintain connections with people in Russia. One of their two sons had died when he was 21 and they were uninterested in adopting a newborn or young child. They became involved with a program that hosted children from orphanages in Russia through their church in Atlanta. Although they did not adopt the child they hosted, they eventually adopted Leonid, who had also been part of the program. Leonid was 15. He regularly called the orphanage where he had lived for four years, spoke at length with boys and girls there who were his friends, flew periodically to San Antonio to visit another boy from his orphanage, and also spent time with Natasha, who had been adopted from Russia by another family in Atlanta.

The adoption "stories" or fragments of them that RA adoptive parents shared with their children, sparked their children's interest in their preexisting social ties. The loose ends left behind were a principal reason that Gena and Larisa wanted to go back and to adopt and that Leonid kept in touch with the people from his past. It was a way for them to reestablish and keep alive those links, to create more coherent structure from the fragments that the narratives conveyed and to integrate multiple facets of their developing sense of self. The children undertook much of the work of nurturing these links, though their adoptive parents helped by supporting them emotionally and contributing needed economic resources. Hilda's case was unique in that she took the next step, permanently validating Larisa's connection to Gena by incorporating her into their family as a "sister."

The ways that RA adoptive parents "storied" their children led them to express their confusion, such as trying to figure out exactly what it meant to be a "tummy baby" rather than a "heart baby." Seven-year-old Billy seemed to be trying to understand why "the lady" who gave birth to him did not "need him." His adoptive mother told me:

> One night when we were saying our prayers, my 7-year-old (adopted at five months from Russia) said out of the blue, "We really need to say a prayer and thank the lady whose tummy I was in . . . you know, the one that didn't need me." I almost lost it right there. It broke my heart when he said that. I told him that God has many ways of making families. There are women that are

meant to be mommies and can't have babies, and women that have babies that aren't supposed to be mommies. God knows just who belongs with who and he sorts it all out.[6]

Billy was sorting through what it meant for him to have become "a gift" from God to his adoptive mother and that the lady who had given him birth "didn't need him." His adoptive mother, hearing this, did not try to explain further because she felt she did not have sufficient information about his birth mother, and she found it easiest to let God be the arbiter of the exchange that had taken place.

RA adoptive parents who pursued searches for information about their children's birth parents—a booming cottage industry in Russia—often found what they wanted but then were even more anguished about whether to share it with their children. The details of their children's early years included parents who suffered from alcoholism, drug addiction, and impoverished conditions without social welfare resources. They found out that some parents had left their young children alone at home when they went to work (something that many adoptive parents were appalled by), they discovered siblings and half-siblings (presenting yet another dilemma), and some developed a nagging suspicion that the information they had received might not be entirely accurate. Almost all of them had decided to keep such information to themselves until if and when their children asked for more details about their birth families or wished to undertake a search.

This kind of information was not usually part of the narratives the adoptive parents shared with their children, although they shared it with me. Jean had just begun telling me her daughter Marya's narrative, whom they had adopted at age 6:

We really wanted a little girl, and so we talked about how we went to Russia to find her and that we had gotten this video about this little girl named Marya, and we joke because in the video she had this big, huge dress on with these big, huge ponytails. She wore these tights, and she spent all her time scratching her legs and scratching her neck. And we just knew from the minute we saw this video that she was the one for us 'cause she was just who she was. (RA12)

She suddenly halted her narrative and told me how difficult things were for Marya despite her having "assimilated real well":

She has some, like, not-great memories of something her mom—she says her mom made her do all the cleaning, and her mom hit her. . . . Last summer, she was in my closet hitting a pillow 'cause she was angry with her birth mother. . . . I told her about how my father was never around in my life, and how there's some point where you just sort of forgive them. They did the best they could. And I just said, "You know, your mother did the best she could. She took care of you as long as she could. She loved you enough to bring you to the orphanage, to make sure you were well taken care of," and that kind of thing. So I think she goes between being mad at her, but she doesn't carry around [her early memories of her birth mother] like she was carrying the weight [of the world] on her shoulders. (RA12)

Some RA adoptive parents had trouble comprehending the enormous gap in economic standing and resources between their children's birth families and their own upper-middle-class background. Others were aware of the systemic economic and political conditions that structured people's lives in Eastern Europe, which contributed to the institutional practices in bleak state-run orphanages, but nevertheless tended to pass moral judgment on those conditions.

The silences within narratives constructed by RA adoptive parents about the cultural, economic, and political conditions in which birth families raised their children in Russia had repercussions for RA adoptees, as Marilyn Freundlich (2000: 116–17) attests to: "There are parents who seek to adopt from Russia or Eastern Europe in order to have a 'Caucasian child without a birth parent' and to obviate the need to acknowledge the cultural or national heritage of their adopted child . . . This view of international adoption as a 'simpler' way to adopt is fraught with difficulties for the child and the adoptive family."

In general, if their children looked different ("non-Caucasian"), RA adoptive parents thought they should make more effort to create a diverse cultural environment for them. Almost none of them participated in cultural events after they returned from Russia, although more parents joined organizations such as FRUA as a support network, particularly if they had special-needs children. Otherwise, they felt they did not need to do anything.

A minority, like Helen and Josh, were unusual in the efforts they made to incorporate cultural aspects of Russia into their narratives. Helen was an anthropologist, and she and Josh celebrated exoticism. By calling attention to the unique aspects of their adoption, Helen's approach hinted at a kind of essentialist orientalism that has been critiqued by Edward Said (1978). At the same time, though, they were trying to challenge the idea that adoption lay outside what was socially acceptable, something they could have easily decided not to do because of the ability of many children adopted from Russia to pass. They were also grappling with their son Emil's sense of loss and his awareness of how much they did not know, counterpoised to their celebration of adoption.

> Helen: Right from the beginning, we viewed adoption as something to be celebrated, not something not to talk about. . . . He realizes at a fairly deep level that it's an important part of his identity. We played up the publicity value of adopting a child from a different place in the sense that we wanted to make a symbolic statement that this was a very exciting thing for us to do and for people in general to do, and that we were going to do what we could to celebrate that we had this child from a different place. First, the adoption announcement was a map of the Black Sea with Krasnidar highlighted, and on it, in Russian, were the words, "Emil (Russian middle name) (Last name), born such and such a date and adopted such and such a date," and you open it up and there's a map of M. (U.S. State) and T. (U.S. city) highlighted, and you know, the same thing in English. We took the kids' pictures that year for Christmas. We brought back a vest for Joseph [Helen's stepson] and a cute little Russian girl's outfit for Anna [their biological child] complete with head-dress and for Emil, we had a bright red shirt that was trimmed in the Russian style. The picture made its way into the newspaper, and again, it had a lot of value because it was unusual among people that we knew to adopt from Russia. And for a lot of people, to adopt, period.

I pressed further to find out what Helen and Josh had actually told Emil and what he wanted to know. Helen told me:

> He wants to know about his mother and, unfortunately, we don't know much other than her name; and we can sort of calculate how old she is and we talk about how, if at some point, after he reaches 18, he would like to try to see if he could reach her and meet her, then we will support him in that, but there are no guarantees and that we don't know what her life is like now. . . . So that's how we explain it and, you know, we get the same question again, and do the same whole thing all over again. A lot of tears. A tremendous feeling of abandonment which he can't articulate, but we try to say things like, "You're here with us now. We don't know why your mother, your birth mother, chose to give you up for adoption, but chances are she did it because she loved you and wanted you to have a better life. . . . So those kinds of things are hard for anybody to hear, least of, especially, a child. We just try to hug him and let him

know that we love him. And you know, there have been a few times I've been told that I'm not his mother and [she laughs], you know, we get over that. He's certainly aware that there is a difference, but at another level, we have a kind of joke. I used to have a perm and Emil has very curly hair and the strangest thing is that we look alike, and when I came back on the plane from Russia with this baby, at least four people on the plane asked me. They knew we were ... there were a bunch of adopted kids, but they looked at us and they just thought, we were the spitting image, so when we got home after, we'd meet people that didn't know us and they would say, "Oh My Gosh," and they didn't even know he was adopted, and they would say, "Wow, you two really look alike," or "Your son looks just like you." And sometimes to be flip, I would say, "Well, Um. I've got a perm and Emil's adopted." And they didn't know what to do with that! (RA9)

Helen's narrative more resembled those of CA adoptive parents though she was not interested in "Russifying" Emil through language training or other cultural activities. She was proud of Emil's birthplace; she openly discussed his birth relatives in Russia; and, at the time she and Josh adopted Emil, she saw herself as a kind of "poster child" for a new practice—transnational adoption. She also publicly highlighted the paradox—almost making a joke out of it— that physical resemblance between her and Emil and family-making through adoption in America could go together.

Personal storytelling acquired more meaning for all children when they included anecdotes, which created a sense of shared temporal dimension between the past in which the child was placed, and the adoptive parents. They turned into "conversational stories [that] were about and had to do with the people who were telling them and hearing them" (Miller et al. 1990: 293). It did not so much matter if these were "good" or "bad" or involved mishaps, but rather that they became a kind of witnessing and corporeal emplacement for the child. For example, Grace talked about how Sonia cried when she first saw Grace and her husband and took a long time to warm up to them; Jarett [the son they adopted] was "doing kissy-kisses" and therefore "maybe trying to tell us something" (RA7); adoptive mother Holly explained that Alisa "liked to hear little stories about her adoption," such as "You were always flapping your arms up and down" (RA11), and Jean's daughter Marya had "big, huge ponytails, wore tights, and spent all her time scratching her legs and scratching her neck" (RA12). Out of context, these might seem insignificant details but the children savored them as they actively listened to their narratives.

To reprise, the major "broken links" in RA adoptive parents' adoption narratives were that they rarely discussed adoption or integrated it elaborately through storytelling or ritual. Reinscribing more traditional views of adoption and of family in America, their mention of Russia and Russian cultural heritage was subdued.

An important shift became apparent, however, when RA adoptive parents encountered their children's special needs. These were sobering and daunting, the consequence, at least in part, of their having chosen to adopt from Russia, where children were most likely to be white and look like them. Their children's special needs made them more conspicuous as a family, and led them to become more open about sharing that their family had been formed through adoption. Finally, in their narratives, most RA adoptive parents conveyed overtly or more covertly key tropes of rescue and negative images of the conditions from which they had extricated their children. Their children's comments and reactions to the narratives they listened to varied. A few were proud of their narratives; some were making their way into the future without a story to tell; others carried with them secrets they could not easily share; and still others expressed a degree of vulnerability, confusion, anger, shame, and longing, coupled with a relief that they were "now" safe.

Private Stories and Public Faces: Being Black in White

The narratives of AA adoptive parents dwelled on why their child's birth mother (a few included the birth father or other relatives) was unable to care for them; the idea of "growing" babies; and the conclusion that "you have to share that mom title, I guess" (AA4). One AA adoptive parent went so far as to describe the relationship with her daughter's birth family as an example of "co-parenting." AA adoptive parents found it challenging to arrive at appropriate classificatory terms and labels for their complex family formations, which included birth parents, birth stepparents, foster parents, and their respective adopted and biological children and grandparents.

Dolly's narrative for her son, Pearson, emphasized his birth mother's single status when she and her husband adopted him as an infant, but also acknowledged that he had three half-brothers. The social construction of race through kinship ties and practices figures prominently in Dolly's narrative and in Pearson's reactions to it. Pearson, at age 9, imagined his birth mother as white because his adoptive mother is; he articulated, in an incipient way, a positive view of biculturalism, and he appeared to have embraced the value his adoptive parents placed on a family that begins with a married man and woman, which Dolly conveyed in her narrative.

> I explained that his birth mother and birth family were down in Missis-
> sippi, and we knew at that time . . . that you have three half-brothers down
> there—and they're older than you—and your birth mother. And he told me
> when he was very, very small, "Mom, whenever I think about my birth mother,
> I picture a white lady because my mom is white." . . . I said, "No, she's got beau-
> tiful brown skin just like you," . . . we didn't have any pictures to look at, which
> makes it hard. Every time I talk to Annabelle [Pearson's birth mother], I tell
> her, "I need you to send us a picture." So then he can look at the picture and
> say, "Well I have this feature or that feature that looks like my birth mother and
> my older brother." We didn't go into the circumstances of his father. . . . He was
> too little for that, but just that she had a very hard decision and that she cried
> a lot and she missed him [Pearson] a lot and . . . she had told the worker there
> were a couple of different placements that were offered to her. Another one
> was a single woman, and I think I may even know who that woman is; but she
> chose my husband and me because we had been in a stable marriage for a long
> time and she really wanted Pearson to have a mom and a dad. At that time she
> was not married, so we said, "You know your birth mother Annabelle wanted
> you to have a mom and a dad and that was part of her decision to place you
> with us." Now that he's old enough, I've explained that Langston [his birth
> father] is married to some other lady, and he's like, "Well that's not very nice."
> And he's more focused on his birth mother than on the birth father. In fact, he
> talks more about Annabelle's husband, you know the man whom she married,
> who is her two younger sons' father, than about his birth father. He's more
> interested in David [Annabelle's husband] because David is part of that family
> that his birth mother is in, and his other sons. (AA17)

Pearson told me himself, "I don't have a really high opinion of my birth father." He had little contact with his birth family and found the hardest thing about being adopted "never getting to see my birth family" and the best thing "getting to have a point of view of kind of being like a white person and also being like a black person." He spoke with Annabelle from time to time, and she had reiter-ated to Pearson, "You can call me any time, and if you have a question you can call me and ask me a question." Dolly concluded, "he knows there's somebody else down there that loves him and that there's brothers down there, and I think it gives him an added sense of security to know that they're there, and then if he's mad at me he can always say he has a spare mother down in Mississippi."

Pearson was open about his adoption. He had participated in a local radio program on transracial adoption and a local television station had interviewed him at his family's house.

When I asked Clare if she shared any kind of narrative with her children Melea and Chaz about their adoptions and life histories, she said:

> I think about that constantly, actually. Melea knows her story probably better than some people know [theirs]. She knows she was adopted. She's been to The Cradle [adoption agency]. She knows where that's at. She knows she has a birth mother. She doesn't know she has three other birth siblings. . . . We kinda told her that in passing, but that has definitely not registered. And Chaz is only two, but he knows his mom, and he calls her Mommy Latisha. And actually he sees her regularly, about every two, three weeks. He just kinda goes with the flow as far as two mommies. (AA13)

AA adoptive parents negotiated tensions in their everyday lives and in their narratives because many of them had adopted more than one African American child whose early histories diverged in accessibility and detail. AA children quickly began to compare and contrast their narratives, acutely aware of differences in their backgrounds and that they had greater or lesser amounts of information than other AA adoptees. Their adoptive parents had to figure out how to mediate these interactions. Although doing so was hard for them, it meant that the children could jointly engage and reflect on their stories.

Denise had adopted Rachelle and Mindy, both as infants, from two different birth families. They were eighteen months apart in age. For Rachelle, Denise explained, "We tell the story of how . . . here was a nice lady named Charma who had a baby growing in her belly, and she knew that she was taking care of the baby until . . . she was ready to meet her mom and dad; and we talk about that and when we met each other. We always tell it with humor . . . to lighten it just a little bit" (AA16).

Mindy's story was more complicated, creating tensions between Rachelle and Mindy. Rachelle's mother, Charma, had decided she did not want to have anything to do with Rachelle until she was 18, whereas Mindy's birth relatives wanted to be involved in her life. At the same time, Mindy's adoption narrative excluded the horrific reasons she had been removed from her birth family, but Mindy regularly visited some of her birth relatives. Rachelle always wanted to hear about Mindy's birth family, but Mindy did not want Denise to tell her story: "It's interesting because Rachelle'll say, 'Okay, now tell me Mindy's story,' and I'll say, 'Well, we need to ask Mindy first 'cause that's hers, you know?'

And [then we'd ask], 'Mindy, you wanna hear it?' 'Nope.' I feel kinda bad for her. We always said we thought it would be hard for Rachelle not knowing. . . . Rachelle's birth mom said, 'Find me at 18.' But she never left a letter, never left a picture, nothing. Mindy's birth mother signed the papers, saying, 'I don't want you looking for me,' but then decided she wanted open contact."

Mindy's case was a difficult one, and Denise and Noel knew they were in uncharted waters as they tried to figure out how to balance Mindy's desire for openness with her need for security and safety. Mindy's birth mother, Kanika, had been raped by a family member when she was 12, and her birth father was in jail. Yet Kanika, along with other birth relatives—grandparents, in-laws, and Mindy's stepfather—desired contact with Mindy. Denise explained:

> We met Mindy's birth relatives at Mindy's first birthday. . . . We met on her second, and then—they call and we send pictures and things like that, but then they missed [her birthday]. . . . Mindy . . . has a difficult time when she sees them . . . so recently . . . we've made the decision that . . . they need to really decide what they wanna do. She's a very smart child, and they need to decide— either you're in or you're out. . . . I think it's almost easier for Rachelle because it's kind of abstract. She grew in somebody else's stomach. . . . But for Mindy, she has a visual, and she actually gets scared if she sees anybody who looks like her birth mother. And she started going through separation anxiety with me. . . . So at this point where the relationship's gonna go, I don't know. . . . Rachelle's a little young still, I mean but she kinda processes that Mindy has a birth mother and hers is unknown . . . . It's an interesting concept that's going on now in our house. . . . We talk about Charma and Kanika all the time. And as a matter of fact, I just started a book drive in Charma's name, and so we've been talkin' a lot more about her. And when we've gone and met Kanika a few times, Rachelle says, "Can we, can we meet Charma?" And it's a little heartbreaking, but I say to her—and here, I should preface this, I am um, estranged from my parents, so I don't see my parents unfortunately. And um, I think it's interesting how your life experience might help ya, you know, down the line with your kids. We simply say, "You know, sometimes you getta meet, you know, the person whose belly you came out of and sometimes you don't," and we tell her, "Hopefully if you wanna meet her one day, you'll be able to." So, that is a little difficult, but my kids have said some things that I, I think kids are way wiser than we think they are. (AA16)

While Denise and Noel could not share everything with Rachelle and Mindy about the conditions of their respective adoptions, they tried to be open; they recognized that their children felt sorrow, loss, fear, and anger; and they were trying to become more adept at drawing and maintaining boundaries. As they created stories together and practices to accompany them, Denise drew heavily on her own life history, and that too became a bond between her and Rachelle.

As dramatic as these cases were, they were not uncommon. Brandy and Roy had adopted a sibling group, and the narrative she decided to share with them was also bleakly honest:

> Our current narrative is pretty much that the birth mom for the older three tried to be a good mom, but because she has mild mental retardation it was very hard for her to learn how to be a mom, and often she would forget to feed the babies or change the diapers, and sometimes she would forget that babies shouldn't be left alone and she would leave . . . and you can't do that to babies. . . . She tried really hard to learn but she just couldn't because she had brain damage from her birth mom, who drank a lot of alcohol when she was pregnant, and she had no one to turn to 'cause her birth mom had died and she had no brothers and sisters and no grandmas and grandpas and there was nobody to help her. And after a year the caseworkers decided it was too dangerous for the babies to stay in the house . . . so they were moved to a house down the street from her so that she could still see them every day.. . . . They spent another year working on how to be a good mom and she still couldn't get it, so the caseworker decided that these babies needed to be adopted by somebody who knew how to take care of babies, and their birth mom agreed that she wanted her kids to grow up safe and healthy and with somebody who knew how to be a mom. And, we haven't gotten into the birth father's role yet. (AA10)

One boy I interviewed, Jerrick, age 12, was born in Chicago and still lived near his birthplace. Once or twice a year he would get together with members of his birth family. He was distressed that his birth dad was in jail and told me that he was "happy, sad, and mad" about being adopted. When I asked him what he knew about the people or place from which he was adopted, he described both as "bad and poor" (AA6).

One conclusion AA children drew from their life circumstances in conjunction with their narratives was that they were situated in an awkward position in the midst of white privilege, in contrast to the condition, in most instances, of their birth relatives. As they grew older, this awkward positioning became increasingly problematic for them to sustain. AA adoptive parents were aware that the narratives they created for their children were flexible and that what they would deliberately include and exclude would change over time. This was because of the ongoing interactions and possibilities of interaction with birth family members, and the pressing need for adoptive parents to prepare their children to navigate American racial waters. CA adoptive parents, in contrast, were only just beginning to realize that their children, too, would be swimming in rough waters.

Unlike a generation ago, AA adoptive parents knew that even as they could not directly experience what their children did, being black in America *and* white and black in their families, they needed to figure out ways to approximate knowing and acting on how that burden felt for their children in a fashion that went beyond white "goodwill" (Rush 2000: 37). Some did this in the ways they constructed their narratives as well as in their everyday behavior. They took more steps across class, kin, and racial boundaries than did CA and RA adoptive parents.

The early years of Agnes and Drew's two adopted children, Aamina and Joshua, with their birth families, included abuse, jail, multiple partners, and little knowledge in Joshua's case about his birth father. After telling me her adoption narrative, Agnes went on to describe the challenges their family faced, focusing on issues of race:

> One of the things that I try to remind myself pretty regular is that I only think about race when I think the kids are having some kinda problem or when they're dealing with somebody and I think somebody's dealing with them that has to do with race; but the kids, they deal with race with every interaction because they bring it with 'em; and I would never have been aware of that if we didn't have kids of another race. I never would've realized that every time I have an interaction with an African American person, they're thinking that race is an issue, even if I'm not. They can't walk away and pretend that that interaction didn't have anything to do with race, even if it didn't, because it does for them. So I think it just has really broadened who I am as a person and how I look at the whole world. In a lotta ways, I would not have been able to have that perspective if I hadn't had a baby in my arms that was a different color. (AA19)

For Agnes, "race as an issue" was not about color but about her realization that it was impossible for her to maintain a multiculturalist position with respect to race.[7] Pointing out that while there were more similarities than differences among all families—e.g., disabilities, injuries, learning issues—for Agnes, there was nevertheless a whole list of things that they had faced as an AA adoptive family—being the white mother of a six-foot tall African American boy who happened to be her son; black kids taunting her daughter that white parents were not her "real" parents at school; people coming to the door and doing a double-take because neither parent was black. She concluded, "That's a problem that you have, you know, with people feeling that somehow your family is artificial, and I think Joshua feels that race is a big issue for him; and he's right. He's a black male, and race is a big issue for them." (AA 19)

Amber, who had experienced transformations similar to Agnes's as the mother of African American children, had taken her awareness one step further. Moving away from either a simple anti-racist or feminist position, as a single mother she had decided to dedicate her energy to working with underprivileged kids in areas of education, protection from domestic abuse, housing, and creativity (see Crenshaw 1991: 1256). She explained,

> I'm committed to teaching in the inner-city schools . . . which people are just shocked and appalled at. And I do believe that my mentoring of these girls, even if it's changing [only] three lives, it's a start, and it's something you can do and make a real difference in someone's life. I don't think it's about black people; it's about poor people and poor girls who happen to be mostly black in Chicago. I mean, I've signed on with all these programs like the literacy program, and then I did a photo project with a homeless shelter, and I'm all about the disenfranchised who happen to be black. (AA5)

Discussion

What can we learn from these narratives? What assumptions are embedded in them? What do they exclude? On what grounds do they offer alternative discourse and models of family formation and ties? While some of the distinctions among the adoption narratives I have described above are sharp, others are blurry. The blurring is the product of the belief among Americans that in understanding one's place in the world and one's connections to others, biology still matters. This is apparent in all of the narratives, even when adoptive parents wanted to make it not matter and creatively tried to arrive at new ways of explaining their ties to their children.

It is intriguing to think about how children understood the contrast that adoptive mothers made between "tummy babies" (brought into family membership through labor pains, pregnancy, and giving birth physically) and "heart babies" (brought into family membership through the primacy of affect, culturally defined as love, a nonbiological process of affiliation that gave birth to a family. Heart babies became family members through sustained efforts by adoptive parents and birth parents, reflected in reams of paperwork, years of waiting, extensive travel, big expenses, broken hearts, chaotic lives, poverty, and government policies. Similarities among the narratives are also apparent: inequalities between sending and receiving families and regions undergird all of them.

In contrast to the narratives of CA and RA adoptive parents, AA adoptive families dealt with complex and multiple family histories and connections. Children eventually challenged the initial efforts of adoptive parents to connect broken links through the narratives they constructed. The stuff of adoption narratives did not substitute for loss but nevertheless gave children something to pin their curiosity, hopes, dreams, and sometimes their grief on.

The more noticeable shake-ups in cultural assumptions about family-making occurred when adoptees embarked on their own searches for knowledge, personhood, and belonging. The impetus for these searches began in conjunction with the narratives adoptive parents shared with them. Peggy Miller described "personal storytelling" as a resource for younger children "to the extent that the growing child resists, accedes to, seizes upon, or in some way, makes use of the self-relevant messages embodied" in the stories (Miller et al. 1990: 294). As adoptees searched, they involved their adoptive and birth families; they struggled with legal obstacles; they spent hours making sense of document trails or the lack thereof; they collaborated increasingly with other adoptees; and for many of them, the revisions they made to their narratives were not so much a gradual process as they were a momentous upheaval.

7 Doing School
Family Trees and Playground Banter

The effects of power are frequently intangible, inscribed on the body. They organize and distinguish permissible and transgressive behavior, and stratify people according to how they talk, dress, or look, for example. Michel Foucault has written about how qualities such as madness (2006), sexuality (1978, 1985, 1986), and citizenship are defined through techniques of what he calls "governmentality" (1970, 1991), arguing that even as these qualities and how they are socially viewed may be redefined, their meanings and significance are elaborated, reinforced, and, literally, impressed upon the body. He calls this process "biopower," showing that institutions such as schools, hospitals, and court systems do not solely exert power hierarchically or through laws and regulations, but even more assiduously by producing knowledge and discourses that are positively internalized by individuals and then actively encourage certain kinds of social behavior. For Foucault, these shifting dynamics, which he documents historically, are efficient mechanisms of social control. In this chapter, we look at how school assignments, playground interactions, and policies to promote tolerance conveyed knowledge and discourse about family-making.

Schools are one of the most powerful influences on children's identity formation in general, and certainly on children who are adopted. The decision about where to send their children to school confronted parents very quickly after they adopted their children. AA parents struggled the most with school choice. Most adoptive parents preferred to send their children to public schools, which they felt were more diverse, and if their child had special learning needs, the public schools could provide them at a lower cost. The exception to this line of reasoning, ironically, was in dense urban areas, such as Chicago and the District of Columbia. Parents wanted to send their children to public school, especially those who had adopted AA children, but the conditions in the schools were not optimal. They lacked a strong tax base, which led to the declining quality of the school and a high student-to-teacher ratio, they often lacked diversity, and there were problems with daily violence. Many adoptive parents of AA children complained about the practice of tracking, which they felt was based on criteria such as race, rather than their children's capabilities.

Becky had been eager to send her son, Kadema, to a public school because she thought he would benefit from its diversity. Although he remained in public elementary school, she remarked: "There's a pattern of behavior . . . who gets recognized, who gets kudos, and who doesn't. . . . That is very clear, and the darker the hue . . ." (AA6).

Betsy and Allen initially sent Maia to a Washington, D.C., public school, but the conditions were horrendous, and they switched her to a private school. They had enough money to send her to a private school, but parents who didn't have that choice had to decide whether to do battle in the schools; and some of them did. They confronted school administrators who had automatically assumed that their children should be put in special education and teachers who ignored bullying and name-calling; and they complained about class assignments that assumed all families were connected biologically.

Brandy tried to deal with many problems in the public schools, and she also decided to keep her kids in them:

> The public school, it's close and convenient, and I really looked at the diversity of the student body. . . . I was raised in public school. My dad was a teacher in a public school. So I have a sort of personal family bias towards public school. But when I talked to a co-worker and now close friend who's African American, W., he says, "Go, get the best education there is!" And he went to private schools, and certainly they are far more diverse then they were at the time when he was growing up. . . . But he said the big difference was [for African American children at that time], "You got to go home to your black parents." My kids will come home to me. And I want them to be in an environment where there is a lot more diversity. The middle school that my eldest son is now going to is more diverse in the teaching and the administration. I'm happy with that aspect because it makes a difference in terms of the adult color. . . . It's something like 13 percent African American . . . and I get to volunteer at the school. (AA6)

It was far easier for parents to talk about social commitment to racial diversity than to risk pursuing it, as Brandy had done, in light of the declining quality of the schools and the deleterious consequences when one's children became the target of racial prejudice and stereotyping.

Family Trees

Almost every elementary school includes projects in the early grades that require children to create their autobiographical timeline and family tree. Sometimes teachers approached this with sensitivity. More frequently, it remained a pro forma part of the curriculum. Cindy, a CA adoptive mother, wrote to an online adoption discussion group asking for advice about how to handle her third grader's assignment to create a timeline with her parents:

> We are to create a lifeline [timeline] with pictures or drawings. When completed, this lifeline will be displayed in the school's central area. The examples given for this lifeline are: I was born in *x* hospital weighing *x.x* pounds and *xxx* height. . . . I first smiled at *xxxx* months, I walked at *xxxx* yrs. old, then go through current age followed by: In 2020 I will be *x* old and *xxxx* will be happening in my life. In 2030, *xxxx*. In 2040, xxxx. My daughter has always been very verbal about her adoption history, she shares when she wants to, and she says some things are private. . . . We've had family tree type projects which we have modified to include birth, foster, adoptive parents and sometimes just went with family. . . . My daughter doesn't want any mention of China or her life before joining our family on the lifeline. She doesn't want mention of . . . when I joined my family. . . . She says, "That's private. It shouldn't be hanging on the school wall."[1]

This assignment was clearly designed for intact families formed through biological reproduction. Cindy's daughter's reaction to it projected her desire for privacy but also an internalization of negative sentiments about being from China. Participants in the discussion group suggested ways to modify the assignment, and they also contributed their own stories about timeline assignments. One recommended building a lifeline around particular themes as a way of supporting children in following whatever path they chose. Another explained that her son had wanted to post that he was adopted because his birth parents could not afford to raise him. His adoptive mother was uncomfortable with his decision but thought it important to let him make his own choice about how to explain his lifeline. Several parents suggested that the teacher should be contacted about the assignment, yet not a single participant in the discussion recommended asking teachers or administrators to permanently alter the discourse and structure of the assignment as part of the established curriculum. Parents and children alike, in addition to struggling with the assumption that a "lifeline" would take a linear and straightforward form, also wrestled with their own ideas about what should be private and public knowledge. The conspicuousness of transracial families and the attention that devolved altogether too frequently on the children, as well as the difficulty many children had in understanding adoption, contributed to their desire to keep these matters private.

Many transnationally adopted children did not have information about their families of origin or photographs of themselves as infants. African American children who had been adopted had complex families they could not explain with the vocabulary accessible to them. New referential kinship terms were emerging, some of which they came up with themselves to express their complex family ties, but within the context of a school assignment, children had to be willing to take on the burden of explaining these unfamiliar terms and, in the course of doing so, they might also be faced with revealing more than they wanted to.

> I remember my 12-year-old had to put together a family tree, and you've never known a third-grader more disgusted about it because she had brothers and sisters from her father who she was close to, but they had another mother. I'm divorced. My son's father had two other little boys. I happen to be very close with my son's stepmother; we're very good friends. So I've known her little boys since they were babies. Elsie May has grown up with these little boys who aren't really her brothers. They're her brother's brothers. Does that make sense? How does she identify this woman Susan that she's known her whole life and is very close to? She's not really an aunt if you want to get down to the specifics. So her family tree looks like something. There are lots of bushes and interesting outgrowths. (CA14)

Denise expressed similar frustrations:

> I have such big issues about this . . . because over the years my older children as well always included their brothers and sisters. They would come home from school and they would say, "This friend said to me that that's not really who they are. They must be steps or they must be half." And my kids decided "brothers" and "sisters" was good enough, and the rest of it was really none of anyone's business. I think with them internally they understand that family is what they choose in a lot of respects. . . . It's not a project you can just eliminate. I understand the importance of it. I just think it should be presented in

more of a social context and not as a science thing, a biology thing. Not every kid has access to all of that. Not every kid knows really who their parents are. They go back so many generations, it's not fair to expect them to understand the concepts of all that. But family to them is the people that are in their lives and what they make. That's what they understand. (AA 17)

Denise thought lifeline assignments should be structured to call attention to the living practices that went into family-making rather than to biological and genetic connections alone. She was also working with her children to teach them how to contest their peers when they insisted they use particular kin terms, such as "stepbrother" or "half-sister" instead of "brother" and "sister" to characterize ties they maintained with siblings in their birth families with different parents. The lack of distinctions drawn between kinds of siblings was also a product of the more flexible kin-care among African American families that existed.

Becky, as well, was adamant about advocating for her African American sons when they had these kinds of assignments. She explained to me:

Part of it is being ready to be, or if you are not ready, becoming open to, when your kid comes home and says, "Who am I gonna put pictures of? How should I describe my family?" And for Jerrick, he's consistently said, "I have nine brothers and sisters." And then Kadema was adding, "Because I have ten brothers!" And that's an every-year occurrence. In a middle school, you have six different classes, so it comes up a lot.

One day Jerrick said, "I've got a timeline and I have to start with my birth, and I have to put in a bunch of things and I don't want to put foster care. I know that some people will, but I don't want to put it. . . . " So we were able to say in the car, "How can we talk about this? Let's think of six important things. When you got your capoeira cord,[2] when you became a junior ranger, when you were a coach for Brothers YMCA basketball team. Here are milestones that don't reveal other things. . . . " One day, my older son was in high school biology and the teacher brought up genetics—your earlobes, your tongue twist, and different physical traits, and he [the teacher] said, "by the way, if you're adopted, if you are in an adopted family, deal with it." And that gave me a preview of what was to come. . . . We figure out what you don't have to reveal, what you do want to reveal. It's different because we know Jerrick's birthday. A lot of kids we know who were internationally adopted don't know anything. And so just by doing that, teachers stir it up. Now I have resources. When I went in to the assistant principal, I said, "Hey, here's a copy of *Adoption in the*

Schools.[3] Please add it to your library. Have it as a resource and then I'll follow up with you and the teachers when things come up." (AA6)

Becky's solution to the timeline assignment was to transform it into an "event history"—taking key milestones or events of significance to her children as the basis for building their unique timelines; to allow them to have control over how to share their knowledge; and to take action as an adult with some authority by attempting to educate school personnel.

Adoptive parents also told of teachers who initially assigned students who were adopted or fostered a timeline project that differed from what all the other students were doing. After pressure from parents, one teacher changed her mind and assigned a project to the entire class that entailed looking at the genetic history of one breed of dogs and how that breed was developed. Astonishingly, three years later at the same school in the same grade, the same teacher made the children do the traditional timeline assignment!

Agnes and Drew's first child was African American; their second, Brittany, was Chinese. When faced with a timeline assignment, Brittany protested that she could not do it because she did not have her "biological heritage." Her solution was to focus on Agnes as the center of her lifeline, leaving out her own existence prior to adoption. Agnes was irate, nevertheless. She "wished the teachers, as a team, would've learned that you need to change the assignment. I'm sure Brittany is not the only kid . . . There's lots of examples of genetic things that don't have to be about you and your parents" (CA19).

Gina, remembering her first- and second-grade experiences, told me with exasperation, "It was always family, family. Just the simple exercise of drawing a picture of your family. I felt I was not able to be real about it. Labeling them my mother, father, sister, brother. . . . It was a lie" (AA10). Timeline assignments were also linked to assumptions about the geographic relationship between nationality and birthplace that seem shockingly dated. One child was given a map of the United States and told to mark where she had been born. Instead, she turned it over, drew a map of China, and marked where she was from. Maia, who was African American, was asked to write an essay on "Where I Come From" and, in her mother's words,

> She did a very bizarre poster. She had a picture of the Statue of Liberty. I mean, you could not tell what any of this stuff was. She had to explain it. It was because I'm from New York. And then there was a picture of the Washington Monument, which is obvious—she's from Washington [though she was originally born in Texas]. Then there were Christmas carolers and a Star of David.

When I saw the Star of David next to the carolers, I could understand what it was, but just seeing the carolers, I couldn't. Then there was this St. Paul's Church, which was not the St. Paul's Church where she'd been fostered, but that was close enough, and she explained it. Then there was a picture of a bog, and that was Scotland [where her adoptive father is from] and then there was a picture of Manhattan, and then there was a big map of Africa. (AA8)

Maia completely ruptured the assumption of correlation between birthplace and family configuration and how she was situated in it. Instead, with great ingenuity, she created a collage of different places that, for her, represented her origins and reflected her identity-in-the making.

The children in adoptive families were creative and brave in contesting existing understandings about American families, reinforced by the comportment of school personnel and curricular expectations. Many of them felt they had no choice but to lie, not do assignments, or come up with other ways to do them, sometimes with the help of their adoptive parents. Their conceptualization of family trees and timelines was nonlinear. Their own processes of identity formation served as raw representational materials for them and their peers to begin to reflect on taken-for-granted ideas about family configurations.

For the families I interviewed, the failure of public and private schools to recognize how much family-making had changed—because of divorce, migration, and blended families of all types—was remarkable. Stasis was apparent in classroom assignments, the attitudes of administrators, and in documents. Helen recalled a written questionnaire that the school had sent out that "made no allowances for either adoptive children or stepchildren." She told me, "Of course, since I have one of each, it struck me immediately that the survey needed to be formulated to be inclusive, not exclusive, and I pointed that out" (RA9).

Because the schools had changed little over a long period of time, adoptive parents had to fight to make them realize that they needed to revise their assumptions about family-making that reinscribed notions of the ideal American family. When they pointed out the problematic practices, the schools made it clear that they expected the children themselves or their parents to develop coping mechanisms. Few teachers were aware of the impact of classroom assignments on their students. Some had the skills and vocabulary to help children learn that there were many ways to form families; but teachers and children primarily learned about race, gender, and family formation from adoptive parent volunteers who offered to do workshops or teach a class on the topic. The group Concerned Persons for Adoption prepared a list of alternatives to the usual projects schools assigned to children about their autobiographies, life histories, and cultural celebrations. The list of alternatives provides insight into how schools inadvertently and frequently promote narrowly normative ideas about family configurations that are often correlated with assumptions about class and race.[4]

One adoptive father I spoke to was a journalist. He had been responsible for publishing the first *Teacher's Guide to Adoption* and also co-authored the widely used *Journalist's Guide to Adoption*. Children and parents equated "private" as another way of distinguishing particular lifelines as normative and others as "different" and difficult to "fit" into. Some adoptive parents had begun actively promoting four ways they and their children could respond when they were faced with prying questions. They were called W.I.S.E. Up! (Walk Away; It's Private; Share Something; and Educate Them), developed by the Center for Adoption Support and Education, Inc. (2010) These responses were important ways to protect one's family and children. The parents made it clear that incorporation and birth are possible starting points of a timeline. Such defensive practices would have been unnecessary if the American cultural norm had been that family trees are messy and that children and parents do not necessarily resemble each other, whether adopted or not.

It was hard enough for children in the classroom, but the playgrounds were an even bigger battleground.

Recess

Informally, on the playgrounds and in the hallways, children begin to notice that some children look like their parents and others do not. At a young age, most children do not have the ability to articulate or understand the concept of adoption as one way of forming a family. However, they do have an empirically grounded sense of the social dynamics of belonging. That sense emerges from their interactions with others and bears directly on their sense of self (Mead 1967; Van Ausdale and Feagin 2001; Vygotsky 2004).[5]

How Zelda, Nora's young child, and some of her friends were processing same-sex couples and single parents who had adopted is an excellent example of the concrete logic with respect to sexual orientation and family formation that children employ in trying to make sense of differences. Nora told me:

> The funny thing is, many of Zelda's very good friends have single moms. . . .
> One of her best little friends from preschool has two moms. . . . Her other good
> friend, Josephine, who was adopted from China, has two moms. . . . My friend

Marilyn is also a single mom. So our daughters independently asked us the same question, "How come she has two moms and I don't?" It's almost as if my daughter was somehow thinking that having two mommies is more socially acceptable than having a mom and a dad. . . . Zelda has a little boy in her class, Charles, who has two moms, and I'll tell you a funny story of how Zelda grows and thinks. Last year, we were talking about Charles, and I said, Oh, yeah, I was talking to Trina, one of the moms. Zelda asked, "Who's Trina?" I said, "Trina is Charles's mom." She looked at me, she was dead serious, "No, Myrna is his mom!" I said, "No, Zelda, remember Charles has two moms, Trina and Myrna. She looked at me and said, "Charles is a boy. He can't have two moms. He has to have two dads." (CA11)

As much as these dynamics of belonging were about what constitutes a family, far more frequently they were about looking alike or different in a very basic way. Children who looked different were frequently teased mercilessly, a practice that grew more relentless as they approached high school. This was true whether or not they were adopted. Many parents whose "cute" kids received oohs and aahs when they were little were unprepared for the reality of the school playground or, later, the cafeteria. They did not know how to prepare their children. When their children approached adolescence, they were often unaware of what their child was experiencing in school, and the boundaries of public and private that the children erected could not easily be crossed by parents.

Adoptive parents gave many examples of teasing related to family formation and race. Winnie reported that one of her daughter's classmates told her, "Your parents threw you in the trash can. That's what they do in China" (CA29). Children, in general, faced taunts about their hair texture (if they were African American), their skin color, and their eyes (Chinese American), queries about who their "real mom" is, and general name-calling about being adopted.

Shannon was adopted from China, and her two older sisters were Fred and Lisa's biological daughters. They had a fierce loyalty to each other as siblings and felt responsible when Shannon was teased in racial terms at school:

They get very defensive. My oldest, Candice, is looking for a fight. Some kid said something about Chinks. Candice is a big strong girl with a big mouth to match. She got right in his face, spoiling for a fight . . . The middle one is more fearful. There was a story about kids who went up to a Chinese girl and started slanting their eyes, and her question was, "What are we going to do if they do that to Shannon?" Then Candice said, "Well, I'm going into the school, and I don't care how young they are, I'm going to smack them." (CA6)

Candice went out of her way to protect Shannon from racist teasing, but, of course, this kind of behavior more often than not went completely unnoticed, or was punished. Dolly described what happened to her son at school:

> We sent Pearson to a Lutheran school that was the only religious school in town. . . . He was the only black person, not only in the class but in the entire school, and we felt like this was not a healthy environment for him. . . . He knew he was being treated differently and I remember one incident that I witnessed. When he and his little classmates were standing in the hallway and the kindergartners walked by and one of the kindergarten boys reached out and rubbed Pearson's hair because he has the textured African-American hair, and this kid hadn't seen this up close before and he just reached over, and Pearson didn't like that and he told me later, he said, "Mom, I'm not a dog, you know you can't pat me on the head like that." And I said, "You know that isn't right for somebody to just do that to you. They're not your friend and you don't want 'em to do that." And then you know when we'd go out, people would go out of their way to prove they weren't prejudiced by being overly friendly to him and things like that. . . . I said, "You know, sometimes Pearson there will be people that don't like you just because of the color of your skin, and that's called racism, and that's a problem that they have and they might say things that are mean." (AA17)

Dolly moved Pearson to a different parochial school where, thus far, he had not had further difficulties. However, at his new school there are no black administrators or teachers to serve as role models for him. Pearson's experiences are precisely what makes critics of transracial adoption irate. Although Dolly put him in a different school, she worried that the lack of other black role models would not be good for Pearson.

Amber was well aware that Ashley could not easily handle playground teasing on her own. So she worked hard to role-model appropriate responses for Ashley because she knew that much of what took place on the playground was out of view and earshot of teachers and wanted Ashley to be able to defend herself. She stated matter-of-factly,

> I know there's going to be issues when it comes to race. With my daughter, it's much more conspicuous. So kids ask [why mother and daughter are not the same color] on the playground now, and that's stuff that I've tried to prepare myself for ahead of time. Hopefully, Ashley picks up on my response enough that when she gets older, it will just come naturally to her. No denying that

we're different races, but she can answer to kids on the playground like I do: "Yeah, that's my mom." And the kid, of course, is going, "Well, it doesn't look like your mom, and so I asked you, is that your mom?" And she can say any part of what I've told people. I've said to some kids who've asked, "Well, let's see. I read her stories at night. We eat dinner together. I put her to bed. We go buy clothes, and I bring her to school. I guess that makes me her mom." To get these little preschoolers to conceptualize the fact that we don't match and that's okay. (AA4)

AA adoptive parents were taking these kinds of steps, but the schools were doing much less, formally or informally, to foster a more expansive understanding of family formation that included care-taking. Examples abound of how the social construction of race and its relationship to family-making emerges and is reinforced, often in a cruel fashion, inside and outside the classroom. These examples are not confined to children whose families are formed through adoption. Greater attention to formulating discourse and assignments to acknowledge the kinds of families that now exist in America would go a long way toward changing some of these exchanges. Children who are adopted have come up with some excellent ideas about how these changes could be made.

Affinity and Diversity

Why in the world would I think about being Chinese? I don't sit there in class thinking, "I'm Chinese, Miss Fern." I just do my work. She says this with the utmost conviction, my fourth grade daughter. Never mind that just moments earlier, we'd been pooling our memories to reconstruct a cluster of year-old encounters in the school hallway involving fifth-grade boys and some unpleasant racial taunts. She couldn't remember if there were four or five boys, if most were white or if half were black. All she could remember was that these older boys thought her Chinese looks were "stupid or funny" and that she told them, "That's your problem, not mine." "Do you remember how you felt at that moment about being Chinese?" I ask. . . . "I just thought I was a normal person." "Do you remember how you felt about the boys?" "Yeah. I wanted to kill them." Bewildering stuff, this business of race. Make too much of it, and you risk grooming your child to forge an identity based on other people's insensitivity and ignorance. Make too little of it, and you risk failing to prepare your child for life in a country that every ten years maps its racial boundaries in such meticulous detail that the 2000 Census offered 63 different options.
—Smolowe (2005: 93–94)

In the United States, as in many parts of the world, identities are politicized, and cultural differences have become a key idiom through which political struggles unfold. To think of identity itself as the end of these struggles, however, is to take identity politics as a given, rather than to critically probe its effects (Hale 2006: 17).

Schools are primary institutions through which ideas about family and race are filtered and where these struggles happen. Classical racism—systematically equating particular aspects of physical appearance with biological inferiority—has been nominally replaced by an endorsement of cultural rights and intercultural equality. In practice, the school environment, a reflection of ongoing dynamics in society broadly, more resembles what one might call a partial multiculturalism, one that celebrates a diverse range of cultural practices and rights but that, nevertheless, tends not to recognize or respond to ongoing modes of marginalization. Ana Anagnost alludes to this kind of multiculturalism as "embracing diversity as a way of containing difference" (2000: 391).

Multicultural ideologies and diversity may be "good to think with" (Segal and Handler 1995: 392–93) and may allow schools (as well as parents) to instrumentally "vanish" existing class or racial differences. On the other hand, the goals of multiculturalism may foster practices and products that give minority groups greater possibilities for social and political enfranchisement, and that embrace diverse cultural practices and "physiognomic variation"—Crayola Multicultural Crayons, for example, which are welcomed by children of color and their parents. New practices and ideologies are small steps in the face of major structural boundaries enacted by children, administrators, and teachers alike in schools. Their effects were refracted in the choices that adoptees and their adoptive parents made.

"Post-blackness" has also been introduced into the schools as an alternative to multiculturalism and to critical race theory with its emphasis on the need for shared black identity. Touré (2011), in *Who's Afraid of Post-Blackness: What It Means to Be Black Now*, interviewed a wide range of black figures and found that duality, code-switching, and comfort in interethnic relationships were all part of the greater malleability of identity that blacks in America feel. The controversial stance Touré takes is that while black identity is rooted in the racial history of being black in America, the centrality of blackness no longer needs to constrain African Americans' identity. Orlando Patterson (2011: 1, 14), cites Henry Louis Gates's argument, however, that "post-black" does not mean postracial. Post-black identity resides in the need to live with and transcend new and subtle but pervasive forms of racism. There is "a new racism, always lurking in the shadows, the secret decisions of whites resulting in lost opportunities blacks never knew about or even thought possible. There's a sense of malevolent ghosts darting round you, screwing with you, often out of sight, but never out of mind." This complex new racism is hazardous because its existence is the null case, the *lack* rather than the *presence* of evidence. Yet it is a sensation that is widely reported and is reflected in some of the shifts under way at schools that are directed toward children from a young age.

In some of the schools attended by adopted children, "diversity," so long equated with rectifying marginalization through multiculturalist practices, was being replaced by "affinity" task forces in order to combat discrimination. When I asked about this in one elementary school, I was told that the former notion of diversity was too polarizing. Affinity was more inclusive. The origins of affinity groups lie in social movements, emerging alongside or out of them. Such groups make efforts to be nonhierarchical and trusting; they are allied with each other because they have something in common other than a single issue, and they form networks and ties with other groups with whom they share similar characteristics, histories, or experiences.

The affinity groups that were forming in schools included parents and children and met periodically. I documented the activities of one affinity group over two years and followed some of the children and parents who participated in it. Initially, it seemed unlikely that such groups would call into question the discourse and distinctions that emerge on the playground or the more formal discourse and boundaries channeled through classroom assignments, in part because the group included only non-whites and very few African Americans. The approach they were taking tended to reproduce a celebratory, multicultural discourse about diverse cultures. However, after the first year, the participants initiated a new program they called CODE, "Conversations on Diversity and Equity." The purpose of CODE was to provide a safe space for discussion of how students' identities—race, gender, religion, sexual orientation—influenced their experiences at the school. More important, it intended to facilitate conversations of this nature throughout the school, including interviews with students and faculty.

Contemporary social scientists emphasize the meaninglessness of race as biological —that is, it is a social construction. Yet, as Sandra Patton points out, knowing that racial distinctions are not biologically grounded, but rather social constructions that

> do not dismantle the racial foundation of the legal and political infrastructure of the United States. Racial categorizations are inscribed in our identities and institutionalized in the state-regulated discourse of birth certificates and "non-identifying information," school records, and census forms. Cultural understandings of race and racial difference shape our perceptions of ourselves and those in our social worlds. (Patton 2000: 60)

Patton's remarks echo what Justine, a 12-year-old adopted from China, told me when I asked her whether she planned to participate in the affinity group at her school. After thinking about it, she told me that she felt affinity groups emphasized race and cultural differences, and that they ignored what she thought was much more important—the interactions, not among children labeled as African American or as Asian American, but *between* them and non–African Americans or Asian Americans. She thought what counted was how people, in general, behaved toward each other. Being able to share similar experiences and struggles might serve as a basis for transformative action; but Justine's thinking, as a child, also calls attention to the need to move from talk to behavior to institutional transformation.

Discussion

Schools are but one site where debates such as those described above were unfolding, but because children spend many years in school from a young age, schools played a key role in how they absorbed ideas about social identity and family-making, and about the significance of racial differences. While powerful ideas about family configurations, sexual orientation, and racial matching continued to percolate and dominate school settings, children and parents were contributing alternative approaches to the mix of American families. As children contested school assignments about their lifelines or family trees, they began to use kin terms in a metaphoric way to depict the social relationships that made them "family." How they drew, articulated, and acted on what they understood as their family diverged from more institutionalized ideas about kinship.

Anthropologist Julian Pitt-Rivers (1973: 3, 5) observed that the metaphoric use of kin terms "may be functional or strategic," but he also makes the point that the existence of these metaphoric kin terms does not depend only on biological ideology. If one traces the emergence of some of these metaphors, as I have done here, their very use exhibits "complex interactions (symbiotic, parasitic, dominant, subordinate, competitive) with ordinary kinship ones." The increasing presence of alternative family models in schools, the emergence of new referential kin terms, the struggles over privacy, the gradual reassessment of what it means to be a mother, and the reevaluation of the effectiveness of countering playground roughhousing with multicultural celebration called into doubt the kinds of biological assumptions that have long underpinned dominant ideas about family-making as they are enacted in schools.

8 The Anchors of Virtual Communities

Belonging is located in knowledge. . . . how knowledge circulates, not only in terms of secrets but also how the principles behind the circulation of knowledge in families and communities underlie the production of identities
—Ilana Gershon (2003: 246)

The Internet plays a significant role in how members of adoptive families acquire knowledge and mull over and enact practices as adoptive families. They participate in forums, chat rooms, blogs, and listservs that cover almost every imaginable aspect of their lives. Relatively little qualitative research has been done on the impact of the Internet on adoptive parents' daily lives, particularly with respect to adoption issues, although a number of social scientists have pursued textual analyses of Internet content and images (see Anagnost 2000; Cartwright 2003; Castells 1996; Edwards 1997; Jenkins, Thorburn, and Seawell 2003; Turkle 1995).

It is difficult to trace these interconnections since the uses people make of the Internet in their lives may transpire over long periods of time and in many different settings. It is easier to see the impact of online resources on political mobilization, for example, than on identity formation and cultural understandings and practices related to family formation. In the former case, one is more able to point to concrete outcomes.

Tom Boellstorff (2008), in his ethnography of the virtual world, *Coming of Age in Second Life*, argues that virtual and actual worlds should not be conceptualized in a dualistic fashion and that virtual worlds, whenever possible, should be viewed as stand-alone "cultures." The ways that adoptive parents participate in virtual worlds differ from the description in *Coming of Age in Second Life*, which Boellstorf discusses in light of graphic capabilities, a game-like framework, rules, currency, and avatars.

My purpose in this chapter here is far less ambitious than Boellstorff's. It is simply to show the permeability between the interactions and exchanges that parents engage in, using Internet media and their actual world interactions and exchanges, with respect to questions surrounding adoption.[1] I examine the principles and cultural logic that structure these interactions and exchanges and describe how virtual interactions and dialogue have led adoptive parents to embrace new networks and communities, to think in a different way about their own families and how to raise their children, and, in turn, to air their changes in thinking via the Internet.

While the idea of viewing the worlds enacted within cyberspace as their own culture is intriguing, I would argue that it is of more importance to recognize the interactive dimensions between the spatial and temporal context of these worlds and to understand how they "bleed" into one another. Anthropologists Daniel Miller and Don Slater (2000: 10) make the point that an ethnographic approach to the Internet recognizes that individuals articulate a version or versions of themselves with electronic media and that they may also be transformed through their encounters (see also Olaniran 2008: 46). At the same time that one's presentation of self may be highly idealized, Miller and Slater's research shows that the articulation itself has "expansive potential" and, in specific instances, "one can become what one really thinks one really is (even if one never was)."

In like fashion, people's immersion in specific Internet media can transform Internet networks themselves. On the other hand, the utopian and libertarian promise of the Internet must be counterbalanced by the fairly common practice of human beings to deepen their sense of self or reinforce it through their selective participation in Internet networks. Miller and Slater (2000: 18) caution that "the Internet sometimes becomes primarily a means of repairing allegiances to older identities." The real question for Miller and Slater, and for this project, is "how freedom and normativity are linked rather than sundered in these newer media of social interaction."

The Internet is far from being a democratic medium, despite its potential. Economic and political forces shape the construction of both virtual and actual domains, and mediate how aspects of adoption are received and processed by adoptive parents (Estes 2008; Boczkowski 2004). As Castells states, "Technology does not determine society: it embodies it. But nor does society determine technological innovation: it uses it" (1996: 5, fn. 3). On the Internet people operate within networks that transcend their immediate location, placing them in wider cultural, political, and economic flows. One question to ask, then, is how people understand their emplacement and, in turn, how that understanding affects their subsequent positioning within Internet networks and their lives outside of those networks (Miller and Slater 2000: 18; Escobar 2000: 57).

Many Internet networks are hierarchical, and they also operate according to specific rules and with cultural norms. For example, some are more open than others; some condone and others forbid certain behaviors and discourse; and sustained participation in particular networks results in behavior that is akin to "ritualistic storytelling." Those who participate over long periods of time become familiar with expected protocols, ways of asking questions, posing problems, providing answers or solutions, and, in general, engaging in online interactions (Adams and Smith 2008: 16).[2]

These characteristics foster a feeling of "in-group" culture and create categories of participants whom Bolanle Olaniran (2008: 47) distinguishes as "tourists, minglers, and devotees." Some may be "surfing" and have a "shallow interest" in the network; others have a "token interest" but have strong social ties with other network participants, and still others have strong ties and a passionate interest in the network's or group's activities. These distinctions may also constitute a kind of hierarchy. Rarely do devotees or minglers readily embrace a totally novel approach to the group subject matter. More likely, should they become dissatisfied enough with the prevailing group culture, they will withdraw or seek or start another group. In fact, Kevin Robbins (2000: 91) cautions that the healthy democratic processes that constitute social life require "antagonism, a vibrant clash of political positions, and an open conflict of interests," and he contrasts these dynamics with the prevailing perception of computer-mediated communities in virtual space as domains of "order, refuge, and withdrawal."

Ana Anagnost (2000), Lisa Cartwright (2003), and Paul McIlvenny and Pirkko Raudaskoski (2005) have analyzed how economic and political forces, the goals and desires of adoptive parents, and the power relationships in which they are embedded mediate adoptive parents' access to, reception of, and interpretation of Internet discourse. For example, even as people increasingly rely on the Internet, there remain significant class barriers to participation. Birth parents, even in open relationships with adoptive parents, are less likely to be active in cyber-discussions in which adoptive parents are participating, although they are increasingly using email to stay in touch with adoptive family members (Brassard 2008).

A second example, which I expand on in Chapter 9, has been articulated by adoptees themselves, who note that in many domains—virtual and actual—the voices of adoptive parents have dominated and the perspectives and concerns of adoptees have remained unheard. Adoptees have begun to create their own websites and listervs, asking who has the right to exert authority and power in structuring how adoptive families are defined and viewed, and using cyber-resources to explore the possibilities for creating communities they imagine. For adoptive parents, cyber-resources and channels of communication serve more transparently instrumental purposes, yet even for them, the Worldwide Web has become a place where they air concerns and dilemmas specific to their families that in the past might have remained private rather than public.

Public Domains of Intimacy

The remarkably public nature of postings by adoptive parents—what Ann Anagnost (2000: 397) calls the "intimate public sphere," is a hallmark of cyber-communication. Methodologically, the Internet, as product and catalyst of globalization, has created a peculiar domain of gazes. Adoption has always occupied a netherland of public and private concern, intimate business, and state regulation. This blurring of boundaries permeates American culture today and is notably pronounced for very specific reasons in the sphere of adoption.

In familiarizing myself with adoption sites for this research, I found posted excruciatingly intimate details about the lives of families, their predicaments, and difficulties; frequently, family members also publicly posted photos of their children. Two major observations struck me about this blurring of public and private domains. The postings were an effort to create constructive community, initially out of relatively thin air. Yet a false sense of insularity accompanied some of these postings by adoptive parents, such that it seemed they paid little regard to what they might mean for their children's futures.

Initially, this was my concern: what will the children think about what is being written about them or about their photos gazing back at them as they grow into adulthood? It seemed ironic to me that the emotional and cultural cachet attributed to children as priceless (Zelizer 1985) was inspiring the public airing and scrutiny of highly personal dimensions of their lives. Now, several years later, it appears to me that the range of subjects addressed—the careful confessions, the fury, desperations, vulnerability, and the joy that permeate these postings by adoptive parents and their children, and even occasionally by birth parents—suggest that the participants regard these sites as among the safest places they can voice their concerns and obtain information (see also Vance 2008: 153).

At the same time, the vanishing of boundaries between what is public and what is private is indicative of a broader cultural reassessment that, with rare exceptions, assumes everything is available for public consumption and tends toward a high degree of self-referential expression. Interestingly, because many kinds of Internet media constitute "public letters written to a group," they may also entail more self-censorship than does private letter writing (Vance 2008: 155). Robbins (2000: 91), reflecting generally on this phenomenon, labels this self-referential dimension as a kind of "autistic logic"; and Wilbur (2000: 47) similarly finds that "the experience of dislocation in time and space. . . . can help individuals see their own identities in a different perspective."

One blog I followed had been fashioned by an adoptive parent and her child, and they both regularly contributed to it, sharing their daily experiences, particularly those that touched on adoption and identity. The blog was advertised on several Yahoo sites and was open to comments from visitors. Lack of privacy did not seem to bother most participants. In fact, as I discuss below, increasingly, virtual community participants tried to convert those interactions into face-to-face meetings. Not least of these transformative moments was the active learning that occurred as participants in virtual networks came to feel comfortable airing queries and asking for advice, which they then put into practice and reported on.

Reading the postings constituted a novel form of participant-observation for me as an anthropologist. It was different from my prior experiences of participant-observation where, usually, I took time to gauge the sensitivity of topics, or the person with whom I was speaking could decide to shut down and walk away if my behavior or questions were too intrusive. In the virtual setting, unless someone announced their intention to leave the discussion, I might have no idea why someone dropped out of an online conversation.

While Arturo Escobar (2000: 62–64) views virtual communities as "vibrant new villages of activity" that do not necessitate a new branch of anthropology, he recognizes that they constitute "unprecedented sites of articulation of knowledge and power." The combination of speed, range, anonymity, and the complex political and cultural economy of information that circulates in virtual space makes it difficult to systematically research and analyze ethnographically. For example, one mother I spoke with who kept a blog was adamant about protecting her daughter's privacy and was the exception that proved the rule:

> Right, in fact, we're gonna keep the blog up until the end of the year, and then she's getting old enough now I think I'm going to switch to a password-protected venue. Not that anyone has specifically threatened us. We haven't gotten any weird searches or anything, 'cause I check our stats and stuff. There hasn't been any freaky Googling or anything, but she's just getting old enough now. I don't talk about anything personal in there. We talked about our trip

to China, but for example, the personal details of her story we share with no one outside of our immediate family. . . . Any personal details . . . we just don't share those as far as her story, other than just the general she was in foster care. That I don't mind sharing, but just the details of her coming into that situation are things that we don't really share. Some people have no problem doing that, and I've seen people post their kid's stories on the Internet, and that's a decision for each family to make. I just feel that the one thing she really owned when she came to us was her story. That was hers. (CA8)

Economic and Political Contours

Anagnost (2000: 214)) found that CA adoptive parents used Internet resources from the time of referral to the immediate post-adoption period to reinforce the privileged middle-class position that gave them "the right to form families as a middle-class imperative" and therefore permitted them to pursue adoption as a specific kind of immigration. They celebrated adoption via Internet images and communication, emphasizing culture and material objects connected to their child's birthplace to fill in missing links in their child's life history. And skillfully, if subconsciously, they converted transnational circuits of commodity exchange into ambivalent gifts—ambivalent because the relationships between them and their adopted children were mediated by the Chinese state and people rather than through personal relationships. As a consequence, Anagnost concluded that despite the embrace of multiculturalism and the "imaginary resolution of identity construction" that adoptive parents' Internet communications appeared to signify, in reality, the Internet facilitated their ability to seal themselves off from the larger question of the complex row that adoptees—their children—would have to hoe as "multiraced subjects" in the United States whose positioning resembled that of many other Asian American immigrants.[3]

Since Anagnost wrote those words in the year 2000, things have moved slowly, but they have changed. Increasingly, adoptive parents are confronting issues on the Internet and in their everyday lives that Anagnost had found they were utterly blind to just a few years earlier. The most important changes I found among CA adoptive parents were their participation in debates about child trafficking, their struggles with race and culture as part of their family's identity formation and re-formation after adoption, and their contestation of images of "perfect" and "exotic" little Asian girls that circulated in the American public. CA adoptive parents had also begun to openly discuss online the special needs of their children, though this topic has been the central focus of RA adoptive parents' participation in online groups for many years and has helped them find resources for them and their children.

Many adoptive parents had no idea their children might have been trafficked. Brian Stuy lives in China and runs a business for adoptive parents that tracks down children's "finding ads" and any other information accessible about their children's early years prior to adoption.[4] He also has a website, "research-china.org," where he posts research findings about adoption in and from China. He has actively sought to publicize instances of trafficking. In May 2011, he posted a story that had already broken, exposing the trafficking of thirteen children from Gaoping, Hunan, by the local "Family Planning" agency. The children were then sent to Shaoyang orphanage and adopted internationally. While this was not the first time such an incident had occurred, this time the names of the children and their finding dates were published, making them much more readily identifiable.

Subsequently, Chinese birth parents whose children had been confiscated from them were able to discover that the children had been internationally adopted. Many of them have a desire to know about their children. The publication of the names of the children and their status set in motion a debate that will likely continue. Adoptive parents, on listservs and with each other, discussed privacy issues, what they should tell their children about being trafficked, the rights of their children to know they had been trafficked, whether they should try to contact birth parents, and the rights of birth parents who might not want this kind of exposure. In general, they found themselves struggling to figure out an ethical course of action.[5] The widespread impact of this case is in part due to adoptive parents' participation in cyber-communications.

The economic and political contours that shape virtual and actual communications are complex, dialectical processes. Participating in the world of cyberspace does not automatically lead to the revolutionary creation of new subjectivities or cultural practices among adoptive family members who are using it. Robbins (2000: 2) makes the point that virtual communities do not consist of real people or real communities; they are an "invocation of community" but not "a production of sociality." This is true, but if one does have the opportunity to follow a virtual community over time and also talk or interact with participants in that community, one can sometimes trace how sociality, political action, and changes in cultural practices emerge. Hardly revolutionary, the process is usually gradual and somewhat unpredictable (Castells 1996; Boczkowski 2004; Rheingold 2000). A virtual community can be viewed as a translocal space in which ideas and relations meet, circulate, and are in the process of becoming, in a geopolitical context that is not level. Further, different kinds of adoptive families used Internet resources in distinctive ways, as I discuss below. Regardless of the differences among them, adoptive parents did not use cyber-resources in the same ways that their children did. There were marked contrasts in how they viewed privacy, identity formation, and sociability, and in their dreams and fears.

To find out if, through their participation in cyber-communications, adoptive parents challenged any of the social boundaries and discourses of power that structure family-making, I spoke with them about how they used the Internet. I also followed blogs, discussion groups, and listservs. I found that most adoptive parents used cyber-resources for information retrieval and communication, while their formation of new kinds of community and social networks was usually a result of their participation in particular cyber-groups.

When I began this research in 2006, adoptive parents rarely examined the categories, terms, and classifications that they used in speaking about adoption. This changed gradually. Their cyber-communications became more reflective, and they more often debated issues. More adoptive parents were challenging the structure and content of mediated discourse and images circulating on the Worldwide Web and were, therefore, less unreflexive in embracing them. They were also simultaneously obtaining information that was less available via the mainstream media or television networks.

The ripple effects of these new types of communication were obvious. Adoptive parents were putting more of their concerns and questions openly on the table and into action. They were scrutinizing the legitimacy of the adoption process itself, how to conduct searches for birth relatives while preserving birth parent privacy, the appropriateness of particular adoption rituals and the labels attached to them (such as "Gotcha Day," discussed in Chapter 9), and how to handle racist family members or social prying. More generally, they were questioning their own cultural assumptions about openness and the adoption narratives they had constructed.

Although the transformative impact of adoptive parents' cyber-communication was usually not dramatic, their efforts to rethink ideas about culture, about race, and about geopolitical inequalities, and their willingness to entertain debate about these topics, has encouraged their children to strike out in unpredictable and innovative ways to build their identities and to rethink their understanding of who they are. In short, these were fluid, dynamic, and non-dyadic processes.

Actual and Virtual Community-Making

Virtual communities structured the choices of prospective adoptive parents, especially as they contemplated whether to adopt and from where to adopt. Anthropologist Lisa Cartwright examined and analyzed the construction of websites, where many parents received and processed their initial information about adoption. She looked at the systems of classification that adoption agencies, for example, used in posting photos of children from all over the world. Some of these websites allowed prospective adoptive parents to create their own portfolio of "favorite" children. Cartwright also notes that, in some countries, such as Kazakhstan, children were classified into two groups, those that were more "European" looking and those that were more "Asian" looking. In another instance, she found that a reputable U.S. adoption agency had placed a child from Russia in the category of "special needs" apparently solely on the basis of his skin color, which was black. In looking at these websites over time, Cartwright concludes that "classifying systems are internally inconsistent and changeable because they must keep up with the political changes that impact identity formation at a time when the very categorical system that made 'nation' the most meaningful relative to 'identity' is in flux" (Cartwright 2003: 92–93).

These virtual representations of adoption appeared to objectify children, unconsciously or subconsciously, yet at the same time they conveyed powerful systems of classification, grounded in ideal notions of age, gender, or race. Further, these systems, often bound up with how a nation represents itself to itself, were projected even as people who lived within those imagined communities might be questioning the representations.[6]

McIlvenny and Raudaskoski (2005: 66–67) studied adoptive parents from Denmark. They systematically analyzed how a child that was to be adopted was scaled and "resemiotized" (acquired new meanings) via the Internet, and documented how the Internet structured the prospective personhood of a child. Children-to-be-adopted could be scaled downward, to become more object than subject, represented by legal documents that had to be filed in order to begin the adoption process, medical statistics, growth curves, probabilities of particular illnesses, and a changing timeline linked to travel groups or waiting parents. Prospective adoptees could also be scaled upward gradually with photographs or videos of the child, descriptions of the child's physical characteristics and personality, the attribution of a name, and an emerging bond with other people including the prospective adoptive parents, the child's caretakers, and playmates and cribmates in the orphanage. Likewise, the development of blogs that began with familiar aspects of the adoption process could become progressively more detailed.

The ways that adoptive parents communicated on the Internet led to the emergence of shared ideas about landmark moments in the adoption process: the waiting period (submission of documents, completion of the home study, approval by an adoption agency, referral); the wait to travel; the trip itself; transferring and receiving the child; and the critical stage of attachment and bonding. In the case of domestic adoptions, these milestones included completion of the birth mother's pregnancy and legal relinquishment of the child by birth parents and relatives. Internet participation and cyber-communication among adoptive parents continued throughout the child's early years, ebbing and flowing; but when the child became a teenager these communications subsided, with a few exceptions. This was when the children themselves became far more active users of cyber-communication to discuss aspects of their adoption.

The oldest adoptive parents I spoke with all wished they had had access to Internet resources when they embarked on adoption. In general, I found that CA and RA adoptive parents relied far more than AA adoptive parents on Internet resources right from the start. The information they culled from their searches became the basis for selecting an agency to work with as well as for deciding from what country to adopt. The following is a typical example of how adoptive parents used the Internet to retrieve information:

> I can't imagine doing this without the Internet. It would have been terribly lonely and challenging. We started ahead of time. We created a Yahoo group, and for six months we talked online about things we learned, and when we got referrals, we exchanged information, met up with each other, and coordinated our trip arrangements. By the time we got to the hotel, we knew a lot of people virtually. (CA4)

Ellen, who lived in Maryland, explained how she decided on adoption and how she picked Russia in what was an impressively random but hardly uncommon fashion:

> We started meeting people who adopted, and I had gone to a conference up in Minnesota . . . about making choices. . . . I had just turned 40. . . . I was freaking out. So I was flying home, and there was this woman sitting next to me. . . . We started talking, and she shared with me the adoption story of her infant daughter from Russia. It was a very inspiring conversation, and I said,

"You know, we thought about it, but now that we're 40 we really don't want an infant. I can't even put my head around that, changing diapers." And she said, "Well, there are lots of older children available as well."

I came home and started Googling stuff, you know, information, and every corner we turned it was always Russia. I had looked domestically, just to find out the general information, and then I Googled "international adoption agencies, Maryland" and three agencies came up, Baltimore, Columbia, MD, and one was in Dunkirk, MD, which was ten minutes up the road, and I live in a very rural county. So I went, hmm, I'm listening. I called and spoke to the agency owner. (RA2)

Ironically, many prospective parents used the global Internet to find a local agency, and they frequently selected a particular agency not because of its track record, cost, or the support services it offered, but because it was conveniently local and was ranked high enough on the Google search engine that it appeared prominently in a search.

Cyber-communities and Families

Anthropological and social definitions of "community" abound. The "Chicago School" made analogies between "community" and "organism," arguing that communities existed within physically bounded space in an ecological context.[7] Another definition of community is a network that brings people together despite only indirect connections between them. Yet another definition has emerged as a consequence of the growth of information technologies: a community can be created from large-scale interactions among people who are primarily linked by common identities but minimally by networks of interpersonal relationships (Appadurai 1996; Calhoun 1991; Escobar 2008; Hannerz 1996; Latour 2007).[8]

Many parents have created virtual as well as physical "reunion communities" on the basis of having adopted their children from the same country or orphanage. Adoptees have also begun participating in these spaces, contributing their voices and opinions to the mix, and converting these connections into physical gatherings and cultural and intellectual productions, phenomena I discuss in Chapter 9. The reach of the Internet has facilitated new kinds of communications and connections, financial and otherwise, not only among adoptive parents and their families, but also between adoptive families and the orphanages from which they adopted their children. They have begun to keep track of who is traveling where and when, and are able to send photos and updates of their children, as well as donations for the orphanages and for foster parents. Jeanne Marie Laskas wrote:

> The Yahoo group was wonderful because I got to look at pictures of other babies adopted from Huazhou that people had posted and also I got to hear how everyone loved Miss Peng, the orphanage director, whom many had met and thought to be an angel. (Laskas 2006: 39)

The use of these modes of communication by families gained momentum because of the mysteries, anxieties, longing, and uncertainties that adoptive parents were experiencing, as well as their impatience. After adoption, their communications became more complex, a way to craft kinship ties through projected shared experiences. Parents who initially made these connections have now introduced a "new" tradition in which same orphanage children are labeled "siblings" or "cousins." In more than one case, a nascent virtual community formed because prospective parents expected to adopt from the same orphanage. Subsequently, actual communities materialized that resembled a novel kind of extended family.

Lola and Caren were part of a group of prospective adoptive parents who had traveled to China to adopt their children. The Internet initially connected this travel group, which then bonded in the course of their adoption experiences. Lola told me that when Caren, a single mother, became ill with throat cancer after the group returned, the group members rallied to take care of her child. Before Caren died, she turned over guardianship of her child to one of the families in the group, who then readopted the child into their family. Lola describes the experience of being a member of this travel group as akin to sharing in the collective birth of their children; she also saw travel group members as being analogous to siblings or, in relation to their children, "aunts" and "uncles," a term that already was in common usage in the United States to refer to parents' closest friends who had developed a special relationship with their children:

> They're family [the travel group]. By the time you've been through two weeks you've given birth with these people . . . . One of our members, the one that we became the closest with, her name is Caren. . . . She was a single mom . . . and she was totally from nowhere around any of us. . . . and she was adopting the youngest baby in our group. . . . We hung out with Caren. . . . And after we got home she was diagnosed with throat cancer. . . . We thought she wasn't going to make it for a while . . . when we all met at the FDI reunion . . . a year after

our adoption. . . . And then she was diagnosed with lung cancer. The month with us was so strong. I mean I really felt like Caren was a sister, and so she asked if I could come help her while she got her chemo treatments in Reno. Gina and I went to Reno for a week and took care of Daisy while she was getting treatment. . . . Caren was about to die and she moved to Vermont, and her sister had decided that she couldn't keep Daisy even though she was the guardian. . . . The bond was just so strong that she asked our travel group if any of us would adopt Daisy. . . . And Caren has passed away and little Daisy is living with the O'Haras just outside of Indianapolis. . . . I think all of us still think Daisy was ours. I mean a part of us will always think—what does Daisy like. . . . You know the difficulties of raising twins because that's pretty much what they have now. (CA5)

A second growing area of interest to CA adoptive parents has been establishing possible sibling connections among children who have been adopted internationally by different families. Initially, they relied on commonalities in physical appearance by searching through images posted on the Web, and then pursuing DNA testing that establishes probable but not certain proof of sibling links. (Without DNA from birth parents, certainty cannot be established.) In cases where a probable relationship has been confirmed, adoptive parents have begun to more deeply question the circumstances that led to the adoption of the children. In addition, although they have not created what are known as joint families, more than a few families have moved in order to live closer to each other and interact more regularly. When this has not been possible, they have tried to meet up periodically throughout the year.

In one case, two families who had adopted their children from China and given them the same first name discovered the children were twins. The families had first corresponded with each other on a Yahoo group before adopting their children. After adopting, one family posted a photo of their daughter via the same Yahoo group and the other family realized she looked just like their own daughter. Although maintaining their relationship has been arduous, the two families now consider themselves "twin laws"; they travel regularly between Chicago and Birmingham to visit each other, spending their money and vacations to bring the twins together; the two children communicate weekly and each feels incomplete without the other (*Newsweek* 2009).

Tracy, a single mother who had adopted her daughter from China, told me that she and other families who had adopted from the same orphanage participated in an Internet forum; through that forum they had come to know a woman in China who kept all of them informed about the orphanage and served as the intermediary between adoptive families and orphanage personnel. When Tracy first joined the forum, she did not know this woman's role:

> I recently found a group of people who adopted from the same orphanage on the Web, and through that, all of a sudden this woman started wanting to know all this stuff about my daughter, and she was from the orphanage. . . . My wall went up. Who are you? Why do you want to know this? 'Cause she's like, "What's your daughter's Chinese name? Where do you live? What do you do?" all this real personal information. One of the other moms that I know at one point said, "You know, I feel like they are trying to keep track of everybody and exactly where they are." She was suspect of it. So I put up this red flag . . . and then all of a sudden I realized that everybody loves this woman in this Internet group, and I just had not been in on the conversations with her. . . . So anyhow, I apologized. . . . Mei [the woman] was trying to come over here, and people are willing to sponsor her. She is working in the bookstore in the orphanage. . . . She is Chinese herself. . . . So I told her who I was and what Sabrina's [her daughter's] name was, and she sent me an e-mail back and said, "So and so here at the orphanage remembers her!" I was like, oh my. . . . She teaches English over there as well, so part of her goal is to come over here so she can learn English better to take back, I think. She wants sponsors here, and there was a couple in Canada who . . . ended up starting a Family Group and they would mail out stuff every once in a while with pictures and stories and whatever to Mei. . . . When I contacted Mei, I said, "I understand that the orphanage has changed, and do you have pictures?" So she sent me the old orphanage front and inside, and then she sent me the pictures of the new, which I had already seen before from somebody else. I was able to show them to Sabrina. . . . She's also sent pictures of people in their costumes, so it's been kind of nice. I was really kind of touched that she told me that that worker was still there and does remember Sabrina. (CA24)

Tracy also had used the Internet to locate a Chinese language and culture school run by Chinese Americans, which she and her daughter attended. As a newcomer to the site who was unaware of others' positioning in it, Tracy went through a learning process; her experience demonstrated the power of the Internet to create bridges, not only between adoptive parents and the orphanage, but between past, present, and future. Mei, the Chinese woman working in the orphanage bookstore who hoped to study in the United States, helped further the connections between adoptive families and their children. This scenario was somewhat unusual, but is likely to become more common in the future, as more adoptees seek to reestablish connections with their birthplace.

From the Ether to the Ground

The density of local ties created distinctive functions for listservs and means of connection. Adoptive families from the same town tended to use message boards to arrange gatherings with each other, to become better acquainted, and to organize events throughout the year. The connections between families that were linked through message boards around the United States or in other countries remained more tenuous. They more often used boards and listservs to facilitate therapeutic discussion, to vent frustrations, and to search for information. All of the families used Internet resources to help them obtain information and advice about specific issues or problems. Brandy explained:

> I go to different parent support boards. I have one for kids with issues—you know, psychiatric issues. The INSITE one I told you about for kids that are adopted and there are people on there that have done the whole broad spectrum of adoption and infertility treatments. Everything from embryo adoptions to foster parent, international, newborn, family . . . I'm trying to think what else. Every so often I'll search just on whatever issue we're dealing with, like black hair care. (AA10)

Many adoptive parents highlighted the differences between their virtual networks and communities and their actual social community of friends. Penny explained that her "best friend" and that "most of [her] friends" now were also adoptive parents with children from China but that she preferred a small support group more than the larger ones fostered by Internet boards:

> We did have a bit of association with Families with Children from China . . . but it just got so big and we ended up having our own group. In fact, there are maybe five families who adopted children from China in our church . . . and we know all of them. So, we sort of have our own little network and don't have to go to the bigger group. The last picnic we went to had maybe 200 people there, and although it was great fun to see all these little beautiful Chinese kids running around, most girls, it was a little overwhelming. (CA14)

Her sentiment was reiterated by other parents. They used the Internet to seek practical or therapeutic information, but their social life, which had indeed changed after adoption, revolved around members of their travel group and smaller, transracial playgroups or enduring friendships with other families who had adopted children, regardless of where they were from. Most also maintained their prior friendships with people who had no direct link to the adoption process. CA families, especially, participated in gatherings or fostered friendships for their children based on country of origin, even when they had little in common with the parents themselves.

Parents also quickly realized that having in common a child adopted from a particular country did not mean that they shared enough other values and interests to form genuine friendships. Although they would participate in actual gatherings arranged through virtual connections for the sake of their children, their relationships with these other adoptive parents at occasional events differed qualitatively from their close friendships. Alise outlined these distinctions quite clearly:

> What was probably on TV was some worst-case scenarios in one area or another, and that's what upsets me. That's what people still think is foster care. So thank God for the Internet 'cause that's where I've gotten. . . . you can find a group that works with adopting children, being a white family or whatever kind of family . . . , and adopting a child, getting them raised, and learning how to deal with their hair and skin. Tons of information is exchanged between whole groups of us. In fact, [in] Australia, England, I have some people I would consider to be friendly with in other countries. . . . That's been a very great source. The Internet has helped me find other kinds of support when it comes to foster care and adoption. A forum is a real good idea because you can get a lot of information about foster care and adoption from any particular stage or whatever agency. To actually hear what people's experiences are makes you realize that just because you adopted a child doesn't mean you're part of an adoption community. I had that idea initially. I thought people would be like-minded. And that isn't true. This is [as] individual as anything else. So you learn that people have adopted for all kinds of reasons. Honestly, I look at some of those people and I go, "Wow, they're not emotionally on the same page about this as I am." Just the fact that we've adopted doesn't necessarily give us stuff in common. (AA4)

When I asked Helen if she used the Internet for different things related to adoption, in marked contrast to most other parents, she stated: "No. And maybe this is a poor choice on my part, but I'm not in the adoption business anymore" (RA9). Helen did not view adoption as a process that required any attention subsequent to the adoption itself. Instead, it was a point in time. She also thoughtfully noted that perhaps her attitude (and that of her husband) would have been different if (a) they did not already have two biological children; and (b) they were younger. She contrasted her case with that of a good friend who was an older parent and whose child, also adopted from Russia, was his only one.

Gretchen, who was grappling with her daughter's special needs, told me:

> The biggest thing I wish I had known about was the Internet resources. The prospective families who are on, reading the boards every day, seeing the issues, hearing how families are dealing with them, or not, seeing what it does to marriages, they have a better chance of going in truly more prepared than we were. . . . I had never heard of FRUA [Families for Russian and Ukrainian Adoption]. . . . I got on the bulletin boards and that was an eye-opener. . . . I finally had to get off of it because I was just escaping to it. . . . When reality here got too rough, I would go down and read about people who were worse off than me. (RA8)

Helena reiterated Gretchen's embrace of Internet resources, although she used them primarily before adopting her children with Bessie, not afterwards:

> The Internet is so full of resources. Between 2000 and 2003 is a world of difference in that regard. Had it not been for the Internet, I don't know if we would have thought about international adoption. . . . We never thought that after our experience in the late nineties that any domestic adoption was an option for us, so we decided to go through, started looking at our options for children, and it was on the Internet that we realized international was something we should look into. (RA15)

For parents, and for children who were not yet adolescents, a sense of community was more likely to form via the Internet if those families lived near each other. If parents were more dispersed geographically—connected on listservs because they lived in the same county or their children came from the same orphanage—their interactions were limited to special occasions and sometimes monthly playdates.

Many parents acknowledged that they only half-heartedly participated in Internet message boards because the network was too large and amorphous. They preferred smaller networks in which they could activate the ties they initially established via the Internet for other purposes, especially friendships and reunions. Parents also found that the rhythm of Internet media tended to be inconsistent and was often too slow and sporadic for their liking. That is, participation ebbed and flowed, questions and comments went unanswered, and they preferred sustained relationships. This was not a view shared by all. Some liked the flexibility and anonymity, the "lurking" that participation in such media permitted, especially if they were trying to decide whether to adopt and from where, or if they were searching for physical or mental health information.

One of the most difficult aspects of researching virtual communication networks is that they are dynamic. When I began this research in 2006, there was almost no discussion of heritage journeys, the structuring of adoption narratives and rituals, or connections to birth parents among CA adoptive parents. By 2010, the discussions had become painful, lively, probing, and sometimes very contentious concerning what adoptive parents should tell their children about their birth mother/parents, especially if adoptive parents had very few facts to tell them.

Extended debates rage about how adoptive parents should explain the process by which they adopted their children. Should the word abandonment, relinquishment, or adoption plan be used? Is it permissible to invoke God as the great designer of the plan by which a family in the United States adopted a child from China or Russia? Is it reasonable to be concerned about "time-outs" as a practice that might rupture a fragile bond of attachment? How much contact should take place with birth parents who may have had problems with different kinds of abuse? Should adoption be celebrated or mourned on a specific day, and how? Should negative information about a child's birth country be shared with her, or should knowledge be filtered so that the child initially has only positive sentiments about her heritage? And rather than adopt, might it be more ethical to provide resources so that birth parents could keep their children? Sometimes participants were shut down by moderators because the debates became so heated.

The tone of cyber-dialogues has shifted as well, because some parents have adopted more than one child, because children are reaching adolescence and have successfully challenged the narratives their adoptive parents originally constructed, and because some adoptive parents now consider themselves experts. These shifts suggest that social boundaries *are* being questioned, if somewhat tenuously. Some of the assumptions that underpin the taken-for-granted ways that families form and that gloss over inequalities and racism are being reevaluated. One major change I discerned was that some adoptive parents are reassessing their positions because their children are encouraging them to do so.

One exchange, portions of which I cite below, illuminates these kinds of debates. It took place on an active and open adoption forum. The language used in the exchange reveals the "code" that these groups developed in their communications. Newcomers had to figure out how to decode shorthand such as A-parents (adoptive parents), TAs (transracial adoptees), and OTOH (on the other hand), a more generic expression. Terra, a long-time participant began by pronouncing that she was "still surprised that rather than learning from the mistakes of others and from the adoptees themselves, A-parents felt they knew better." Jill, another long-time participant and mother of an adult adoptee, had been following and engaged in matters connected with adoption for forty years. She agreed with Terra:

> Me Too!!!. . . . I have given up on trying to make today's newly adopting parents understand that things really haven't changed all that much in the past forty years of adoption! A-parents today so want to believe that somehow they can do parenting of an adopted children in some way that eliminates the pain and loss and "issues" that previous generations of adoptees have experienced. For me, I knew TAs when I was in high school (graduated in 1980) and they went to "culture camp" and I know "OURS" magazine came out in the late 60's or early 70's (today it is called *Adoptive Families* magazine) and that shift from "just raise them as if they were born to you" had really changed from the 50's and 60's very long ago. . . . the adult adoptees of today (like my daughter . . . those in their 20's and 30's) really were raised exactly like people raise adopted kids today and guess what? They still have pain, they still have loss, they have issues, and as teens and adults—as Terra said—they share it, blog it, and speak about it (and not always in ways a-parents of young kids want to hear).[9]

The reaction to Jill's position was, while not harsh, emphatic. Jennifer responded,

> I would beg to differ that things aren't different. "Attach China" didn't exist, adoption trauma therapists didn't exist, the shift of parenting style to a much deeper awareness of the issues surrounding transracial adoption didn't really start to take place until the 70'-80's, the education requirements for AP's [adoptive parents] were pretty minor, and access to adult adoptees with opinions was limited. The tools to help an adoptee and their adoptive family deal with expressions of their loss were not widely available. The wave of new media has made opinion sharing, as Terra pointed out, that much easier and often more thoughtless.
>
> The positive side is that perhaps the greatest change in adoption is the availability of forums for adult adoptees to reach others, talk about their losses, share their feelings, and be acknowledged. The new media has made reaching out for help easier too. I just Googled "Adoption Therapy" and got 20 million results.[10]

While acknowledging that virtual media resources had been a great boon to participants in adoption, Jennifer cautioned that they had also made it easier to engage in overgeneralization and sectarian slurs because one could simply find the group one felt most comfortable with and easily ignore arguments and positions one disagreed with. She recommended that "it would be more accurate to say, 'SOME AP's' rather than tarring all AP's who adopted within the last 2 decades with the same brush. Yes, the idiots are out there, and they always have been (I've seen no indications that the idiot quotient has changed in the last 50 years). They just have better tools to get in your face."

Michele chimed in, supporting Jennifer's position:

> While there are AP's who do things as they were done 30 years ago, there are a significant number who don't. How many AP's in the 80's took their kids on homeland trips? How many made sure they learned their birth language? How many talked about adoption? How many made an effort to raise their children in a diverse environment? I listen to and value what adult adoptees say. I learn from them and I respect their truth. I am indebted to them. OTOH, my kids attend a Chinese immersion school. That is huge for them! At 9 & 10 years of age, they are fluent in Mandarin. They live Chinese culture at school. The school is half Caucasian so they see members of the majority culture valuing Chinese culture and language. And because their teachers are all native language speakers, they have adult Asian role models.[11]

Because so many of these discussions are occurring online, it requires indirect research to find out if they are having any impact on what parents are actually telling their children and whether they are following through with some of the suggestions and practices proposed and discussed there. The jury is still out on the impact of the Internet on how adoptive parents are thinking about race and class. The increase in heritage camps and journeys suggests that parents are channeling their anxieties about adoption in a different way, finding it acceptable *not* to exclude and truncate originary ties, but these ties take the form of "heritage" and "culture" rather than actual family connections. Some of them (and, admittedly, it is impossible to arrive at specific numbers) have come to recognize that the heteronormative nuclear family model in America is a construct whose time has come to be reassessed by recognizing that family formation may entail "commerce, sentiment, intuition, accident, or simply common sense" (Ahluwalia 2007: 58). The rush of parents to protect their children by incorporating them into a safe and secure family does not do away with children's sense of displacement and their nagging internal queries about where they come from or where they belong.

Betty stressed that she needed more than Internet advice. She needed a group that she could turn to cope with everyday interactions. She had cultivated ties with "an awesome group of ladies that have adopted from the same agency that we've adopted through. . . . We have a transracial adoption playgroup." When I asked if the children were black, she said that "every single one was biracial, all mixed up with something." She credited the group with helping her to figure out appropriate language with which to respond to unsettling questions from her family:

> They were a huge, huge, support to me. Like, when one of my nieces—this was our Thanksgiving dinner this past year—we're sitting down and that first bite of food in my mouth and the 10-year-old niece says, "Why was Melanie adopted?" Ten seconds couldn't have passed and I'm swallowing the bit of food, I'm formulating my response, and my 7-year-old niece said, "'Cause her real mother didn't want her," and I was like, "No, no that's not right. Melanie's mother did want her. She wanted her to have a good life and she wanted her to be healthy." (AA9)

Betty went on to describe how one of her nieces, a 15-year-old, subsequently wanted to date an African American boy but her mother (Betty's sister) would not allow it. The sister acknowledged that "they loved Melanie" and that "she was part of family" but would not allow interracial dating. Betty turned to her group for support because she found "it hard to take."

Two-thirds of AA adoptive parents I interviewed were more likely *not* to use the Internet to establish actual connections with other African American families, culture, and individuals. They portrayed themselves as "hands-on people" (AA16). When encouraged by a friend to participate in an "interesting dialogue that you might like," Deborah's response was, "I basically don't go on. I think Internet friendships are weird" (AA15). Over and over, they spoke instead of going to great lengths to create "a mixed arena" for their children where their children could see and interact with other black people. They mentioned turning to telephone directories, other families, acquaintances, and neighbors, to find black babysitters, hair dressers, pediatricians, and churches. Allen explained how he and his wife had found a babysitter for their daughter in Washington, D.C.

> We flailed around for a year. . . . Then we moved here and . . . there's an assisted-living place up the way, and we called the manager and asked if they could recommend one of the people there. And they recommended this

woman. . . . She was in her late sixties. . . . We talked on the phone. . . . What she said was, "I want you to know that I'm colored," which sort of floored me because I hadn't heard anyone use that term in so long and basically I didn't know what to say, so I said, "So is our daughter." And they hit it off and she decided Maia needed a black grandmother and she's become that, and Maia actually does things with her grandchildren. She considers them to be her cousins and so that's very nice. (AA8)

Alisa explained that "you might end up driving two hours for a tax appointment so that your 3-year-old can have a look at a black man. It sounds silly, but then she's young enough where I develop a relationship with this black man, [and] in a few years I might know his family and children." Alisa, who had adopted an African America child and also had two white children, attended two churches in Illinois:

We go to a Christian community church . . . very open to transracial families. And that fits a certain need. And we also go to another church that is almost exclusively African American, but also very open to helping us support adoptive families. So we're the minority there and that's good for us. . . . I remember my son saying, "My gosh, Mom. I think I feel uncomfortable." I said, "What do you think your sister would feel if she gets older and she's the only one in a white church here in our town? And it gives them stuff to think about. So my kids have kind of been pushed into some issues that they might not have otherwise been. (AA4)

One of the more powerful commentaries on the distinctions that some AA adoptive parents drew between participation in Internet groups and on-the-ground community work came from one of my informants.[12] She was tireless in trying to make adoptive parents realize that they had to move beyond their comfort zone in providing the resources their children needed, that they had to stop assuming that other African Americans would want to help their children just because they were also African American, and that they themselves had to engage in the hard work of forging social ties with African Americans and the other African American community. The irony is that she posted her response on an Internet group and, interestingly, a group dedicated to Chinese adoptive parents. She explained that she had gone to great effort to deepen her relationships with African Americans, writing about the time that she took her own transracially adopted African American sons, along with five of their friends, all transracially adopted African Americans, and four adult African American

chaperones to attend a rodeo in which the star was an African American cow-
boy, Bill Pickett. Her purpose was to "provide black transracial adoptees with
the opportunity to have fun at an event that celebrates the achievements of
black cowboys and cowgirls among a predominantly black audience (without
their white adoptive parents tagging along)." She had some advice for other
transracial adoptive parents who were trying to find role models and mentors
for their children:

> Here is my answer. . . . I did not RECRUIT African American mentors. I
> CHOSE to live in a multicultural neighborhood. . . . I enrolled my eldest
> son in the neighborhood school which has a majority of "minorities." At the
> school, there is a YMCA program which my eldest son has attended since
> kindergarten. Through my work, I became acquainted with African Ameri-
> can coworkers. One of my coworkers invited me to bring my son to *capoeira*,
> a Brazilian martial art. Over the past three years, my family has actively
> participated and our friendship has grown. I am also a member of FAIR
> (Families Adopting in Response), an all-volunteer organization for adoptive
> families. At a writing workshop two years ago, I met a young man who led
> poetry and writing workshops. He is African American, like my sons, and
> was adopted transracially as a kid. The four wonderful men who agreed to
> chaperone the event to the Bill Pickett rodeo have had a presence in my life
> and the lives of my children for years. My relationship with each of these in-
> dividuals has deepened over time. So, there is no quick fix or box of "instant
> chaperone" or "instant mentor." My advice is for adoptive parents is to do it
> for yourselves. Our kids will share the benefits of the personal relationships,
> knowledge, and activities that develop. Making skin-deep connections mo-
> tivated out of a desire to match a . . . mentor [ethnically or racially] with the
> children we chose to adopt is one of the shallowest reasons for trying to make
> contact with the members of our children's communities of origin. That is
> my opinion. I'm interested in the views of adoptive parents, birth parents,
> adults who were adopted and anyone else on this list because of an interest in
> cross-cultural adoption.[13]

She then quoted from an earlier post, critiquing how adoptive parents tried to
forge relationships for the sake of their children:

> What makes us think that we're such great catches as friends/acquaintances for
> people of color? After the typical moaning and groaning about why did I wait
> so long? I hear white adoptive parents conducting an inventory of the black

(or Hispanic or Chinese or Korean) people they know with an eye to recruiting a mentor for their young child, preteen, or teen. The one black Dad on the soccer team or baseball team or whatever is usually brought up. What makes some white adoptive parents think that an individual would want to devote his or her limited leisure time with our kids? What too often comes across to me in these types of conversations is that the goal is to bring people of color into the social circle of the adopted children of color, not the white adoptive parents. No wonder some kids start getting pissed off at their parents during the teenage years. Imagine how awful it must feel to be isolated in your family and community. Lest I sound too much like I've got my act together, let me assure you that I've got a long ways to go myself. I do want to urge white adoptive parents to do more than lurking—it's time to start working on relationship building in the real world, and not just on the Net.[14]

AA adoptive families made a stark contrast to RA or CA adoptive families because, while they had adoption in common, almost all of them thought that questions of race, as well as the hurdles of the regulatory system for purposes of fostering and adoption in the United States, were more important than adoption in the social relationships, friendships, and communities they established, although they did participate in adoption-related Internet groups. They realized that information was only the first step for them in forging substantive organic relationships with African Americans who could become part of their family's daily life as friends and neighbors.

Adoptive parents also found that, despite having common interests with online group members, meeting each other did not automatically enable community. In fact, it could constrain ties as people discovered they did not like each other or clashed over political and religious issues. As Appadurai pithily notes, "One man's imagined community is another man's political prison" (1990: 5–6). Nevertheless, the dialectical interaction between virtual and actual connections sometimes produced long-lasting dense ties that fostered greater support and sociability among parents and children. This was especially true if they lived in communities of 30,000 or less. They knew each other by name, they commiserated over their local school curriculum and practices, they stepped in to help each other during difficult times or crises, their children shared common constructed memories, and, in many cases, their families mirrored each other in physical appearance.

Some adoptive parents preferred investing in community formation mediated by information technologies, while others expressed a preference for creating community based on day-to-day struggles and investment in forming and sustaining ties, as well as engagement in local battles and social activism. Yet these two modes of community-making are not dichotomous. Rather, I believe that a wide range of media representations and Internet connections feed into the mix that governs how adoptive parents make community in their neighborhoods and daily lives, even when they themselves eschew direct engagement in discussion forums. That is, what circulates through the media may influence how they revise their values and practices or reinforce them, even though they prefer to enact those values and practices through more tangible social networks.

Likewise, their everyday activities—at school, on the playgrounds, with their children at night, in the grocery stores—may lead some of them to seek out advice and evidence of shared struggles on the Internet. In the latter case, self-selection happens rapidly and simultaneously. Common vocabularies and symbols emerge that make it possible to create a shared identity, even though these online groups are large and not connected by direct interpersonal relationships.

Demographics played a prominent role in shaping adoptive parents' participation in virtual and actual communities. Older adoptive parents, those with only one adopted child, and those without preexisting networks that included children eagerly welcomed becoming part of an adoptive parents' group with characteristics similar to their own, and the Internet provided the resources to easily do that. One father became active online with an adoptive parents' group whose children all came from China. The six couples in the group have all become good friends, interacting regularly, traveling together, and meeting up in different parts of the country periodically. Similarly, Wilma, who had adopted from China, stressed that the adoption network of families with children from China had served as a lifeboat for her:

> I feel so sensitive about my age. . . . I was 43. I have these little kids. And all of their peers, those mothers, were in their 20's. . . . I couldn't access that social network at all. And consequently, I felt very isolated. In the Chinese adoptive network community, those parents are old. . . . I just felt more accepted. I was never badly treated by any of the younger parents. . . . I just felt like I had screwed up. . . . It was the adoption network of people that made it more easy for me. . . . And my husband, Rutledge, has said, and I agree with him, there are people in our network that we've held on to that we would never have been friends with. . . . There was nothing else in our lives that would have made our lives intersect. . . . The only thing we had in common seemed to be these little

girls from China. . . . You know, people who wouldn't have voted the same way we do, whose economic position is different from ours, or whose educational opportunities were different from ours. So, yeah, I think our network has definitely changed a great deal. (CA30)

Given the influential impact of interconnectivity on human behavior virtually and actually, I wondered if the networks that emerged might lead to collective activities that addressed questions of racism in the United States, the different state laws governing domestic adoptions, child trafficking, or even school curricula. Few adoptive parents were involved in activism related to these topics, although several had started giving workshops and seminars on transracial adoption; some were attending adoption conferences as a group; and four AA adoptive mothers were suggesting that their neighborhood library and school acquire specific resources that provided role models for children and for mixed adoptive families.

In grappling with issues of race, AA adoptive families took actions that they thought enhanced the well-being and individual security of their children by having them interact regularly with other children and individuals of color. Yet only a few seemed aware that even as they worked hard to create a social world that included people of color, their knowledge of black culture was highly circumscribed. This was also true of CA adoptive parents. Lisa, a CA adoptive mother, urged other CA adoptive families to move from talk to action. She put it this way: "We need to get together and talk specifically about the issues we're facing. Eventually, we need to do something. . . . If not, we will slip back into our white world. I always call it 'our white privileged world'" (CA6).

Discussion

Almost all transnational and transracial adoptive parents took advantage of Internet resources to meet their needs and desires as adoptive families. One mother put it succinctly:

> No one should go through this process without a lot of quality time on the Internet. From chat groups like this, to personal blogs, to getting the Denver developmental milestones . . . the information available is invaluable. There is a lot of chaff for the wheat . . . but the ones who spend the most time beating the straw are the best able to recognize the chaff. (RA11)

The Internet has had three major effects on the lives of AA, CA, and RA adoptive parents in the context of family-making. The most obvious is that the information and images circulating on the Internet structure how adoption processes unfold and what adoptive parents expect. The Internet reinforced the idea that one could approach each stage of adoption in a particular way, with emphasis on how stages, children, and prospective and adoptive parents are represented.

The second effect of the Internet is the calling into question of existing cultural assumptions about normative family formation in the United States, such as the meanings of heredity or biological relatedness and the meanings of affiliation or alliance, and their relationship to each other. Parents are more openly discussing these matters and seeking alternative language, practices, and coping mechanisms. Although it is difficult to trace the evolution of people's thought processes, I have followed some participants in discussion groups who have revised their own assumptions over time. The three most important areas where this is occurring are: openness in adoption; an awareness of the corruption and criminality in the legal system, facilitated by adoption brokers and attorneys; and the painful realization by upper-middle-class white mothers of the systemic racialization of American society and its effects on them as a family and on their children. Nevertheless, recognition and action need to be distinguished, and few adoptive parents had moved from recognition to engagement in confronting racism beyond their children's personal experiences.

Last but not least, the Internet has fostered the formation of tangible communities that have endured over time. Weekly and annual social gatherings among adoptive families provide a sense of belonging and intimacy that distinguishes them from other kinds of networks.

Using Internet resources, adoptive parents began to reevaluate the meanings of existing social boundaries and created new kinds of communities. The impact of their efforts on their children are the next part of the story. Many CA adoptive children at the time of my research, for example, were approaching adolescence and just beginning to air their views, experiences, and reactions to their parents' experiments through books, blogs, message boards, and filmic media.

In the next chapter, I examine the children's responses to their adoptive parents' efforts in the course of growing up, spinning out their own social networks, and elaborating their symbolic worlds.

9 The Children's Search and the Formation of Diasporic Communities

At the moment, I have decided that I may feel deeply the loss of my biological parents, extended family, village, native language, food, customs . . . ancestors' graves, and the place where my umbilical cord was cut and placenta buried, while still enjoying and marveling in the love of my adopted parents, siblings, friends, health, education and other opportunities. I feel that my ever-present loss . . . a homesickness, an empty place at the table—will and should never be ignored or denied, and to speak this loss is not to be ungrateful, unappreciative, or unthankful for my chance to live.

—Rachel Quy Collier (2006: 213)

"You know Mom, I wish you could be brown like me." He didn't say, "I wanna be white like you." He said, "You know it'd be great if you could be brown like me."

—Child adopted by AA17

i've been struggling with these issues for years but i've never been able to find an answer. How does a transracial adoptee like me find her heritage????? i live in a very rural, White community and most african-american culture is no where near me. i've tried internet, meeting new people, etc.. . . . i still have that emptyness in me. my parents did not bring me up to be knowledgable about my own people. i'm becoming desperate, does anyone have advice at all?

—Lena

The ways that adoptive parents "storied" their children through place-making and adoption narratives set the stage for adoptees to reflect on their own identities. Adoptive parents furthered this process by enacting adoption rituals, enrolling their children (and sometimes the whole family) in culture camps, and by taking heritage journeys. Their children, as they grew into young adulthood, in turn, began to embark on activities they thought crucial to building their sense of self, family, and belonging, such as quests for birth relatives, heritage journeys that constituted circuits rather than one-time searches or sightseeing ventures, and gatherings and reunions with other adoptees in the United States and in their birth countries. Drawing on interview materials and participant-observation, excerpts from adoptees' postings on websites and blogs, documentaries they made, and their personal accounts and memoirs, I trace this dialectical process to show how some of these searches for identity were unfolding.

There were striking differences among the three groups of adoptees in their searches for identity and community when they reached adolescence. CA adoptees were the most energetic in founding and participating in activities for adoptees and their families, especially those intended for international and transracial adoptees. Fewer AA adoptees participated in activities specifically designed for them. Instead, they sought out forums and activities aimed at all people of color who were adopted. They were also likely to interact regularly with other African American children, adopted or not, whereas if CA adoptees interacted with other Chinese American children, they were usually adopted as well. RA adoptees were less visibly and publicly engaged in any of these activities, and few participated in adoptee, international, or transnational adoptee blogs or discussion forums. However, the conversations I had with RA adoptees suggested they did have questions and concerns but were not raising them publicly. They sometimes posted in FRUA newsletters, attended culture camps, or went on heritage journeys.[1]

Memories and Longing

In an anthology of autobiographical accounts of Korean adoptees Adam reported his immediate sensation when his mother returned from Korea with photos of his birth family:

> I was almost 14. . . . I think I pretty much basically detached my mind from my body. . . . The most immediate thing I saw were people who looked like me. It was really the first time that had happened. I'd always kind of wondered what they looked like and where I had gotten some of my traits from, my body shape, my stature . . . I saw that they are all about my size and had a very similar build to me. If I spoke Korean, my voice would have sounded like theirs. And, it was . . . quite something. (Lee et al. 2008: 10)

The activist voices of Korean American adoptees who felt their adoptive parents had been clueless about their needs have encouraged this generation of adoptive parents to do more cultural work for their children to facilitate connections with people who look like them, or to substitute cultural knowledge for biological connections. They are bringing the global into the local through their awkward searches for knowledge about their children's cultural heritage and their stumbling efforts to move beyond proclamation to action. In this same spirit, they have collaborated with their children in creating new rituals that acknowledge their children's connections to other places and people from their earliest days. They have flocked to culture camps, a flourishing new industry that sometimes targets adoptive families, sometimes solely their children. And more recently, adoptees have developed their own versions of teen culture camps.

Paul Connerton distinguishes between "personal memory claims" and "habit memories." For Connerton, personal memory claims contribute to identity formation through links to a personal past in which "persons have special access to facts about their own personal histories." He explains that "personal memory claims . . . are critical to my self-description, because my past history is a rich resource for my conception of my self; my self-knowledge, my view of my character and potentialities. . . . All these past actions were located somewhere. There is a vital connection between my personal identity and a variety of backward-looking states" (Connerton 2009: 141). In contrast, he says, habit memories are "performative acts" (140). In the absence of access to many facts about their personal histories, transnational and transracial adoptive families have resorted to performative acts, digital networks and media, and archives of material objects as ways to create links to the past and a context for who they are and who they are becoming, not a minor undertaking.

JetLoakman wrote in her blog about how she became aware of the narrow role models and images depicted in the media and objects accessible to her. It was not until she discovered *National Geographic* that she experienced a sensation of liberation through exposure to the range of settings and people of color depicted in the magazine. Nevertheless, she came to realize that the diverse images and novel rituals she learned about there might have very different goals—in *National Geographic*'s case a celebration of exoticism for purposes of encouraging consumption—than what she read into them (Lutz and Collins 1993). There are few models for transnational and transracial adoptees to emulate as they try to create "habit memories" integral to their identities, and they are learning to approach those that do exist with a degree of wariness, as JetLoakman recounts:

> When I was growing up, there were only caucasian people selling me stuff . . . and only caucasian people were being "sold." To be successful it seemed that one had to be pretty, blue-eyed, and blonde. Asians were servants or dolls in the background to lend a sense of colonial exoticism that bordered on eroticism. This affects us when we look for someone to become—especially when we are vulnerable and searching for "who we are." When we grow up amongst our own "culture" and "race," it's apparent that we could become our father, mother, aunt, uncle, cousin, neighbor, etc. When we grow up in a new world where we are possibly only a handful in the community—then where should we look to see what we might become? Just background or can we be fore-ground? The "models" I see today are a little more varied but still, one should

question what is being sold to you—not just the gizmo but more importantly its marketing to YOU of YOU.[2]

New Rituals and Culture Camps

Adoptive families have crafted novel ceremonies and activities, akin to rites of passage, that convert narratives to practices, first through small rituals that memorialize their connection to their child's birth family and culture, and then through what some have come to call "culture camps." One of the most well-known rituals that CA adoptees participate in, and that now extends to all internationally adopted children, is called "Gotcha Day," the day when they were put into the arms of their adoptive parents by a nanny or foster mother. The excerpt below describes Gotcha Day rituals:

> Well-known in the adoption community, "Gotcha Day" is the first day a parent spends with his or her newly-adopted child. Chicago's *Spectrum Press* has declared September 15th as International "Gotcha Day," one day each year when families who have come together through international adoption celebrate their coming, and being, together.... This September 15th, more than 21,000 new families each year have a new reason to celebrate. "I fondly recall the day I became the mother of my two sons," says Margaret L. Schwartz.... "A family's first day together is both exciting and nerve-wracking. Every emotion from frustration to elation makes International 'Gotcha Day' worthy of celebration."[3]

Schwartz's (2005) memoir, *Pumpkin Patch: A Single Woman's International Adoption*, about her adoption of two children from the Ukraine, generated intense debate about how appropriate "gotcha" was to describe the day, given that it projected an impression of children as commodities to be possessed and exchanged. Adult adoptees made it clear that they were not fond of the word, despite what it was intended to celebrate: Hanna Sofia Jung Johansson pointedly asked, "What is being celebrated [on Gotcha Day]? Parenthood and the new family, I guess. But do adoptive parents acknowledge their child's losses at the same time? 'Gotcha' for parents means 'lost-ya' for children who have been separated from familiar faces, smells, and surroundings." Another adult adoptee, Eun Mi Young, was equally blunt. "While endearing to adoptive parents, 'Gotcha' is downright disrespectful to adoptees," she says. "What does this term imply? We use it when we grab someone who is running from us, or when we save someone from something, or when we're playing a game. We shouldn't use it for an event that recalls the loss of culture, country, and birthparents."[4]

While adoptive parents and the public at large have generally portrayed Gotcha Day as a day of celebration, adoptees viewed it more as a time for grieving and memorializing their lost birth families, especially their birth mothers. The conscious motivation among adoptive parents for ritualizing the day they adopted their child was not so much to suppress feelings that adoptees might have about their origins on this day, but to project a new habitus about family formation through international adoption. Many parents made the observation that because this was a new celebration, it was evolving.

The modification of Gotcha Day to include ceremonies of both celebration and memorialization occurred because of criticism by adoptees. CA adoptees preferred to dedicate the day they were adopted to their birth parents (usually the mother) by lighting a candle or constructing an altar on which they burned incense. They reflected on the paradox that they were "sad and happy"; they wished they did not have to feel "lucky," but they also appreciated that their adoptive parents were formally recognizing the day they were adopted and the role their birth mother may have played in that process.

"Entrustment ceremonies" and variants of "candle ceremonies" have also spread to "mark transitions" and acknowledge "losses and gains, joy and sadness, and the present and future." I saw one enacted at an annual meeting of the North American Council on Adoptable Children. Each candle signified a facet of the adoption process—one to honor birth relatives and separation from birth siblings and the difficult decisions they made; a second to honor adopted children and adults; a third for adoptive parents; the fourth for waiting parents; and the fifth for children awaiting a permanent family. The ritual had a paradigmatic structure and dominant symbols, but like many effective rituals, its healing power, eliciting both joy and sadness, derived from its flexibility and the polyvalence of the symbols and practices (Turner 1967). I saw candle ceremonies performed in small groups and large auditoriums, and participants spoke about holding candle ceremonies on specific occasions in the privacy of their homes or in religious settings such as churches, synagogues, and Buddhist temples.

Ai Mei Li and her adoptive parents made a journey to China. While the "heritage" dimension of their journey played a role, the opportunity for Mei Li to memorialize her ties to her birth parents was more significant:

Almost eight years after she had been abandoned after dark under a spruce tree in a police training camp in central China, Mei Li Isaacson wrote a letter to her first family. "I am called Ai Mei Li. I just want to say hello. I want you to

know I love you and here are some pictures of me and my new family." Mei Li
wrote the letter in Chinese, a language she has been studying for three years in
a bilingual school with daily half-day Mandarin immersion in San Francisco.
That day, a crowd of neighborhood children and a few adults gathered to
watch as she and her American parents put the letter and some photographs
into an envelope and tied it to the tree. Among the photos was one of three-
day-old Mei Li bundled in the flowered blanket in which she had been found.
Mei Li's father, Bob Isaacson, insisted on leaving them on the tree, however:
"It doesn't matter if they remove the pictures," explained Bob. "We just want
to tell her mother she did the right thing. Her child is alive, happy, living in
America, and learning Chinese. This is the most we can do." The retired civil
engineer felt he had "a karmic obligation to help remove a scar from their
souls that must certainly be there." As they drove back to their hotel, one of the
visitors saw a sad and tired-looking woman walking along the dusty road. She
looked like an elder version of Mei Li. But what could they say to her? No one
would admit to abandoning a child. The Isaacsons will probably never know
Mei Li's birth mother. There wasn't even a note. "Our primary purpose for the
trip was to open a door for Mei Li to her roots that she can walk through when
she is older if she chooses," her father explained later. "We don't want to bring
her up Chinese, but as an American who is fully aware and proud of her origins." "We want her to have familiarity with Chinese culture and friends and
feel positive about it," agreed her mother, Ginny Stearns, "and have the tools to
go deeper into it or walk away from it all if she chooses."[5]

A key turning point in adoptees' identity formation occurred when they
attended heritage or culture camps. These have sprouted all over the United
States in the summer and, more recently, in sending countries, some tailored
for adoptees from a particular country, others for all transnational adoptees,
and still others for all adoptees. Some adoptive parents attended the camps.
CA adoptive families whose children came from the same Social Welfare Institute (orphanage) sometimes made a point of going together to these heritage
camps and thought of themselves as constituting an "extended family." Most
of the camps were for children between 4 and 17 years old. At last count, there
were thirty-four major camps operating in eighteen states.[6] One camp in Colorado, in operation since 1991, described its mission in the following way:

> Chinese Heritage Camp is a family camp with programming for each member
> of the family. Campers from toddlers to grandparents participate in classes
> and workshops taught primarily by Chinese Americans who enthusiastically

share their expertise with adoptive families. Asian American counselors serve as role models and mentors to the children as they participate with them in cultural classes while adult family members attend cultural and adoption related workshops ranging from Chinese cooking and customs to the blessings and challenges inherent in our adoptive families.[7]

In listservs, blogs, and newsletters, and in interviews, the children and young teens stressed that they had benefited most from camps they attended by themselves without their adoptive parents hovering at their back. They described the camps as opportunities to "commune" with others like themselves without making any "effort." They said they experienced a "silent understanding," a glimmering of "peace." It was not so much what they did at these camps that they valued, but rather being there without their parents, who had expectations for what their children should get out of the camps. They could shed the feeling of being "engineered."

CA adoptee Ellen had told me of her annoyance with "being forced" to be someone that she was not. At 15, she desperately wanted to quit doing Chinese dance in a group her mother had enrolled her in at age 5. Among the earliest of adoptees, she disliked being forced to take the class because she felt that "it sets me apart from my friends." She lived in a suburb of Virginia where the density of CA adoptees was high. Nevertheless, her feelings were typical of many teens who want to fit in. Her mother insisted she continue because she strongly believed that "one day Ellen will appreciate her connection to her culture." The superimposition of culture on physical appearance was something many transracial international adoptees came to resent.

At culture camp, adoptees discovered they could confide in others who shared similar feelings, especially confusion about their identity, and they did not have to keep their guard up. Crystal explained, "I really can't explain the difference between camp and when my mom had tried to get me to go to other support groups. I guess at camp I felt like I didn't have my mom watching over my back. I wouldn't have to go home to my mom and tell her what I did . . . I was very inspired to learn more about the country that gave me birth." Emily Rappeport, age 10, of Reisterstown, MD, summarized her experience: "We got to do tai chi and Chinese writing. And no one looked at me for being different because, for once, I wasn't."[8] (Hainer 2005).

Three CA adoptees, Qiu Meng, Celena Kopinski, and Hope Goodrich, whose parents had helped found Families with Children in China in 1993, had regularly attended a culture camp and had been friends since they were young.

They returned to the camp as counselors because they felt that their role as mentors would make a huge difference for younger adoptees. They reflected on their experiences while they were growing up as one principal reason they had come back as counselors. Qiu Meng described her experience: "We're related. . . . We don't have to be like, 'Oh, you're adopted?' or 'Oh, yeah, I'm Chinese.' It's just easy." She remembered "how hard it was to talk about painful things" when she was younger, and how "children at school would stretch their eyes upward and tease" her, concluding that "there aren't a lot of children who can talk openly and easily about things like that. So it feels good to be able to help them." Rituals were a part of culture camp activities. At this particular camp, the campers gathered in a circle at the end and were linked to each other with a string. Each camper went home with a section of the string. Qiu Meng kept hers on the wall of her bedroom.[9]

One young CA adoptee explained what she loved about culture camp by contrasting her experience there with middle school:

> Today was a hard day[;] imature people kept making Chinese jokes at me. . . . Here in America sometimes I think people just can't picture being adopted from halfway across the world. . . . Having a friend that is a Chinese adoptie [*sic*] is different. There's just a certain bond between the two that clicks. I don't get along the same way with my adoptie friends as my American ones. . . . What gets me through the hard times is talking to my China adoptie friends.[10]

In these settings, at least for a brief time, mimesis and menace dissolved, and carrying those memories with them, adoptees felt transformed. Their mirror became other adoptees like them. They did not have to feel guilty about being lucky or, ironically, be passionate about Chinese (or any other) culture to satisfy their parents' substitution of culture for originary ties to their birth families.

One of the most interesting culture camp experiments for children adopted from China was called "Adopteen," established in 2008 and organized by teen adoptees from China. Approximately sixty teens attended the 2012 four-day camp. Although adult chaperones were there, the "Teen Committee" had chosen the topics for the sessions, and adoptees ran them with the express goal of creating an environment in which adoptees could "share openly without adult interference" and maybe "even get some long-pondered questions out into the open," as they put it. In reviewing the topics, I thought it unlikely they would have occurred to adult organizers, yet they were of importance to adoptees themselves; they included "Fashions of Chinese Minorities," "What Is the Adoption Process," and "Doing Make-Up on Asian Features."[11]

RA adoptees also enjoyed "culture camps," though fewer attended them. Ben, who went to the Colorado Heritage Camp at age 8, was glad to have "met many kids adopted from Russia, Romania, and Ukraine" and to be able to "send money back to one of the orphanages in Russia." He felt it was important that his cousin, a domestic adoptee, be at the camp with him because he "thought it was good for him to learn about different cultures and also talk about being adopted" (FRUA 2008: 12).

Marina had been adopted from Russia at age 4. She told me that at age 18 she used culture camp as an opportunity to exorcise the frustrations she had faced over the years, dealing with all the class assignments and invasive queries about adoption and about Russia. With impressive agency, she put together a project for camp attendees:

> I got the idea to do a presentation on my adoption because it has a tendency to come up occasionally in conversation. When this happens, it seems that I am hitting the "replay" button and saying the same information over and over. So . . . I volunteered to do this. . . . One weekend when I was home with my family, we went through the videos, photo albums, and all the documentation surrounding my adoption. It had been a long time since we had reviewed all this information. There were a few surprises, things I had either forgotten about or didn't understand previously. This process brought back feelings of being unwanted and unloved. Even though I can rationalize that this isn't true, the feelings still tend to emerge from deep inside me. . . . Without positive affirmation, I have a tendency to slip back into these old feelings. . . . The overall reaction to my presentation was positive. There were students from Russia in the audience and they found it fascinating. Even though they lived in Russia, they didn't understand any of this nor were they aware of the plight of the many children living in orphanages. . . . Going through this process had a very positive effect on me . . . I felt safe while presenting to this audience. (FRUA 2008: 12)

Far fewer camps were designed for African American adoptees. Many AA adoptees attended "Pact" camps or "Camp for Me." The philosophy of Pact camps was to begin the hard work of transracialization among adoptees and their adoptive parents. In both of these camps, many of the counselors were adult adoptees. Pact camps were open to all adoptees, but focused more on the needs and questions of transracial adoptees. During the six years Dr. John Raible, an adult adoptee, had attended the camp as a counselor, he had seen remarkable changes in the practices of those who had attended it. He saw "families making life-changing decisions for their children, for example, about relocating and choosing to attend more racially diverse schools and houses of worship." They were "willing to learn about black hair care and how to do braids, rather than chopping off hair that feels unmanageable due to their lack of experience," and he found that families were more "receptive to hearing the hard knowledge about living as a person of color in a still racist society . . . acknowledging that their adopted children of color need to be around people who look like them." He also found that adoptive parents were working toward "more openness in adoption, for example, by establishing ongoing relationships with their children's birth families . . . becoming advocates for open records and adoption reform" and "grappling with how to live ethically as a multiracial family, and with what transracial adoption and race mean to the white children in their families." In short, he concluded that adoptive parents were "shouldering some of the burdens of being adopted, such as the emotional toll of surviving orphanages, foster care, and birth mother relinquishment, and other early traumas. . . . standing in solidarity with adoptees of color as allies in the struggle to transform racism."[12]

Culture camps were a giant step forward in forging a sense of community among adoptees. For the first time, as one young man exclaimed, "we are in the majority and we have something in common with everyone." The camps had different objectives and moral orientations. Some were not adoptee-centered; they included cultural activities but also interwove adoption discourse built on ideas of "rescue" and "gratefulness." The best camps took seriously the needs and desires of adoptees, and if adoptive parents were involved, the family activities were more adoptee-focused. Adoptees basked in being able to be themselves or, if they were first-timers, getting a glimpse of what it *would* be like to be themselves. The camps conveyed cultural knowledge that adoptive parents of adoptees had also been transmitting, allowing attendees to reconsider that knowledge in a new context—in a community of their peers rather than their adoptive parents, whose authority was hard to escape. Many culture camps thus nurtured the emergence of a new view that recognized in "the other" a whole self. It became a "good enough" mirror for adoptees.

The Meaning of Connections

Judith Modell (2002: 69) asserts that "the shifts in adoption are not creating new forms of families, just new ways people can gain knowledge about their own families." Modell is right that adoption practices still swim in the current of biology, especially when it comes to the desire among young teens and adults to search for birth relatives—usually their birth mother—in order to feel whole or know someone who looks or acts like they do or who shares their DNA.

While little research has been done in this area, these reflexive moments appear to occur less frequently in other cultures where boundaries do not rigidly differentiate among individuals that nurture a child. For example, Janet Carsten (2004) observed that:

> It was precisely the obvious contrast between Western adoption, which signals the full relinquishing of parental rights on the part of birth parents, and Malay fostering, which is both very frequent and does not involve the assumption of exclusive parental rights, that motivated me to undertake research on adoptive reunions in Scotland. . . . It is hard to imagine a Malay adult who has been fostered in childhood seeking out her birth parents. . . . This is most obviously unlikely because the connections to birth parents would have been maintained alongside those to foster parents." (Carsten 2004: 104–6)

Sandra Patton points out that in the United States searches are "viewed as an expression of a universal human need" and that those who are not curious about roots are "repressing their true selves." She found that "search literature and television discourse discussed search as a sort of rite of passage for adoptees, a *rebirth* through the rewriting of the origin narrative. While the discourse was fueled by the loss that most adoptees feel, it was also infused with the power of biological and genetic ways of explaining the "nature" of identity" (Patton 2000: 109).

Adoptive parents and children alike exhibited this compulsion to explain the "nature" of identity, yet little has been written about how the views and actions of adoptive parents shaped their children's subsequent decisions. Even when adoptees rejected their adoptive parents' efforts to explain race or adoption or to link them to their birth culture or birth families, as young adults they were nevertheless better equipped to strike out on their own searches and paths than an earlier generation of adoptees had been. They began to find their comfort zone by working both with and against the impulses and practices of their adoptive parents whose essentialization of Chinese or black culture, for example, ironically facilitated their processes of identity formation. This was true of Catie B., whose curiosity about her roots in China eventually led her to participate in a ten-month study-abroad program in Beijing:

> Upon arriving in China . . . I felt very American. . . . However, ever since I was little I was very interested in China. I could never forget the country of my ancestors. When I was four years old, I went with my mother to China to adopt my younger sister. Since I was so young, the memories from that first trip back to China have mostly faded, but I still have photos to help me remember. Each

time I flipped through those photo albums, I became even more interested in learning about China.[13]

Adoptees who "looked different" also yearned to see themselves in their family physiognomies. Yet this desire was not a simple one. Repeatedly, adoptees mentioned, in the same breath, wanting to look like someone and feeling "a hole," "a void," or "something missing." Adolescence was the time when questions surrounding identity *and* the desire to fit in typically occur in the United States, but adoptive parents reported these questions and sentiments far earlier among their children. When the adoptees entered their teen years, they intuitively felt they were missing something, but it was not until they began to search that they could articulate what they wanted. When they were younger, they often expressed this as a desire for a sibling or friend from the same place or who looked like them, not so much for *cultural* reasons but so that they would not be the focus of attention and, in the case of African Americans, especially, so that they could share what they felt about living in a white, racialized society (Baden and Raible 2010, 2011).[14]

Wrestling with shadow identities—glimmers of connections with their birth parents and information about their roots—came to the fore in different contexts and at different times for adoptees. Many children were not initially interested at all in searching for their birth parents or their shadow lives. The sharp contrast between the daily experiences of AA adoptees and those of their white adoptive parents spurred them to search, even though they did not know exactly what they were searching for. Transracial adoptees, both women and men, shouldered a double burden during adolescence because of the stress of transracial dating. In addition, transracial adoptees became fatigued by negotiating how they felt on the inside and how they looked on the outside. They could not bring the two together and they searched in hope of resolving the contradiction. As Sandra Patton (2000: 13) notes, "The experiences of African American adoptees raised in White families are often similar to those of international adoptees raised by White parents. . . . Both . . . report a disjuncture between the ways they experience themselves in their families and the racist treatment to which they are subjected in public. . . . and both draw on a repertoire of cultural meaning systems in charting their course through life."

Being Lucky, Being Plucky

Many adoptees were disturbed by the social pressure on them to "feel lucky." In an article in *The New Yorker* about organ donation, Larissa MacFarquhar (2009) writes that organ donors and recipients have sentiments that closely resemble those of adoptees in certain circumstances. She says that those who have given and received kidneys through the national donor program and those who used a website that allowed donors to choose to whom they wanted to give their kidney have very different experiences. As I read the article, I felt I was reading about adoption dynamics. By the time I reached the end of the article, MacFarquhar was bringing both processes together, using the example of adoption to describe the ambivalent sentiments of altruism that shaped how donors and recipients in the dance of organ transferral felt.

In organ donations facilitated by the Internet, the logic of the market lurked. Recipients, it seemed, could more easily exploit vulnerable populations and undermine public trust in the equitable allocation of organs. Less anticipated, the exchange itself had the capacity to "bind the donor and the recipient together, sometimes with love, sometimes with guilt, or gratitude." It could shift bonds and create feelings of obligation and oppressive control that so overwhelmed the recipient that they could no longer face the donor (MacFarquhar 2009: 43). Some people found that "in some quasi-animistic way, the dead beloved survived in the body of the recipient" (44).

The donation of an organ to another human being is not the same thing as adopting a child. No one need know that one has received or given an organ, whereas in the case of transracial adoptions, in particular, the dimension of exchange has a visual dimension. Yet similarities exist between the two—the anonymity of donor and recipient, and in many cases altruism and obligation, encapsulated in adoptive parents' narratives and social commentary. The burdens of gratitude and the sadness and anger about abandonment are such that adoptees often feel that they do not have the right to express their mixed sentiments about their adoptive and birth parents. This is true whether or not adoptive parents themselves expected their children to be unconditionally loyal and perfectly behaved. The sense of feeling "lucky" to have acquired a "forever family" created anxiety among adoptees about abandonment, guilt about having questions about their adoption, and anger about being different. If adoptive parents fused the notion of "luck" with the idea that God "meant" the adoption to be, the sense of oppression and unspoken power dynamics at work were intense indeed. Eleanor, a poised 12-year-old commented to me, "If my parents had adopted me because God told them to, that would be really sad. It would make me feel as if *they* didn't really want me."

When children decided to search, their decision was complicated by the American idea of "family" itself as a primal "gift" that had to be reciprocated. As

Marcel Mauss (1990) showed long ago, gift-giving spins out webs of obligation through exchange, which become the basis for society. Hence, even as parents might acknowledge their "selfish" motivations in deciding to adopt a child so they could have a family, their adoption narratives created conditions for children to feel obligated by gratefulness to them. At the same time, adoptees experienced guilt because they longed for initial connection with their birth and foster parents. JetLoakman alluded to this, as did many other adoptees:

> I had rationalized how being an adoptee was a blessing and my fate, and how grateful I was for the love my adoptive parents gave me. My adoptive parents were my parents—no doubt—but to meet my birth mother was amazing. . . . As I meet more of my family . . . I see a lot of them in me . . . the bad bits as much as good bits! Maybe it's my own desire to be connected like this. . . . I call my adoptive mum my "A-mum" and Annie was my birth mother, my "B-mum."[15]

Signe Howell argues that it is "precisely the juggling act of keeping both biology and sociality as meaningful but not hopelessly contradictory, that represents the main challenge" for adoptive families (Howell 2006: 82), and children wrestled hard with this juggling act, especially after they reached adolescence. One young woman, adopted from China, laid out how she regarded this juggling act and the discourse that accompanied it:

> I'm going to be honest; I have a strong dislike towards the term "adoptive parent," because I do not consider my birth mother and birth father to be my "real" parents. They don't even know me except, perhaps, for a memory in their minds of my birthday. I have no apparent ties with them, other than through my blood and genetic tendencies. I always struggle over the nurture over nature question of my different characteristics. . . . being a clean person seems to be nature; my family is quite messy while I need my environment to be neat and organized all the time. Also, it seems that my love for art, and even more, my passion for music is also a "natural" tendency, but maybe I was the only one to stick to my interest. Of course, I would want to compare myself with my birth parents if I ever could, to see whom I look like, to see if I can find any similar behavior or quirk in myself that they had. The truth is, it is virtually impossible to find my birth mother, who most likely gave a fake name on the hospital forms she filled out. It is most likely I'll never find her, but unlike most adoptees today, I do have the pleasure of knowing more about them, such as, my birth mother liked ice skating, playing badminton—and most telling—singing, which is one of my greatest passions and joys, so I do

like to think I've "inherited" that. Oh dear, as I write, I find so many problems with these terms, they always seem to be connecting directly to an emphasis on a blood-tie relation. . . . the word heritage itself implies a blood tie to a place of origin. So that's enough of that![16]

So what form did the children's searches take as they looked for mirrors that reflected themselves? Below, I first discuss the searches of transnational adoptees and then turn to those of AA adoptees. Although they were similar in some ways, the searches by AA adoptees were easier geographically and more likely to produce knowledge about their birth families; for many transnational adoptees, their parents had thought that heritage journeys could provide answers to their identity searches.

Return Journeys, Searches, and Homecomings

As metaphor . . . and metaphors go to the heart of what human beings are . . . there is absolutely nothing wrong with the idea of ghosts haunting the living. . . . It's simply a statement about our relation to the past, and to the parts of the past we haven't managed to cope with.[17]

One of the first steps parents who had adopted transnationally took in order to connect the missing links in their children's past was to go on a "heritage journey." Heritage journeys began with the coming of age of Korean adoptees and have steadily gained momentum. They were often organized by or had some existing association with agencies that facilitated adoptions. This made sense since the agencies already had relationships and contacts in place in the country. The journeys were often labeled as "motherland tours," a not-so-subtle allusion to substituting place and culture for a tangible connection to a child's birth mother. For transnational adoptees, heritage journeys served many of the same functions that searches for birth relatives did for domestic transracial adoptees. In both instances, the journeys entailed "returning," but in a nonlinear way.

Heritage journeys were undertaken by individual families or groups of adoptive families. They were a money-making venture for agencies that promoted and managed them. They also brought foreign exchange to orphanages and welfare institutes, and to countries which profited from the industry of tourism that accompanied heritage journeys. Yet these journeys were not solely about the commodification of culture. "Genealogical tourism . . . where essence becomes enterprise" could also be a "mode of reflection, of self-construction, of producing and feeling" a sense of rootedness and belonging to a particular culture (Comaroff and Comaroff 2009: 9). The Comaroffs note that "heritage, of course, is culture named and projected in the past, and simultaneously, the past congealed into culture" (10). In a similar fashion, adoptive parents, in the search to construct for their children a sense of cultural belonging, went on heritage journeys with them.

These journeys followed a predictable, orchestrated pattern. In China, they included sightseeing at major tourist sites in order to learn about ancient and modern China, and a visit to their children's orphanage. If families were traveling as a group, they separated to visit their respective orphanages, and reunited afterwards. At the orphanages, they were welcomed by several officials—the director and other administrative personnel. In exchange, the families, instructed by the organizers of the journey, offered small gifts of appreciation to orphanage personnel and, possibly, a more substantial donation to the orphanage. Sometimes, families were allowed to "tour" the orphanage and interact with children there; if a visiting child was lucky, she might reunite with one or more of the nannies that had cared for her and remembered her; and even more rare, she might see her foster mother or caretaker again. Families were also frequently allowed to "go back" to the site where their child was first found, the "abandonment" or "finding" site.

The sentiments this experience produced were not the same for every child. Maia was born in Hangzhou, and after she was adopted had spent most of her life in the Midwest. She returned to Hangzhou in 2005 with her adoptive parents at the age of 11. That trip was mostly an eye-opening experience of travel and being exposed to new things—"the thrill of bargaining, drinking tea from a fancy cup, riding a boat on a lake." Maia did not feel that Hangzhou held much significance for her, even though she visited the site where she had been found as an infant, went to her orphanage, and saw the note her birth mother had left in her clothes. What she most remembered about the day she visited her finding site and orphanage was "going to a small store close to the orphanage and buying their entire stock of baby diapers. We gave the diapers to the orphanage, which was much in need of them."[18]

When Ellen, age 13, first returned to China, she was deeply disturbed by the impoverished economic conditions in China in contrast to American notions of progress and modernization. She viewed her birthplace as backward and underdeveloped and was embarrassed rather than pleased by the photos her parents had lovingly taken, documenting daily life in China when they had gone to adopt her in the early 1990s. She made another trip in 2000 and was less upset when she saw that parts of China had been dramatically modernized and was now more like the United States (CA10).

When families traveled in a group, the children appreciated the security of being with each other because, although they looked Chinese, they were not, and as I learned in my own heritage journey with our daughter, curious stares and chatter were the order of the day, especially if one traveled into rural areas. Nevertheless, the children began to appreciate more nuanced dimensions of Chinese culture that went beyond (and against) their exposure in the United States to stories and activities related to Chinese culture. The most dramatic moment came for many children when they compared and contrasted the beauty of China, as conveyed to them in the United States, with the reality of China. As breathtaking as particular sights were, it dawned on them that China was struggling with pollution, crowds, a lack of infrastructure, and a population of 1.3 billion. While this somewhat superficial knowledge challenged their prior romanticized images of China, it also highlighted, again, the idea that because they had been adopted, they were "lucky" not to live in these difficult circumstances.

It was moving and frightening for children to visit their respective orphanages. However kind and welcoming the orphanage personnel were, the conditions were bleak and many of the children were not healthy. As one girl put it, "It wasn't very cozy." If they were traveling with siblings and visiting two orphanages, not infrequently one child would have information from the orphanage about their past; the other would have none or very little. Sometimes, neither child found information about their early years. Places that had been documented in photos and that their adoptive parents had told them about, had changed, sometimes dramatically. In my daughter's case, the entire orphanage had been torn down and only one small building remained; the playground was completely overgrown; only special-needs children remained at the site, and a new high-rise "welfare institute" was being constructed for both children and the elderly.

When children found one or more of the caretakers who remembered them and called them by a special nickname—"big eyes" or "two bottles"—they did feel as if they had "connected," and they welcomed any kind of knowledge about their past that was proffered to them. A few of the visiting adoptees mentioned the pleasure they experienced interacting with children in the orphanage, holding their hands, playing with them, or being allowed to carry one of the infants. These moments allowed them to re-enter a past that they were busily constructing in the present.

Mei Mei had only recently begun to investigate her roots, but she wrote that "the minute I set foot on Chinese soil, I experienced a primeval gut reaction, a sense of belonging. It was as if, buried in my unconscious, a shadowy, ghost-like world, had laid hidden, waiting to emerge." Mei Mei's ghost world haunted many adoptees. What they did not know, what they had read into their adoptive parents' narratives, what they saw before them, all held out the prospect of their "could have been" and "could be" lives.[19]

Return or heritage journeys could be disconcerting and exhausting as adoptees sought to integrate them with the prior memories or fantasies they had embraced and absorbed. One family, after their daughter's first return journey, decided that they would go back every four years so that the experience would be interactive as their daughter changed and her birthplace changed. In Mei Mei's case, she felt she had reached a peace about her roots. She decided that she was "fortunate" to have had "two mothers and two fathers," and although parts of her past remained "shrouded in mystery," she concluded that, "in my "unrelenting pursuit of connections, I have magically pieced together the disparate pieces to complete the mosaic of my life."[20]

Maia returned to Hangzhou five years after her first heritage journey. It was an entirely different experience for her. She did not visit her orphanage or go to her finding spot. However, wherever she went, she felt haunted by the presence of her birth mother and father and her alter-identity. In her blog, which she expected to publish as a memoir, she described what she felt when she was traveling by bus into a rural, tea-growing area:

> I know that farmers are hard at work, backs bent double as they pick the valuable leaves. I could just as easily be one of them. Or maybe they're my mom or dad. . . . I was in the city of my birth, and even though I didn't spend much time there, every shopkeeper I talked with, every street cleaner I saw, every tour guide whose voice amplified over a grainy little speaker clipped on her belt, I thought, "That could be my family." This shopkeeper charging me for a mango—this could be my father. And instead of bargaining down from such an exorbitant rate, I would fish in my wallet and pull out a ten *yuan* bill. . . . I found myself unable to handle so many emotions and relegated them all to a small box. . . . It was only after we left the city that I began tentatively . . . sorting through the jumble. I tried and gave up. So the little box got put back in the corner until this past fall. . . . I pulled it out once again . . . and tried again. . . . I made the realization that there really is no way to sort through everything that you feel from an experience so complicated as going back. Sometimes you just have to love the mess of contradictions you will never completely understand or quantify.[21]

JetLoakman kept the name her birth mother had given her and, unusually, eventually found her birth mother because of a short film she had made about her own adoption and posted on the Internet. She described her heritage journey as a search for biological connections and for a place that she could feel comfortable in:

> We may have grown up in the West, but I think there is a part of us that does want something from our biological past. Maybe it's like salmon who go back to the river they were hatched from, maybe it's something in our DNA that needs a particular latitude and longitude, maybe it's about finding a place that we can hold in our heart that is "ours" and not "theirs." . . . In 2002, I finally met my birth mother. . . . I finally found what I looked like. . . . Strange to say this, but I had no real conception of what I looked like. Whilst I saw other female Asian faces and body types and I tried to imagine how someone might see me, I couldn't. But meeting Annie—I saw my future face and through my half-sisters, I saw a possible past.[22]

For legal reasons, few Russian adoptees returned to Russia before they turned 18. RA adoptive parents were worried that Russian authorities or birth families would attempt to keep their children in the country or that their sons might be drafted. Nadine went at age 19. She visited the hospital where she had been housed and concluded, "I didn't need to do any soul searching. I didn't need to fill a void. I just wanted to see it." In contrast, Bellany had wondered about her roots since the age of 4. Her adoptive parents helped her locate her birth mother, and from the time Bellany was 10 they exchanged letters. At 17, Bellany returned to Russia against her adoptive mother's wishes. Accompanied by her adoptive father, she spent ten days with her birth family, which included a sibling. What meant the most to her was that "they had the same eyes and rosebud mouth that I had. When you're adopted you don't have that at all. I had a kind of physical connection with them." She was simultaneously struck by the poverty she encountered: "You read about poverty, but when you see it, especially when it's your own family. . . . It's kind of amazing to think, "what if I had lived that life?" After her visit, she continued to Skype periodically with her birth family and hoped that someday they could visit her. She concluded, "It's not like I want to live with my birth family. I know that this family comes first. . . . It's just something I had to do. It's part of me."[23]

Anthropologist Mary Douglas (1966: 40) argues that cultures use classification systems that distinguish that which is pure and clean from that which is polluted. Should the two mix, it creates cognitive anxiety. That which is polluting may threaten the entire system of social order and therefore must be bounded, actively cordoned off. It is considered "matter out of place." Some adoptees, upon returning from their journeys, viewed them as "extremely negative," in part because they disrupted the order of their lives. They did not want to ever go back, and they experienced their fabricated roots in a more alienated fashion. I write "fabricated" because these roots were the result of the efforts of adoptive parents, in conjunction with the heritage and genealogical tourism industry, to craft cultural attachment in ways that were far from organic. Others, catalyzed by similar experiences, recalibrated their fabricated memories and their internalization of "being lucky and special" and the structure and content of their classification systems began to change. They converted what had been limited to shadows, images, sealed boxes, and discomfiting sensations into more concrete, nuanced ties with people and places in China or Russia.

Barbara Yngvesson and Susan Bibler Coutin (2006) studied the experience of "going back" among transnational adoptees. They discuss how a structured personal life or timeline, in which gaps were papered over with documents, was called into question by return journeys. These journeys really had no destination or endpoint. Instead, they were made up of multiple affiliations and documents, piecemeal and originary, and those that "jutted into the future." Because they had nonlinear reference points they always suggested alternative trajectories, and one point did not connect to another. They were "unclear," had "gaps," and might not "really be a path at all." In their words, "from one point on this path, other points can be seen, but dimly, as when peering through translucent glass. If time were linear, this path would be transparent. When individuals move along this path, however, they move across as well as through time. As a dimension of space, time assumes a planar as well as a linear form" (Yngvesson and Coutin 2006: 183).

All of the adoptees Yngvesson and Coutin interviewed for their study found that going "back" made them feel "strange" (2006: 183–84). It was "less a journey with a clear end point (or a clear point of origin) than a network of referents" (Yngvesson and Coutin 2006, quoting Latour 1999: 310). The paradox that Yngvesson and Coutin describe has set in motion a growing movement among adoptees to make multiple return journeys (rather than just one), and to stay for longer periods of time in their country of origin. Many of them were pursuing activities to raise money or purchase toys and other needed items for their orphanage; some were raising scholarship funds to send Chinese girls in rural areas to high school; and even more of them were working in orphanages during the summer. Return journeys have also led to annual reunions of adoptees in the United States and in their countries of birth, thus creating another strand to be woven into their identity formation. Korean adoptees, who were among the first to begin holding annual reunions, are now also holding periodic reunions in Korea.[24] A similar pattern is visible in the developmental trajectories of AA adoptees who have returned to Africa or who, as young adults, have decided to live in black neighborhoods or affiliate with black college student groups.

Irene Sege wrote an article in the *Boston Globe* about three teens who began volunteering in an orphanage in China. Jenna, one of the girls, explained her motivation: "I always wanted to thank the people at the orphanage for taking such good care of me. I wanted to show them that when the babies go away they're not gone for good." The three girls worked in a "Little Sisters" program in Wuhan Province with children with severe disabilities, others who were on the verge of being adopted, and a boy who had lived in the orphanage since age 9. At 18, he was going to the University of Science and Technology. Guastella, one of the girls, wondered whether they had they passed their birth parents in the street and concluded, "There's a part of me that's now filled in because I've gone back and seen my first home."[25]

The activities adoptees pursued in their circuit journeys differed from the annual rituals they had performed as children or the material objects emblematic of China or Russia they had received as gifts or purchased as symbols of their attachment to their birth origins. They were finding ways to return gifts through labor that benefited their birth country and its people and that could conceivably lead to ties that would grow over the years. They were also acquiring a renewed interest in the "Chinese" or "Russian" part of their identity and had moved from experiencing this in a limited way. One teen described to me what happened to her after she visited China: "Being adopted in a white family on the East Coast and growing up contributed to my denying my Chinese ethnicity until I went on a long search to China. Now I am definitely more accepting of myself as a Chinese and an American person."

Some who returned more than once to China decided, after all, that it was a good idea to learn Chinese and were less resentful of their adoptive parents' efforts to immerse them in Chinese culture. They were motivated to participate in study-abroad programs and learn Mandarin. Others began to explore how they could incorporate both sides of their identity as equally relevant to who they were.

This pattern was just beginning to appear among CA adoptees who were reaching college age. The acceptance among adoptees of the "Chineseness" and

"Americanness" of their identity resembles Korean American adoptees' embrace of being "twinkies." One Korean American adoptee described this, not as a derogatory term but rather as a descriptive one—"a yellow sponge cake soaking up American culture surrounding it" with a "white interior." She explained she was constantly being misinterpreted, misread, and stereotyped, but had concluded that she "should not feel shame for not embodying my birth culture. I use forks and wear western clothes; I see myself mirrored in my parents; my physical characteristics are Asian; I wear children's-sized shoes; I have loving parents. I am a twinkie and don't want to be anything else. My twinkified body gives me a voice." She felt that it was more through her "performance" that she embraced her identity and "plays" with people's expectations (Bacon 2010).[26]

Openness, Class, and Searches

A startling figure was released in 2012 that an estimated 95 percent of U.S. infant adoptions now have some level of openness between birth and adoptive parents, unlike earlier decades, when such contact was routinely denied. According to a report published by the Evan B. Donaldson Adoption Institute, based on 4,400 recent adoptions from 100 agencies, "55 percent of domestic infant adoptions are 'fully disclosed,'" such that birth and adoptive families "know each other" and "typically have ongoing, direct contact." Another 40 percent are "mediated," with families exchanging letters and pictures through intermediaries without having direct contact with each other. Five percent remain closed or confidential. The adoptive parents have medical information about the biological parents, but no other identifying information (Siegel and Smith 2012).

For AA adoptees, the increasing openness of adoptions in the United States and the probability that their birth families resided in the United States made their searches more likely to be successful than those of CA or RA adoptees. They could also be traumatic, if they discovered, as they sometimes did, that their birth relatives had little or no interest in sustaining a relationship with them. This was true for all domestic adoptees who undertook searches.

Class differences also intervened between birth families and adoptive families and sometimes became insurmountable. In describing geopolitical inequalities between sending and receiving regions and families in transnational adoption, the term "poverty" is often used. In domestic adoptions, more frequently "class" is used. Although geographic proximity might provide AA adoptees with more access to black culture and more open relationships with their birth families, as Christine Ward Gailey (2010) describes in *Blue Ribbon Babies and Labors of Love*, class differences threw up hurdles between AA adoptive and birth families, exacerbating adoptees' identity struggles. For AA adoptees, these collisions involved how discipline was conducted; how conflicts were resolved and expectations determined; the uncomfortable place of privilege adoptees occupied; and adoptees' acknowledgment of the physical and gendered sexual abuse that may have driven their adoption in the first place. AA adoptees snatched what they could—similarities in speech, skills, and physical appearance—yet might be unable to stitch up the wound that led them to search in the first place. AA adoptees who had been able to interact with birth family members from a young age were more able to connect more missing links.

Missing links were not solely about biological connections. AA adoptees were seeking to find out who they were as black persons in America and to solve the conundrum of what constituted choice. Their adoptive parents harbored a secret hope that, brought up with "white values," they would not suffer the racial discrimination leveled at American Americans. The search of AA adoptees for identity was more complex than either embracing their birth families (though that was important) or embracing their blackness. Especially when they reached college, AA adoptees struggled to situate themselves as black or white—that is, whether to ally themselves with black Americans even though, perhaps, they didn't speak or dress like many of them. One adult AA adoptee with whom I spoke, Maudie, told me, "I always thought of myself as black, but people would say, 'You're not really black.' I still hear it today. It bothers me that people don't think of me as black. I don't know the nuances of being black. I'm a wife, a mother, I have my religion, and these are just as important as being black but I think it is really important to have connections with people who have the same background."

AA adoptees searched for an identity that permitted them to be black—and more than black, to be black and their own person. Dennis Leoutsakas (2010), alluding to the shift in discourse from "melting pot" to "salad bowl" to describe ethnic and racial mixing in the United States, wryly commented, "What happens if you are both tomato and piece of lettuce? What do you do in this salad bowl?" This was not an easy question for AA adoptees to answer, and they did not answer it the same way. In their journeys, they came to embrace their blackness and their positioning as adoptees, but also their right to embody a much more fluid notion of culture, race, and ethnic identity.

In a film about transracial adoption, Noah, who lived in Vermont, one of the least ethnically diverse states in the United States, said, "I didn't really think about it [being black] much when I was little. When you get older it sucks. We were outcasts." His sister, Angeli, a 27-year-old teacher, was also adopted and African

American. Both she and Noah had their cars searched; they were followed around in malls and generally regarded with suspicion. Noah concluded, "Apparently I'm threatening." And Angeli reflected, "It was interesting to be treated as a common criminal." On the advice of a friend of hers who was also an African American teacher, she decided to keep her teaching materials in her car as a sign to the police of who she was because, as she said, "They don't know my accomplishments." As long as Noah and Angeli were *within* their families where they and their adoptive parents openly discussed adoption and race, they were fine. However, as soon as they ventured into the wider world, they were exposed regularly to experiences that forced them to live on an emotional fault line (Farber 2009).

Lisa Marie Rollins (2011), an AA adult adoptee, was the founder of a major African American adoptee group and a popular performer who developed a solo show, *Ungrateful Daughter: One Black Girl's Story of Being Adopted by a White Family . . . that Aren't Celebrities.* She tried to explain the complex emotions of AA adoptees who loved their adoptive parents yet were subject to virulent racism:

> For the record, I love my parents. I love the HELL outta my parents. I would
> not be able to do what I do without my parents and without my aunt and
> uncle who provide me with emotional, financial, and spiritual support. . . .
> I am grateful. Even as I counter, resist and push back against the discourse
> of gratefulness in adoption, I am thankful, I am blessed that my family is my
> family. . . . I like my life and I resist and push back at the same time. I can
> be both without shame. Me loving my parents and my larger family, doesn't
> preclude me from critiquing their racism and . . . how white privilege is a
> microcosm of larger systems.[27]

In Gina Samuels's interviews with twenty-three AA adoptees, only two had experienced black cultural immersion experiences early in their early childhoods. Because most of the families in her study lacked access to immersion in African American culture, they reacted forcefully to their adoptive parents' practices when they were older. They moved into black neighborhoods and embarked on searches for their birth families to discover their blackness. Andy found that his move to a black neighborhood when he went to college made a huge difference in his sense of well-being, even though he had lived in a diverse suburb and attended a racially diverse high school:

> It was priceless. . . . it was what I always wanted and never had. . . . when I was
> a kid . . . to be submerged in black people where a white person would be the

minority. And it was just . . . nice. It filled that gap and that question that I always had. That was one of the best things I came out of college with. (Samuels 2010: 32)

Phil Bertelson made a powerful film in 2001, *Outside Looking In: Transracial Adoption in America*. It conveyed his conflicting experiences growing up, from his own perspective as well as that of his birth and foster parents, his siblings, and his nephew, also a transracial adoptee. His parents had embraced a color-blind stance that ignored the transracial dimension of their family. They thought that by inculcating their children with particular kinds of values, they would be accepted by society. Bertelson's mother commented, "I don't see you as a black person. I see you as my family." When Bertelsen reached adolescence, he discovered a sharp dichotomy between the outside world and the sheltered utopia within his family. Instead of a sense of safety and security, he felt increasingly insecure. Eventually, Bertelson fully embraced his roots as an African American and then made it his job to socialize his transracial nephew in a way that he thought was more appropriate. He took him on a frenzied journey (in retrospect, he called it "force-feeding") to New York City and Harlem, a journey that left his nephew embarrassed, bewildered, and even more reticent about accepting his roots. Bertelson gradually came to realize that he was imposing on his nephew his own disappointments and losses. It remains to be seen what his nephew will make of the journey he took with Bertelson as he grows older.

Kevin Hoffman's (2010) journey differed from Phil's. Growing up in Detroit, he was surrounded by many other African Americans at his school and in his neighborhood. He described the experience as "a racial balancing act" in which he "learned to talk black" (yet another form of passing) and feared being called out for talking "proper" (57). His friends in high school educated him about black traditions and culture, and he felt accepted until he realized the gap between his experiences and how people, including his white teachers, "see my friends and me" (91).

His introduction to prejudice was matched by his parents' efforts to shield him from their own experiences of racism—his father was turned down for a series of jobs as a minister because of his mixed family. Kevin was "forever grateful" to them for bolstering his self-confidence by hiding the knowledge of their ordeals, which he says "would have crippled me." He, in turn, returned the favor by "shielding Mom and Dad" (Hoffman 2010: 91).

When he reached college, he became "a minority every day, all day . . . a shock to my system. . . . The majority of the blacks on campus did not want me around and the whites did not want me around either. The fear of being caught in the gap between the two was a real fear." He described "moving through college" like "walking through a minefield, scared that my next step could end in an explosion I would never hear" and he regretted "that the shade of black that I chose to show was the shade so many of my white friends had seen on TV and in the movies. . . . At that age, I didn't have the energy to speak for an entire race" (Hoffman 2010: 128).

It was in "the solitude of college" that he decided to "venture out and see if he could find his mother . . . to try to stitch together fantasy and reality." His birth mother was "the treasure" he sought, but he was very hesitant because he worried he would "somehow betray the ones that have loved me unconditionally" (Hoffman 2010: 132). Eventually, he learned details about his birth family from his adoptive parents and his non-identifying records; and for the first time, he realized "a foreign thought. There is someone out there that looks like me. After years of being the different one I can comprehend the thought that there is someone who shares my DNA" (134). His search ended at that point, "not with a hug." Instead, "the urgency to dig for his "lost treasure" was replaced by "the need to digest" what he had learned (135–36). He began to feel whole, finally, when he married an African American woman and had a child, again sharing "DNA with someone I know" (150). He still dreamed of connecting with his birth mother, especially to introduce her to her grandson and to thank her for the choice she made. He viewed his adoption experience as successful, but his experience "growing up black in white," also the title of his memoir, made him hide and prevented him time and again from realizing his potential. He put brakes on himself. His search led him to recognize these facets of who he was (162–64).

Other young AA adoptees who went on searches for their birth families described them as "a journey" and "a grieving process." Darrell/DMC, who did find his birth mother and siblings, began by asking, "Who wants to start a book on Chapter Two?" and concluded that "healing wounds sometimes causes pain. Sometimes truth has to be spoken in order for true communication and healing to begin. What keeps me doing what I am doing is other adoptees, who tell me that what I am doing keeps them sane." He added, "Ya'll keep me sane too . . . telling me your stories, telling me about your struggle to find your birth parents and their rejection or inability to accept you."[28]

Avery Klein Cloud, the African American daughter of lesbian parents who were Jewish and lived in New York, was a high-achieving athlete and doing well in high school. She had two adopted siblings, an older brother from Korea, and a younger brother who was also African American. Her adoptive parents were supportive and open-minded. She was the only black girl in her class in middle school. In high school, there were no white students, but almost all the teachers were white. She began to feel increasingly "out of place" and as if she was a "wrong person." Eventually, she decided to embrace her blackness, got her hair braided at a black beauty salon, began a serious relationship with a black boyfriend, and learned what "oreo" meant.

Avery also embarked on a painful search for her birth mother who, after responding to one letter, never answered her again. She felt her adoptive parents did not understand who she was or her world as she delved more deeply into her African American side. They did not "fit into her life." She began switching between her adoptive and birth name; she contemplated leaving high school and became estranged from her adoptive parents, living on her own and not attending their wedding. She had been very close to her brother, but they drifted apart, and he enrolled in Princeton. Her brother felt that Avery's search was not "personal" but rather a quest to "individuate" herself more. Eventually, Avery reached an uneasy peace, accepting both that she had the right to search and that her adoptive parents, however "not good enough" she felt they had been, had given her the support and empowered her to search to find out if she had gotten "certain characteristics" from her birth mother." Eventually, she concluded, "I am the person my parents raised me to be, but I am also my own person and I am learning about that person every day." She put on hold a future reunion with her birth mother, returned home to her adoptive parents, and accepted an athletic scholarship to Delaware State University (Opper 2009).

Despite their many variants, patterns are apparent in these accounts. All selves are multifaceted, at once individuated and socially constructed, but in each case described above, a transitional period, defined by emotional withdrawal, self-deprecation, and blame, followed the experience of loss and displacement, and then led to a growing awareness that race mattered in a way that their adoptive parents could never understand or experience. With that awareness, adoptees still questioned where they came from, why they were abandoned or unwanted, and entertained fantasies of reunions with birth family members (Leoutsakas 2010).

Not all adoptees had a desire to search for their birth families, however. Instead, searches could take many forms—searches for self, for others like themselves, for emplacement. In the course of searching, as DMC commented above, adoptees made sense of their lives through new stories that they began to tell about themselves.

AA and CA adoptees have increasingly challenged the geology of race and class structures by sharing what they know with other adoptees, mentoring, pushing older generations to reassess their prejudices, and embracing a moral responsibility to deliberately unlearn what had been bequeathed to them. Kevin Hoffman, for example, turned to activism in embracing his blackness and began mentoring other AA adoptees and adoptive family members. Many adoptees, when they reached adulthood, decided to change their names to more prominently feature their connection to their birth families.

Adoptees stressed that having the option to draw on what constitutes Chinese or African American cultural essences was important to them. Being a "cultural chameleon," as one CA adoptee described it, was not superficial multiculturalism but rather meant understanding that identity in America (and likely in many other places) was a product of a personal quest for who one was in interaction with who one was thought to be in the public's eye. Jane Jeong Trenka, Julia Chinyere Oparah, and Sun Yung Shin, in *Outsiders Within*, remark that, as adoptees, "we are trying to reinvent ourselves and the world. . . . We are not objects but rather subjects in our own histories" (2006: 15).

Anthropologically, the ways that transracial adoptees conceptualized or talked about their identity formation incorporated the deep-seated cultural value of individual voluntarism, along with the ongoing tensions in America among individual rights and free will, equal rights for all, and the conditions that created class inequalities and prejudice. AA adoptees recognized that this was a tightrope they walked in a deeply personal fashion, yet their common experience of walking the tightrope lent itself to shared community among them and to revised narratives through which they could conceptualize who they were.

The Worldwide Web: Blogging and Networking

An explosion of narratives constructed by adoptees about their feelings and experiences have begun circulating in blogs and websites on the Internet, in documentary and commercial films, in daily shows and soap operas, and in print form.[29]

Many adoptees wanted to build connections with "elsewhere" that were both imaginary and concrete. Their Internet posts were intentionally public, a means of sharing experiences and information among themselves, and of building a safe place, whose locus initially was virtual.[30] Natalie Cherot (2006: 2) suggests that the communities adoptees are forming give us insight into how they perceive themselves within the structure and strictures of international and transracial adoption. As "community intellectuals" and "claim makers," their "versions of adoptive truths have "the capacity to be transformative" and "to be a legitimate voice in adoption policy." She explains,

> Developing out of a diasporic consciousness and a common history, international adoptees create an imagined community . . . in which they narrate their life stories, disidentify with exclusive membership in white communities, and forward hybrid identities. The self-identifying community's face-to-face and Internet pedagogical storytelling allow for the emergence of an alternative collective history and an expression of agency separate from adoption agencies, orphanage workers and adoptive parents. Global flows of communication, including listservs, instant messaging, and multiple user chat rooms, have facilitated international adoptees' ability to imagine themselves as part of a transnational community of adoptees and as connected with larger diasporic communities. (Cherot 2006: 8)

Cherot's description resembles Bruno Latour's "actor centered networks."[31] In the early twenty-first century, these networks span the globe with varying degrees of impact on people's values and practices. It is usually not until transformations are well under way that the networks themselves become singled out as significant in facilitating changes.

In what ways were diasporic communities forming among adoptees? New shared ideas and practices about family formation were materializing from virtual exchanges that also fostered periodic gatherings, conferences, friendships, and mentoring relationships. In tandem, these catalyzed even more virtual interactions. The very act of being able to engage in these forums empowered adoptees to claim new cultural ground on which to build their identities, define and experience membership in their families, and create a collective network of friends.

International adoptees were the most active participants in the formation of diasporic communities, but AA adoptees, who had had little contact with others in a similar position in the past, were finding these experiences exciting and helpful as well. One AA adoptee spoke of the profound transformations she experienced when she attended a conference in Oakland, California, "Adopted and Fostered Adults from the African Diaspora" (AFAAD) in 2009 that had been widely publicized on the Web. She stressed that it was the first time she had been in a room with so many people who looked like her, who had grown up in similar circumstances—in white families—and who were close to her in age. Although her mother had tried to connect her with black hairdressers and other transracial adoptees, she grew up with a sense of deep insecurity and vulnerability. The gathering caused her to revisit painful memories that had prevented her from fully living in the present or looking toward the future. She had often simply given up—on friends or jobs, or building a career for herself. The gathering, which included a healing circle, served as a catalyst for her to let go of some of her pain, and to consider the possibility of making transformations in her life, and she felt it would be extremely useful to establish a black or transracial adult adoptee support network.[32]

Sharing common experiences in the present about the past allowed this AA adoptee to begin to make her way into the future and to move from a passive sense of discomfort to active engagement, which has included building a support network for adult adoptees. Currently there are blogs for tweens, teens, and adults, for Chinese American women, transnational adoptees, and transracial adoptees; there are also country-specific forums and search sites.

As in the virtual communities in which adoptive parents participated, I found there were dominant adoptee voices participating in the forums and exchanges on the Internet that were gradually recognized by everyone, but the exchanges seemed to allow for people to express themselves about any number of concerns. While I did not know *who* these individuals were, I was able to learn something about them because many of them participated in a sustained manner over a long period of time—they constituted nodes in a network that could be envisioned as hierarchical. Those who regularly blogged or posted actively contributed to creating a "culture" of communication, and although they could not be identified as three-dimensional persons, their voices, the issues they were struggling with, and their positions on many issues became recognizable.

Diasporic community-building played out in different ways in these contexts. To be part of a forum with subtopics was one thing; to be part of a transnational network of Chinese adoptees blogging and planning for a worldwide gathering was quite another. The latter constituted a nascent culture of transnational adoptees, one likely to expand over the years to come. Participants used these sites as places of refuge and to vent and grieve; as networks through which some of them got to know each other and then met personally; and as sites where they felt comfortable contributing their autobiographies in great detail—not simply the routines of their daily lives. They hosted periodic gatherings, which were gaining momentum as the most innovative dimension of adoptee identity formation and community-building, in contrast to generations past and the work of adoptive parents.

The "One World Chinese Adoptee G2 Links Blog," for example, celebrated its first anniversary on February 14, 2011. Founded by eight "One Worlder" Chinese adoptees on February 14, 2007, they call themselves "G2" to refer to "Global Generations," and many of them prefer to call themselves "G2's" rather than "adoptees." Their site is, in their words, "the first global group created by and for Chinese adoptees around the world." The first Chinese Adult Adoptee Worldwide Reunion took place in September 2010.[33] The postings on "One World" brimmed with excitement. The participants range in age from their twenties to their sixties and come from three continents.

Another major site, "AdoptionTalk" originally was intended for those involved in some way in adoptions from China, but its commentaries, blogs, and compiled websites had come to cover a far broader spectrum. Its banner proclaimed: "Talking about adoption, birthparents, abandonment, race, and China with my kids. That's not all we talk about—but reading this blog, you'll think it's all we do!!!!!" It included blogs posted by birth parents, adoptees, adoptive parents, instructional resources, newsworthy items, and an impressive array of online resources that could be accessed.[34] These sites and the gatherings and reunions that emerge from them have found their inspiration in part in the experiences of Korean adoptees. The latter had almost no support from their adoptive parents as they struggled with identity issues, racism, and loss growing up. As young adults, they became pioneers in establishing such networks (Kim 2010; Palmer 2011). CA adoptees were following in their footsteps.

Yet another example, the Yahoo group International-Adopt-Talk (I-A-T), permitted adoptive parents to "lurk" and then participate after a month. One of their major points was that adoptees have not easily been able to express themselves or their points of view because of the power that their adoptive parents have exerted. I-A-T has been criticized by some adoptive parents as a forum for bitter adoptees with a chip on their shoulder. Yet, in my review of their postings, I found that the frankness of adoptees and adoptive parents alike brought many hidden concerns and fears out into the open and resulted in more than one adoptee or adoptive parent reevaluating their assumptions.[35]

Equally significant were blog participants' observations that such transnational networks were transforming their everyday lives and mixing with them. Many had found ways to articulate the strangeness of the comfort and familiarity of the routines of eating dinner, going to school, playing sports, and, most frequently, leading the lives that many white middle- and upper middle-class families live, in contrast to the their unique status as transracially and transnationally adopted children. The fact of initially being disembodied by their virtual connections—possibly embracing an ideal self—was liberating for many of them, whose first social interactions had demanded awareness of physical differences in appearance and connections.

Participants contributed to events and practices related to adoption—making films, holding conferences and symposia, writing songs about the culture of adoptees, exploring what it meant to be Asian American through poetry, and creating additional on-the-ground groups such as "Adoptees United at New York University," the first adoptee organization established at that university. One such example was posted on the site by a Chinese American adoptee who was participating in an adoption conference at MIT called "Secret Histories, Public Policies":

> From the moment I stepped into the plenary session on day one, I felt as if I had slipped into a new world. To be in the same space with hundreds of adoptees of all ages and ethnicities, birthmothers, adoptive parents, women, men, all sharing their unique stories through film, poetry, essays, autobiographical fiction, installations, authentic tellings and performances, was overwhelming and deeply poignant. I feel privileged to find myself surrounded by strangers who speak the same language, who have embarked on similar journeys, who "know" and "understand" without having to explain. My heart is full, my mind whirling with images, as intimate accounts of loss, pain, yearnings, searches, dreams, stunning discoveries, joy and sorrow resonate, some eerily familiar, others leading to new perspectives, possibilities, interpretations.[36]

One of the most interesting aspects of these virtual communities was the power of the visual images they posted. These images projected in condensed fashion the complexity of who adoptees were, how they thought about the paths they had taken, and where they were situated. They conveyed a sense of emplacement and represented, far better than linear narratives, how they imagined themselves as individuals and families.

Forging Links:
Working toward Becoming and Reaching for Home

The dizzying range of virtual networks formed by adoptees raises an important question: How were adoptees building a *shared* sense of community? The interactions between public and hidden transcripts that James Scott (1992) sketched vividly in *Domination and the Arts of Resistance* offer a useful way to understand the paths that adoptees were taking to identify themselves as a community. Scott argues that, in unequal relationships, public transcripts emerge from those in both dominant and subaltern positions. These public transcripts suppress alternative interpretations and practices, which take place offstage, hidden from view. Public transcripts are what those in power want the public to see and what those who are, relatively speaking, in a subordinate position, want those in power to see. However, hidden transcripts emerge in conjunction with the interactions that take place in the public eye. Public transcripts create constraints within which both parties with more and less power are forced to interact. Offstage, however, hidden transcripts flourish to greater or lesser extents, depending on the degree of freedom, opportunity, and segregation. In addition to tracing the existence of these hidden transcripts, Scott asks how they become shared and subsequently serve as the basis for challenging the status quo. His question indirectly points to if and how heterogeneity (such as that which flourishes on the Internet) may be subsumed by more overarching common concerns and practices in making challenges to the status quo.

As I have argued throughout these chapters, the production by adoptive parents of carefully crafted and well-intentioned adoption narratives and practices gave rise to adoptees' hidden transcripts, ironically through what was often a very public medium, the World Wide Web. In these, adoptees challenged, or at least questioned, what their adoptive parents were communicating and providing, especially once adoptees moved into the wider world. Eleanor, who got to the point when she was "not even remotely interested in Chinese things at this time of my life," created a blog so that other CA adoptees could apprehend a somewhat different and broader understanding of China and of adoption that took account of the broader social struggles of people of color in the United States.

Another young CA adoptee, Kitty, started a book club for adoptees. Like Eleanor, Kitty felt her parents had pushed her too hard to "be" Chinese. She felt that the book group allowed her to process her connections to China (or not) in a more nuanced and realistic fashion. Her view was, "You find your own path and when you are ready to seek it, you do." Keesha, an AA adoptee, reported that her "detachment from . . . personal self" diminished when she began to participate in social media and groups that included people of color. When adoptees took their "hidden transcripts" into the public realm, they could use them to build an alternative worldview and sense of shared identity (Kim 2005; Palmer 2011; Prebin 2009).

A sense of shared community also materialized when, through their circuit journeys, adoptees reduced the exoticism of their birth countries and worked against political and economic inequalities by undertaking volunteer activities with foster mothers, orphanages, and welfare institutes. Others advocated in the United States for further openness in adoption practices and policies and programs that would lessen the likelihood of relinquishment (fully giving up a child for adoption). These activities were emblematic of adoptees' awareness that their place(s) in the world spanned the globe even though much of their everyday lives might unfold in one physical locale.

Another phenomenon shared by many adoptees was the embrace of adoption as a mode of family-making. A minority of children who had been adopted rejected adoption as a bad practice, particularly if it took place across racial lines. However, in my review of secondary sources and interviews with children as young as 8, and up into their thirties, I found that the vast majority fully expected to adopt at least one of their children, if not all of them; CA adoptees specifically wanted to adopt girls rather than boys. They were profoundly aware that being a girl child or a mother in China led to frightening and painful consequences, for them, as well as for birth mothers, even if they, as children who were adopted, "turned out all right" in the end, as one 11-year-old commented to me. Hence, the shared desire among CA adoptees to adopt girls was partly a way to channel their own pain. Their positive embrace of adoption as a way to make their families was mixed with these sentiments.

The structure and substance of family that they envisioned did not conform to the normative American family configurations of the time. Not only did they assume their families might be transracial; they also expected they would be a mix of biological and nonbiological relatives.[37] Margaret Mead (1978), as a participant in and prescient observer of the turbulent 1960s in the United States, challenged the usual assumptions of anthropologists about socialization processes. She argued that parents and grandparents would find themselves learning from their children, in a reversal of the taken-for-granted older-to-younger socialization and enculturation process. Today this reversal seems unsurprising, given the rapidity of technological changes that have rained down.

In the culture of adoption, reverse socialization processes appear to be a primary catalyst of the transformation of family configurations. In the course of finding their places, metaphorically and physically, in the world, adoptees find themselves resisting racism, biologism, and crusading xenophobia. As adoptees and others increasingly challenge such ideologies and concomitant practices, those who embrace them may become even more recalcitrant about accepting alternative kinds of family-making. The statements and practices of evangelical fundamentalist groups such as Focus on the Family and the American Family Association are examples of these reactions. Yet there are key moments when a culture itself is in the throes of transformation and upheaval. It is thus inevitable that adoptees will shoulder some of the burdens of bringing about those changes, and that they will serve as bridges in the process. The very historical context in which they are situated makes this impossible for them to avoid.

By participating in virtual and non-virtual activities, the adolescent and young adult adoptees I studied were creating novel meanings of self, family, and belonging. The communities they were forming challenged existing taboos, narratives, and cultural assumptions, and adoptees were helping each other arrive at revised narratives and practices that could communicate what it meant to live in disparate and multiple worlds. They were engaged in restoring themselves through restory-ing themselves.

Barbara Ballis Lal (2001: 159) argues that adoptive parents tend to essentialize identity, equating physical appearance with cultural heritage and identity. She contends that identity formation is much better understood as a dynamic process in which adoptees "do" identity. The adoptees in this study, as they grew out of childhood, were drawing on multiple models and reference points to structure their identities in a nonlinear fashion. All of them had to take account of their status growing up in upper-middle-class, white, privileged families, fusing it with other dimensions of their lives. Some adoptees might come to characterize themselves not as multicultural but as transethnic—with an understanding of the gendered, racial, and political economic context in which they move. Others, such as Darrell, Lisa, Andy, and Noah, embraced blackness. And still others were seeking comfort as consummate code-switchers who were biculturally adept. AA and CA adoptees, if they had the chance, might find facets of themselves mirrored in the experiences of nonadopted Chinese Americans and African Americans. Last but not least, they acknowledged a shared bond of adoption that they enacted through numerous avenues with other adoptees.

One fervent hope of teen and adult adoptees in the early twenty-first century was their desire *not* to be categorized and classified by labels *and* their simultaneous desire that society recognize that their identities have been shaped by the experiences of adoption, racial and class differences, loss, and the reality that their roots are grounded in affect and ties of blood (of which they might never have full knowledge). Although the steps they were taking were not choreographed, they were patterned (Palmer 2011).

The seemingly personal experiences they aired publicly via virtual and non-virtual means provided the raw material for adoptees to refashion themselves and to realize that many of their experiences, positive and negative, were shared rather than unique. The "dances" they were improvising also brought to the general public a more profound recognition of the hurdles that all Americans face—of segregation, of gendered and economic inequalities, and of cultural parochialism. The cultural assumptions they had been exposed to and socialized into, the already established narratives their adoptive parents had shared with them, the discourses of power within which they struggled at school and on the playground, and their knowledge of pages taken from "Chapter One" of their lives all set the stage for how their dances unfolded, sometimes alone and sometimes in tandem.

While present and past do not necessarily mesh easily for transnational and transracial adoptees, this generation has more resources available to it to reconnect broken links and move between worlds in ways that were almost impossible to envision in the past.[38] The framework of the American family is, if not being torn down, being revised to include members who do not look like each other, who may or may not be connected to each other by blood ties, and who have roots, loose ends, enduring ties, and attachments to multiple regions.

Conclusion

Ties That Bind

I began the research for this book by asking about the cultural assumptions and practices of adoptive parents and their children as they engaged in family-making through transnational and transracial adoptions in the United States. I wondered as well about the agency they have exercised in challenging these assumptions. I view my conclusions not so much as a termination, but as a step forward on an unpredictable trajectory. That the future is unpredictable is telling. We often wish for arrows to point us in the right direction, a product of our own participation in progressive modernity perhaps. However, social transformations operate *through* conflicts, setbacks, tensions, and sudden breakthroughs.

Pierre Bourdieu (1977) suggests that what we take for granted in our daily lives—calendars, the layout of houses, or the labor done by men and women, respectively—exerts the most power over us. When people begin to wonder about and call into question the reasons for an existing cultural *habitus* or particular mores, frames shift. Bourdieu notes that when these heterodox ways of thinking and activities and begin to make themselves known and felt, unsurprisingly, the forces of orthodoxy also surge forth. This elegant yet abstract model begs the question of how heterodoxy arises, where, and by whom, and what its consequences might be. Bourdieu himself argued that "improvisations" eventually could bring about more substantive shifts in the culturally grounded, symbolic systems that people took for granted.

Twenty years ago or so, in, say, the early 1990s, most adoptive parents in America assumed that assimilation was the best and most appropriate path for the children they adopted, and that it mattered not what had preceded their incorporation into a new family. Little regular communication took place between adoptive parents and their children about their children's past or the culture and circumstances of their birth families or countries; how the children felt about looking different from the other members of their family; or how Americans, in general, thought about families formed through adoption. Agency brokers and social workers took account of class, religion, and color in matching prospective parents and adoptees, and along with adoptive parents, kept papers hidden; religious institutions that took in unwed mothers promoted certain kinds of families and discouraged others; and international adoption, apart from adoptions from Korea, were low in number and hardly discussed in the public media. Stigmatization was part and parcel of adoption, reinforcing structural boundaries between what Americans were comfortable with and what they considered ambiguous and therefore threatening about the ingredients that went into family-making. And adoptees internalized this stigmatization. The anger and self-doubt experienced by an earlier generation of Korean adoptees and by AA adoptees that they began to articulate as adults became critical to some of the shifts under way in adoption practices on the part of adoptive parents and their children.

As the twenty-first century unfolds, the institutional framework and the discourses of power and knowledge about transnational and transracial adoptions remain fraught. Even as adoption figures go up and down, geopolitical inequalities continue to structure adoption practices. These inequalities are sometimes justified by religious ideologies; they are underpinned by racism, nationalism, the unwitting embrace of color-blindness, the suppression of information, and truncated memories. The decision of the Russian government to call a halt to adoptions from Russia to the United States in 2012 dramatically called attention to how adoption could be used for purposes of diplomatic sparring over issues that had little or nothing to do with adoption itself or with children's rights. The American public has also come to reluctantly acknowledge that however much it wishes it were otherwise, children have been treated as commodities and that forming a family, as intimate an undertaking as some might desire it to be, is subject to corruption, public exposure, and criminality. These dimensions of adoption have been amply documented.

Sociologist Bruno Latour reflects on the desire among people for solutions, recipes, and conclusions that are elegant, straightforward, and simple. Yet life does not work that way and certainly not on a terrain that is as complex and bumpy as that across which family-making through transnational and transracial adoption unfolds. In his words,

> It would be incredible if the millions of participants in our courses of action
> would enter the social ties through three modes of existence and only three: as

a "material infrastructure" that would "determine" social relations like in the Marxian types of materialism; as a "mirror" simply "reflecting" social distinctions like in the critical sociologies of Pierre Bourdieu; or as a backdrop for the stage on which human social actors play the main roles like in Erving Goffman's interactionist accounts. None of those entries of objects in the collective are wrong, naturally, but they are only primitive ways of packaging the bundle of ties that make up the collective. None of them are sufficient to describe the many entanglements of humans and non-humans. (Latour 2007: 84)

Adoptive parents and their children have encountered the conditions that structure adoption as we have described them above. Many of them have also tried to transform them, some more than others, and always with varying degrees of success. Among the shifts we can point to are: the signing and ratification of the Hague Convention, despite the difficulties entailed in enforcing its stipulations; the easing of restrictions in obtaining U.S. citizenship for international adoptees; the informal discussions about adoption in all sorts of venues; the legalizing of gay marriage in nine states and the District of Columbia between 2004 and 2013; the increase in gay couple and single-parent adoptions; the growing openness of adoptions; and the emergence of expansive kinning that goes beyond bonding among those who share blood.

Judith Modell draws contrasts between the power of discourse communicated to children that they are "chosen" and the equally powerful reality of "losing" a child, the unspoken part of the adoption narrative. Openness in adoption between birth and adoptive families is transforming important aspects of transnational and transracial adoption, even as inequalities and biologism still color open adoption. The interactions between birth and adoptive families call attention to the conditions that give rise to "the option of adoption" and to loss. More adoptive and birth parents are taking the path toward open adoption. As they do so, it has dawned on them that, while having a "mirror" to look into and "knowing one's origins" carry great weight, the connections that are forged with birth families do not take away from the power of nurturing in family-making.

In more anthropological terms, heredity, on the one hand, and alliance or affiliation on the other, remain key principles in American family-making through transnational and transracial adoption. Nevertheless, heredity, especially for adoptees, is less about the primacy granted to "blood ties" and descent, and more about mimesis and knowledge. At the same time, alliance or affiliation has acquired value in the form of the sustained nurturing on a daily basis on the part of adoptive parents. Some adoptive parents and adoptees have gone further, embracing the idea of multiple nurturers and connections across a wide array of "kin" whose significance and presence in the daily life of adoptive families vary. While the latter remains a nascent cultural practice, evidence for it is found in the development of new referential kin terms, for example.

The reflections of adoptees and their adoptive parents throughout this book convey the turbulence surrounding American ideas about family at this moment in time. Sally Falk Moore (1987: 728) writes about challenges that face scholars when they try to point to social or cultural changes under way because form and content do not necessarily change in tandem. What appears as evidence of continuity may actually indicate a process undergoing change. That is, an old social form or structure—for example, the structure of a narrative—may stay the same, but its content may begin to subtly or dramatically shift. Or, a new form or structure may appear but convey traditional content. Old forms may be used as vehicles for introducing new substance, or new forms may be used to reassert old substance. It is only through close attention to ongoing social processes that we may become aware that new cultural mores are in the making (Moore 1987; Hobsbawm and Ranger 1983).

The purpose of this volume has been to train our attention on the salient ways that Euroamerican adoptive parents in the United States have engaged in family-making, and to convey how their CA, RA, and AA children, as they grow up, are responding to and critiquing their efforts. Most of the adoptive parents in this study realized that their children live with rejection and loss, and with dreams, fantasies, and hopes that accompany them as they walk through life. Some CA adoptive parents responded to this realization by creating images and narratives about China; others tried to link the future to unknown pasts and people by making return journeys and incorporating Chinese and Chinese American culture into their lives; and still others succeeded in forming friendships with Chinese Americans and in making connections to China more than a mode of cultural tourism—a journey or camp that they attend sporadically.

RA adoptive parents appear to remain wedded to a more biologically grounded model of family-making than either CA or AA adoptive parents. This is evident in their desire to adopt white children, an option that they argue better ensures their family's privacy and prevents their children from being conspicuous. It is also reflected in their preference for adopting infants so that bonding will happen more easily between adoptive parents and children. At the same time, RA adoptive parents usually have more information available to them about their children's birth families and struggle with whether and how to share that information. Because of the high number of RA children with special needs, many of them revised their initial plans to keep their adoptions private and secret and became pioneers in being more open about them, especially in working together with other parents to get diagnosis and treatment for their children.

AA adoptive parents, in the midst of white privilege, have faced a difficult and rocky road in their efforts to cross both class and racial lines. They have incorporated black culture into their lives, but have encountered hurdles in creating real friendships with African Americans, living in mixed neighborhoods, sending their children to diverse schools with African American students, teachers, and administrators. Although CA adoptive parents have generally viewed crossing these borders as more cultural than racial, they too are coming to recognize that, like it or not, their children will experience racism. While a kind of cultural tourism still characterizes border crossings of transnational and transracial families, adoptive parents' recognition that they must do more is just one of the steps on their trajectory toward becoming families of color.

All human social life requires classification to create order. Otherwise, chaos would reign. Hence, we establish classification systems that create exclusion from and inclusion in one or another category. Mary Douglas (1966) wrote that these systems help people avoid uncomfortable and sometimes threatening ambiguities. Yet the categories are linked to one another in complex ways, creating multiple and far-reaching connections and hierarchical relationships. The simultaneity of activities within these categories and the pressures exerted upon their borders may shift the boundaries of the cultural categories through which the world's material is filtered.

Among the many controversial dimensions of transnational and transracial adoption as a mode of family formation in the United States is the embrace of color-blind multiculturalism, usually reinforced in school settings. There are adoptive parents in all three of the categories examined here who remain more comfortable embracing the myth of the melting pot, the harmonious mosaic, or the salad bowl gently tossed. Diametrically opposed to this position are those who think that interracial family formation through adoption is deadly, a mode of abduction, imperialism, and cultural genocide.

At the heart of this debate stands the elephant in the room with a very long memory. The elephant in the room *is* the assumption that it is impossible to move beyond black and white in America. If we cannot move beyond it, can we move into it? By acknowledging and understanding the history and consequences of being black in America, and then acting on that knowledge, some adoptive parents have begun to make a dent in the economic, political, and cultural segregation that colors daily life and expectations. They have begun talking and moving across these boundaries, sustaining discussions in forums over long periods of time about painful topics, engaging thorny issues, confronting schools, and trying to change their own behaviors. Their families resemble less a given than a work in process, less a closed circle than a network whose density thins out as it expands—across residential neighborhoods, churches, playgrounds, grocery stores, sports arenas, and schools. It also stretches over oceans and national boundaries.

And what of the children they have adopted, especially as they come into their own? Some are becoming political activists, following in the footsteps of other adult adoptees, especially Korean adoptees and African American adoptees, in trying to expose unequal power relationships between children of color and what they call "the white adoption industry." Others are less intent on challenging these inequalities and more focused on figuring out ways to knit together multiple and partial facets of their identity. Whichever route they take, they are calling attention to their own ideas of family-making, openly acknowledging nature and nurture as fundamental to who they are.

In addition to moving the experience of loss from private and secret places *within* adoptive families to public ones via virtual communities, adoptee gatherings and reunions, circuit journeys, documentaries, memoirs, and mentoring relationships, they are trying to encourage open discussions of enduring ties and broken links in family-making. Jennifer Bao almost wistfully and dreamily shared her feelings about her identity-in-the-making:

> My body is the question mark. I live inside the mysterious geometry of its gracious, gorgeous curves. Yet I do not know it. I do not know its wellspring, its eternal source. I cannot see its constellation dotting the midnight sky, reflecting light back to me so I can trace its soft shape in the womb of the universe, to show me, to protect me, to gently guide me towards a future that can rest in familiar faces, to a past that can lean into soft, neat layers, elegant extensions and bodily histories of myself and of my ancestors.
>
> Sometimes my heart sinks when I think that these question marks seem destined to follow me forever like quiet shadows lurking, spying. The key is to use these question marks to your advantage. Take them. Embrace them. Explore them. Challenge them. And most of all, love them. Unconditionally. Ambivalence is the form and fabric of my life. What kinds of question marks surround you? Follow you? How do your question marks fill your life with mystery, frustration, intrigue and, most of all, the gift of prescient possibilities?[1]

AA adoptees and CA adoptees have embraced in a positive fashion what many regard as pejorative labels such as "oreo," "twinkie," and "banana" to refer to their feelings about adoption and their sense of self. For example, adoptees begin as "angels," and through a transubstantiation process they become, in one case, sweet, bi-colored, creamy, and white on the inside and black and crusty on the outside—or in the other case, yellow on the outside. Feeling white within, saturated by the values of white middle- and upper-middle class households, yet perceived as black or "Asian." What differs from an earlier time is that transracial domestic and international adoptees of this generation have more resources to feel secure in exploring multiple facets of their identity, inside and out. Rutledge Dennis argues that,

> Understanding where they are situated in the cultural collective is important for individuals and groups, especially in restricted societies where some groups are excluded and segregated. Being rejected by the larger society, smaller groups must find the wherewithal to create and build their own cultural foundations from which their cultural values and institutions are rooted. In segregated bicultural societies, groups must develop comprehensive institutional patterns whereby they are taught and they, in turn, teach ways of knowing the culture, ways of creating and adding to features of the culture, and ways to insure that individuals and groups within the culture may affirm an identity and identification. (Dennis 2008:41)

What does this mean for adoptees? While many of them *have* experienced the security of a white, upper-middle-class upbringing, they have had to work hard to build the foundations of which Dennis speaks within a milieu characterized by physical distance, structured inequalities, and ideologies of exoticism. How do adoptees "cross the cultural threshold . . . where there are class, caste, and racial and ethnic lines separating groups"? (Dennis 2008: 41).

Young adult transracial and transnational adoptees are building on their conviction that they are more than how they are perceived or originated. Their adoptive parents' efforts to incorporate connections with their children's birth cultures and birth family member and communities—including the selective memory-making devices they have used to craft their adoption narratives—provide some material for grounding their children's identities, even as the latter come to embrace or reject that material in a dynamic fashion. Gailey, writing about the experiences of AA adoptive families, concludes that "what makes adoptive kinship different in practice" is not so much a lack of "shared substance" but rather "a call to address, validate, and integrate unshared histories as they affect relationships and human potentiality in the present." Whether they are formed through birth or adoption, all "families" must intertwine their histories in the process of acknowledging and perpetuating (or sometimes rejecting) their kinship with each other. Gailey found that the key was to recognize that kinship practices "articulate social hierarchies" (2008: 151–52). Adoptive parents, in turn, may subvert these hierarchies, they may reinscribe them, or they may live uncomfortably with them, struggling to decide whether to reject or accommodate them. These are key steps that have a bearing on their children's identity formation and sense of comfort.

The words of one CA adult adoptee reveals how she combined a sense of security with an ability to understand "birth" in a fresh and constructive fashion:

> Where were you born? People can be physically born via hospital, house, anywhere really, and then they can be born emotionally in places that they feel that they come alive. Although there is no information about how I was born, or where I was born, I was physically born in Jiangsu province, China. After coming to America, I truly came alive when my mom and I made that special mother-daughter bond. That wasn't the only place where I was truly born. I feel alive and born when I travel, and I feel alive and born when I dance and sing. I also feel alive when I am with friends and family and I enjoy their company. Again, making that connection between physical birth and emotional birth is very important for me as a Chinese adoptee, for when I feel alive, nothing is stopping me from achieving my dreams, or being happy with my life and myself. That I feel is the most powerful kind of birth, one that makes you feel like you can do anything and enjoy life moment by moment.[2]

Biculturalism does not sufficiently capture the experiences and perspectives of the groups of adoptees in this study. It comes closest for AA adoptees. CA adoptees, rather than shifting between or feeling comfortable in *two* groups— Chinese and white—pull on the threads that constitute intertwined networks diffused throughout American society as well as across the globe and into the ether. The meetings and exchanges of transnational, transracial adoptees attest to a more dynamic and less concrete mode of community and identity formation. RA adoptees, thus far, do not appear to be explicitly contesting normative family formations in America, but they too have experienced loss. Those who did know more about their adoptions also looked forward to circuit journeys and interacting more regularly with children who remained in orphanages or with members of their birth families.

While some adoptees have embraced networks and coalitions that reject adoption altogether, the majority appear to be empowered by their growing ability to shape public discourse, to voice their critiques, to arrive at satisfying and creative narratives of who they are and who their families are. They find these narratives compelling and are sharing them with other adoptees. And they are more comfortable with multiple facets of their identity, which *include* but are not limited to losses, frustrations, and anger.

Adoptees are also formulating new symbols and putting them into action. They have been creating new ceremonies—rites of passages as well as healing rites—that acknowledge their social identities as transracial and transnational adoptees. At its annual conference in 2008, AFAAD—Adopted and Fostered Adults from the African Diaspora—included a cathartic and powerful healing ceremony in which all adoptees put something on an altar from their life "journey." One by one, adoptees placed on the altar photos of themselves with their adopted siblings and family members, birth family photos, or other things that were meaningful to them. They then wrote on hearts the names of people they wanted to remember, including people who had died or about whom they knew nothing. As one adoptee explained, "We can't come here and just be people in our heads. We are affected deeply in our hearts and spirits." After placing the hearts on the altar, they lit candles. Each candle symbolized something to heal from or be released from.[3]

All of this movement, does it lead anywhere? History has shown that non-linearity is more characteristic of processes of change. It is thus dangerous to predict, but I would venture to guess that, in the years to follow, the families that CA and AA adoptees make and grow will diverge from those within which they were nurtured. This is already happening. Some will "look" the same and act the same, but many more will comprise members, near and far, whose relationships and activities are based on affinity (not through marriage alone), filiation, and consanguinity, and the content of these relationships will be far more varied and elastic than it is now. These will be understood to be kin ties, emotionally and formally. The activation of relationships among adoptees themselves may be sporadic and discontinuous, but the communities they form will provide them with the fortitude to continue to contest the hierarchies of culture, race, place, class, and gender. They will also continue to wrestle with the challenges of confronting entrenched ideologies and crossing great distances and high borders.

Appendix

Characteristics of Adoptive Families Interviewed

Code	Respondent		Partner		Status	Income	Biological Children		Adopted Children			Location*		
	Sex	Age	Sex	Age			Sex	Age	Sex	Age	Age when adopted	State	Type	City Pop.
AA1	M	37	F	45	Married	$90,000			1 F	2	infant	VA	Suburban	128,923
AA2	M	30	F	29	Married	$50,000			2 M	1, 2 mos.	infants	CO	Rural	129,872
AA3	F	31	M	30	Married	$100,000			1 M	8 mos.	infant	CA	Urban	101,124
AA4	F	43	M	55	Married	$80,000	2 M, 3 F	16, 26, 20, 32, 30	2 F	3, 18 mos.	infant; fost-adopt.	IL	Suburban	6,335
AA5	F	47	M	51	Single @Adopt.	$35,000			1 F	2	2 mos.	IL	Urban	2,869,121
AA6	F	41			Single	$66,000			2 M	11, 16	3, 5.5	CA	Urban	36,457,549
AA7	F	43	M	41	Married	$80,000	1 F, 1 M	18 and 16	2 F, 1 M	6, 4, 3	infants	WI	Rural	14,153
AA8	F	52	M	65	Married	$50,000	1 M, 1 F	36, 34	1 F	12	infant	DC	Urban	581,530
AA9	F	34	M	36	Married	$80,000			1 F	1	infant	SC	Rural	2,743
AA10	F	38	M	38	Married	$75,000			2 M, 2 F	7, 7, 9, 12	8 mos., 4, 5, 2	IL	Suburban	17,771
AA11	F	32	M	33	Married	$35,000			2 M	3.5, 2.5	infants	CO	Rural	2,000
AA12	F	32	M	31	Married	$120,000			2 F	2, 10 mos.	infants	IL	Urban	2,869,121
AA13	F	48	M	48	Married	$200,000	2 F	22, 18	2 F	4.5, 1.5	infants	IL	Suburban	27,896
AA14	F	26	M	26	Cohabiting	$55,000			1 F	9 mos.	infant	UT	Suburban	179,894
AA15	F	42				$85,000			1 M	4	infant	NY	Rural	923,459
AA16	F	42	M	43	Married	$95,000			2 F	5.5, 3.5	infants	IL	Rural	162,184
AA17	F	50	M	50	Married	$60,000	1 M	20	1 M	9	infant	NE	Suburban	629,294
AA18	F	48	M	46	Married	$200,000			1 M, 1 F	2, 7 mos.	infants	MA	Suburban	83,829
AA19	F	46	M	52	Married	$120,000			1 M, 2 F	16, 13, 10	2 mos., 7 mos., 1	TX	Urban	786,386
AA20	F	34	M	35	Married	$190,000	1 M	21 mos.	1 F	2	infant	DC	Urban	581,530
CA1	F	42	M	43	Married	$150,000	2 F	7 and 8	1 F	4	11 mos.	DC	Urban	581,530
CA2	F	46	M	45	Married	$160,000			1 F	2	10 mos.	VA	Suburban	128,923
CA3	F	43	M	45	Married	$150,000			2 F	8, 8 (twins)	2, 2	VA	Urban	189,453

Code	Respondent		Partner		Status	Income	Biological Children		Adopted Children			Location*		
	Sex	Age	Sex	Age			Sex	Age	Sex	Age	Age when adopted	State	Type	City Pop.
CA4	F	45	M	45	Married	$150,000			1 F	2	17 mos.	DC	Urban	581,530
CA5	F	33	M	35	Married	$70,000			1 F	3	10 mos.	KY	Rural	27,408
CA6	M	40	F	40	Married	$160,000	2 F	14 and 12	1 F	4	1	NY	Rural	10,295
CA7	F	50			Single	$55,000			1 F	6	16 mos.	AK	Urban	270,951
CA8	F	32	M	39	Married	$70,000			1 F	2	11 mos.	WI	Rural	4,479
CA9	F	35	M	35	Married	$80,000			1 F	3	9 mos.	PA	Urban	1,479,339
CA10	M	56	F	52	Married	$170,000	1 M, 1 F	19 and 13	1 F	15	10 mos.	VA	Suburban	14,453
CA11	F	42			Single	$55,000			1 F	7	11 mos.	MA	Rural	57,107
CA12	F	50	M	55	Married	$135,000	2 F, 1 M	11, 22, 25	1 F	5	2	ID	Urban	190,117
CA13	F	39	M	39	Married	$70,000			2 F	7, 5	10 mos., 1	VA	Suburban	19,279
CA14	F	55	M	59	Married	d.k.			2 F	10, 13	d.k.	VA	Suburban	1,010,443
CA15	F	39	M	41	Married	d.k.			1 F	2	11 mos.	VA	Suburban	1,010,443
CA16	F	50	M	52	Married	100,000+	2 M, 2 F	29, 20, 23, 20s	2 F	4, 3	18 mos., 3	VA	Suburban	169,599
CA17	F	46	M	48	Married	$75,000			1 F	3	13 mos.	DC	Urban	581,530
CA18	F	52	M	49	Married	100,000+			1 M	6	9 mos.	VA	Suburban	1,010,443
CA19	F	49	M	49	Married	$75,000			2 F	3, 2	14 mos., 1	VA	Suburban	56,407
CA20	F	45			Single	100,000+	1 F	29	4 F	9, 10, 11	8.5, 2, 6.5, 3	VA	Suburban	54,994
CA21	F	60s	M	60s	Married	d.k.			1 F	9	3	VA	Suburban	21,498
CA22	F	45	M	51	Married	100,000+	1 M, 3 F	20, 18, 16, 28	1 F	5	d.k.	MD	Suburban	26,064
CA23	F	51			Single	100,000+			2 F	6, 3	d.k.	VA	Urban	189,453
CA24	F	55			Single	$62,000			2 F	10	8.5 mos.	VA	Suburban	1,010,443
CA25	F	34	M	44	Married	$70,000			1 F	3	9 mos.	KA	Rural	12,000
CA26	F	45	M	57	Married	$125,000	1 F	21	1 F	3	1	VA	Suburban	39,162
CA27	F	55			Single	$70,000			1 F	12	4 mos.	KY	Urban	248,762

Code	Respondent		Partner		Status	Income	Biological Children		Adopted Children			Location*		
	Sex	Age	Sex	Age			Sex	Age	Sex	Age	Age when adopted	State	Type	City Pop.
CA28	M	46	F	37	Single at adoption	$65,000	1 F	10 mos.	1 F	6	9 mos.	MA	Suburban	20,331
CA29	F	53			Single	$150,000			2 F, 2 M	13, 10, 7, 3	6 mos., 6 mos., 4, 3	MD	Suburban	56,397
CA30	F	56	M	60	Married	$120,000	2 F	40, 37	2 F	13, 12	4 mos., d.k.	VA	Suburban	26,665
RA1	F	d.k.	d.k.	d.k.	Married	d.k.	1 M, 1 F	14, 12	1 M, 1 F	3, 4	d.k.	OR	Urban	538,544
RA2	F	42	M	42	Married	$300,000	1 M	15	1 F	9	8	MD	Rural	600
RA3	M	55	F	51	Married	$200,000	1 M	28	1 M	16	15	GA	Urban	423,019
RA4	F	46	M	50	Married	$80,000			1 M, 1 F	7, 5	9 mos., 11 mos.	AL	Rural	2,521
RA5	F	45	M	46	Married	$260,000	1 M	13	1 F	9	18 mos.	VA	Suburban	21,498
RA6	M	45	F	50	Married	$200,000			2 M	12, 9	3, 18 mos.	DC	Urban	581,530
RA7	M	46	F	50	Married	$400,000			1 F, 2 M	10, 9, 8	2, 10 mos., 4	NJ	Suburban	38,977
RA8	F	49	M	55	Married	$150,000	1 F	11	1 F	5	2	VA	Suburban	41,041
RA9	F	50	M	51	Married	$293,000	1 F	21, 12	1 M	9	1	MI	Urban	911,402
RA10	F	58			Single	$35,000			2 F	15, 16	5, 7	TX	Urban	1,214,725
RA11	F	48	M	52	Married	$200,000			2 F	8.5, 4.5	7 mos., 15 mos.	VA	Suburban	21,498
RA12	F	48	M	56	Married	$200,000			1 F	10	6	CA	Suburban	4,389
RA13	F	44	M	53	Married	$145,000			1 M	12	3	VT	Rural	7,705
RA14	F	40	F	41	Cohabiting	$195,000			1 M	6	15 mos.	DC	Urban	581,530
RA15	F	51	F	48	Cohabiting	$270,000			2 M, 1 F	9, 13, 4	2.5, 6.5, 10 mos.	MD	Urban	71,452

*City/county omitted to protect confidentiality of interviewees and their families.

Note: Fost-adopt. = the parent(s) began by fostering a child or is fostering a child with the expectation that if things go smoothly they will have the option to adopt the child; d.k. = don't know.

Source: Population figures for resident of families taken from U.S. Census Bureau, *State and County Quick Facts, 2011*, http://quickfacts.census.gov/qfd/index.html.

Notes

Introduction

1. To avoid cumbersome language, throughout the text, unless otherwise specified, "adoptive parent(s)" denotes "Euroamerican" and "American" adoptive parents in the United States. I also refer to the families whose members I interviewed as CA, RA, or AA to indicate that they include children adopted from China or Russia, or African American children adopted transracially within the United States.

2. Babb (1999) and Bowie (2004) offer excellent compendiums of cross-cultural adoption and fostering practices.

3. In addition to cross-cultural studies of adoption and fostering, such as the ones described here, there are a number of anthropological studies that document the means by which kin are made through activities that transform them, sometimes suddenly, more often gradually, into relatives. Fonseca (2003, 2009) has shown how children circulate among families in poor *favelas* in Brazil, while Leinaweaver (2008), Van Vleet (2002, 2008), Walmsley (2008), and Weismantel (1995) have provided case studies of how kin ties develop through the circulation of children and through activities, such as feeding and nurturing, in the Andean highlands of Ecuador, Peru, and Bolivia. Howell (2003, 2006) has focused on cases of transnational adoption and the means by which children are transubstantiated into kin.

4. "Sending country" refers to a country that is the source of children adopted by "receiving" adopting parents in another country, in this case the United States. There are usually marked economic inequalities between poorer sending and wealthier receiving regions that are central to ethical debates about adoption practices.

5. U.S. Department of Health and Human Services 2010.

6. See also Evan B. Donaldson Adoption Institute, "Benchmark Adoption Survey: First Public Opinion Survey on American Attitudes toward Adoption," 1997, http://www.adoptioninstitute.org/survey/baexec.html (accessed Jan. 25, 2013); Children's Bureau, AFCAR (Administration for Children and Families, U.S. Dept. of Health and Human Services), "Race/Ethnicity of Public Agency Children Adopted 10/1/2001 - 9/30/2002," http://www.acf.hhs.gov/programs/cb/resource/race-2002 (accessed Jan. 25, 2013); U.S. Department of State, "Statistics: Intercountry Adoption," May 23, 2011, http://adoption.state.gov/about_us/statistics.php (accessed Jan. 25, 2013).

7. Kreider's (2011b: 108) analysis, using the U.S. Census Bureau's American Community Survey, found that in 2008, of approximately 1.6 million adopted children, 350,209 (22 percent) were

adopted interracially; of those, 18 percent (63,016) were black children adopted by white parents. In addition, another 10.8 percent (37,659) were mixed (black and white) adopted by white parents; and 33.5 percent (117,184) were Asian or Pacific Islanders adopted by white parents.

8. In the United States, public agency adoptions take place through government agencies and are usually cheaper than those transacted either through private agency adoptions or as private adoptions. Public agency adoptions often involve children who are older or who have special needs. Private agency adoptions are funded by private organizations. They are more likely to employ stricter criteria for prospective parents because of the high number of waiting parents. Private adoptions are not arranged by an agency and are legal in most but not all U.S. states. Lawyers usually mediate, and final court approval is almost always needed. Most of the time, these are expensive and can be quite complicated because of the high probability of interaction between adopting and birth parents, and the longer waiting period that many states allow that permits birth parents to reflect on whether they wish to revoke their consent for adoption (Riley and Van Vleet 2012: 10). Private adoptions are more likely to involve the transferral of infants from birth to adopting parents.

International or transnational adoptions take place across boundaries between countries. They are complex because they are simultaneously subject to the laws of each country involved, including immigration laws, and, in some cases, international laws. They may also be costly if expenses for paperwork, travel, and donations to orphanages are tallied, but the range varies greatly. Children adopted through transnational adoption range in age from very young infants to much older children. The degree of openness in all of these adoptions differs according to legal contracts and more informal arrangements. In fact, initial decisions to keep birth records sealed or to comply with the termination of any link to birth parents may shift as children grow up and adoptive and birth parents themselves change their views.

9. The best source for up-to-date information and analysis on adoption figures comes from the *Adoption Fact Book V*, prepared by the National Council for Adoption (Roseman, Johnson, and Callahan 2011; see also Selman 2009; Riley and Van Vleet 2012); for transnational adoptions, the U.S. Department of State keeps the most accurate figures: "Statistics: Intercountry Adoption," May 23, 2011, http://adoption.state.gov/about_us/statistics.php (accessed Feb. 8, 2013). The Evan B. Donaldson Adoption Institute strives to maintain statistics on domestic and transnational adoptions, as well as foster care and foster care to adoption statistics ("Foster Care Facts," 2007, http://www.adoptioninstitute.org/FactOverview/foster.html (accessed Feb. 8, 2013).

10. Coutin, Bibler, Maurer, and Yngvesson (2002: 182) note, however, that, while it might appear that transnational adoption operates in a neocolonial fashion unidirectionally, "sending" nations also view adoptable children as one mechanism they can use to expand their national reach and resources in a kind of "reverse colonization."

11. David Herszenhorn, Andrew Kramer, and Erik Eckholm, "Russian Adoption Ban Brings Uncertainty and Outrage," *New York Times*, December 29, 2010. http://www.lexisnexis.com.mutex .gmu.edu/hottopics/lnacademic/ (accessed Feb. 8, 2013).

12. Gailey (2010), Rothman (2005), Rush (2000), and Dalmage (2006: 210–24) delineate the centrality of race and class in structuring adoption in America. Gailey (2006b: 71–88) describes how distorted and deleterious cultural images and representations of adoption and adoptive families circulate in American popular culture. Patton (2000) discusses similar themes from her vantage point as a transracial adoptee herself. Modell (2002) has traced how inequalities in race and class, and cultural assumptions about exchanges, gifts, and openness structure relationships between birth and adoptive families across racial and class lines. Many of these authors are themselves adoptive parents.

13. Lynette Clementson and Ron Nixon provide an excellent synthesis of how adoption gets filtered through the lens of race in the United States in "Overcoming Adoption's Racial Barriers,"

Aug. 17, 2006, *New York Times*, http://www.nytimes.com/2006/08/17/us/17adopt.html?_r=2&ref=
lynetteclemetson&pagewanted=all (accessed Feb. 8, 2013). Castañeda (2002) also delves into how
problematic it is to assume that race will not matter in mixed families in the United States.

14. It would have been methodologically elegant to include adoptive parents and children who
resemble the normative model of the American family. Their very desire to be invisible, however,
means they are difficult to access and few actively participate in listservs. The exception is children,
especially those seeking birth parents, and I have had a chance to look at their postings and to compare and contrast them to the children who participated in my research.

15. The composition of a group participating in a recent China heritage journey was telling.
While there were two gay couples, only one publicly acknowledged their status. The other represented themselves as part of a group of three friends traveling together.

16. In a stimulating debate about the ethical concerns surrounding ethnographic research and
the oversight of institutional review boards, Lederman (2006: 482–491) discusses the gray zones
that emerge from research that she calls "informal" or "subterranean" because it is not framed off
in any particular fashion from one's usual activities and does not entail departure to a field site
away from home. Others have called attention to how problematic it may be to use the concept "informal" to describe ethnographic research. They argue that whether or not ethnographic research
spills over into everyday life and interactions, it nevertheless requires special skills, a simultaneous
detachment, involvement, and ongoing analysis, a commitment to protecting the rights of subjects,
and a recognition that field work does not require a focus on the exotic (see also Brenneis 2006).

17. In the best of situations, I would have interviewed teens and adults in sufficient numbers
from each subcategory, and done extensive participant-observation with the adoptive families and
their children who are the subjects of this book, but they were not all accessible. Not all adoptees are
readily identifiable; furthermore, many do not want to identify themselves as such.

18. To protect the confidentiality of participants in these forums and blogs, they are only identified by their user names, and whenever possible I have asked permission to use their posts. I have
also used pseudonyms to protect the identities of everyone I interviewed or who participated in
online surveys.

19. Religious beliefs have been central to ethical debates about adoption, usually in the context
of institutionalized theological positions (Freundlich 2000; Jackson 2005). However, the concept of
popular religiosity, always important in child welfare policies, has received little anthropological attention in understanding practices of family formation. The works of Roof (1993) and Williams
(1999), addressing popular religiosity in a historical context, have assisted me in this analysis. There
is no clear-cut division between participating in religious institutions according to their concomitant belief systems, on the one hand, and what is called here "religiosity," on the other. But religiosity tends to comprise individually tailored beliefs in mysticism, faith, fate, and spirituality and to
place less emphasis on prescriptive, institutional practices, experiences, and beliefs.

20. The idea that the taken-for-granted nature of family formation among non-adoptive families is distinct from the activities that come to constitute "belonging" among adoptive families, especially those that are formed transnationally has been the subject of extensive anthropological
research (Bowie 2004; Carsten 2004; Dorow 2006; Gershon 2003; Howell 2006; Jacobson 2008; Lal
2001; Modell 1994; Rothman 2005; Volkman 2005a; Wegar 2006; Yngvesson 2004). Recent works
on adoption have examined the ways that adoptive families approach "kin-making" through means
other than "blood ties" and biological metaphors (Howell 2006).

21. Anthropologists are beginning to document the experiences of adoptees. Yngvesson
(2004), Yngvesson and Mahoney (2000), and Yngvesson and Coutin (2006) have analyzed how
paper trails and documents intervene in the journeys and return journeys of Swedish adoptees and
in their identity formation. Kim's (2005) work focuses on the relationship between nationalism and

heritage journeys for Korean adoptees. In her more recent ethnography (2010), she addresses these same questions, but more than any other work on adoption, hers is resolutely multi-sited. She follows how Korean adoptees, moving between Korea and the United States, are arriving at alternative kinship practices and building their identities in ways that avoid the dualistic or binary thinking that is prevalent in American and Korean kinship models and ideologies.

Chapter 1

1. "Convention on the Rights of the Child," November 12, 1989, United Nations, http://treaties .un.org/Pages/ViewDetails.aspx?src=TREATY&mtdsg_no=IV-11&chapter=4&lang=en (accessed Jan. 26, 2013).

2. Hague Convention on Protection of Children and Cooperation in Respect of Intercountry Adoption, 2006. Federal Register, February 15, 2006, final rules on "Hague Convention on Intercountry Adoption; Accreditation of Agencies and Approval of Persons under the Intercountry Adoption Act of 2000 (IAA)" (22 CFR, Part 96), U.S. Department of State, Federal Register 71(31): 8064–8161, http://www.gpo.gov/fdsys/pkg/FR-2006-02-15/pdf/06-1067.pdf (accessed Feb. 8, 2013).

3. By putting "orphan" in quotation marks, Briggs is calling attention to the fact that many children who are adopted have been legally categorized as orphans but often have living relatives who are no longer able or willing to care for them.

4. Children's Bureau, AFCAR, "The Multiethnic Placement Act of 1994, P.L. 103-382," 2004, http:// www.childwelfare.gov/systemwide/laws_policies/federal/index.cfm?event=federalLegislation .viewLegis&id=46 (accessed Jan. 31, 2013).

5. National Association of Black Social Workers, "Position Paper: Preserving Families of African Ancestry," 2003, http://www.nabsw.org/MServer/PreservingFamilies.aspx (accessed Jan. 31, 2013).

6. Each adoptive family interviewed has been assigned a source code. Hence, AA5 is a parent who has adopted an African American child. The Appendix provides further details about the members of each family and their respective characteristics. Here, for example, AA5 refers to a 46-year-old female who was single at the time of adoption but later married.

7. Abraham McLaughlin, "Americans Are Bringing Home Baby—Increasingly from Africa," Dec. 4, 2003, *Christian Science Monitor*, http://www.csmonitor.com/2003/1204/p01s03-woaf.htm (accessed Jan. 31, 2013); U.S. State Department, "Statistics: Intercountry Adoption," May 23, 2011, http://adoption.state.gov/about_us/statistics.php (accessed Jan. 31, 2013).

8. Dawn Davenport, "Born in America, Adopted Abroad," October 27, 2004, *Christian Science Monitor*, http://www.csmonitor.com/2004/1027/p11s01-lifp.htm (accessed Jan. 31, 2013). Ethiopia has become a sending region of choice for many Americans because the children are thought to be Christian; this is an example of religious matching.

9. Clifford Levy, "Russia Calls for Halt on U.S. Adoptions," *New York Times*, April 10, 2010.

10. Barbara Demick, "Chinese Babies Stolen by Officials for Foreign Adoption," *Los Angeles Times*, Sept. 24, 2009, http://www.latimes.com/news/nationworld/world/la-fg-china-adopt20-2009 sep20,0,618775,full.story (accessed Jan.31, 2013); see also John Leland, "For Adoptive Parents, Questions without Answers," *New York Times*, Sept. 18, 2011.

11. Attachment theory has found that children's emotional development and long-term healthy social relationships are negatively affected if infants do not experience bonding with a primary caregiver in their early years of life, usually between birth and 2 years of age.

12. Jerng's excellent exegesis of how transracial adoption and adoptees have been portrayed over two centuries in classical American literary accounts, shows how "claiming" was represented through adoption practices between Native Americans and captive whites, between freed slaves and whites, and more recently in accounts of transnational and transracial adoption in the late

twentieth century. He makes the point that "race is not so much a given as it is something that gets materialized through the uncertainty of relating the individual to the social contexts that precede and condition it. . . . Adoption reminds us that racial identity is located in that space of anxiety and insecurity between the world and self in which social norms are continually in flux" (Jerng 2010: 122).

13. Adoption Parenting Yahoo Group, "We're Buying Domestic: *Modern Family* Premiere," Sept. 22, 2011.

Chapter 2

1. Zelizer (1985: 11) states that "the expulsion of children from the 'cash nexus' at the turn of the past century, although clearly shaped by profound changes in the economic, occupational, and family structures, was also part of a cultural process of 'sacralization' of children's lives. The term sacralization is used in the sense of objects being invested with sentimental or religious meaning."

2. Pew Research Center for the People and Press, in collaboration with the American Association for the Advancement of Science, "Public Praises Science; Scientists Fault Public, Media," July 9, 2009, http://people-press.org/report/528/ (accessed Jan. 31, 2013). See also Pew (2010).

3. According to the Pew Forum on Religious Life (2009: 2), "Religiously mixed marriages are common in the United States, and the survey finds that the link between being in a religiously mixed union and attendance at multiple types of services is a complex one. Overall, people in religiously mixed marriages attend worship services less often than people married to someone of the same faith. But among those who attend religious services at least yearly, those in religiously mixed marriages attend multiple types of services at a higher rate than people married to someone of the same religion."

4. Karen McCowan, May 10, 2007. "Adoption Unites Two Families," *Register-Guard*, http://www.thefreelibrary.com/Adoption%20unites%20two%20families.-a0163405699 (accessed Jan. 31, 2013).

5. Smolin (2012) argues that neither Christian nor Jewish founding documents (the Bible and the Talmud) regard adoption positively. He makes a distinction between caretaking and adoption, in a legal sense, which he argues, almost never occurred in the Bible and Talmud. He also stresses that in the few instances of formal adoption in these documents, they did not unfold as assumed by those who embrace adoption today in the United States. In the Bible, adoption is primarily used as a metaphor for the vertical relationship between human beings and the adoption of God; in the Talmud, it would be highly unusual to remove a child from its patrilineage, except in the case of levirate marriage.

6. "The Gift of Adoption," http://moving2germany.blogspot.com/ (accessed Jan. 31, 2013).

7. Amy Eldridge, "Matching," April 14, 2004, RaisingChinaChildren, http://groups.yahoo.com/group/RaisingChinaChildren/message/13593 (accessed Jan. 31, 2013).

8. Since 1992, more than 60,000 Russian children had been adopted by U.S. citizens, and between 1996 (when records began to be kept) and 2013, nineteen of those children died in the United States as a result of abuse. In addition to these cases, others have been reported in which adoptive parents have sent their children back to Russia or abandoned them (Clifford Levy, "Russia Calls for Halt on U.S. Adoptions." *New York Times*, April 10, 2010). The acquittal of manslaughter of one father, whose young son, adopted from Russia, died in 2008 of heat stroke because his father left him in a parked car for nine hours, served as the catalyst for Russia to ban adoptions by U.S. citizens. Russia argued that that case, along with the other deaths, were equivalent to the violation of human rights that Russia was being sanctioned for by the United States. The numbers of deaths of Russian adoptees in the United States are small, but must be contextualized in light of the loss and disruption those children had already suffered (David Herszenhorn and Andrew Kramer, "Russian Adop-

tion Ban Brings Uncertainty and Outrage." *New York Times*, Dec. 28, 2012; Shuster 2012). At the same time, as I have stressed, the Russian Duma and Putin himself were using adoption as a political football rather than to improve the welfare of Russian children who were in state institutions or who had been adopted in the United States.

9. Anisia, "Panic," May 17, 2006, *Transracial Adoption or Placement*, http://groups.yahoo.com/group/Transracial_Adoption_or_Placement/message/3505 (accessed Jan. 31, 2013).

10. Kelly, "Panic," May 17, 2006, *Transracial Adoption*, http://groups.yahoo.com/group/Transracial_Adoption_or_Placement/message/3506?var=1&l=1 (accessed Jan. 31, 2013).

11. Holt International Children's Agency was one of the first agencies involved in international adoption. It began its work in South Korea immediately after the end of the Korean War in 1953. In "First Person Plural," Deann Borshay Liem (2000) documents her adoption from a Korean orphanage by her Euroamerican parents through Holt. Her adoptive parents were dissatisfied with the behavior of their church minister but still wanted to do something in the way of "good" and "charity." They began by supporting Deann in Korea and eventually adopted her. Her impoverished Korean mother had been pressured three times by a man next door working for an orphanage to turn Deann over to him for the orphanage, and she finally did. She was switched with another child originally intended for Deann's adoptive parents and only much later found her Korean family.

12. Dr. James Dobson, "Caring for the World's Orphans," *Family Talk with Dr. Dobson*, Feb. 11, 2011, http://www.oneplace.com/ministries/family-talk/listen/caring-for-the-worlds-orphans-163471.html (accessed Jan. 31, 2013). See also Vance (2005) on "foreign adoption ministries."

13. The mission of the Russian Orphan Lighthouse Project has been to help "orphans ages 7–15 years old to experience 10-day, fun filled trips." They go on "Vacation Bible School trips where kids stay with prospective adopting hosts." They advertise that "more than 600 children have found Christian homes through our program. We believe God sustains our work, and it is only through Him that it has blossomed." They also take prospective adoptive families to Russia, where they spent time with older orphans. As of Jan. 31, 2013, the organization had taken down its website because of the ban on Russian adoptions, but details about its projects are found on other sites, such as Rainbowkids.com, "The Voices of Adoption," http://www.rainbowkids.com/ArticleDetails.aspx?id=251 (accessed Jan. 31, 2013). One of the RA adoptive families I worked with had begun thinking about adoption after volunteering to host an older Russian boy through their church.

14. Most frequently, the black churches they attended were either AME (African Methodist Episcopal) or some variant of National Baptist. There are many denominations of black churches.

15. "National Jewish Population Survey 2000–01: Strength, Challenge and Diversity in the American Jewish Population," pp. 4–5, http://www.jewishfederations.org/local_includes/downloads/4606.pdf (accessed Feb. 1, 2013).

16. Andy Newman, with Michael Luo. "A Chinese Orphan's Journey to a Jewish Rite of Passage." *New York Times*, March 8, 2007.

17. Eighty-seven percent of scientists stated that humans and other living things have evolved over time and that evolution is the result of natural processes such as natural selection. Yet just 32 percent of the public accepted this as true (Pew Research Center 2009).

Chapter 3

Portions of this chapter were originally published in Linda J. Seligmann, "The Cultural and Political Economies of Adoption Practices in Andean Peru and the United States," *Journal of Latin American and Caribbean Anthropology* 14, no. 1 (2009): 115–39

1. Horridge (2011: 83) elaborates on the substantive and structural content of scrapbookmaking by adopting gay and lesbian parents: "The ways in which gay adopters choose to represent themselves through the construction of their waiting profiles may or may not be at odds with the

ways in which they present themselves in everyday life. My research found that most gay adopters are 'coached' through the direct placement open adoption process by lawyers and hired 'facilitators' and often re-frame different aspects of their identities according to the assumed expectations and desires of waiting birthmothers. These re-presentations of selves are believed to be crucial to the success of direct placement open adoptions and play an important role in the task of identifying a birthmother."

2. Naming processes in American adoption are complex, especially as names simultaneously contribute to a sense of personhood or selfhood and incorporation into larger units. In adoption, both the individual child and the larger units into which they are incorporated are differentiated. The naming process, which is itself dynamic, must both differentiate and be inclusive.

3. Elizabeth Olson, "Families Adopting in Vietnam Say They Are Caught in Diplomatic Jam." *New York Times*, Feb. 11, 2008.

4. "Keep Chinese Name Poll," initiated Jan. 17, 2005, Raising China Children Yahoo Group, http://groups.yahoo.com/group/RaisingChinaChildren/surveys?id=1601987 (accessed Feb. 10, 2013).

5. Yannie Fan, "Farewell Letter," June 9, 2000, http://www.usaweb1.com/chinatrip/farewell.htm (accessed Feb. 1, 2013).

6. SWIs serve not just as orphanages but also as caretaking facilities for elderly Chinese who need assistance. The younger and older generations interact with each other in these homes rather than remaining socially isolated.

7. Once the parents submitted citizenship papers in the United States, the children received U.S. passports.

8. Adoptshoppe.com and Tapestry Books are two online companies that market lifebooks, specifically for families with children who have been adopted. They differ from the baby books and even the lifebooks targeted to adoptive families found in mainstream stores like Hallmark, which are usually structured for two-parent households. While there is considerable room for flexibility, adoption specialists have encouraged parents to focus on the following questions when they put together lifebooks: who gave birth to the child; why birth parents could not raise the child; the passage from birth parents to foster parents to orphanage and other caretakers; how children got their names; where they lived and what it was like; what their room looked like; whether they shared it with anyone; who they lived with; what their daily life (food, toys, friends) was like; their health; why they were not adopted sooner (if the child is older); whether they had special needs and how they were taken care of; whether they have biological siblings; whether their birth parents or relatives are alive. See Myra Alperson, "A Link to the Past: An Adoption Scrapbook Lets Parents and Children Create a Sense of History and of Belonging," 2001, http://www.adoptivefamilies.com/articles.php?aid=529 (accessed Feb. 10, 2013).

9. The work of Chatham-Carpenter (2009) complements Dorow's (2006) on the adoption narratives of CA adoptive parents and the common themes that emerge from them. Chatham-Carpenter examined lifebooks, blogs, and the act of writing letters to unknown birth parents.

10. The "red thread of destiny" is invoked by many participants in adoption from China. It is from a Chinese legend, originally alluding to lovers, that an invisible red thread binds those who are destined to meet. This idea has been extended to the red thread of destiny binding children from China to their adoptive parents.

11. Julie, "Where Did Everyone Go?" #293659, Apr. 17, 2010, *Adoptive Parents China*, http://groups.yahoo.com/group/a-parents-china/message/293659 (accessed Feb. 10, 2013).

12. Sue, "Support Groups/FCC Complaints," April 3, 2005, msg. 6, *China Adoption Race Matters* (CHaRM), http://groups.yahoo.com/group/CHinaAdoptionRaceMatters/(discontinued website).

13. Sasha, "Culture, Hot Dogs, Baseball and Fireworks," March 10, 2005, msg. 5, *China Adoption*, http://groups.yahoo.com/group/CHinaAdoptionRaceMatters/ (discontinued).

14. There is substantial evidence of pervasive trafficking and abduction of children for international adoption. Understandably, this evidence flies in the face of what was once thought to be an orderly, uncorrupted process and has created ethical dilemmas and anxiety for adoptive parents and distress for birth families who are attempting to locate their children. See Sharon LaFraniere (with Edy Yin, Shao Heng and Shi Da), "Officials in China Seized Infants for Black Market, Parents Say," *New York Times*, August 5, 2011; Sharon LaFraniere, "Officials Say They Saved 81 Babies from Child Traffickers," *New York Times*, July 28, 2011; Liu Linlin, "Alleged Child Trafficking Involving Family-Planning Officials in Hunan Province…" *Global Times*, May 10, 2011.

15. Tobias Hubinette (Lee Sam-dol), "A Critique of Intercountry Adoption," 2006, http://www.transracialabductees.org/politics/samdolcritique.html (accessed Feb. 10, 2013); and John Raible, "An Open Letter to Parents of Mature Transracial Adoptees," Reprint from Pact: An Adoption Alliance, Fall 2003, http://nysccc.org/family-supports/transracial-transcultural/voices-of-adoptees/an-open-letter-to-parents/ (accessed Feb. 10, 2013).

16. In fact, Johnson (2004) and Johnson, Wang, and Huang (1998, 2005) are among the few researchers who have studied how children become available for adoption in China, offering concrete tales that contrast with most adoption narratives. Their research finds that many Chinese families courageously and informally adopt abandoned girls, who do not exist legally since they are unregistered. Because many families wish to "complete" their families with a girl if they only have a son, families who must give up healthy daughters at about six months of age often "abandon" them close to home on the doorstep of a family they think might wish to have a daughter. In only a few cases did women make the decision to abandon their child themselves. In about a quarter of the cases the decision was made by men; and in the rest, jointly. They also documented that social welfare institutes (orphanages) had successfully placed healthy children with Chinese families until the Chinese government further restricted the practice in the interest of population control and more stringent birth planning. As a result, orphanages had to accept and care for a greater number of children. Johnson and her co-authors create a very different, far more nuanced, and less Manichean depiction of the history and practices that lie behind infant girl abandonment in China.

Chapter 4

1. The two quotations that start this chapter are responses by RA adoptive parents to a query I made on the FRUA (Families for Russian and Ukrainian Adoption) Yahoo forum, asking about the ways that they thought about their children's birthplace. FRUA also held an annual conference with sessions on different aspects of adoption from Russia and published a newsletter. I was fortunate to get to know one of the officers of FRUA who was very generous with her time. She permitted me to interview her and meet her family, and introduced me to other adoptive families with children from Russia. Starting in 2012, the FRUA forum decided to permit only those who had adopted children from Russia or the Ukraine to participate in the forum. Hence, to protect the privacy of those who responded, I am not including their names. "Russian Adoption," July 15, 2005, Families for Russian and Ukrainian Adoption (FRUA), http://chat.frua.org/ (accessed May 18, 2006), and have only provided the date when the responses I received were posted.

2. The misuse of the term "Caucasian" was common among RA adoptive parents. While they equated it with white, in fact, it refers to people of the Caucasus mountains rather than to skin type or a particular race. Historically, it became a politicized and racialized term between 1917 and 1965 central to U.S. immigration policy, such that Middle Eastern and North African populations were labeled Caucasian and nonwhite to distinguish them from European "white" immigrants and to prevent the former from becoming naturalized citizens. Since Caucasian refers to "white" in the context of U.S. adoptive parents of Russian children, I use "white" in the text except when quoting others.

3. In 2011, the total cost of adoption ranged from nothing to over $40,000, with foster care adoptions costing between 0 and $2,500; private agency adoptions from $5,000 to over $40,000; independent adoptions from $8,000 to over $40,000; and intercountry adoptions between $7,000 and 30,000. In 2010, private adoptions of white infants could cost as much as $100,000. Some expenses are incurred by all adoptive families, including home-study expenses and court costs. Court costs ranged from $500 to $2,000; legal representation cost between $2,500 and $12,000. Certain countries have additional fees, including child foster care, parents' travel, escorting fees, children's medical care, translation fees, foreign attorneys, passport fees, and visa processing (Child Welfare Information Gateway, "Cost of Adopting: A Factsheet for Families," 2011, http://www.childwelfare .gov/pubs/s_cost/s_costs.pdf (accessed Feb. 11, 2013). See also "ASFA Identified as Having Most Impact on Changing Public Child Welfare," and "Optimism about Race Relations Found Key to Social Workers' Attitudes," Feb. 2005, *Evan B. Donaldson Institute Newsletter*, http://www.adoption institute.org/newsletter/2005_02.html#optimism (accessed Feb. 11, 2013).

4. May 22, 2010, FRUA, http://chat.frua.org/.

5. January 8, 2006, FRUA, http://chat.frua.org/.

6. "Russian Adoption," July 15, 2005, FRUA, http://chat.frua.org/.

7. "Russian Adoption," July 16, 2005, FRUA, http://chat.frua.org/.

8. Ibid.

9. Ibid.

10. A comprehensive study performed by the University of Minnesota found that Eastern Europeans and Russians in particular had the world's highest per capita alcohol consumption, and that the risk to the fetus during pregnancy was not widely appreciated, particularly among impoverished and/or chemically dependent women who were the most likely to voluntarily or involuntarily lose parental rights. Consequently, many if not most orphans placed from Eastern Europe, and Russia in particular, were at risk of intrauterine alcohol exposure. The University of Minnesota's statistical evaluation of children adopted from Eastern Europe confirms an unusually high incidence of FAS and FASD among them. Diagnosing FAS can be difficult, but the symptoms include specific facial features, especially with respect to the nose and lips; small brain circumference; height and weight that do not progress over time; delays in development and/or cognition; motor dysfunction; language deficits; and disordered socialization. Many of these characteristics are also present, at least initially, among children who have been in institutional settings from infancy, hence the difficulty in immediate diagnosis. "Fetal Alcohol Syndrome Research," International Adoption Medicine Program, 2008, http://www.peds.umn.edu/iac/IACservices/research/fas/ home.html (accessed Feb. 2, 2013).

Chapter 5

1. That is, some AA parents believed that parents adopting from China, in particular, were motivated by stereotypes about "model minorities" *and* latent prejudice against African Americans. Rothman (2005: 245), citing Yan (2003), argues that "Asian Americans and Latinos will move into 'whiteness,'" while there will be no assimilation of African Americans. Yan concludes "that the main racial issue in the United States has been and will continue to be the divide between blacks and whites. Thus a black/nonblack dichotomy is the best way to approach race in America, rather than the more typical white/nonwhite dichotomy."

2. Some birth parents who did not want any kind of openness with adoptive families changed their minds over time. And adoptive parents told me of cases in which birth parents wanted to either decrease or increase their contact.

3. Kin care in the black community is too often viewed in a celebratory light when, in fact, it

is a huge burden that exists because of the lack of alternative childcare arrangements available to them (Solinger 1992).

4. Goffman (1963) focused on social interactions but paid less attention to how they were embedded in and shaped by the structural contexts in which they unfolded.

5. Brandy, who had foster-adopted three African American children, in her concluding remarks to me recognized how crucial it was to change adoption practices in precisely the way that Perry argues would truly disrupt racism. Brandy's remarks fell well outside a multiculturalist position: "Just that, in an ideal world I'd like to see all the kids that are coming out of foster care placed transracially, and that includes the white kids into black homes, because from what we have noticed the more people that truly—like our kids, for some people are the very first black people that they've ever spoken with—realize that they are human and they are just like their kids, I think that is about the only way that racism is going to end when everybody is related to somebody who is black. Then it's real" (AA10).

6. Smith, Jacobson, and Juárez (2011), in a study of the experience of racism among transracial adoptive families in the United States, found that racial slurs and discrimination were still prevalent. They found that the Euroamerican parents and their adopted African American children, whether young or grown, without exception, had experienced discrimination, and almost all parents, and children over the age of 5, had heard the "N" word.

7. Margie, "Saturday with Alison and John," March 22, 2009, *Third Mom*, http://thirdmom .blogspot.com/2009/03/saturday-with-alison-and-john.html (accessed Feb. 11, 2013).

8. The Rev. Dr. Martin Luther King Jr. called Sunday morning church service the most segregated hour in America. In 2011, there are more mixed and white people attending black churches. Susan Saulny, reporting on the degree of "racial mixing" through intermarriage, found, for example, at Grace Temple Ministries, a neighborhood black church in Mississippi, there were many mixed race families. The pastor was white, the assistant pastor black, and the arts pastor Latino. The pastor's message in the sermon she attended was "Let us not be guilty of thinking as the culture and society decides." Susan Saulny, "Black and White and Married in the Deep South: A Shifting Image." *New York Times*, National Section, March 20, 2011.

9. CHarM is the acronym for "ChinaAdoptionRaceMatters," a Yahoo group that has since ceased to function. "Talking to Kids about Racism," msg. 1578, Jan. 22, 2006, CHarM, http://groups .yahoo.com/group/CHinaAdoptionRaceMatters/. While most participants were adoptive mothers of Chinese children, a small number who had adopted African American children participated in significant ways that opened the eyes of CA adoptive parents to racial issues that would affect their children. I use pseudonyms here to protect those who posted.

10. Kelly, "Transracial Adoption or Placement Question," April 11, 2006, msg. 3243, *Transracial Adoption or Placement*, http://groups.yahoo.com/group/Transracial_Adoption_or_Placement/ message/3243 (accessed Feb. 12, 2013).

11. "Juneteenth" takes place on June 19 to commemorate the ending of slavery in the United States and African American freedom. It has expanded as a holiday in which participants place emphasis on African American freedom and achievements. It originated in Galveston, Texas, in 1865.

12. Children adopted from China and other parts of the world are also perceived as racially different, but the inflection of adoption tends to carry more weight than racial difference. In the case of China, the notion of model minority and the stereotypes that are coupled with it intervene.

13. Two trends may contribute to this acceptance: the rise in mixed-race children; and intermarriage across race and ethnic lines. Susan Saulny reported in a *New York Times* article that, according to census figures, in the ten years between 2000 and 2010 the number of mixed-race children in America rose by 50 percent, to a total of 4.2 million. Overall, the total number of Americans who self-identify as mixed-race went up an astounding 134 percent, to 1.8 million. Since the

mixed-race population is "overwhelmingly young," these numbers translate into more mixed-race peers for all children, especially in southern and midwestern states, where increases in numbers of mixed-race Americans have been "far greater than the national average." Susan Saulny, "Census Data Presents Rise in Multiracial Population of Youths," *New York Times*, National Section, March 25, 2011. A Pew Charitable Trust study also found that "about 15 percent of new marriages in 2010 crossed racial or ethnic lines, double the rate from three decades ago." Wendy Wang, "The Rise of Intermarriage: Rates, Characteristics Vary by Race and Gender," *Social and Demographic Trends Project, Pew Charitable Trust*, Feb. 28, 2012, http://www.pewsocialtrends.org/2012/02/16/the-rise-of-intermarriage/ (accessed Feb. 3, 2013). In a summary of the study, Morello writes, "Intermarriages comprise 8 percent of all marriages now, up from just 3 percent in 1980. And most Americans tell pollsters they are untroubled at the prospect of intermarriage in their own family." Further, the study found that "the share of whites who marry 'out' of their race has more than doubled since 1980, to 9 percent. The percentage of blacks who marry nonblacks has more than tripled, to 17 percent." See Carol Morello, "Intermarriage Rates Soar as Stereotypes Fall," *Washington Post*, Feb. 15, 2012, http://www.washingtonpost.com/local/intermarriage-rates-soar-as-stereotypes-fall/2012/02/15/gIQAvyByGR_story.html (accessed Feb. 13, 2013). A cautionary note is in order, however, in that most of the "mixing" has been the consequence of immigration and the influx of people of Asian and Hispanic descent; and a much higher percentage of black men than black women have intermarried; they were three times as likely to intermarry as black women.

Chapter 6

1. Ochs and Capps (1996) provide an overview of approaches to life stories and narratives. Bruner (2004); Peacock and Holland (1993); Brenneis (1988); and Miller et al. (1990) also offer discussions of storytelling in light of structuring devices, typologies of narratives, the use of narrative instrumentally in disputes, and how stories intervene in the social construction of the self. There is also a robust anthropological literature on life histories and their interactive dimensions, but that genre differs from adoption narratives told by parents to their children. Life histories are usually told by informants to anthropologists. In both cases, however, as we discuss here, power relationships and deliberate choices about what to include and exclude intervene in the interaction itself.

2. It is a truism that people tell stories and that stories are told to them. Children's stories and films in which the central character is an orphan affect all children, but perhaps have impacts on adopted children in ways that we do not yet understand well. The representation of the orphan as "in need" or "bad," or as one who eventually is incorporated into a fairy-tale dream of a better life, has circulated for centuries. Surely these tales of orphans permeate the consciousness of Americans of every generation.

3. Sweetman's doctoral dissertation is on the formation of memory among adoptees from China.

4. Children differ from one another in their curiosity, and we do not hear from adoptees who are not curious about the gaps or "ghosts" in their narratives. For the curious ones, their parents' narratives and the documents they discovered led them to wonder, almost obsessively, about what was missing in their narratives and catalyzed them to search for answers. Two excellent examples of this are depicted in the documentaries *Off and Running* (Opper 2009) and *First Person Plural* (Liem 2000).

5. It may be that it was too threatening or frightening to explicitly include birth parents as "family" through speech precisely because the children had already recognized that "the norm" was one or two parents, not three or four. It was equally likely that the meaning of parenthood, for them, emerged from the daily interactions that constituted relatedness. At the same time, actions

speak louder than words, and several CA adoptees remembered their birth mother on the day that they were adopted by burning incense or lighting a candle.

6. May 8, 2008, *FRUA*, http://chat.frua.org/.

7. Agnes's growing awareness of the centrality of race in social interactions in America is similar to a point that Sharon Rush makes in her memoir, *Loving across the Color Line: A White Adoptive Mother Learns about Race*. Rush points out the paradoxical dangers of color-blindness among "whites of goodwill."

> To be color-blind in the context of racial differences means, at best, that a White person sees Blackness but doesn't devalue it or discriminate on the basis of it. But this presents a paradox, a paradox every White person who adheres to color-blindness must confront: Seeing racial differences is inevitable, but if seeing racial differences does not cause one to discriminate against Blacks, then why pretend there are no Blacks in society? The only reason a White person needs to avoid acknowledging a Black person's Blackness is to avoid negative (discriminatory) behavior by the White person toward the Black person. This is a silly trap for unwary White people of goodwill who adamantly insist that they would never knowingly and intentionally discriminate against Blacks anyway. (2000: 37)

Rush concludes, "My daughter and all mulattoes present special challenges for many people who condemn interracial Black/White relationships. Naturally, falling in love with a person of color does not mean a White person will understand racism or be motivated to help end it" (2000: 136).

Chapter 7

1. Cindy, "Looking for Suggestions: Lifeline 3rd Grade Assignment," January 8, 2010, *Adoptive Parents China*, http://groups.yahoo.com/group/a-parents-china/message/292909 (accessed Feb. 13, 2013).

2. Capoeira is a Brazilian martial art developed by descendants of African American slaves with Brazilian influences, and which has different ranks.

3. *Adoption in the Schools* is a comprehensive analysis prepared by the Evan B. Donaldson Institute (2009) of current school practices and how they should be modified to take account of the experiences of the high number of children who are members of adoptive and foster families.

4. Concerned Persons for Adoption, "Information for Educators/School Personnel on Adoption," 2009, http://www.cpfanj.org/resources/Section_for_Educators.pdf (accessed Feb. 6, 2013).

5. In *The First R: How Children Learn Race and Racism*, sociologists Van Ausdale and Feagin (2001) set themselves the task of discerning exactly how children, through their interactions, constructed categories and, specifically, ideas about race. Building on Mead's (1967) and Vygotsky's (2004) approaches, they argue that children always learn in a social context but that most prior research on children's attitudes about race has been distorted by an adult-centered or -initiated context. They found that if the adults (with their dyadic interactions with children, formalized testing, and awkward interviews) were removed, children built their understanding of the world, and of race and ethnicity, through interactive language and physicality with each other, and a wide array of cues from daily life, including those that circulate in institutional settings such as school.

They spent a year observing a preschool class of fifty-eight 3-to-5-year-olds, documenting the extraordinary range of ways in which children processed race and skin color. Examples included what it meant when parents had two different colors of skin, why the words "black" and "white" were used in some cases but Chinese or Japanese was used in others, whether skin color was permanent, and how color correlated with culture or language. They concluded that concepts of race and racism were present even among very young children when they played and interacted with each other, and sometimes because of the ways teachers were implementing anti-bias programs, but that the children had difficulty grasping what they meant and how to use such terms and relationships.

The results of their study created controversy, specifically over whether such young children, developmentally, should be taught about race and racism. Wright's (1998) popular *I'm Chocolate, You're Vanilla*, which some parents and educators prefer, opposes introducing racial awareness to young children. A large percentage of adoptees and their parents have rejected Wright's perspective because they believe that children need to be able to understand why they are being teased and to have the language and skills to respond in ways that do not diminish their self-image.

Chapter 8

1. I adopt Boellstorff's (2008) distinction between "virtual" and "actual" worlds and his logic that "actual" means something different than "real." That premise suggests that virtual worlds are not real, a premise not borne out by the many ways that both worlds together shape our current social existence, politically, economically, and culturally.

2. Adams and Smith (2008) discuss how to define "electronic tribes," whose principal constituents, for them, are people, purposes, protocols, and technology, and how such tribes behave. Relevant to this discussion of the ways that adoptive families use the Internet, they emphasize that a major reason individuals "aggregate" to form such Internet networks is "information sharing and the exchange of life experiences." They hazard that the "continuous flow of information defines the essence of electronic tribes" (p. 18).

3. Although Anagnost (2000) states that her findings are based on her review of cyber-communications, in fact, much of what she analyzes is taken from her participant-observation, in general, of adoptive parents of Chinese children. The creation of memory books and gift exchanges are two examples of practices that do not take place via the Internet. It is true, however, that Internet discourse may influence parents, especially mothers, to make memory books and how to make them.

4. Since 1999, orphanages in China have been required to publish a provincial newspaper advertisement for children that are brought to their orphanage. These are known as "finding ads," and they include information about where and when the child was found and which orphanage is taking care of them. Many of them include a photo, likely the earliest taken of the child.

5. Stuy's website, http://www.research-china.org/ (accessed Feb. 7, 2013), includes both a public and a subscription blog. Links to the newspaper articles that broke open this particular case, and the detailed list of the children who had been trafficked, are found on his public blog, Brian Stuy, "Shaoyang, Hunan Birth Parents Seek Contact with Adoptive Families," May 9, 2011, http://research-china.blogspot.com/2011/05/shaoyang-hunan-birth-parents-seek.html (accessed Feb. 7, 2013).

6. Although I have little information available about how sending nations themselves classified children for adoption, it was apparent that the United States, China, and Russia, for example, used their own systems to children for adoption. These systems remain silent, hidden behind the photos that surfaced virtually. Regulations set by different countries in part reflected their classification systems. China's rejection of single, same-sex, or obese parents, and its age requirements, were not only about the welfare of the child but also about the ideal physical and social status of persons in China. One Chinese liaison who worked for a U.S. adoption agency told me that infants were distinguished by location of the ears and the distance of the eyes from the forehead. At the same time, classification systems, whether in the United States or elsewhere, remained opaque, in part because they were undergirded by ideological constructs.

7. A good overview of major variants and the history of the Chicago School is provided by Becker 1999.

8. Adams and Smith (2008: 11–20), in their edited volume *Electronic Tribes*, prefer to refer to such virtual networks as "tribes" rather than "communities" because they argue that those who "be-

long" to them have shared interests and, unlike communities, tribes "incorporate both utopian and dystopian formations. They are easily accessible and are not subject to spatiotemporal constraints." There remains considerable debate about how the best term to use to describe such networks.

9. Jill, "Adoption Today," July 9, 2011, msg. 56879, *Adoption Parenting Group*, http://groups .yahoo.com/group/adoptionparenting/message/56879 (accessed Feb. 7, 2013).

10. Jennifer, "Adoption Today," July 10, 2011, #56889, *Adoption Parenting*, http://groups .yahoo.com/group/adoptionparenting/message/56889 (accessed Feb. 7, 2013).

11. Michele, "Adoption Today," July 10, 2011, msg. 56892, *Adoption Parenting*, http://groups .yahoo.com/group/adoptionparenting/message/56892 (accessed Feb. 7, 2013).

12. This informant remains anonymous here because, although she agreed to be interviewed and participated enthusiastically, for many of the same reasons that she elucidates below, she asked that I not use her interview material. However, she agreed to permit me to use what she had posted online.

13. Anonymous AA mother, quoted from an online blog post.

14. Ibid.

Chapter 9

1. A research project such as this one does not reach closure. As this book was going to press, the views of RA adoptive parents on open adoption had begun to shift toward supporting their children in searches and establishing ongoing relationships with members of their birth families in Russia.

2. JetLoakman, "My New Nat Geo Mag . . . ," *One World Chinese Adoptees Links Blog*, Dec. 24, 2009, http://www.chineseadoptee.com/2009/12/my-new-nat-geo-mag.html (accessed Feb. 7, 2013).

3. Sandra Pesmen, "'Gotcha' for Good," *Chicago Sun-Times*, August 29, 2005.

4. Karen Moline, "Get Rid of "Gotcha," 2010, *Adoptive Families* (online version), http://www .adoptivefamilies.com/articles.php?aid=1266 (accessed Feb. 7, 2013).

5. Ruth Lor Malloy, Dec. 18, 2002, "The First Family," *City Weekend*, http://ruthlormalloy.com/ firstfamily.htm (accessed Feb. 7, 2013).

6. "Summer Culture Camps and Adoption Camps for Kids and Families," *Adoption.com*, http://camps.adoption.com/ (accessed Feb. 7, 2013).

7. "Chinese II," *Heritage Camps for Adoptive Families*, http://www.heritagecamps.org/what-we -do/the-camps/chinese-ii.html (accessed Feb. 7, 2013).

8. Michelle Hainer, "Foreign Culture Brought Home: Adoptees Discover Themselves at Camp." *Washington Post*, May 3, 2005.

9. Lynette Clementson, "Adopting in China, Seeking Identity in America," March 23, 2006, *New York Times*, www.nytimes.com/2006/03/23/national/23adopt.html (accessed Feb. 7, 2013).

10. Jazz, "Friendship," Dec. 18, 2009, *One World*, http://www.chineseadoptee.com/2009/12/ friendship.html (accessed Feb. 7, 2011).

11. Adopteen, http://www.chinaadopteen.org/ (accessed Feb. 7, 2013).

12. John Raible, "Benefits of Pact Camp," 2009, *Pact's Point of View*, https://www.pactadopt .org/app/servlet/documentapp.DisplayDocument?DocID=141 (accessed Feb. 7, 2013).

13. Catie B., "Roots," June 16, 2011, *China's Children International Blog*, http://cci-chinas children.blogspot.com/2012/03/roots-catie-b.html (translated from Chinese, Mar. 18, 2012) (accessed Feb. 7, 2013).

14. Although I have no systematic research data, in my interviews with parents and children and in participant-observation I found that children articulated these desires as early as age 6, and by age 8 experienced a deep sustained sense of grief and loss, as well as a desire for knowledge about missing family members.

15. JetLoakman, "Somebody's Child: A Riposte," January 14, 2010, *One World*, http://www .chineseadoptee.com/2010/01/somebodys-child-riposte.html (accessed Feb. 7, 2013).

16. Sabrina, "This Is a One Life Stand," Dec. 30, 2009, *One World*, http://www.chineseadoptee .com/2009/12/this-is-one-life-stand.html (accessed Feb. 7, 2013).

17. Pat Barker, acclaimed author of the "Regeneration" trilogy, in which she documents the lives of soldiers who participated in "The Great War," made this comment in an interview (Fraser 2008: 41).

18. Maia S., "Heritage Trip: Back to Hangzhou," March 18, 2012, *One World*, http://www.chinese adoptee.com/2012/03/heritage-trip-back-to-hangzhou-maia-s.html (accessed Feb. 7, 2013).

19. Dorow (2006) offers the most systematic account of the "ghosts" that haunt adoptions of children from China.

20. Mei-Mei, "What Is in a Name?" March 10, 2012, *One World*, http://www.chineseadoptee. com/2012/03/what-is-in-name_10.html (accessed Feb. 7, 2013).

21. Maia S., "Heritage Trip . . . ,"March 18, 2012, *One World*, http://www.chineseadoptee .com/2012/03/heritage-trip-back-to-hangzhou-maia-s.html (accessed Feb. 7, 2013).

22. JetLoakman, "Somebody's Child . . . " January 14, 2010, *One World*, http://www.chinese adoptee.com/2010/01/somebodys-child-riposte.html (accessed Feb. 7, 2013).

23. Tara Bahrampour, "Born Abroad, Adopted Teens Find Home in Multiple Lands." *Washington Post*, Jan. 21, 2012, http://www.washingtonpost.com/local/born-abroad-adopted-teens-find-home -in-multiple-lands/2012/01/18/gIQAVvr8GQ_print.html (accessed Feb. 7, 2013).

24. Several anthropologists have studied how Korean adoptees have made an impact on Korea's views of international adoption (see Kim 2003, 2010; Palmer 2011; Prebin 2009). The Korean government has encouraged them to participate in cultural gatherings in Korea and created television shows on which adoptees reunite with their birth parents. Jennifer Kwon Dobbs reported that in 2011, the Korean government, in response to the circuit journeys of Korean adoptees, and for reasons of nationalism, changed its law to permit adoptees to retain dual citizenship ("Ending South Korea's Child Export Shame," June 23, 2011, *Foreign Policy in Focus*, http://www.fpif .org/articles/ending_south_koreas_child_export_shame) (accessed Feb. 7, 2013). Korean American adoptees view these efforts on the part of the Korean government with skepticism. For them, it appears much more like a combination of nationalistic fervor and an economic agenda than a genuine interest in the lives of the adoptees who were deliberately rejected by the Korean state and by Koreans for many years. At the same time, community-building among Korean adoptees has gained momentum and strength from the reunions themselves. It is unclear whether China's government is motivated by similar objectives.

Louie (2001) explains that anyone who looks Chinese *is* Chinese (of higher or lower status, perhaps). While mainland Chinese viewed CA adoptees with a combination of patriotic nationalism and economic pragmatism on their return journeys to China, unlike Korean adoptees who were forcibly assimilated and whom Kim (2003) describes as "deterritorialized," CA adoptees were more familiar with China and their Chinese cultural heritage. They were also more aware of the conditions that structured gender, class, and race conditions in both the United States and China. How this knowledge will affect their sentiments toward the Chinese government remains to be seen.

25. Irene Sege, "The Point of Return," August 30, 2008, *Boston Globe*. http://www.boston.com/ lifestyle/articles/2008/08/30/the_point_of_return/ (accessed Feb. 7, 2013).

26. Stephanie Cho and Kim So Yung (2006) also describe the often painful challenges for transracial adoptees of bringing together multiple facets of their histories and identities without being compelled to belong to one category or another.

27. Lisa Marie Rollins, "Negotiating Guilt, Activism/Performance and Family," February 6, 2010, *A Birth Project Blog: Transracial Adoption from One Black Girl's Perspective*, http://birth

project.wordpress.com/2010/02/06/negotiating-guilt-activismperformance-and-family/ (accessed Feb. 7, 2013).

28. *My Adoption Journey,* by DMC, 2006, http://www.me-dmc.com/index.cfm/pk/view/cd/NAA/cdid/5654/pid/4814, VH1 Television, Viacom International (accessed Feb. 7, 2013).

29. Gailey (2006b) has done a close analysis of the position and functions of "orphans" in films. Increasingly, one finds shows about aspects of adoption in the popular media. Examples include ABC's *Find My Family,* Fox's *Who's Your Daddy?* Hallmark's *Adoption: Real Families, Real Stories,* and Freddie Mac's *Wednesday's Child. Mei Magazine* has become a very popular publication for CA adoptees, and there are many newsletters tailored to niche groups that attest to the growing cultural communication among communities of adoptees. Mark Jerng (2010) also shows how orphans are depicted historically in American literature and the ways they not only represent cultural anxieties and uneasiness about differences in race and class but also become the vehicle for resolving or controlling them.

30. See "Ethnically Incorrect Daughter Adoptee Blogs," 2011, http://ethnicallyincorrect.wordpress.com/ (accessed Feb. 7, 2013).

31. The idea that one should explore what society *is* through emergent networks rather than begin with the assumption that a society has concrete or even empirically discernible boundaries is hardly a novel idea to anthropologists. Members of the Manchester School, for example, while they were more interested in the materialization of structures than the circulation of ideas and practices, relied on this conceptualization of society to explore how knowledge circulated and institutions emerged from networks.

32. AFAAD, an all-volunteer organization founded by Lisa Marie Rollins in 2008, holds annual conferences. It does not permit non-adoptees to participate in sessions, with the exception usually of one large public education event.

33. "One World: Chinese Adoptee Links Blog, http://www.chineseadoptee.com/ (accessed Feb. 7, 2013).

34. "AdoptionTalk," http://chinaadoptiontalk.blogspot.com/ (accessed Feb. 7, 2013).

35. I do not have permission to quote from these exchanges, but the topics from this Yahoo group forum, International-Adopt-Talk@yahoogroups.com (accessed Feb. 7, 2013), include the following: whether affection differs between parents and their children who are adopted and biological; the failure of adoptive parents to recognize the struggles of their children and move from simple acknowledgment to changes in lifestyle, including activist intervention in schools and neighborhoods; the pain of identity issues when transracial adoptees reach dating age; the willingness of adoptive parents to ignore what it would mean for their children to have no knowledge of their birth families when they embarked on adoption; and the ease of adoption construed as monetary transactions. The debates acknowledge vulnerability on the part of both adoptees and adoptive parents, and they rarely escalate into what is known virtually as "flaming"—when exchanges get out of control and result in insults and deliberately targeted harmful discourse.

36. Mei-Mei, "Adoption Conference at MIT: Secret Histories, Public Policies," May 1, 2010, *One World,* http://www.chineseadoptee.com/2010/05/adoption-conference-at-mit-secret.html (accessed Feb. 7, 2013).

37. These shifts roughly mirror broader demographic trends in American society, as reported by the 2010 Census. Among transracial adoptive families, fully 84 percent included at least two siblings adopted transracially. Also, while the non-Hispanic white population is still numerically and proportionally the largest major race and ethnic group in the United States, it is growing at the slowest rate. During the first ten years of the twenty-first century, the Hispanic population and the Asian population grew considerably. Another fast-growing population were those who considered

themselves to belong to more than one race. Overall, the U.S. population has become more racially and ethnically diverse over time (Humes, Jones, and Ramirez 2011).

38. Availability of resources and access to information are closely linked to the middle-class and upper-middle-class economic status of most transnational adoptive parents.

Conclusion

1. Jennifer Bao Yu, "Monday Musings, The Smell of Magic," April 12, 2010, *One World*, http://www.chineseadoptee.com/2010/04/monday-musings-smell-of-magic.html (accessed Feb. 8, 2013).

2. Julia, "Nobody's Child Question 4: Where Were You Born?" Feb. 2, 2010, *One World*, http://www.chineseadoptee.com/2010_02_01_archive.html (accessed Feb. 8, 2013).

3. Adopted and Fostered Adults of the African Diaspora Gathering Healing Session," 2008, http://vimeo.com/22112754 (accessed Feb. 8, 2013).

References

Adams, Tyrone L., and Stephen A. Smith, eds. 2008. "A Tribe by Any Other Name." In *Electronic Tribes: The Virtual Worlds of Geeks, Gamers, Shamans, and Scammers*, edited by Tyrone L. Adams and Stephen A. Smith, pp. 11–20. Austin: University of Texas Press.

Adopted and Fostered Adults of the African Diaspora (AFAAD). http://afaad.wordpress.com/about/.

Ahluwalia, Pal. 2007. "Negotiating Identity: Post-colonial Reflections on Transnational Adoption." *Journal of Global Ethics* 3(1): 55–67.

Alber, Edmute. 2004. "The Real Parents Are the Foster Parents": Social Parenthood Among the Baatombu in Northern Benin. In *Cross-Cultural Approaches to Adoption*, edited by Fiona Bowie, pp. 33–47. London and New York: Routledge.

Alperson, Myra. "A Link to the Past: An Adoption Scrapbook Lets Parents and Children Create a Sense of History and Belonging." http://www.adoptivefamilies.com/articles.php?aid=529 (accessed Feb. 3, 2013).

Anagnost, Ann. 2004. "Maternal Labor in a Transnational Circuit." In *Consuming Motherhood*, edited by Linda L. Layne Janelle S. Taylor, and Danielle F. Wozniak, pp. 139–67. New Brunswick, NJ: Rutgers University Press.

———. 2000. "Scenes of Misrecognition: Maternal Citizenship in the Age of Transnational Adoption." *Positions* 8(2): 389–421.

Anderson, Astrid. 2004. "Adoption and Belonging in Wogeo, Papua New Guinea." In *Cross-Cultural Approaches to Adoption*, edited by Fiona Bowie, pp. 111–26. London and New York: Routledge.

Appadurai, Arjun. 1996. *Modernity at Large: Cultural Dimensions of Locality*. Minneapolis: University of Minnesota Press.

———. 1990. "Disjuncture and Difference in the Global Cultural Economy." *Theory, Culture, and Society* 7: 295–310.

———, ed. 1986. *The Social Life of Things: Commodities in Cultural Perspective*. Cambridge, UK: Cambridge University Press.

Babb, Linda Anne. 1999. *Ethics in American Adoption*. Westport, CT: Bergin and Garvey.

Bacon, Gina. 2010. "The Life of a 'Twinkie:' Performing Race as a Korean Adoptee." Paper presented at "Voices of International Adoptees: Narratives of Race, Identity, and Orphaning," Intercounty Adoption Summit 2010, University of Waterloo.

Baden, Amanda, and John Raible. 2010. "Sibling Relationships in Transracial Adoptive Families: Influences of Race and Adoption." In *Sibling Development: Implications for Mental Health Practitioners*, edited by Jonathan Caspi, pp. 287–317. New York: Springer.

Bargach, Jamila. 2002. *Orphans of Islam: Family Abandonment and Secret Adoption in Morocco*. Lanham, MD: Rowman and Littlefield.

Bartholet, Elizabeth. 1996. "International Adoption: Propriety, Prospects and Pragmatics." *Journal of the American Academy of Matrimonial Lawyers* 13(2): 180–210.

———. 1993. *Family Bonds: Adoption and the Politics of Parenting*. New York: Houghton Mifflin.

Becker, Howard S. 1999. "The Chicago School, So-Called." *Qualitative Sociology* 22(1): 3–12.

Berman, Karen. 2003. "Adopting from Eastern Europe 101." In *An International and Non-Traditional Adoption Reader*, edited by Lita Linzer Schwartz and Florence W. Kaslow, pp. 173–85. New York: Haworth Clinical Practice Press.

Bertelsen, Phil. 2001. *Outside Looking In: Transracial Adoption in America*. Directed by Phil Bertelsen, produced by Katy Chavigny, edited by Emma Joan Morris.

Blassnigg, Martha. 2009. "Review: Memory against Culture. Arguments and Reminders, by Johannes Fabian." *Leonardo* 42 (5): 456–57.

Boczkowski, Pablo J. 2004. *Digitizing the News: Innovation in Online Newspapers*. Cambridge, MA: MIT Press.

Boellstorff, Tom. 2008. *Coming of Age in Second Life*. Princeton, NJ: Princeton University Press

Borneman, John. 2001. "Caring and Being Cared For: Displacing Marriage, Gender, Kinship, and Sexuality." In *The Ethics of Kinship: Ethnographic Inquiries*, edited by Johannes Faubion, pp. 29–46. Lanham, MD: Rowman and Littlefield.

Bourdieu, Pierre. 1977. *Outline of a Theory of Practice*. Trans. Richard Nice. Cambridge, UK: Cambridge University Press.

Bowie, Fiona, ed. 2004. *Cross-Cultural Approaches to Adoption*. London: Routledge.

Bowker, Geoffrey C. and Susan Star. 1999. *Sorting Things Out: Classification and Its Consequences*. Cambridge, MA: MIT Press.

Boyarin, Jonathan. 1994. "Space, Time, and the Politics of Memory." In *Remapping Memory: The Politics of TimeSpace*, edited by Jonathan Boyarin, pp. 1–38. Minneapolis: University of Minnesota Press.

Brassard, Shaina. 2008. "Transnational Adoptions and Identity in the United States." B.A. thesis, Latin American and Latino Studies, Vassar College, Poughkeepsie, New York.

Brenneis, Donald. 2006. "Partial Measures. Commentary on AE Forum: IRB's, Bureaucratic Regulation, and Academic Freedom." *American Ethnologist* 33(4): 538–40.

———. 1988. "Telling Troubles: Narrative, Conflict and Experience." *Anthropological Linguistics* 30(3 and 4): 279–91.

Briggs, Laura. 2006. "Making 'American' Families: Transnational Adoption and U.S. Latin America Policy." In *Haunted by Empire: Geographies of Intimacy*, edited by Ann Laura Stoler, pp. 244–65. Durham, NC: Duke University Press.

Bruner, Jerome. 2004. "Life as Narrative." *Social Research* 71(3): 691–710 (originally published in *Social Research* 54(1), Spring 1987).

———. 1968. *Processes of Cognitive Growth: Infancy*. Worcester, MA: Clark University Press.

Calhoun, Craig. 1991. "Morality, Identity, and Historical Explanation: Charles Taylor on the Sources of the Self." *Sociological Theory* 9(2): 232–63.

Carp, E. Wayne. 2004. *Adoption Politics: Bastard Nation and Ballot Initiative 58*. Lawrence: University of Kansas Press.

Carsten, Janet. 2004. *After Kinship*. Cambridge, UK: Cambridge University Press.

———. 2000. *Cultures of Relatedness: New Approaches to the Study of Kinship*. Cambridge, UK: Cambridge University Press.

Cartwright, Lisa. 2005. "Images of 'Waiting Children': Spectatorship and Pity in the Representation of the Global Social Orphan in the 1990s." In *Cultures of Transnational Adoption*, edited by Toby Alice Volkman, pp. 185–212. Durham, NC: Duke University Press.

———. 2003. "Photographs of 'Waiting Children': The Transnational Adoption Market." *Social Text* 21(Spring): 83–109.

Castañeda, Claudia. 2002. *Figurations: Child, Bodies, Worlds*. Durham, NC: Duke University Press.

Castells, Manuel. 1996. *The Rise of the Network Society*. vol. 1, *The Information Age: Economy, Society and Culture*. Oxford: Blackwell.

Center for Adoption Support and Education (CASE). 2010. *Wise Up! Powerbook*. Burtonsville, MD: CASE.

Čepaitienė, Auksuolė. 2009. "Children, Individuality, Family: Discussing Assisted Reproductive Technologies and Adoption in Lithuania." In *International Adoption: Global Inequalities and the Circulation of Children*, edited by Diana Marre and Laura Briggs, pp. 208–22. New York: New York University Press.

Chatham-Carpenter, April. 2009. "Living in the West Facing East: Communicating with Our Adopted Children about Their Homeland." Paper prepared for China Association for Intercultural Communication & Association for Chinese Communication Studies International Conference on Intercultural Communication between China and the World, Beijing Foreign Studies University, Beijing, China, June 11–14, 2009.

Cherot, Natalie. 2006. "Transnational Adoptees: Global Biopolitical Orphans or an Activist Community?" *Culture Machine*, vol. 8, http://www.culturemachine.net/index.php/cm/article/view Article/46/54 (accessed Feb. 7, 2013).

Cho, Stephanie, and Kim So Yung. 2006. "Transracial Adoption Should Be Discouraged." In *Interracial America: Opposing Viewpoints*, edited by Eleanor Stanford, pp. 185–90. Detroit, MI: Green Haven Press.

Collier, Jane, and Sylvia Yanagisako. 1989. "Theory in Anthropology since Feminist Practice." *Critique of Anthropology* 9(2): 27–37.

Collier, Jane, Michelle Rosaldo, and Sylvia Yanagisako.1997. "Is There a Family? New Anthropological Views." In *The Gender/Sexuality Reader*, edited by Roger Lancaster and Micaela di Leonardo, pp. 71–81. New York: Routledge.

Collier, Rachel Quy. 2006. "Performing Childhood." In *Outsiders Within: Writing on Transracial Adoption*, edited by Jane Jeong Trenka, Julia Cyinyere Oparah, and Sun Yung Shin, pp. 207–20. Cambridge, MA: South End Press.

Comaroff, John L., and Jean Comaroff. 2009. *Ethnicity, Inc.* Chicago: University of Chicago Press.

Connerton, Paul. 2009. *How Modernity Forgets*. Cambridge, UK: Cambridge University Press.

Coutin, Susan Bibler, Bill Maurer, and Barbara Yngvesson. 2002. "In the Mirror: The Legitimation Work of Globalization." *Law and Social Inquiry* 27(4): 801–43.

Crenshaw, Kimberlé. 1991. "Mapping the Margins: Intersectionality, Identity Politics, and Violence against Women of Color." *Stanford Law Review* 43(6): 1241–99.

Dalmage, Heather. 2006. "Interracial Couples, Multiracial People, and the Color Line in Adoption." In *Adoptive Families in a Diverse Society*, edited by Katarina Wegar, pp. 210–24. New Brunswick, NJ: Rutgers University Press.

Dawkins, Richard. 2006. *The God Delusion*. New York: Bantam Books.

De Certeau, Michel. 1984. *The Practice of Everyday Life*. Trans. Steven Rendall. Berkeley: University of California Press.

Dennis, Rutledge. 2008. "Biculturalism and the Dialectics of Identity." *Biculturalism, Self-Identity and Societal Transformation Research in Race and Ethnic Relations* 15: 31–48.

Dorow, Sara K. 2006. *Transnational Adoption: A Cultural Economy of Race, Gender, and Kinship.* New York: New York University Press.

Dorow, Sara K., and Amy Swiffen. 2009. "Blood and Desire: The Secret Heteronormativity in Adoption Narratives of Culture." *American Ethnologist* 36(3): 563–73.

Douglas, Mary. 1966. *Purity and Danger: An Analysis of the Concepts of Pollution and Taboo.* London: Routledge.

Edwards, Paul. 1997. *The Closed World: Computers and the Politics of Discourse in Cold War America.* Cambridge, MA: MIT Press.

Escobar, Arturo. 2008. *Territories of Difference: Place, Movements, Life, Redes.* Durham: Duke University Press.

———. 2000. "Welcome to Cyberia: Notes on the Anthropology of Cyberculture." In *The Cybercultures Reader,* edited by David Bell and Barbara M. Kennedy, pp. 56–76. London: Routledge.

Estes, Brian. 2008. "Writing the War: Military Institutions, Military Blogs, and Social Networks in the Iraq War." Master's Thesis, George Mason University.

Evan B. Donaldson Adoption Institute. 2009. "Adoption in the Schools: A Lot to Learn. Promoting Equality and Fairness for All Children and Their Families."

———. 2008. "Finding Families for African American Children: The Role of Race and Law in Adoption from Foster Care," http://www.adoptioninstitute.org/research/2008_05_mepa.php (accessed Feb. 5, 2013).

———. 1997. "Benchmark Adoption Survey." http://www.adoptioninstitute.org/survey/baexec.html (accessed September 15, 2012).

Fabian, Johannes. 2007. *Memory against Culture: Arguments and Reminders.* Durham and London: Duke University Press.

Farber, Jeff, Filmmaker. 2009. *Living on the Fault Line: Where Race and Family Meet.* Community Family Media.

Fine, Gary, and Kent Sandstrom. 1988. *Knowing Children: Participant Observation with Minors.* Qualitative Research Methods Series, 15. Newbury Park, CA: Sage.

Fogg-Davis, Hawley. 2002. *The Ethics of Transracial Adoption.* Ithaca, NY: Cornell University Press.

Foner, Nancy, ed. 1987. *New Immigrants in New York.* New York: Columbia University Press.

Fonseca, Claudia. 2009. "Family Belonging and Class Hierarchy: Secrecy, Rupture and Inequality as Seen through the Narratives of Brazilian Adoptees." *Journal of Latin American and Caribbean Anthropology* 14(1): 92–114.

———. 2003. "Patterns of Shared Parenthood among the Brazilian Poor." *Social Text* 21(1): 11–27.

Foucault, Michel. 2006. *The History of Madness.* New York: Routledge.

———. 1991. "Governmentality." In *The Foucault Effect: Studies in Governmentality,* edited by Graham Burchell, Colin Gordon, and Peter Miller, pp. 87–104. Trans. Rosi Braidotti. Chicago: University of Chicago Press.

———. 1986. *The Care of the Self,* vol. 3, *The History of Sexuality.* Trans. Robert Hurley. New York: Random House.

———. 1985. *The Uses of Pleasure,* vol. 2, *The History of Sexuality.* Trans. Robert Hurley. New York: Random House.

———. 1978. *The Will to Knowledge,* vol. 1, *The History of Sexuality.* Trans. Robert Hurley. New York: Pantheon.

———. 1970. *The Order of Things: An Archaeology of the Human Sciences.* New York: Random House.

Franklin, Sarah, and Susan McKinnon, eds. 2001. *Relative Values: Reconfiguring Kinship Studies.* Durham, NC: Duke University Press.

Fraser, Kennedy. 2008. "Ghost Writer: Pat Barker's Haunted Imagination." *New Yorker,* May 17.

Freundlich, Madelyn. 2000. *Adoption and Ethics: The Role of Race, Culture, and National Origin in Adoption.* Washington, DC: Child Welfare League of America.

FRUA (Families for Russian and Ukrainian Adoption). 2008. "Focus on Kids." Summer Newsletter.

Gailey, Christine Ward. 2010. *Blue-Ribbon Babies and Labors of Love.* Austin: University of Texas Press.

———. 2006a. "'Whatever They Think of Us, We're a Family': Single Mother Adopters." In *Adoptive Families in a Diverse Society*, edited by Katarina Wegar, pp. 162–76. New Brunswick, NJ: Rutgers University Press.

———. 2006b. "Urchins, Orphans, Monsters, and Victims: Images of Adoptive Families in U.S. Commercial Films, 1950–2000." In *Adoptive Families in a Diverse Society*, edited by Katarina Wegar, pp. 71–90. New Brunswick, NJ: Rutgers University Press.

Geertz, Clifford. 1972. "Religion." In *The International Encyclopedia of the Social Sciences*, edited by David Sills, vol. 13, pp. 398–406. New York: MacMillan and the Free Press.

Gershon, Ilana. 2003. "Knowing Adoption and Adopting Knowledge. Review Article." *American Ethnologist* 30(3): 439–46.

Ginsburg, Faye, and Rayna Rapp, eds. 1995. *Conceiving the New World Order: The Global Politics of Reproduction.* Berkeley: University of California Press.

Goffman, Erving. 1963. *Stigma: Notes on the Management of Spoiled Identity.* New York: Simon and Schuster.

Gottlieb, Alma. 2009. "Who Minds the Baby? Beng Perspectives on Mothers, Neighbours, and Strangers as Care-takers." In *Substitute Parents: Biological and Social Perspectives on Alloparenting in Human Societies*, edited by Gillian Bentley and Ruth Mace, pp. 115–38. New York: Berghahn.

———. 1994. *The Afterlife Is Where We Come From.* Chicago: University of Chicago Press.

Graeber, David. 2001. *The Anthropological Theory of Value: The False Coin of Our Own Dreams.* New York: Palgrave Macmillan.

Graff, E. J. 2010. "The Baby Business," *Democracy* 17. http://www.democracyjournal.org/17/6757.php.

Green, Sarah, Penny Harvey, and Hannah Knox. 2005. "Scales of Place and Networks: An Ethnography of the Imperative to Connect through Information and Communication Technologies." *Current Anthropology* 46(5): 805–26.

Gupta, Akhil, and James Ferguson, eds. 1997a. *Culture, Power, Place.* Durham, NC: Duke University Press.

———. 1997b. "Culture, Power, Place: Ethnography at the End of an Era." In *Culture, Power, Place*, edited by Akhil Gupta and James Ferguson, pp. 1–32. Durham, NC: Duke University Press.

Hagan, Jacqueline María. 1994. *Deciding to Be Legal: A Maya Community in Houston.* Philadelphia, PA: Temple University Press.

Hale, Charles. 2006. *Más Que Un Indio: Racial Ambivalence and Neoliberal Multiculturalism in Guatemala.* Santa Fe, NM: School of American Research.

Hannerz, Ulf. 1996. *Transnational Connections: Culture, People, Places.* London: Routledge.

Harvey, David. 1990. *The Condition of Postmodernity: An Enquiry into the Origins of Cultural Change.* Oxford, UK: Blackwell.

Heelas, Paul. 1996. *The New Age Movement: The Celebration of the Self and the Sacralization of Modernity.* Oxford, UK: Blackwell.

Herman, Ellen. 2008. *Kinship by Design: A History of Adoption in the Modern United States.* Chicago: University of Chicago Press.

———. 2002. "The Paradoxical Rationalization of Modern Adoption." *Journal of Social History* 36(2): 339–85.

Herzfeld, Michael. 1992. *The Social Production of Indifference: Exploring the Symbolic Roots of Western Bureaucracy*. Chicago: University of Chicago Press.

Hobsbawm, Eric, and Terence Ranger, eds. 1983. *The Invention of Tradition*. London: Cambridge University Press.

Hoffman, Kevin D. 2010. *Growing Up Black in White*. Toledo, Ohio: The Vine Appointment Publishing Company.

Hollingsworth, Leslie Doty. 2003. "International Adoption among Families in the United States: Considerations of Social Justice." *Social Work* 48(2): 209–17.

hooks, bell. 1992. *Looks: Race and Representation*. Boston: South End Press.

Horridge, Lynn. 2011. "Finding Kinship in the Twenty-First Century: Matching Gay New Yorkers with Children through Adoption and Fostering." Ph.D. dissertation, The Graduate School and University Center, City University of New York (CUNY).

Howell, Signe. 2006. *The Kinning of Foreigners: Transnational Adoption in a Global Perspective*. New York: Berghahn.

———. 2003. "Kinning: The Creation of Life Trajectories in Transnational Adoptive Families." *Journal of the Royal Anthropological Institute* (NS) 9: 465–84.

Hubinette, Tobias. 2007. "Bodies Out-of-Place and Out-of-Control." In *Proceedings of the First International Korean Adoption Studies Research Symposium*, edited by Eleana Kim, Kim Park Nelson, and Lene Myong Petersen, pp. 147–64. Seoul, South Korea: Dongguk University.

Humes, Karen R., Nicholas A. Jones, and Roberto R. Ramirez. 2011. "Overview of Race and Hispanic Origin 2010." Washington, DC: U.S. Census Bureau.

Ishizawa, Hiromi, Catherine T. Kenney, Kubo Kazuyo, and Gillian Stevens. 2006. "Constructing Interracial Families through Intercountry Adoption." *Social Science Quarterly* 87(5): 1207–24.

Jackson, Timothy, ed. 2005. *The Morality of Adoption: Social-Psychological, Theological, and Legal Perspectives*. Grand Rapids, MI: W.B. Eerdmans.

Jacobson, Heather. 2008. *Culture Keeping: White Mothers, International Adoption, and the Negotiation of Family Difference*. Nashville: Vanderbilt University Press.

Jacobson, David. 2003. "Step-Families in Cultural Context: Problems in Middle-Class U.S. Stepfamilies." *Ethnofor* 16(1): 31–42.

Jenkins, Henry, David Thorburn, and Brad Seawell, eds. 2003. *Democracy and New Media*. Cambridge, MA: MIT Press.

Jerng, Mark. 2010. *Claiming Others: Transracial Adoption and National Belonging*. Minneapolis: University of Minnesota Press.

Johnson, Kay. 2004. *Wanting a Daughter, Needing a Son: Abandonment, Adoption, and Orphanage Care in China*. St. Paul, MN: Yeong and Yeong Book Co.

Johnson, Kay, Huang Banghan, and Wang Liyao. 2005. "Chaobao: The Plight of Chinese Adoptive Parents in the Era of the One-Child Policy." In *Cultures of Transnational Adoption*, edited by Toby Alice Volkman, pp. 117–41. Durham, NC: Duke University Press.

———. 1998. "Infant Adoption and Abandonment in China." *Population and Development Review* 24(3): 469–510.

Khabibullina, Lilia. 2009. "International Adoption in Russia: "Market," "Children for Organs," and "Precious" or "Bad" Genes." In *International Adoption: Global Inequalities and the Circulation of Children*, edited by Diana Marre and Laura Briggs, pp. 174–89. New York: New York University Press.

Kent, Stephen. 2003. "Spiritual Kinship and New Religions." *Religious Studies and Theology* 22(1): 85–100.

Kim, Eleana. 2010. *Adopted Territory: Transnational Korean Adoptees and the Politics of Belonging*. Durham, NC: Duke University Press

———. 2005. "Wedding Citizenship and Culture: Korean Adoptees and the Global Family of Korea." In *Cultures of Transnational Adoption*, edited by Toby Alice Volkman, pp. 56–80. Durham, NC: Duke University Press.

———. 2003. "Korean Adoptees and the Global Family of Korea." *Social Text* 74 21(1): 57–81.

Kim, Jae Ran. 2006. "Scattered Seeds: The Christian Influence on Korean Adoption." In *Outsiders Within: Writing on Transracial Adoption*, edited by Jane Jeong Trenka, Julia Cyinyere Oparah, and Sun Yung Shin, pp. 151–64. Cambridge, MA: South End Press.

Klein, Naomi. 2007 *The Shock Doctrine: The Rise in Disaster Capitalism*. New York: Metropolitan Books.

Knowlton, Linda Goldstein. 2011. *Somewhere Between*. Docurama.

Kreider, Rose. 2011a. "Internationally Adopted Children in the U.S.: 2008." In *Adoption Factbook V*, edited by Alisa Roseman, Charles Johnson, and Nicole Callahan, pp. 81–96. Baltimore, MD: National Council for Adoption.

———. 2011b. "Interracial Adoptive Families and Their Children: 2008." In *Adoption Factbook V*, edited by Alisa Roseman, Charles Johnson, and Nicole Callahan, pp. 97–114. Baltimore, MD: National Council for Adoption.

Lal, Barbara Ballis. 2001. "Learning to Do Ethnic Identity: The Transracial/Transethnic Adoptive Family as Site and Context." In *Rethinking Mixed Race*, edited by David Parker and Miri Song, pp. 154–72. London: Pluto Press.

Landsberg, Alison. 2004. *Prosthetic Memory: The Transformation of American Remembrance in the Age of Mass Culture*. New York: Columbia University Press.

Landgren, Magnus, Leif Sevensson, Kerstin Strömland, and Marita Andersson Grönlund. 2010. "Parental Alcohol Exposure and Neurodevelopmental Disorders in Children Adopted from Eastern Europe." *Pediatrics* 125(5): 1178–85.

Lamont, Michèle, and Virág Molnár. 2002. "The Study of Boundaries in the Social Sciences." *Annual Reviews in Sociology* 28: 167–95.

Larsen, Elizabeth. 2007. "Did I Steal My Daughter?" *Mother Jones* (Nov./Dec.): 53–59.

Laskas, Jeanne Marie. 2006. *Growing Girls: The Mother of All Adventures*. New York: Bantam Books.

Latour, Bruno. 2007. *Reassembling the Social: An Introduction to Actor-Network-Theory*. Oxford, UK: Oxford University Press.

———. 1999. *Pandora's Hope: Essays on the Reality of Science Studies*. Cambridge, MA: Harvard University Press.

———. 1993. *We Have Never Been Modern*. Cambridge, MA: Harvard University Press.

Le, Huynh-Nhu. 2000. "Never Leave Your Little One Alone: Raising an Ifaluk Child." In *A World of Babies: Imagined Childcare Guides for Seven Societies*, edited by Judy DeLoache and Alma Gottlieb, pp. 199–220. Cambridge, UK: Cambridge University Press.

Lederman, Rena. 2006. "The Perils of Working at Home: IRB 'Mission Creep' as Context and Content for an Ethnography of Disciplinary Knowledges." *American Ethnologist* 33(4): 482–91.

Lee, Barb. 2008. *Adopted: When Love Is Not Enough*. Carbondale, CO: Point Made Films.

Leinaweaver, Jessaca. 2008. *The Circulation of Children: Kinship, Adoption, and Morality in Andean Peru*. Durham, NC: Duke University Press.

Leinaweaver, Jessaca, and Linda J. Seligmann. 2009. "Introduction." Special Issue of the *Journal of Latin American and Caribbean Anthropology* 14(1): 1–19, "Cultural and Political Economies of Adoption in Latin America."

Leoutsakas, Dennis. 2010. "Internationally Displaced Children: Causes, Care, and Social integration." Paper presented at the session "Voices of International Adoptees: Narratives of Race, Identity, and Orphaning," Intercounty Adoption Summit 2010, University of Waterloo.

Lévi-Strauss, Claude. 1962. *The Savage Mind*. Chicago: University of Chicago Press.

Lewin, Ellen. 2006. "Family Values: Gay Men and Adoption in America." In *Adoptive Families in a Diverse Society*, edited by Katarina Wegar, pp. 129–45. New Brunswick, NJ: : Rutgers University Press.

Liem, Deann Borshay. 2000. *First Person Plural*. Documentary. Point of View.

Liu, Xin. 2000. *In One's Own Shadow: An Ethnographic Account of the Condition of Post-Reform Rural China*. Berkeley: University of California Press.

Louie, Andrea. 2001. "Re-Territorializing Transnationalism: Chinese Americans and the Chinese Motherland." *American Ethnologist* 27(3 May): 645–69.

Lugo, Alejandro, and Bill Maurer, eds. 2000. *Gender Matters: Re-reading Michelle Z. Rosaldo*. Ann Arbor: University of Michigan Press.

Lutz, Catherine, and Jane Collins. 1993. *Reading National Geographic*. Chicago: University of Chicago Press.

Ly, Phuong. 2005. "Adopting a New Way of Life: Chinese Children Shift Families' Culture." *Washington Post*, Feb. 17.

MacFarquhar, Larissa. 2009. "The Kindest Cut." *New Yorker*, July 27, pp. 38–51.

McIlvenny, Paul, and Pirkko Raudaskoski. 2005. "Mediating Discourses of Transnational Adoption on the Internet." In *Discourse in Action: Introducing Mediated Discourse Analysis*, edited by Sigrid Norris and Rodney J. Jones, pp. 62–72. London: Routledge.

Malkki, Liisa. 1997. "National Geographic: The Rooting of Peoples and the Territorialization of National Identity among Scholars and Refugees." In *Culture, Power, Place*, edited by Akhil Gupta and James Ferguson, pp. 51–74. Durham, NC: Duke University Press.

Marre, Diana, and Laura Briggs, eds. 2009. *International Adoption: Global Inequalities and the Circulation of Children*. New York: New York University Press.

Massey, Doreen, and Pat Jess, eds. 1995. *A Place in the World?* Oxford, UK: The Open University, Oxford University Press.

Mauss, Marcel. 1990 [1967]. *The Gift: The Form and Reason for Exchange in Archaic Societies*. Trans. W. D. Halls. Foreword by Mary Douglas. New York: Norton.

Mead, George Herbert. 1967 [1934]. *Mind, Self, and Society from the Standpoint of a Social Behaviorist*, edited and with an introduction by Charles W. Morris. Chicago: University of Chicago Press.

Mead, Margaret. 1978. *Culture and Commitment: The New Relationships between the Generations in the 1970s*. New York: Columbia University Press.

Melosh, Barbara. 2002. *Strangers and Kin: The American Way of Adoption*. Cambridge, MA: Harvard University Press.

Miller, Daniel, and Don Slater. 2000. *The Internet: An Ethnographic Approach*. Oxford, UK: Berg.

Miller, Peggy, Randolph Potts, Heidi Fung, Lisa Hoogstra, and Judy Mintz. 1990. "Narrative Practices and the Social Construction of Self in Childhood." *American Ethnologist* 17(2): 292–311.

Modell, Judith. 2002. *A Sealed and Secret Kinship: The Culture and Practices in American Adoption*. New York: Berghahn Books.

———. 1994. *Kinship with Strangers: Adoption and Interpretations of Kinship in American Culture*. Berkeley: University of California Press.

Moore, Sally Falk. 1987. "Explaining the Present: Theoretical Dilemmas in Processual Ethnography." *American Ethnologist* 14(4): 727–36.

Múñiz, Vicki. 1998. *Resisting Gentrification and Displacement: Voices of Puerto Rican Women of the Barrio*. New York: Garland.

Nader, Laura. 1972. "Up the Anthropologist: Perspectives from Studying Up." In *Reinventing Anthropology*, edited by Dell Hymes, pp. 284–311. New York: Pantheon Books.

Nash, Jennifer. 2008. "Re-thinking Intersectionality." *Feminist Review* 89: 1–15.

Newman, Andy, with Michael Luo. 2007. "A Chinese Orphan's Journey to a Jewish Rite of Passage." March 8. *New York Times.*

Newsweek. 2009. "The Power of Two." December 2.

NPR (National Public Radio). 2007. "Mother and Son Offer Transracial Adoption Insights." Steve Inskeep, Host. Morning Edition. www.npr.org/templates/story/story.php?storyId=12136864 (accessed March 31, 2013).

Ochs, Elinor, and Lisa Capps. 1996. "Narrating the Self." *Annual Review of Anthropology* 25(1): 19–43.

Olaniran, Bolanle. 2008. "Electronic Tribes (E-Tribes): Some Theoretical Perspectives and Implications." In *Electronic Tribes: The Virtual Worlds of Geeks, Gamers, Shamans, and Scammers,* edited by Tyrone L. Adams and Stephen A. Smith, pp. 36–57. Austin: University of Texas Press.

One World Chinese Adoptees Links (CAL G2). www.chineseadoptee.com.

Opper, Nicole. 2009. *Off and Running.* Documentary. ITVS (Independent Television Service) and NBPC (National Black Programming Consortium).

Ortiz, A. T., and Briggs, Laura. 2003. "The Culture of Poverty, Crack Babies, and Welfare Cheats: The Making of the Healthy White Baby Crisis." *Social Text* 76: 39–57.

Palmer, John. 2011. *The Dance of Identities: Korean Adoptees and Their Journey toward Empowerment.* Honolulu: University of Hawai'i Press.

Patterson, Orlando. 2011. "Race Unbound." *New York Times Book Review,* pp. 1, 14, September 25.

Patton, Sandra. 2000. *Birth Marks: Transracial Adoption in Contemporary America.* New York: New York University Press.

Peacock, James, and Dorothy Holland. 1993. "The Narrated Self: Life Stories in Process." *Ethos* 21(4): 367–83.

Perry, Twila A. 1993/94. "The Transracial Adoption Controversy: An Analysis of Discourse and Subordination." *New York University Review of Law and Social Change* 21: 33–108.

Peters, John Durham. 1997. "Seeing Bifocally: Media, Place, Culture." In *Culture, Power, Place,* edited by Akhil Gupta and James Ferguson, pp. 75–92. Durham, NC: Duke University Press.

Peterson, Kristin. 2001. "Be/longings." In *The Ethics of Kinship: Ethnographic Inquiries,* edited by James Faubion, pp. 234–49. Lanham, MD: Rowman and Littlefield.

Pew Forum on Religion and Public Life. 2010. "Religion among the Millennials: Less Religiously Active than Older Americans, but Fairly Traditional in other Ways." Washington, DC: Pew Research Center. February.

———. 2009. "Eastern New Age Beliefs Widespread: Man Americans Mix Multiple Faiths." Washington, DC: Pew Research Center.

Pitt-Rivers, Julian. 1973. "The Kith and the Kin." In *The Character of Kinship,* edited by Jack Goody and Meyer Fortes, pp. 89–105. Cambridge, UK: Cambridge University Press

Portes, Alejandro, and Rúben Rumbaut. 2006. *Immigrant America: A Portrait.* 3rd edition. Berkeley: Universtity of California Press.

Prebin, Elise. 2009. "Looking for "Lost" Children of South Korea." *Adoption and Culture* 2: 223–61.

Rheingold, Howard. 2000. *The Virtual Community: Homesteading on the Electronic Frontier.* Rev. ed. Cambridge, MA: MIT Press.

Riley, Nancy, and Krista E. van Vleet. 2012. *Making Families through Adoption.* Los Angeles: Pine Forge Press.

Robbins, Kevin. 2000. "Cyberspace and the World We Live In." In *The Cybercultures Reader,* edited by David Bell and Barbara M. Kennedy, pp. 77–95. London: Routledge.

Rollins, Lisa Marie. 2011. *Ungrateful Daughter: One Black Girl's Story of Being Adopted into a White Family . . . that Aren't Celebrities.* Written by Lisa Marie Rollins; directed by W. Kamau Bell.

Roof, Wade Clark. 1993. *A Generation of Seekers: The Spiritual Journeys of the Baby Boomer Generation.* San Francisco: Harper San Francisco Press.

Roseman, Alisa, Charles Johnson, and Nicole Callahan, eds. 2011. *Adoption Factbook V.* Baltimore, MD: National Council for Adoption.

Rosenberg, Merri. 2006. "Jewish Moms, Chinese Daughters." *Lilith* (Spring): 24–28.

Rothman, Barbara Katz. 2005. *Weaving a Family: Untangling Race and Adoption.* Boston: Beacon Press.

Rush, Sharon E. 2000. *Loving across the Color Line: A White Adoptive Mother Learns about Race.* Lanham, MD: Rowman and Littlefield.

Said, Edward. 1978. *Orientalism.* New York: Vintage Books.

Samuels, Gina Miranda. 2010. "Building Kinship and Community: Relational Processes of Bicultural Identity among Adult Multiracial Adoptees." *Family Process* 49: 26–42.

Schein, Louise. 1998. "Forged Transnationality and Oppositional Cosmopolitanism." In *Transnationalism from Below*, edited by Michael P. Smith and Luis Eduardo Guarnizo, pp. 291–313. New Brunswick, NJ: Transaction Publishers.

Schneider, David M. 1980. *American Kinship: A Cultural Account.* 2nd edition. Chicago: University of Chicago Press.

Schwartz, Margaret. 2005. *The Pumpkin Patch: A Single Woman's Adoption Journey.* Chicago: Spectrum Press.

Scott, Eugenie C. 2004. *Evolution vs. Creationsim: An Introduction.* Westport, CT: Greenwood Press.

Scott, James C. 1992. *Domination and the Arts of Resistance: Hidden Transcripts.* New Haven, CT: Yale University Press.

Scott, Joan. 1988. *Gender and the Politics of History.* New York: Columbia University Press.

Segal, Daniel, and Richard Handler. 1995. "U.S. Multiculturalism and the Concept of Culture." *Identities* 1(4): 391–408.

Seligmann, Linda J. 2012. "Traditions and Transitions: From Market Women in the Andes to Adoptive Families in the U.S." In *The Restless Anthropologist: New Fieldsites, New Visions*, edited by Alma Gottlieb, pp. 123–37. Chicago: University of Chicago Press.

———. 2009. "The Cultural and Political Economies of Adoption Practices in Andean Peru and the United States." *Journal of Latin American and Caribbean Anthropology* 14(1): 115–39.

Selman, Peter. 2009. "The Rise and Fall of Intercountry Adoption in the 21st Century." *International Social Work* 52: 575–94.

Sharp, Lesley. 2006. *Strange Harvest: Organ Transplant, Denatured Bodies, and the Transformed Self.* Berkeley: University of California Press.

Shuster, Simon. 2012. "Why Has Moscow Passed a Bill to Ban U.S. Adoption of Russian Orphans?" Dec. 20, *Time*. http://world.time.com/2012/12/20/why-has-moscow-passed-a-law-to-ban-u-s-adoption-of-russian-orphans/ (accessed Feb. 8, 2013).

Siegel, Deborah, and Susan Livingston Smith. 2012. *Openness in Adoption: From Secrecy and Stigma to Knowledge and Connections.* New York: Evan B. Donaldson Adoption Institute.

Simon, Rita J., and Howard Altstein. 2002 [1992]. *Adoption, Race and Identity: From Infancy to Young Adulthood.* New Brunswick, NJ: Transaction Books.

Simon, Rita J., and Rhonda M. Roorda. 2000. *In Their Own Voices: Transracial Adoptees Tell Their Stories.* New York: Columbia University Press.

Siu, Helen. 1994. "Cultural Identity and the Politics of Difference." In *China in Transformation*, edited by Tu Wei-Ming, pp. 19–44. Cambridge, MA: Harvard University Press.

Smith, Darron, Cardell K. Jacobson, and Brenda G. Juárez. 2011. *White Parents, Black Children: Experiencing Transracial Adoption.* Lanham, MD: Rowman and Littlefield.

Smith, Michael P. 2001. *Transnational Urbanism: Locating Globalization.* Oxford: Blackwell.

Smith, Susan, Ruth McRoy, Madelyn Freundlich, and Joe Kroll. 2008. *Finding Families for African*

American Children: The Role of Race and Law in Adoption from Foster Care. New York: Evan B. Donaldson Institute.

Smolin, David. 2012. "Of Orphans and Adoption, Parents and the Poor, Exploitation and Rescue: A Scriptural and Theological Critique of the Evangelical Christian Adoption and Orphan Care Movement." *Regent Journal of International Law* 8(2).

Smolowe, Jill. 2005."Color Her Becky: Grappling with Race." In *A Love Like No Other: Stories from Adoptive Parents*, edited by Pamela Kruger and Jill Smolowe, pp. 93–104. New York: Riverhead Books.

Solinger, Ricki. 1992. *Wake Up Little Susie: Single Pregnancy and Race before Roe v. Wade.* London: Routledge.

Spar, Deborah. 2006. *The Baby Business: How Money, Science, and Politics Drive the Commerce of Conception.* Boston: Harvard Business School Press.

Sorosky, Arthur D., Annette Baron, and Reuben Pannor. 1978. *The Adoption Triangle: The Effects of the Sealed Record on Adoptees, Birth Parents, and Adoptive Parents.* Garden City, NY: Anchor Press.

Stack, Carol B. 1974. *All Our Kin: Strategies for Survival in a Black Community.* New York: Harper and Row.

Stephen, Lynn. 2007. *Transborder Lives: Indigenous Oaxacans in Mexico, California, and Oregon.* Durham, NC: Duke University Press.

Stoller, Paul. 2002. *Money Has No Smell: The Africanization of New York City.* Chicago: University of Chicago Press.

Straub, David. 2008. "The Adoption of Chinese Children by Jewish Families and the Effect on North American Jewish Identity." In *The Jewish-Chinese Nexus: a Meeting of Civilizations*, edited by M. Avrum Ehrlich, pp. 227–36. London: Routledge.

Stryker, Rachael. 2000. "Ethnographic Solutions to the Problems of Russian Adoptees." *Anthropology of East Europe Review* 18(2): 79–84.

Sweetman, Sarah. 2013. "Forging Family: Construction of Memory in U.S. Adoption from China." Doctoral dissertation, George Mason University.

Touré. 2011. *Who's Afraid of Post-Blackness? What It Means to Be Black Now.* New York: Free Press.

Traver, Amy. 2007. "Homeland Décor: China Adoptive Parents' Consumption of Chinese Cultural Objects for Display." *Qualitative Sociology* 30 (3): 201–20.

Treide, Dietrich. 2004. "Adoptions in Micronesia: Past and Present." In *Cross-Cultural Approaches to Adoption*, edited by Fiona Bowie, pp. 127–142. London: Routledge.

Trenka, Jane Jeong, Julia Chinere Oparah, and Sun Yung Shin, eds. 2006. *Outsiders Within: Writing on Transracial Adoption.* Cambridge, MA: South End Press.

Turkle, Sherry. 1995. *Life on the Screen: Identity in the Age of the Internet.* New York: Simon and Schuster.

Turner, Victor. 1967. *The Forest of Symbols: Aspects of Ndembu Ritual.* Ithaca, NY: Cornell University Press.

U.S. Census Bureau. 2003. *Adopted Children and Stepchildren: 2000.* Census 2000 Special Reports. Washington, DC: U.S. Department of Commerce.

U.S. Department of Health and Human Services. 2010. Administration for Children and Families, Administration on Children, Youth and Families, Children's Bureau (AFCARS), "The AFCARS Report," January 13. http://www.acf.hhs.gov/programs/cb/resource/afcars-report-16 (accessed Feb. 8, 2013).

———. 2004. *How Many Children Were Adopted in 2000 and 2001?* Washington, DC: National Adoption Information Clearinghouse.

U.S. Department of State. 2011. "Statistics: Intercountry Adoption." http://adoption.state.gov/about_ us/statistics.php (accessed Jan. 25, 2013).

Van Ausdale, Debra, and Joe R. Feagin. 2001. *The First R: How Children Learn Race and Racism.* New York: Rowman and Littlefield.

Van Vleet, Krista E. 2008. *Performing Kinship: Narrative, Gender, and the Intimacies of Power in the Andes.* Austin: University of Texas Press.

———. 2002. "The Intimacies of Power: Rethinking Violence and Affinity in the Bolivian Andes." *American Ethnologist* 29(3): 567–701.

Vance, Deborah Clark. 2008. "'Like a Neighborhood of Sisters': Can Culture Be Formed Electronically?" In *Electronic Tribes: The Virtual Worlds of Geeks, Gamers, Shamans, and Scammers,* edited by Tyrone L. Adams and Stephen A. Smith, pp. 143–58. Austin: University of Texas Press.

Vance, Karen. 2005. "Church Adoption Programs Reach around the Globe." *Cincinnati.com,* July 16, 2005, Metro Section, B2. http://news.enquirer.com (accessed Oct. 26, 2005).

Volkman, Toby Alice, ed. 2005a. *Cultures of Transnational Adoption.* Durham, NC: Duke University Press.

———. 2005b. "Embodying Chinese Culture: Transnational Adoption in North America." In *Cultures of Transnational Adoption,* edited by Toby Alice Volkman, pp. 81–116. Durham, NC: Duke University Press.

Vygotsky, Lev. 2004. *The Essential Vygotsky.* In collaboration with Jerome Bruner, Robert W. Rieber, and David K. Robinson, eds. New York: Kluwer Academic/Plenum Publishers.

Walmsley, Emily. 2008. "Raised by Another Mother: Informal Fostering and Kinship Ambiguities in Northwest Ecuador." *Journal of Latin American and Caribbean Anthropology* 13(1): 168–95.

Wang, Leslie K. 2010. "Importing Global Childhoods into a Chinese State-Run Orphanage." *Qualitative Sociology* 33(2): 137–59.

Waters, Courtney. 2008. "Study Focuses on Interracial Adoption," Jan. 14, *BYU NewsNet,* http://newsnet.byu.edu/story.cfm/66915.

Wegar, Katarina, ed. 2006. *Adoptive Families in a Diverse Society.* New Brunswick, NJ: Rutgers University Press.

Weismantel, Mary. 1995. "Making Kin: Kinship Theory and Zimbagua Adoption." *American Ethnologist* 22(4): 685–704.

Weston, Kath. 1991. *Families We Choose: Lesbians, Gays, Kinship.* New York: Columbia University Press.

Wilbur, Shawn P. 2000. "An Archaeology of Cyberspaces: Virtuality, Community, Identity." In *The Cybercultures Reader,* edited by David Bell and Barbara M. Kennedy, pp. 45–55. London: Routledge.

Williams, Peter W. 1989. *Popular Religion in America: Symbolic Change and the Modernization Process in Historical Perspective.* Urbana: University of Illinois Press.

Wills, Jenny Hei Jun. 2007. *Broken Lines: Transracial-Transnational Asian Adoption and the Insufficiency of Witnessing the Trauma.* Proceedings of the First International Korean Adoption Studies Research Symposium, pp. 235–51. Seoul, Korea.

Wolf, Eric. 1982. *Europe and the People without History.* Berkeley: University of California Press.

Wolf, Margery. 1992. *A Thrice-Told Tale.* Stanford, CA: Stanford University Press.

Wright, Marguerite A. 1998. *I'm Chocolate, You're Vanilla.* San Francisco: Jossey-Bass.

Yanagisako, Sylvia, and Carol Delaney. 1995. "Naturalizing Power." In *Naturalizing Power: Essays in Feminist Cultural Analysis,* edited by Sylvia Yanagisako and Carol Delaney, pp. 1-24. NY: Routledge.

Yance, George. 2003. *Who Is White?: Latinos, Asians and the New Black/Nonblack Divide.* Boulder, CO: Lynne Reiner Publishers.

Yngvesson, Barbara. 2005. "Going 'Home': Adoption, Loss of Bearings and the Mythology of

Roots." In *Cultures of Transnational Adoption*, edited by Toby Alice Volkman, pp. 25–55. Durham, NC: Duke University Press.

———. 2004. "Going 'Home': Adoption, Exclusive Belongings, and the Mythology of Roots." In *Consuming Motherhood*, edited by Linda L. Layne Janelle S. Taylor, and Danielle E. Wozniak, pp. 168–87. New Brunswick, NJ: Rutgers University Press.

Ynvgvesson, Barbara, and Susan Bibler Coutin. 2006. "Backed by Papers: Undoing Persons, Histories and Return." *American Ethnologist* 33(2): 177–90.

Yngvesson, Barbara, and Maureen Mahoney. 2000. "'As One Should, Ought and Wants To Be': Belonging and Authenticity in Identity Narratives." *Theory, Culture and Society* 17(6): 77–110.

Youngblood, Denise. 2001. "Rainbow Family, Rainbow Nation: Reflections of Relatives and Relational Dynamics in Trinidad." In *The Ethics of Kinship: Ethnographic Inquiries*, edited by James Faubion, pp. 47–70. Lanham, MD: Rowman and Littlefield.

Zelizer, Viviana. 2005. *The Purchase of Intimacy*. Princeton, NJ: Princeton University Press.

———. 1985. *Pricing the Priceless Child*. New York: Basic Books.

Zerubavel, Eviatar. 2006. *The Elephant in the Room: Silence and Denial in Everyday Life*. Oxford, UK: Oxford University Press.

Index